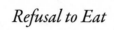

Refusal to Eat

Refusal to Eat

A CENTURY OF PRISON HUNGER STRIKES

Nayan Shah

UNIVERSITY OF CALIFORNIA PRESS

University of California Press
Oakland, California

Library of Congress Cataloging-in-Publication Data

Names: Shah, Nayan, 1966– author.
Title: Refusal to eat : a century of prison hunger strikes / Nayan Shah.
Description: Oakland, California : University of California Press, [2022] |
    Includes bibliographical references and index.
Identifiers: LCCN 2021025582 (print) | LCCN 2021025583 (ebook) |
    ISBN 9780520302693 (hardback) | ISBN 9780520972568 (ebook)
Subjects: LCSH: Hunger strikes—History. | Prisoners. | Medical ethics. |
    BISAC: HISTORY / World | POLITICAL SCIENCE / Human Rights
Classification: LCC HM1281 .S47 2022 (print) | LCC HM1281 (ebook) |
    DDC 303.6/109—dc23
LC record available at https://lccn.loc.gov/2021025582
LC ebook record available at https://lccn.loc.gov/2021025583

Manufactured in the United States of America

31   30   29   28   27   26   25   24   23   22
10   9   8   7   6   5   4   3   2   1

CONTENTS

ILLUSTRATIONS

PREFACE

In February 1989, I traveled to Durban, South Africa. I was twenty-two years old, just graduated from college. The purpose of my visit to apartheid South Africa was to study religion and community in fifth-generation Indian South African communities.

However, when I arrived in South Africa, I was overtaken by the news of the hunger-striking detainees who were engaging in bodily protests against the apartheid regime. From everything I had learned about South Africa from the outside, I was surprised that censorship of such information was not complete. The hunger strikes since January had punctured the secretive detention under which some people were held for up to three years. Short statements—in newspapers, in tabloids, and in magazines designed to teach English literacy to adults—carried the news of hunger strikers being moved into hospitals from secret prisons, and of the daring escapes to European embassies and consulates, filtered through the stringent government censorship. Lawyers, detainee family members, and ordinary people gathered at churches and mosques and in public squares to pray and go on short-term sympathy fasts for the hunger strikers.

In the months after the releases of detainees, I heard one detainee, who had been on hunger strike, share his story. His words still reverberate for me today: "I have endured the worst this regime can throw at me. We will prevail. Apartheid will fail and fall." The audience of labor and community activists and students, many of whom had justifiably feared being detained themselves, was doubtful. However, the mass releases of detainees did swell grassroots opposition and support for a defiance campaign five months later, in September.

The detainee's determination and clear-eyed prophecy struck me. On February 11, 1990, when I had returned home and was a graduate student in

Chicago, the man's words reverberated as I watched, on television, Nelson Mandela's "walk to freedom" after twenty-seven years in prison. The detainee's words in 1989 had foretold the breakdown in the apartheid system's durability—and offered a glimpse into the tenacious resolve and survival of hunger strikers and their vison for a future society.

I returned to South Africa twenty years later and began to ask questions about that signature political moment, which had wider and deeper reverberations than I was able to comprehend in 1989. In the basement of the library of the University of Witwatersrand, I found boxes of documents of grassroots anti-apartheid organizations that had advocated for hunger-striking detainees and their families during that time. The archives revealed the relays of communication among strikers, lawyers, physicians, and prison authorities and offered glimpses into the behind-the-scenes organizing of media campaigns, solidarity fasts, and public demonstrations, as well as the physicians' negotiations over the hunger strikers' hospitalization. In 1989, I didn't know that my trip would lead me to explore the history of hunger strikes. What I knew was that the power of these protests spoke to me and impacted me deeply—and they still do.

ACKNOWLEDGMENTS

Writing this book tested me in every way—as a researcher, as a writer, as a person. It made me confront my sense of ethics and my doubts. Hunger strikes are fundamental fights to control one's own body and spirit. Strikes issue visceral demands to change unbearable conditions. Hunger strikes of the past reverberate in the present. In the here and now, fresh strikes erupt. For those directly involved they are undeniable. At a remove, the strikers may be muffled or ignored, but their bodily defiance reveals elemental insights about the human condition and the chasm between what any society is and what it ought to be. Strikes are contentious and volatile politically, culturally, and socially.

As I kept on inquiring what it takes to hunger strike and why strikers persist, I worried about what justice I could do to human lives embroiled in this life-and-death struggle.

I did none of this alone.

A decade ago, a conversation with my colleague Frank Biess made me reflect on my experiences in South Africa in 1989 when hunger-striking detainees were released into public hospitals. I thank Frank for encouraging me to research and share my thoughts on public emotions and hunger striking for a conference he organized on the History of Emotions at the University of California San Diego (UCSD). An opportunity to return to South Africa led to deeper research and an unexpected invitation to speak at the Steve Biko Center for Bioethics, University of Witwatersrand Medical School. There I met Dr. Yosuf (Joe) Veriava, who treated hunger strikers at the university hospital and researched the ethical treatment and recovery of hunger strikers. I am grateful that he shared private research and papers with me that were held at the Adler Museum.

The physicians, hospital workers, and researchers at the Biko Center—as well as the scholars, health practitioners, activists, and ordinary people who attended the first public talks I gave—made me rethink my assumptions, spurring further inquiry about the long history of hunger strikes in prison and detention. I am grateful to those audiences at my early addresses to the Canadian Society for the History of Medicine in Victoria British Columbia, the Saul O. Sidore Lectures at the University of New Hampshire, and the Wisconsin Institutes of Discovery in Madison.

My research deepened and broadened across the globe as I took on an ever more ambitious scale of case studies. I am so grateful for the assistance and guidance of archivists and librarians in the United States, the United Kingdom, South Africa, Ireland, France, India, and Australia for opening up new arenas of investigation. I am especially grateful to Nancy Oda for sharing a draft version of her father's diary of the hunger strike at Tule Lake camp. Reading its pages and hearing his story from his daughter's perspective deeply impacted my understanding of a prisoner's motivations. Back at home, I benefited from the assistance of librarians and interlibrary loan specialists at the University of Southern California (USC) and UCSD. The research was supported by a UCSD Academic Senate Grant and by USC Dornsife College, and I particularly appreciate the timely support of my department chair, John Carlos Rowe, and vice-deans, Sherry Velasco and Peter Mancall, and Dean Amber Miller.

Several dedicated undergraduate and graduate assistants have assisted in processing archival materials and fact-checking research. My thanks to Jade Matias Bell, Ryan Reft, Nic Ramos, Rosanne Sia, and Emmett Harsin Drager. I benefited from the editorial guidance of Emily Raymundo and Rachel Klein. I am especially grateful for the detailed research and manuscript preparation that Joshua Mitchell did at a key period of intensive revisions and for the intrepid work of Quinn Anex-Ries in locating image rights holders and securing permissions and in manuscript preparation tasks.

Many colleagues have provided spirited criticism, invaluable advice, and generative suggestions to presentations and chapter drafts that helped in my conceptualization and revisions of the book. These included my keynote addresses to UCLA on "Feminism and the Senses: Sense Data and Sensitivity in the Age of Precarity" and on "Geographies of Intimacy" at the Penn Humanities Forum, University of Pennsylvania, and the International Graduate Student Conference on Transatlantic History, University of Texas Arlington; and presentations at Duke University, Harvard University,

McMaster University, Princeton University, Rice University, Washington University St. Louis, San Diego State University, Stanford University, University of California Berkeley, University of California Davis, University of Chicago, University of Michigan, Yale University, American Studies Association, and American Historical Association. At USC, I have benefited from lively exchanges on chapter drafts with the Center for Feminist Research; the Society of Fellows in the Humanities; and the Center for Law, History and Culture. Many colleagues have provided spirited criticism, invaluable advice, and generative suggestions that have informed my conceptualization and revisions of the book: Leora Auslander, Lauren Berlant, Anne Blackburn, Jennifer Brody, Mel Chen, Janet Cowperthwaite, Manan Desai, Juan De Lara, Sally Deutsch, Nan Enstad, Beth Freeman, Cathy Gere, Maca Gómez-Barris, Gayatri Gopinath, Kevin Grant, Inderpal Grewal, Ariela Gross, Daniel Gross, Sofia Gruskin, Jack Halberstam, Ange-Marie Hancock, Kelly Happe, Rosemary Hennessy, Tom Holt, Aniko Imre, Jenell Johnson, Amy Kaplan, Caren Kaplan, Denise Khor, Josh Kun, Susan Lederer, Rachel Lee, Beth Lew Williams, Nancy Lutkehaus, Nancy MacLean, Vic Marks, Victor Mendoza, Durba Mitra, Natalia Molina, Lydie Moudileno, Amber Musser, David Palumbo-Liu, Nathan Perl-Rosenthal, Nancy Postero, Pamela Radcliff, Sumathi Ramaswamy, Chandan Reddy, Amy Rust Higgins, Emily Ryo, Thomas Seifrid, Ashanti Shih, Ian Shin, Sara Sligar, Rebecca Stein, Kyla Tompkins, Zeb Tortorici, Linda Zerilli, and Eric Zinner. In the process of teaching, I learned a great deal from the insights and perspectives of graduate students in my "Body, Power and Politics" seminar and in John Carlos Rowe's "Introduction to American Studies and Ethnicity" seminar, and from the undergraduate students in my "Carceral Geographies" class.

Niels Hooper has patiently stewarded this book at UC Press, and I am grateful for his enthusiasm and his vision of the audiences the book could reach. I wrote and rewrote this book several times over. The changes became transformative through the energizing conversations and vigorous editorial guidance I received from Carolyn Bond, who helped me reimagine and reorganize the book and build it into the book I needed to share with the world. A number of reviewers, both anonymous and known, raised questions and made invaluable suggestions that helped me strengthen and clarify the book's arguments and evidence. I am grateful for the care and attention Patrick Anderson, Neve Gordon, David Roediger, and Parama Roy gave to different manuscripts. My foremost thanks to Antoinette Burton and Regina Kunzel, whose bracing insights about the book's overall architecture and thesis came at a valuable time in the final revision process. This book benefited from Richard Earles's copyediting, Amron Gravett's indexing, and Julie Van Pelt's attentive direction of the book's production. I am particularly grateful to Lia Tjandra for the evocative and bracing design of the cover.

Brief portions of chapters 2, 8, and 10 appeared originally in different form as several research articles that I published in the following books and journals: "Feeling for the Protest Faster: How the Self-Starving Body Influences Social Movements and Global Medical Ethics," in Frank Biess and Daniel M. Gross (eds.), *Science and Emotions after 1945: A Transatlantic Perspective* (University of Chicago Press, 2014), 239–62; "Feeding Hunger-Striking Prisoners: Biopolitics and Impossible Citizenship," in Kelly E. Happe, Jenell Johnson, and Marina Levina (eds.), *Biocitizenship: The Politics of Bodies, Governance, and Power* (New York University Press, 2018), 155–77; "Putting One's Body on the Line," *GLQ: A Journal of Lesbian and Gay Studies* 25, no. 1 (January 2019): 183–87.

My family and friends have supported me in this long research and writing project. I am grateful to have my mother and father's steadfast encouragement and am bolstered by their example of determination and ethics for a just world.

Ken Foster has inspired me throughout. He is always ready to listen to my archival discoveries and quandaries, offer imaginative ideas, and take a pen to my writing. We continue to find new hikes in the mountains and on the coast to ruminate on the complexities of these struggles of bodily defiance and state power and brainstorm fresh approaches to intractable problems. This book exists because of Ken's support, care, and unfailing certainty that this history had to be told and I needed to write it.

In South Africa, going back to 1989, I have many people to thank for their kindness in truly troubled times. I am especially grateful to Jay and Urmila Patel, who took me in, and to the activists I worked alongside at the Durban Housing Action Committee. I am grateful to the friends and communities they introduced me to, how they challenged me to learn firsthand about their struggles for survival, and for the inspiration of their resolute commitments to equity and justice.

Introduction

A HUNGER STRIKE IN PRISON is a protest like no other. There are few proximates or equivalents. If we believe that humans will do anything to survive, then the choice to deprive one's body of food is baffling and alarming. By refusing to eat—for days, weeks, even months—the imprisoned person defies an instinctual imperative to persist. Yet to fight using one's body in this way is at the core of the hunger strike.

The term *hunger strike,* coined in English in the late nineteenth century to describe a type of protest in Russian prisons, circulated and was translated into many languages as the hunger strike became a worldwide form of protest in the twentieth century.[1] The word combination is a paradox. A strike is usually a cessation—a slowdown, no-show, sit-down, or rent strike, in which workers disrupt production or refuse obligations in order to force concessions from an authority. But a hunger strike requires the cessation of the striker's eating. Rather than causing material harm to an adversary, a hunger strike is an alarming exposure of the striker to suffering. Yet it foists the responsibility for the striker's self-destruction onto the state's authority and holds culpable the prison's power.

A hunger strike is distinguished from the more familiar idea of fasting, which, as a practice of abstinence from all or specific foods, stretches back millennia. Fasting is ritual and is often communal in purpose. When some individuals have called their cessation of eating a protest fast, a penitent and purifying self-discipline for the sake of protest, they have insisted on distinguishing its purpose from that of a hunger strike.

By choosing to hunger strike, a prisoner makes a crisis and, more than that, embodies the crisis. Even as the deprivation of food turns violence upon the striker, it is different from taking one's life in suicide or self-immolation, where the result is rapid and immediate death. A hunger strike is a prolonged protest. The hunger strike's lengthening duration is possible only because of the prisoner's determination to overcome the body's signals of hunger and to withstand the pressures of authorities, guards, fellow prisoners, family, and physicians to resume eating. Since the process of bodily deterioration by hunger strike is slow—taking days, weeks, and even months in some cases for grave deterioration and fatality to set in—there is time to respond to the hunger striker and there is opportunity for the striker and his or her allies to leverage the strike to achieve their goals.

Authorities and opponents dismiss hunger strikes as impulse or pique, as inconsequential and not worth attention, or more ominously as acts of manipulation or blackmail. When they do cast the action as grave, it is to accuse the strikers of injury, violence, and harm to the state and society. Above all, the authorities hope for a brief and limited protest. They become anxious as a hunger strike persists and spreads. Reluctantly, government officials must assume responsibility for the hunger striker's life and reckon with how to deflect or mitigate that culpability.

Regardless of opinion, what is true is that the prisoner's striking body takes center stage, attracting inquiry, speculation, and concern. And what the hunger striker wants matters. A hunger strike is rarely the first option of protest in prison. It usually follows protests, petitions, the articulation of grievances, and other strikes. By choosing a hunger strike, the prisoner takes the battle with authorities to a different plane, one that lays bare the stakes of living and dying and tips the advantage to the prisoner.

Hunger strikers claim that they do not seek their death. However, they appear to be ready to die. They reclaim the meaning and course of dying and wield it as a threat, but most significantly as an opportunity to have their demands for change be heard by the authorities and the public. Their persistence puts authorities on notice that the strikers have summoned the resolve to wait out their opponents. The conundrum for the prison is to grab back power over the prisoner, whose very actions drain them of vitality and yet make them a formidable opponent. It becomes a test of who will outlast whom.

Refusal to Eat is an inquiry into what it takes to resist and oppose state power within the precincts of prison and then broadcast that opposition beyond its walls through the unique tool of hunger striking. The hunger strike as a tool has three primary elements. First, the hunger strike marshals the body's elemental material processes: it is the prisoner's personal and political defiance of the state, with the purpose of laying claim to rights the striker has been denied. Second, hunger striking communicates: it speaks to prison authorities and fellow prisoners within the prison and can cross the prison barrier to reach the public outside. Third, the hunger strike has impact: it makes the prisoner and his or her self-starvation matter to whoever hears of it.

Hunger striking takes many forms across space and time, as the chapters of this book illustrate. There is no one format or formula. Each historical instance alters our understanding of its potential purposes and meanings, communicated through a variety of media—speech, writing, murals, banners, acts of demonstration—adapted for speaking from the prison to the public.

Refusing to eat speaks viscerally in a way that is undeniable. People can opt to turn away, deny, criticize, or seek to manage the hunger striker, or they can listen, support, or participate. Whatever the response, the hunger striker's plunge into the unknown summons both allies and adversaries to gather at the precipice of life and death, hopeful and fearful for what comes next.

The power that hunger striking unleashes is volatile, unmooring all previous resolves, certainties, and structures, and forcing supporters and opponents alike to respond in new ways. It can upend prison regimens, medical ethics, power hierarchies, governments, and assumptions about gender, race, and the body's endurance. Whatever its immediate result, it can propel far-reaching and sometimes unexpected effects across the globe and through history.

STATE POWER

Prisoner hunger strikes erupt out of inequity imposed by states that deny rights to people. In the first decades of the twentieth century, hunger strikes erupted out of crises over democracy in a world divided by sprawling empires. Lofty democratic ideals were tested by the swelling protests and rebellions by those denied voice, vote, and participation in governing their society. At the core of this crisis of democracy, states upheld the rights of some and consigned others to rightlessness. Unheard grievances and denied rights spawned protests. States marshaled their powers of police and the courts to subdue political dissent and quell perceived threats to the social order by incarcerating protesters or corralling suspect people. Imprisonment exacerbated further losses of rights, but prisoners found many ways to protest and strike against the prison's rules, routines, and demands. They turned to enacting

disruptions—noisemaking, slowdown strikes, work stoppage, and more—
and one option was the hunger strike.

In the twentieth and twenty-first centuries, prison power scaled up and
expanded across the globe. The powers of criminalization were also broadened. Governments imprisoned and criminalized political opponents
and discredited their protests, and imprisonment became a catchall solution
to harness and suppress political dissent and insecurity.[2] Since the mid-
twentieth century, governments also expanded the use of administrative
detention at an astonishing pace, using emergency powers to abrogate the
right to fair and speedy trial and enabling large-scale, prolonged, and often
secretive detention of political opponents, individuals, and groups branded
as enemies or unauthorized immigrants. Governments justified this exception to their own laws by wielding accusations of terrorism and security
threats, and criminalizing unauthorized migrant entry. For those caught in
its web, indefinite detention fuels despair that there is no way out of incarceration—an evidently intended response designed to deter and punish.[3]

The universality of rights is an aspiration at the core of a modern idea of
the rights of humanity. However, the opportunity to claim rights and have
grievances heard is not universal, because policing and social and judicial
structures have blocked egalitarian rule. What is invariably at stake in a hunger strike is a demand for justice, equity, and fair outcomes that the state has
so far refused to concede. The strike's broader political agenda can include
political self-determination or access to citizenship for communities who are
disenfranchised or whose aspirations are blocked. Or it may be a demand for
inclusion through expanding the electorate or dismantling racial and gender
hierarchies or ending colonial and white supremacist rule while rebuking
those who hold the reins of power.

PRISON POWER

States deploy prison power to solve society's problems by imposing the punitive caging of humans. The prison's power derives from techniques of surveillance and subjection administered by confining, isolating, binding, and
controlling the prisoner's bodily movements and activities. This power to
punish and reform—carceral power—expansively establishes its techniques
of correcting and retraining delinquency across modern institutions such as

reformatories, schools, asylums, hospitals, parole systems, factories, the military, and, at its maximum, prisons and detention camps.[4]

Every dimension of a hunger strike by prisoners is enveloped *in a contest over the prison's power to coerce, regulate, and control human behavior.* The prison responds by dominating, seizing sovereign control over the body and life of the prisoner, and attempting to muffle his or her voice. Prisons sometimes isolate hunger strikers in solitary confinement to reduce their opportunities to organize, strategize, and console each other. Bondage is also used to subdue the restive prisoner. Holding prisoners' arms, legs, and heads with straps and fitting them into a straightjacket or constraint chair are simple technologies to dominate the prisoners' bodies and force compliance. All of these are used against hunger strikers to apply the prison's weapon of forcible feeding. And these technologies of constraint travel freely among a phalanx of institutions: the asylum, the hospital, the prison, the internment camp, and the detention center.

Carceral power envisions total control. Any attempt to subvert or chip away at or wrest the state's carceral power is met with more exertions of power and domination—a bidding up that is asymmetric. When prisoners challenge authority with a hunger strike, carceral power is expended in subduing the human body and obliterating the human spirit. Yet despite all the violence and deprivation inflicted on prisoners, their captors are anxious to prevent a hunger-striking prisoner from dying in their custody. Their threats and coaxing, their indifference and aggressive interventions are invested in keeping the prisoner alive, if just barely, so that his or her death in prison does not make the prisoner a martyr and a legend.

Food—its preparation, delivery, scheduling, and withdrawal—is central to the structuring of prison operations. Food quality, quantity, and distribution are critical measures of prison treatment. The lack of choice in meals indexes unfreedom and punishment. Prison administrators can manipulate food delivery, quantity, and content to discipline prisoners. Guards can withhold or delay the delivery of rations to exert punitive control.

Withdrawal from eating is an avenue for prisoners to assert some degree of control. Wielding this last-resort personal power, prisoners scrape together a measure of sovereignty over their body at the most fundamental level—the right to eat, the right to choose whether or not to eat, the right to refuse when someone tries to force you to eat.

The strikers' grab for this power sets off a fight between themselves and prison authorities. They wield the prison's power of punitive food deprivation against their own bodies. They also challenge the prison's institutional order, demanding a shift of the authorities' attention, resources, and treatment of the prisoners. Their decision to not eat threatens prison structures and procedures that are designed not to let prisoners die but to contain and maintain them.

The physical structures of barbed wire, barricades, walls, and bars separate and confine. The cell's tightly contained internal environment, lacking natural light and ventilation, seals its resident from the larger environment for the sake of security and punishment. The cell both isolates from others and telescopes the surveillance of the prisoner's body, whether directly by guards, by other prisoners, or through the camera.

Despite these attempts to separate and isolate prisoners, hunger strikes spread through avenues of communication among fellow prisoners. A hunger strike is rarely undertaken by just one person. Usually there are several hunger strikers, sometimes hundreds. The prisons try to constrain the prisoners' ability to organize and to break their solidarity. Guards taunt strikers, ridiculing and belittling them for inflicting such extreme violence on themselves. Or they try to persuade them to resume eating by offering better-quality food. Another strategy is picking off more vulnerable prisoners and pressuring them to cease their fasting, with the aim of demoralizing the prisoners who continue the hunger strike.

Hunger striking is used not just by the prisoner voicing defiance; it is also marshaled by the state to identify and strategize what actions to take, who to deploy, and how to subdue this kind of striker. The state and its agents name, diagnose, and define hunger strikes to pathologize and individualize the striking prisoner, to halt the strike's spread, to demoralize and break solidarity between prisoners, and to shut down support from allies—all in the service of quelling prison rebellion and averting rebellion outside.

THE PHYSICIAN'S RESPONSIBILITY

When prisoners go on hunger strike, the prison administration calls in physicians and deploys prison medical staff to treat the strikers. The medical professionals diagnose the deterioration of the body and speculate on how long the person can endure without food. Physicians also conjecture about how bodily endurance might vary by gender, race, age, and class. As the striker's body moves closer to the edge between life and death, there is a new element of urgency: Will the hunger striker continue to fast? How long before medical intervention is essential to preserve life, and will it be given or not? What symptoms and measures mark when the descent to fatality becomes irreversible?

As the hunger strike persists, prisons may introduce force-feeding as a carceral tool to envelop, contain, and control it. Medical staff are necessary to execute force-feeding. So administrators enlist physicians and psychiatrists to examine and diagnose hunger-striking prisoners in order to sanction intervention in the form of force-feeding. This dovetails with the strategy of discounting a hunger strike as the action of a person who is mad, despairing, isolated, and incapable of rational decision-making and thus can be force-fed without his or her consent.

In prison settings, physicians, nurses, and orderlies are likely to approach those they treat quite differently than they would in hospitals and clinics, where compassionate care is the expectation. Historically, prison medical staff's treatment of restive hunger strikers while administering force-feeding has often been brutal and taunting or cold and dispassionate. It has been difficult for physicians and nurses to fully address the hunger-striking prisoner's needs, especially if doing so would defy the prison's order, protocols, and discipline.

Hunger strikes have been the subject of debates among the medical profession, the administrative bureaucracy of prisons, and political circles about how, when, and by what means to implement feeding by force. These debates led to a cascade of doubt and controversy within the medical profession concerning the medical ethics and the physician's role in such settings. Questions were raised by practitioners who believed that the remedy of feeding by force came at considerable psychic, physical, and spiritual cost to the prisoner-patient and to the medical staff.

Medical intervention was supposed to depoliticize the confrontation between hunger striker and prison, but it was rarely neutral. The physician's imperative to save life at all costs confronted the moral imperative of a person's right to control his or her own body.

Hunger striking thus triangulated an ethical and physical battle among prison authorities, physicians, and hunger strikers—replacing terms of living and dying with terms of medical responsibility and judgment. Prison physicians' responsibility to the patient was often outstripped by the demands of their profession and their employer. Across a century, the medical supervision and implementation of force-feeding intensified the dehumanization and alienation of the prisoner.

Protest and political insurgency outside of prison walls often results in imprisonment. Once in prison, the protester-prisoner may choose to continue the insurgency in confrontations with prison guards and administrators, often protesting the conditions, treatment, and justifications of incarceration, but in a larger battle against political inequity and injustice. Their protest is also often tied to claiming status as a political prisoner—a new category of both politics and captivity beginning in the late nineteenth century, when, historian Padraic Kenney argues, prisons became a vehicle for politics. While states had previously used prisons to suppress political challengers, in this era rulers vied with political dissenters to define the status of "political prisoner" and its legitimacy. For prisoners, demanding the status of political prisoner provided them with a strategy to challenge the labels of criminal, terrorist, and rebel being used by the "regimes that imprisoned them."[5]

Political prisoner status set these individuals apart from ordinary, criminal prisoners and meant better treatment in prison and other privileges based on their partisan agenda or political membership. Political prisoners justified claiming these rights because they were waging a struggle politically against state authority, which, they believed, had landed them in prison in the first place. They also often aimed to elevate their particular conflict to the level of politics, batting away the state's aim to criminalize them and to suppress their words and actions into insignificance. Their goal was often to create connections with and help build momentum for political movements outside.

How prisoners are recognized, or not, by the society that cages them is a matter not only of politics, but also of existential uncertainty. From the mid-twentieth century onward, large-scale administrative detention escalated globally as states corralled residents, migrants, and insurgents and stripped them of rights and recognition. Philosopher Giorgio Agamben coined the term *bare life* to explain how the statecraft of using carceral power to cage humans in camps can render those humans barren of social and political recognition, expendable and disposable.[6] Scholars Hannah Arendt and Naomi Paik have noted that the rightlessness detainees experience is used to justify their capture, detention, and coercion. The deprivation of rights, whether in instances of fighting insurgency, terrorism, or unauthorized migration, is governed by the politics of state security.[7]

When prisoners and detainees choose to hunger strike, they reach for a last-resort personal power, seizing command of their bodies from authorities in an act that anthropologist Banu Bargu calls the "weaponization of life," to resist being driven politically and collectively to "bare life."[8] From inside captivity, the prisoner reckons with her own bodily deprivation, clashes with guards and medical staff, and reflects her experience to fellow prisoners and her captors. She also reaches out beyond the prison—to allies, companions, advocates, and family—by finding ways to communicate her voice to the outside world.

By using the weapon of hunger striking, prisoners also gain a new way to *use* their voice. The striking body itself articulates and utters viscerally. And hunger strikers give voice to their experience in spoken and written words, whether conveyed to their fellow prisoners or sent beyond the prison walls— in recorded testimony, in smuggled notes, in interviews with their lawyers.

However, the strikers' ability to be heard is muffled and suppressed by the prison's powers, so prisoners fear that news of their hunger strike will not escape the confines of the prison. They doubt and hope: Does anyone care for my life? If I speak through my body, will people hear, respond, act? Can the government wielding the prison's power be pressured to change course?

Because the captors are loath to publicize information about prisoners, only limited information is released. So even a rumor of a hunger strike makes others—both fellow prisoners and people outside the prison, such as family members, lawyers, and journalists—intent on hearing more. However, outside the prison, the receipt of communication about a hunger strike is rarely immediate. Some information emerges during the strike, but state records are often sequestered for decades—in the case of some of the hunger strikes in this book, for nearly three-quarters of a century. Testimonials may be spoken and written after the strike is over and the hunger striker has been released from prison. Some memoirs, biographies, and investigations are published in the years and decades after the episode. Oral histories are taken decades afterward and in vastly different political contexts.

COMMUNICATING HUNGER STRIKING

One of the most powerful and unstoppable aspects of hunger striking is how it exceeds the boundaries of the prison. Although the prisoner cannot move outside the prison physically, and most observers cannot come in, the hunger strike can cross over the prison walls and cross back, achieving visibility and voice for the unseen and unheard prisoner.

Communication carries the hunger strike over the threshold from the prison to outside. Witnesses—lawyers, journalists, advocates, family, and sometimes other prisoners—can bear witness to the striker's condition, both describing their own experiences in engaging with the striker and representing the striker to others.

Witnesses carry the striker's voice and its cry for assistance and attention to the outside world in the form of interviews, testimonials, smuggled notes, images, and diaries. The communication is not only verbal but also visceral, reflexive, and bodily. It delivers the particulars of a prisoner's voice, their body in deterioration and distress, and the heft and burden of their emotions and sensations. It can deliver the sensibility and rationale for refusing to eat and the dire conditions that fuel the urgency.

Not all communications are successful or impactful; some can fail to deliver or be pitched in ways that miss or mislead their audience. The communication needs to be agile and sensible in delivering claims of grievance and of rights persuasively. One of the early innovations, by suffragists, was using the voices of the hunger strikers themselves in their publications and in the media. A striker's first-person narrative, when available, brings the listener into nearly direct contact with the feelings and bodily distress of hunger striking, as well as the purpose and resolve for the strike.

Journalists broadcast news of the hunger strike through the media to inform the public about the hunger strikers' struggles and the political cause that inspired their actions. The experience of hunger striking during imprisonment is thrust into the public eye in order to pressure the government to curb abusive treatment, improve conditions, ease communication, or grant parole.

For the strikers to succeed, witnesses need to convey the strikers' visceral experiences and win the empathy of the relatively rightful citizens in whose name governments have created the rightless. Identifying self-starvation as both "utterance" and political "speech," scholar Maud Ellmann describes the act of refusing sustenance—food and drink—as "a dialogue whose meanings do not end with the intentions of the speaker but depend on the understanding of the interlocuter."[9] That understanding varies. Some listeners respond with criticism, some with empathy, and some with action. In the streets and on public grounds, those who choose to act as the strikers' allies and supporters communicate through demonstrations, picketing, placards, banners, performances, and sympathy fasts. Each of these forms makes the prison hunger strike visible and manifest outside. In contrast, governments counteract the striker's voices with their own voices of political and administrative concerns, promoting their own actions as defense of law and civil order.

In the twentieth and twenty-first centuries, mass politics and mass media expanded rapidly, prompting innovations in advocacy for striking prisoners. Oppositional mass political movements used expressive emotional and visceral language to motivate political demonstrations in solidarity with the suffering prisoner and to shape the emotions of the public.[10] For scholar Diana Taylor, the witnessing and sharing after the striker's trauma "is a tool and a political project" that challenges listeners to respond, to actively reckon with injustice, and to summon a call to action to raise awareness, change a policy, or enact reparations.[11] Opposition political organizations feature these singular voices in their own media and in the information they furnish to independent news media.

Refusal to Eat aims to explain how these voices emerge, in part by examining the platforms by which a striking body can pierce public consciousness. It explores how hunger striking—a pliable concept, reshaped by different hands for different purposes—came to be intelligible in different societies across the twentieth century, and how it was conveyed as a universal, visceral human experience.

GUT FEELING AND GUT KNOWING

We all know the feeling of hunger, the discomfort and weakness caused by lack of food coupled with the desire to eat. But can we sense hunger in someone else? The involuntary sounds of another's grumbling stomach convey that something is amiss. But its meaning is not clear—it could be indigestion, it could be distress, it could be hunger. Other symptoms may signal hunger in another person—smells, facial expressions, or pallor. In fact, I can only extrapolate your hunger from my own—an inadequate gauge for knowing *your* sensate experience. Even so, we speak of gut knowing and of the sight of someone else's suffering being gut-wrenching, making us feel uneasy and unnerved or distressed.

In communicating the experience of a prolonged refusal to eat, hunger strikers make many attempts to convey to others the feelings and sensations that transpire. Sometimes witnesses assert that they can sense the pain of the striker's body. At other times, both witnesses and critics doubt that such feelings and sensations can be fully known, even when they are anticipated and imagined.

The transmission of gut feeling and knowing from one person to another is the work of visceral body-to-body communication. In the twenty-first century, biomedical science, feminist research, and historical and cultural studies of affect and emotion have investigated the relationship between gut, perception, and feelings that circulate in society and politics.

Recent advances in biomedical science and gastroneurological research have identified the neural sensing capacity of the gut, dubbed the "second brain" by scientist Michael Gershon. This enteric nervous system encases the gut with an envelope of five hundred million neural cells that stretches thirty feet from mouth to anus, exceeding the neural mass in the spinal cord. The gut's reflexes control the breaking down of food through mechanical muscle contractions and chemically through the absorption of nutrients, secretion of enzymes, and expelling of waste.[12] More than 90 percent of the body's serotonin lies in the gut, as well as about 50 percent of the body's dopamine. This intensity of chemical messaging allows us to "feel" the inner world of the gut. Research shows that gut health influences mood and physical and mental illness, but this communication pathway is one-way, with the vagus nerve signaling from the gut to the brain, bringing new insight to common expressions such as "gut reflex" and "gut feeling."

But how does feeling travel from gut to gut, from body to body? Feminist theories of bodily affect have examined how sensory data, sensation, and sensitivity to human suffering can be socially and culturally felt in the sensing and expressing of the gut's neural processes. Scholar Elizabeth Wilson, in her book *Gut Feminism,* draws out the "primitive psyche of the stomach as an example of motive capacity." The network of neural tissue lining our guts "ruminates, motivates and comprehends." This raises the question: What does the feeling of a gut emptied and depleted communicate?[13]

Scholars of affect and emotion examine how somatic responses are communicated between humans intimately, socially, and in public. Sara Ahmed has argued that emotions do not exist in singular bodies but circulate among bodies, aligning on the surfaces of bodies to pull some bodies together and pull others apart, making emotions social and cultural, not simply a matter of individual psychology.[14] Scholar Lauren Berlant has tracked the eruption of visceral feeling from personal to public through storytelling genres that anticipatorily shape experiences and cultural expectations of feelings such as anger, suffering, and disappointment.[15] Historians of emotion have similarly investigated how expressions of feeling are shaped culturally and learned socially through norms, rules, and expectations. They have found that cultural lenses and media influence the ways in which gut feelings erupt, resonate, and convey meaning, heightening some affects and dampening others.[16]

How are emotions shared communally? Feelings of pain, fear, joy, disgust, and shame can transgress barriers to reach some public communities more readily than others. This insight helps explain the basis of solidarity and how it is sustained. Sensing resonances of another's visceral feeling can embolden an individual's ability to endure taunting and pressure from prison administration and guards. Shared visceral feeling can just as well stoke division or dampen morale within and among prisoners during hunger strikes.

WHAT THE STRIKING BODY UPENDS

The ordeal of hunger striking and its aftermath change the body physically and also change what the body means. The body is seen differently; it becomes different, both inside and out. Even as prisoners and detainees who pursue a hunger strike become more and more physically vulnerable and dependent, they continue to claim power over their body, asserting their agency and their political voice.

As a bodily defiance in prison, the act of hunger striking disrupts gender assumptions culturally, confounding the assignment of a fixed gender binary of masculinity and femininity in the defiant bodies. Some women hunger strikers claimed that men lacked the stamina to endure deprivation. Apparently there was a culturally common sense that tried and failed to line up this form of protest with the differences between men and women to explain the kind of fortitude, rationality, courage, psyche, and political consciousness it involved. In the first half of the twentieth century, a number of notable hunger strikers were women. Guards, politicians, physicians, and others were confounded when the cultural and social expectations of gender roles and presentation did not line up with the sex of the bodies of those choosing to hunger strike. For instance, when confronting the British and American suffragists, many onlookers expressed dismay about the women's "unwomanly behavior," commenting that hunger striking is a defiant bodily protest that masculinizes women and then expressing surprise that the women who protested were so feminine. However, when Irish and Indian men took on a hunger strike, critics said their protest was unmanly and passive and that it feminized the men. Expectations that some bodies could endure great pain and privation seeped into the expectations of physicians, the public, and even prisoners about which bodies, by gender, race, or class, could endure longer without food.

This gender switching was in the perceptions of onlookers and witnesses. Critics wanted hunger striking to mean something that lined up gender and body, and they were puzzled when their assumptions were upended. However, the protesters themselves were not confused. They insisted that they were uniquely in touch with the self-sense of their body and who they were.

The cultural switch and inversion of gender may, however, partially explain the ferocity of prison guards, nurses, doctors, and orderlies who directly engaged with hunger-striking prisoners. In early twentieth-century British prisons and in the early twenty-first-century CIA black sites in the Middle East, some of the most disturbing violence enacted on the hunger striker, particularly in the methods of forcible feeding, violated both women and men bodily, using degrading means of sexualized and gender terror and humiliation to force prisoners to submit body, mind, and spirit to prison control. They were being punished for being gender violators.

Hunger striking unmoors other cultural certainties as well. Who are victor and victim? Villain and vanquished? Who and what are rational and unreasonable? Who is right and who is wrong? Who has the power and who does not? How does the perception of bodies as distinct (by race, class, religion, sexuality) change how the fasting body is perceived, known, felt, recognized, and reckoned with?

FOLLOWING HUNGER STRIKING ACROSS GEOGRAPHY AND HISTORY

Refusal to Eat looks at the choice to use hunger striking as a tool of protest and the effects of that choice across geography and time. Hunger striking is a far wider, broader, and deeper social, cultural, and political practice than any one book could possibly undertake. The chapters that follow examine more than a dozen episodes of hunger strikes in depth, including their historical placement in Britain, the United States, Ireland, India, South Africa, Northern Ireland, Israel, Guantánamo (Cuba), Papua New Guinea, and Australia (all in English-speaking contexts). The purpose is not to create a compendium of every strike in history. Instead, *Refusal to Eat* examines the phenomenon of the hunger strike itself, seeking to understand its nature, its motion, its constraints, and how it propels powerful and far-reaching effects.

It explores how embodied defiance is communicated viscerally such that it overcomes prison barriers, becoming arresting and intelligible over time to many different audiences across the globe.

Throughout the twentieth century and into the twenty-first, in prisons, detention camps, university campuses, public squares, and boats, captives and protesters have engaged in hunger strikes. These rich historical studies uncovered the scope of prisoner motivations, the spread of political movements, and the enlargement of state carceral power. Studies of hunger strikes that transpired in the first half of the twentieth century illuminated what historian Kevin Grant calls the role of the "British transimperial network" in transferring and publicizing the tool of hunger striking across the globe.[17] Some books and articles have investigated the development of policies of forcible feeding in prisons across the century.[18] Several important studies of the second half of the twentieth century have examined how prison hunger strikes revealed dimensions of the confrontation with state-sponsored repression, the ethics of medical intervention, and human rights advocacy. These include, in the 1970s and 1980s, the hunger strikes of dissident intellectuals in the Soviet Union and of imprisoned members of the violent Red Army Faction in West Germany; and, from the 1980s into the twenty-first century, the successive hunger strikes of thousands of Kurdish and leftist prisoners in Turkey[19] and the hundreds of indigenous Mapuche prisoners in Chile who enacted hunger strikes.[20] The hunger strikes out of the insurgency in Northern Ireland in the 1970s and 1980s have loomed large on a global stage, shaping both public perception and scholarship on physical and psychological combat in prison.[21] And for the past five decades, hunger striking has been among the arsenal of bodily protests undertaken by migrants and refugee seekers detained in camps in Indonesia, Hong Kong, France, Italy, the Netherlands, Guantánamo, Ireland, and the Bahamas.[22]

The public protest fast, often referred to as a hunger strike, has been employed outside of prison, as have protests against state power, economic concentration, and policies that perpetuate inequality. These have often been solo strikes by a leader such as Mexican American farm labor leader Cesar Chavez, African American comedian and civil rights activist Dick Gregory, Indian farmworker rights activist Anna Hazare, and Attawapiskat chief Theresa Spence in Canada.[23] But others have been efforts of collectives of students, civil rights activists, and environmental activists on specific campaigns to draw public attention and force changes in the policies of businesses, governments, and institutions—such as in the 1990s, when U.S.

university students fought for faculty and curriculum in Chicano studies and Asian American studies.[24]

Cultural studies and anthropology scholars have delivered vital perspective on the performance of hunger striking and how it communicates both viscerally and politically in ways that fluctuate between intimacy and spectacle, between individual and collective. As Patrick Anderson has argued, "hunger striking" is expressed as a "set of gestures, physical actions and choreographies that oscillate in and out of the control of the practitioner" who seizes and inverts the state's powers of "bodily violence" and yet "hovers treacherously on the brink of self-destruction." Delving into how the hunger strike reveals the intricacies of power and the body, these scholars have demonstrated that the inward-turning of the state's tools of violence scrambles and upends the expectations of success and failure.[25] This analysis has been invaluable for my own reflections on the braided dynamic of prison power and striker's voice.

Refusal to Eat is divided into two parts, tracking the history of the state and the crisis over systemic inequalities that have denied participation in democracy and made government unaccountable. Part 1, "Hunger Striking in the Crisis of Imperial Democracy," examines how hunger striking communicates a fight against inequality in the British and American nations and their empires. Chapter 1 examines the British and U.S. transatlantic campaign led by white women for the right to vote and participate fully in the governing of society. The tool of hunger striking is confronted by the state's tool of forcible feeding, the technologies and purposes of which are dissected in chapter 2. In chapters 3 and 4, in Ireland and India, racial and colonial hierarchies and inequities are front and center in the battle of the colonized for a new system of government and political autonomy.

Each of these chapters examines how hunger striking is repurposed to make the hunger strike sensible—in particular, the ways the strikers, their fellow prisoners, their supporters, and journalists experiment with communicating hunger strikes across media to forge networks of solidarity. The hunger strike in this period tells a singular story of an individual prisoner, a political leader, who is tested by imprisonment. These narratives convey the prisoner's life, purpose, and dignity, broadening to larger circles of partisans and onlookers a concern for their welfare that might ordinarily be confined to immediate family.

Self-evidence plainly weighted the experiences of an individual and—better still, a leader—over those of a class or mass of people. The prisoner and his or her advocates molded the hunger strike to achieve the visibility and voice of the unseen prisoner and enfold these features into a wider social and collective narrative. A thorny question decisively characterized the hunger strike: Which persons' and which bodies' grievance and suffering can link a personal agony and a collective social agony?[26]

Early release for the prisoner was the most immediate and instrumental goal of the hunger strike. Bolder political goals were inclusion in the prevailing system of rule and, conversely, backing for national independence—two credible exits from the crisis of imperial democracy.

World War II was a turning point in the history of the state with regard to the capacities and limits of empire and opportunities for democratic rule; as chapter 4 notes, the British Empire scrambled for control in the waning days of its colonial rule of India. Hunger strikes erupted in a range of dimensions before, during, and after the war, each time revealing different paradoxes of race.[27]

The chapters in part 2, "Hunger Striking and Democratic Upheavals," examine these paradoxes as the reality of racial discrimination undermines the ideal of human universalism. Diverse societies governed under empires are in open conflict as state powers reconsolidate. Chapter 5 focuses on one such example, the Japanese Americans in the stockade of Tule Lake Segregation Center and their efforts to break free of detention, imposed without trial or conviction.

The security state, born out of conquest and colonial rule, spread globally during and after the war. Formal empires unraveled through confrontations with anticolonial insurgencies and reluctantly unwound their territorial possessions into new nations. The arming of new nations and insurgencies spawned wars, insurrections, and coups across the formerly colonized world. Allegiances and resources were distributed into a new, bipolar global formation, the Cold War, that reconfigured the war's Axis and Allied powers into communist and anticommunist nations, led respectively by the Soviet Union and the United States. State powers to contain, control, and suppress rebellion and disobedience spread and multiplied. Robust state secrecy mechanisms removed the public from oversight of the growing carceral archipelago of prisons, jails, detention centers, and camps and effectively censored media coverage. By branding prisoners and, increasingly, detainees as enemies and threats to society, the security states could manipulate judicial hearings, deny legal rights, and block recourse to justice.[28]

The hunger strike phenomenon became attached to fights against injustice both in public and in prison. As the phenomenon spread, it was adapted to communicate the massifying of strikes and to embrace both national and transnational networks of solidarity, as well as the amplification of contests in television and digital media. Within new crises, hunger strikes posed a trigger in intractable situations: to upend racial discrimination and repression in South Africa, the topic of chapter 6; as part of the Irish Catholic republicans' fight against British rule and second-class citizenship in Northern Ireland, as discussed in chapter 7; and during fights against indefinite administrative detention in India, Israel, and the U.S. base in Guantánamo, Cuba, the subject of chapter 8. The hunger strike was repurposed and molded to puncture public indifference, amplifying the urgency of life and death in a bid to address entrenched injustice and inequity. Hunger striking accrued new understandings of human rights to life, liberty, and well-being in the wake of state deprivations and denials and sought to subordinate the "supremacy of the nation-state" to "global law" standards and arbiters.[29]

In the 1980s and 1990s, Australia, the United States, and European nations redirected their powers of punitive caging to deter unauthorized migrants from Asia, Africa, the Caribbean, and Central and South America—previously orbits of imperial conquest, colonization, and conflict. Despite international accords to protect and create processes for seekers of refuge, Australia and the United States established criminalization and indefinite caging to address the waves of migrants arriving on their shores and borders unauthorized—as discussed in chapters 9 and 10.

States became committed to securitizing their borders, plunging refuge-seekers into conditions of rightlessness and trapping them in dehumanizing indefinite detention that left them feeling disposable and expendable. They were ensnared by a bureaucracy that refused to release them, irrespective of the facts of their individual cases.

In these settings, hunger striking mutated both in how it was represented bodily and psychically and in the grounds on which lawyers and advocates gained the attention of a national and global audience. Language and political movements centered on rights—both human rights and prisoner rights—burgeoned from the 1960s onward. Yet the challenges were multiple in engaging those on the outside to protest migrant detention, to create temporary relief for the detainees, and to forge political coalitions that might reverse immigration policies that purportedly protected the nation's citizens.

Drawing on archival research into government records, political movements, judicial cases, medical associations, news media, and visual representations, *Refusal to Eat* explores the phenomenon of hunger striking, elucidating how it communicates through media and movements to convey the confrontation taking place within prison walls to the public outside, and from there to other localities and nations.

ENDURING A HUNGER STRIKE FOR THE SAKE OF A DIFFERENT WORLD

Hunger strikers are also, by and large, survivors. Most of the hunger strikers in this book survived the immediate context of their strike. They resumed eating even after weeks and months of starvation. They endured in prison. Many were eventually released, their release being a validation of the justice of their political cause. Many continued to fight and work to see a future different from their own experience.

Hunger striking can take a person to the edge of human endurance. It makes us ponder why people willingly endure such extreme suffering—what makes them resilient in the face of adversity and possible fatality? However, the hunger striker's struggle is centered not only in how long and at what cost she or he can endure, but in whether she or he can force society to listen. In conditions of unfathomable despair, how does the hunger striker nurture hope that it is possible to breach the barriers of incarceration and reach people outside?

This confidence in the powers of communication—that their words and actions could influence others to respond, to meet their demands and thus allow them to set aside their suffering—offers the most poignant glimmer of hope for the witnesses and triumph for hunger strikers. Amid the cacophony of signals, doubts, and precarity they feel in their fasting bodies, hunger strikers exhibit the certitude that they know their own mind and they can reach another's conscience. Hunger strikers seek aid, protection, and community to hold their bodies together, even as they risk their lives. The hunger strike is a kind of mobile externalization of the hunger strikers' individual and collective vision, revealing the fundamentally utopian character of its protest.

Prisoners choose a hunger strike to demand that their voice be heard, that their lives matter. They speak through their bodies in a register that is unmistakable for its claims of sentience and consciousness. No matter how roughly challenged their claims for voice and recognition are, they persevere. How far can a person go to resist the prison's power?

Their actions and their voice disrupt the power and political arrangements around them. They rattle the political order. Domination is unrelenting and unsustainable. Change is imperative, but in what direction? Can we perceive what the striker is reaching for—a sign, a signal, a hunger for a different world?

PART ONE

Hunger Striking in the Crisis of Imperial Democracy

ONE

Suffragists and the Shaping of Hunger Striking

IN 1909 THREE WHITE WOMEN refused to eat when imprisoned for public disobedience. Two of them became British and American national icons; one faded into obscurity.

In July 1909, British suffragist Marion Wallace Dunlop refused to eat for ninety-one hours in London's Holloway Prison. Five months later, in November, American suffragist Alice Paul went on hunger strike for twenty-four days in the same prison. Before Paul's prison sentence began, American Agnes Fair, a street orator supporting the Industrial Workers of the World, was on "starvation strike" for three days in Spokane, Washington. In each instance, the woman's bodily protest within prison walls was an extension of her disobedience to government efforts to curtail speech and deny her political participation. Each was indefatigable, brave, and eloquent in the purpose of her refusal to eat.

UNEASY AND UNFINISHED DEMOCRACY

At the dawn of the twentieth century, both the United Kingdom and the United States were reluctant and uneasy democracies and faced crises of popular discontent. In the nineteenth century, both nations had expanded their power over vast lands and people, yet conspicuously denied vast numbers the political representation reserved for propertied, white male citizens. Now both governments faced vigorous challenges to their denial of political accountability, participation, and rights to freedom of speech. Unpropertied working men and women, propertied women, immigrants, freed black people, colonized peoples, and indigenous peoples all fought for a say in their future. By arms, vote, and voice they sought to participate in governing their society and make the government accountable to their needs and aspirations.

Democracy as practiced in Britain and the United States roiled and agitated in contests and fights in the streets, in the fields, in the mines, in the newspapers, as well as in the legislative halls. The stark imbalance between the small electorates in these avowed democratic nation-states ruled by law and the vast populations they ruled over exacerbated crises over legitimacy and justice. The professed democratic ideals contradicted the reality of the overwhelming majority of adults, who were categorically dispossessed of rights to vote, hold office, be licensed for professions and business, and participate in their governance while being acutely vulnerable to insecurity, violence, and poverty. These inequities underwrote recurrent crises in the lived experience of democracy in both nations—domestically and across their overseas territories, colonies, and protectorates. The questions churned: Who could exercise rule over whom? How much longer would minority rule prevail? Who demanded rights of participation? And who called for the upending of the existing system and its replacement with a new order and a new world?

After retaining the privilege of the vote for male property holders only through the nineteenth century, Britain would grudgingly, after sustained persuasion and militant struggle, cede the vote to working-class men and all women by 1928. Women's exclusion was justified by the assumption that property-holding fathers, husbands, adult brothers, and adult sons could better represent their interests. In 1869, single female property holders were allowed to vote in municipal elections, and some married women were added in 1894, but political parties categorically blocked women and most working-class men from the franchise in national elections. In the nineteenth century, working-class agitation and riots successfully lowered property qualifications for male suffrage. However, even after the third reform act in 1884, less than 60 percent of adult men had the vote. In Britain's world-straddling empire, for every nine persons who were colonized subjects, only one was a resident of the British Isles, further aggravating the acute inequity of who could participate in its parliamentary democracy.

In the nineteenth-century United States, working-class agitation gained voting rights for propertyless white men state by state, and federally, after the carnage of the Civil War, Congress and the states approved a constitutional amendment to extend the vote to black men. From the 1870s into the twentieth century, however, states, municipalities, and federal courts whittled away voting eligibility through poll taxes, literacy tests, culling of voting rolls, naturalization curbs, and violent intimidation. Millions of not only black but also lower-class white, Native, immigrant, and transient men, as well as all women, were denied the exercise of their vote. The arc of U.S. dominion grew across the nineteenth century, and by the century's end— with the annexations of the Philippines, Guam, Puerto Rico, Hawaii, and American Samoa—the "greater United States" held dominion over millions of people to whom it summarily denied access to the levers of political power, while championing democracy. Racial restraints on voting intensified in the twentieth century, with more immigrants being restricted from voting rights. In the federal election of 1912, ten million voted, including women in western states, but the disenfranchised adult population was at least three times as large as the population of voters domestically—not to mention the millions in overseas annexed territories.[1]

Women fighting for the right to vote was one aspect of the broader campaign to expand access to participation in democracy. In the United States, the various women's suffrage campaigns attracted women of all races, ethnicities, and classes. However, wealthy and middle-class white women helmed the national organizational efforts, while African American, conquered Mexican, and Native women, as well as European, Asian, and Caribbean immigrant women, developed their own organizations to demand rights of suffrage for women of their own status. Organizing developed out of transatlantic campaigns for slave abolition, temperance, and workers' rights. Successful efforts in newer western states, such as Wyoming and Utah, required helping men see the partisan political advantage in allowing women to vote.[2]

In mid-nineteenth-century Britain, women's suffrage societies used constitutional methods of petitioning and lobbying members of Parliament to draft legislation to extend suffrage to women. Women's suffrage organizations were founded across Britain, and in 1897, seventeen of these groups banded together to form the National Union of Women's Suffrage Societies (NUWSS) to continue their efforts, despite ongoing defeat. In 1903, Emmeline Pankhurst founded the Women's Social and Political Union (WSPU) at her home in Manchester, gathering women active in the Independent Labour Party in a women-only organization to fight for national suffrage. In 1905 the WSPU managed to convince a member of Parliament to introduce a suffrage bill. Following the failure of the bill in 1907, and in contrast to consultative lobbying of its ally, the NUWSS, the WSPU embarked on a series of campaigns of disruption and disturbance. The attempts at dialogue with British men had failed, and the WSPU shifted its campaign for the vote from parliamentary battle to the streets.[3]

The public demonstrations were intended to rouse publicity and public interest, as newspapers rarely reported meetings and frequently refused to publish articles and letters written by supporters of women's suffrage. On June 21, 1908, two months after Herbert Henry Asquith, an anti-suffragist Liberal, became prime minister, the WSPU organized the Women's Sunday demonstration, where thirty thousand women marched to Hyde Park, drawing an estimated three hundred thousand people to hear eighty women speakers in what was considered the largest political rally in London's history. Even so, a week later, the House of Commons refused a suffrage delegation. Frustrated that their unprecedented public demonstration did not sway members of Parliament, in the ensuing months the WSPU members smashed windows of government buildings and shops, disrupted political banquets and public events, heckled politicians, chained themselves to Parliament, and blew up buildings. Dozens of women were arrested, convicted, and—when they refused to pay fines—sent to prison. When imprisoned, they demanded treatment as political prisoners.[4]

MARION WALLACE DUNLOP AND THE PRISON HUNGER STRIKE

Forty-five-year-old artist and suffragist Marion Wallace Dunlop took her imprisonment to a new threshold of confrontation when she embarked on a hunger strike on July 5, 1909. The genteel feminine appearance of this student of London's Slade School of Fine Art, whose work illustrated popular children's books and was displayed at the Royal Academy, belied a fierce determination. The daughter of a civil servant in British India, she was a socialist and an ardent supporter of women's suffrage, and she joined and led the WSPU's confrontational protests. Wallace Dunlop also had an eye for the theatrical and performative, which she put to good use in 1911, when she was instrumental in designing the Women's Coronation Procession, held on the eve of George V's coronation, to demand the right to vote. The march—the largest ever held in Britain—included the empire's representatives from India, Australia, New Zealand, South Africa, and the West Indies who joined in support of suffrage.

Three years earlier, in 1908, she was arrested twice, first for "obstruction" and the second time for leading a march. On June 25, 1909, she was arrested a third time, in this case on her second attempt to meet with a member of Parliament. Whereas her male companion was allowed to meet with a member of Parliament in the building's Central Lobby, she was permitted to go no further than St. Stephen's Hall, where she stamped a passage from the 1689 Bill of Rights on the wall using an indelible rubber stamp. The passage read: "It is the right of the subject to petition the King, and all commitments and prosecutions for such petitioning are illegal." In her defense in police court, Wallace Dunlop claimed: "I wrote these words because they are in danger of being forgotten by our legislators, and because I intended that they should be indelible." She was found guilty of willful damage, and when she refused to pay a fine, she was sent to Holloway Prison for a month.[5]

On July 5, 1909, in a petition to the home secretary in which she demanded that her status of criminal be redefined as political prisoner, she also declared she was undertaking a hunger strike: "I claim the right recognized by all civilized nations that a person imprisoned for a political offence should have first-division treatment; and as a matter of principle, not only for my own sake but for the sake of others who may come after me, I am now refusing all food until this matter is settled to my satisfaction."[6] She endured ninety-one hours of fasting before being released on grounds of ill health.

On July 9, the day after her release, a letter written by Wallace Dunlop was read out loud at a WSPU meeting and reported in the *London Evening Standard*. In the letter, she described her decision to refuse food as impulsive, without prior planning: "I wondered what I could do to help the cause in prison and I decided to try a hunger strike." Then, as she wrote, she "dogged did it." She emphatically refused food, in the letter describing how she threw "fried fish, four slices of bread, three bananas and a cup of hot milk out of the window" on the first day of her hunger strike. She said remarkably little about the experience of deprivation except that she "really felt hungry" on the first day. Her defiance was emboldened by the way the guards threatened "all the time to 'pump' milk through my nostrils, but never did it." Her response to the prison doctor's entreaties that she resume eating: "'You may feed me through the nostrils or the mouth,' I added; 'but suppose you get 108 women in here on Friday, all requiring to be fed through the nostrils?' At this the doctor's face was a delightful study."[7]

Contemporary journalists, artists, and partisans quickly claimed that Wallace Dunlop's refusal to eat inaugurated the hunger strike as a political

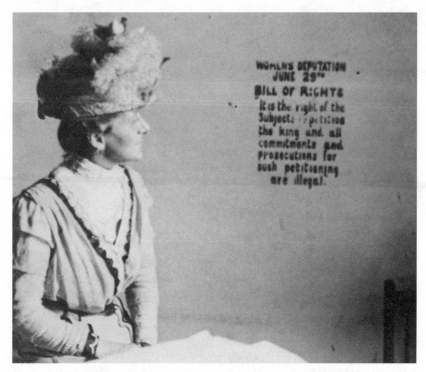

FIGURE I. Marion Wallace Dunlop in St. Stephen's Hall, 1909. © Museum of London.

tool of the twentieth century. They called it new, yet some suffrage supporters and commentators in the weeks after her release remarked that she had adopted the "Russian method of the hunger strike" used by revolutionary prisoners since the late 1870s to fight tsarist repression.[8] One commentator noted: "The only real advance has been hunger-striking which came with its mad bravery from Russia."[9] Indeed, the word *hunger strike* entered the English lexicon as a translation of the Russian word *golodofka,* literally "famine fast," in the writings of American George Kennan, who traveled through Siberia and wrote dispatches for the Associated Press. In British and American newspapers and magazines, Kennan wrote exposés on brutal Russian prison conditions and prisoner revolts in 1889 and 1890, broadcasting news of both female and male political opponents of the tsarist imperial rule protesting their imprisonment and treatment by refusing to eat. His two-volume study on Russian revolutionaries in tsarist prisons in Siberia cemented the association of the Russian anti-imperial and pro-democracy advocates with prison hunger strikes. At the dawn of the twentieth century, international wire services reported periodically on what they called "starvation strikes" by hundreds of imprisoned students and revolutionaries in the Austro-Hungarian Empire. In London, Russian exiles spoke out about their brutal experiences in notorious jails to audiences that included suffragists.[10]

SUFFRAGISTS EMBRACE HUNGER STRIKING AS A WEAPON

Whether Marion Wallace Dunlop was directly inspired by the Russian hunger strikes or not, her hunger strike and subsequent release from prison boosted the fortunes of the suffrage movement. "The star of the Suffragettes is again in the ascendant," announced a column in the British magazine *New Age* a week after Wallace Dunlop's release. "Three months ago the movement had reached its lowest ebb, but today the tide is flowing with them. . . . Miss Wallace Dunlop's 91 hours' fast resulting in her discharge from prison was a masterpiece of ingenuity and tenacity: the public understands hunger."[11] Within a month, George Bernard Shaw reportedly wrote that her actions had "struck a chord which will vibrate to the end of time; . . . when we are dead and forgotten, when this great movement has spent itself and been crowned with victory."[12] Both assessments emphasized that the refusal to eat was a different kind of communicative power, a visceral one that could "vibrate" across space and time and be grasped by the public.

In their memoirs published years later, suffragist leaders gave a heroic luster to Wallace Dunlop's actions and motivations. They heralded her tenacity and noted how her chosen strategy had forced prison officials to respond differently to her. Whereas previously her eating habits had been of little concern, they now received the officials' full attention. Emmeline Pankhurst, in her 1914 memoir, described how the prison governor, physician, and guards had "argued, coaxed and threatened" Wallace Dunlop to eat, but she did not relent.[13] Fellow suffragist and veteran hunger striker Annie Kenney wrote in her memoir, published in 1924, that "Miss Wallace Dunlop went to prison, and defied the long sentences that were being given by adopting the hunger-strike. 'Release or death' was her motto. When asked by the prison authorities what she would have for dinner, her reply was 'My own determination!' From that day, July 5th, 1909, the hunger-strike was the greatest weapon we possessed against the Government."[14]

The WSPU organization harnessed the momentum of Wallace Dunlop's hunger strike, publicizing it and using it to motivate their network of supporters, activists, and donors. They ignited and launched the hunger strike as an essential tool of political protest from prison.

Why did the hunger strike offer such a powerful weapon for disempowered prisoners? Wallace Dunlop's decision to fast was a singular bodily communication. She had effectively turned her persistent petitioning of the government to include women as political subjects, heretofore thwarted and rebuffed, into a bodily refusal that forced prison officials and guards to react. Her determination to refuse meals resonated viscerally with the public, and particularly with suffragists who would later stage their own hunger strikes in prison. Her petition to Home Secretary Herbert Gladstone to be treated as a political prisoner was not accepted, but her threat to refuse food won her early release.

The news of Wallace Dunlop's hunger strike and release spread quickly around London and the world. Proving the potency of the new strategy, fourteen suffragists, convicted on July 9, 1909, the day after Wallace Dunlop was released, resolved to hunger strike. They had been arrested, along with more than a hundred others, on June 29 when thousands of women approached Parliament to support Emmeline Pankhurst in delivering their petition for suffrage to Prime Minister Asquith. Met by three hundred police guards, they were refused and thwarted, and the protest radiated in all directions. Women threw stones and broke windows of government buildings. Not until midnight were the crowds cleared. The magistrate's ruling that the women's right to petition did not "compel" acceptance by legislators reinforced their grievance that they would be ignored until they had the vote.[15] In prison, the fourteen hunger strikers staggered their refusal to eat in successive waves to prolong news coverage. After a few weeks and dozens of newspaper stories, they too were all released.

Hunger striking became an effective weapon against the government and was used in the following weeks by dozens of WSPU prisoners to terminate their sentences.[16] Wallace Dunlop and her fellow suffragists had tapped into a tool that allowed them to extend the duration of women's confrontations with authorities: the first act was suffragists petitioning legislators to bring forward suffrage legislation, and when their petitions were rebuffed, the suffragists confronted politicians and disrupted political events; the second act was street-level battles with the police, arrests, and, in the courtroom, speeches and defiant refusals to pay fines; which led to the third act, which was imprisonment to prove their mettle for suffering. Then the suffragists seized the tool of the hunger strike to force their release, giving them a dramatic fourth act and an opportunity to shame the state.

At the core of what made hunger striking impossible to ignore was the government's fear that the sacrifice of the lives of women in prison would instigate shaming of the government by critics. Even as the government refused to recognize the political status of the prisoners or countenance their political demands, it could not ignore the suffrage prisoners once they went on hunger strike. When Hilda Burkitt went on hunger strike, she warned the prison officials and the government, "If I should die through my fasting, my death will lie at your door, but I am ready to lay down my life, to bring about the freedom of my Sisters."[17]

Not only did Burkitt charge the government as responsible for her potential death; the government officials embraced that responsibility and began to reckon with how to mitigate their culpability. Some men in government felt particularly responsible to protect the white upper- and middle-class women who were at the vanguard of the protests, in spite of the acts of violence and obstruction that had resulted in their imprisonment. Others responded with incredulity, annoyance at the women's insubordinate behavior, impatience to discipline them, or frustration at their resolve. However, they also expressed sympathy and were attentive to the women's emotions and health. They recognized that the women's families, often their social peers, would inquire into and challenge the women's treatment in prison and their deteriorating health in the press, in Parliament, and in person. They made some pretense to the public of treating the women less cavalierly than the poor and working classes were treated in prison.

The possibility of public outrage unnerved government officials in Britain, just as it had in Russia. In 1906, American journalist George Kennan remarked to his readership how even the most "brutally insensible" Russian wardens were alarmed by the "pitiful weapon" of "political hunger-strikers" because of its potential to unleash a firestorm of public outrage and violence. Kennan noted that even in the most secretive regimes, news of hunger striking seeps out of prisons and arouses public fury, uprisings, prison sieges, and assassination threats aimed at prison officials and guards.[18]

The British authorities, in accepting responsibility for the hunger-striking women's welfare, at first required that prison wardens and physicians monitor and document the women's health and communicate that information to the Home Office. Guards were ordered to monitor refused meals, and prison doctors and nurses recorded the prisoners' weight and pulse and made judgments about how to intervene medically. As the strikers weakened and their health became imperiled, the prison wardens, following orders from the Home Office, authorized early release. Eventually, however, they began to consider aggressive responses to keep the prisoners alive, responding to the women's weapon with a weapon of their own.

PRISONS DEPLOY THE FORCE-FEEDING WEAPON

After months of capitulating and releasing fasting women prisoners, in the autumn of 1909, the government followed through on its threat, present since Wallace Dunlop's hunger strike, to feed them using force and justify it as medical necessity. This response set a precedent for subsequent hunger strikes, twisting the hunger strike into an escalating confrontation.

On September 17, nine WSPU members interrupted Prime Minister Asquith's address at Bingley Hall in Birmingham, where all women were denied entry because at similar events that summer, WSPU members had sneaked in and heckled speakers from the audience. Despite security precautions, including evacuating and barricading streets, Mary Leigh and Charlotte Marsh managed to access the roof of an adjacent building. Using an axe, the two women removed slates from the roof, flung them onto the Bingley Hall roof, and damaged Asquith's car on the street below. Other women, who had rented rooms nearby, threw stones from the windows. Police arrested all nine of them. They were tried, found guilty, and given sentences ranging from two weeks to four months imprisonment.

When imprisoned at Birmingham's Winson Green Prison, the women made the now familiar demand for political prisoner status, broke cell windows, and faced the punishment of solitary confinement. As the confrontation escalated, four suffragists resolved to hunger strike. However, it was the government's response, which differed from their response to Wallace Dunlop, that thrust the hunger strike as a weapon into a new vortex of confrontation and ratcheted up political tensions. When Home Secretary Gladstone was informed of the Winson Green hunger strikes, he authorized a new response to hunger strikers: force would be used as necessary to feed them.

The Home Office gave the prison warden a "free hand to take all necessary steps to secure that food be administered artificially" with the "least possible pain or discomfort or danger in event of struggle." The Home Office in addition turned to medical authority and supervision to implement the carceral response, dispatching its medical director to Birmingham and also empowering the prison warden to hire a local physician to advise on the "best means" to feed "(by nostril or mouth)," in order to "avoid prisoner struggle" that could result in "danger and unnecessary pain."[19]

Setting forcible feeding as the new institutional response to refusals to eat led to a cascade of debates and decisions about when to feed the striking prisoners—the first matter being what behavior and condition on the part of the striker should trigger this response. Guards' surveillance and record-keeping of refused meals in a twenty-four-hour period was vital. And once food refusal was identified, prison doctors intervened and monitored each hunger striker's food intake, kept a record of her refused meals, and then delivered a prognosis of her physical condition and a decision of when weakness was dangerous. While similar observations and diagnoses had previously led to hunger strikers being released, now they were used to justify forcible feeding.

While the image of unremitting fasting was paramount in demonstrating endurance and firmness, in fact the prisoners' food refusal was often neither continuous nor consistent. How hunger striking was practiced could be individually adapted, experimented with, and stretched as prisoners reckoned with their own experiences of discomfort and distress. Moreover, women themselves assessed the impact of their fasting and adjusted their actions, all the while calculating in hours, meals, or days the extent of their abstinence. During the month that Hilda Burkitt was imprisoned, she went on several hunger strikes, lasting eighty-six, ninety-one, and twenty-four hours, respectively, and also faced down forcible feeding, in each case pausing to recover and resume eating for a time before renewing her strike. This flexible hunger striking gave prison authorities the impression that a prisoner could relent, was responsive to entreaties and vulnerable to bodily distress, and therefore might stop the refusal to eat at any time. Any voluntary and even temporary acceptance of food and drink by the striker was seen as a victory by prison management. However, the women's recurrent strikes demonstrated how they fine tuned their bodies to endure the rigors of fasting, knowing when they needed to replenish and recover before they resumed striking. This variability was also communal when striking became a relay where each prisoner took a turn and then passed off the strike to the next.

The strikers also explored creative forms of refusal as they were force-fed. For instance, Burkitt refused to be fed by spoon; she would spit out the food and hold "her breath for long intervals" to thwart the orderlies.[20] Sometimes the women verbally refused the feeding but submitted after experiencing the discomfort of the feeding tube. At other times they violently rebuffed the feeding, and prison staff responded with constraint upon their bodies, carrying over bodily binding and restraint techniques from other carceral institutions. Ellen Barwell described how the attendants held her in an armchair, her head grasped from behind, while one compressed her nostrils with a finger and thumb to ensure that she would open her mouth. On another occasion three or four prison attendants held her and tied her down with a makeshift straightjacket of a "blanket folded round her, her wrists and ankles being held by attendants."[21]

SUFFRAGISTS AND MEDIA PUBLICITY OF FORCE-FEEDING

Spotlighting an intimate perspective of the prison experience, the WSPU collected interviews and affidavits from released prisoners to document firsthand the ordeal of being forcibly fed. For instance, after Ellen Barwell and Hilda Burkitt were embraced by family and friends as they emerged through the Winson Green gates after a month's imprisonment, Barwell went home with her father, but Burkitt was taken by taxi to the WSPU offices, where secretary Gladice Keevil took down a statement of her experience of imprisonment and forcible feeding.[22]

These testimonials revealing dramatic confrontations with the guards and medical personnel over force-feeding appeared in the WSPU's pamphlets and its newspaper, *Votes for Women,* and were described in speeches at rallies and meetings. The WSPU also submitted them to mainstream newspapers and magazines. These detailed, harrowing, published accounts in the suffragists' own voices embedded the hunger strike in the horrors of the prison experience, conveying to the public a starkly different impression than the perfunctory official medical reports that were redacted in newspaper accounts and in bureaucratic correspondence. For the historian, weighing the longer suffragist accounts in WSPU materials in the London School of Economics archives against the Home Office case files and newspaper coverage provides a rare personal perspective on the force-feeding experience.

The churn of protest, imprisonment, hunger striking, and forcible feeding persisted month by month for half a decade. From 1909 to 1914, more than one hundred women suffrage activists were force-fed in prisons in Birmingham, London, Liverpool, Dublin, and Dundee. Suffrage leaders regularly publicized these experiences of their fellow imprisoned hunger strikers, effectively making the obscurity and isolation of languishing in prison publicly visible. These testimonials, published both in their own publications and in the broader print media, dramatically changed the public view of and interest in what happens inside prisons.

The suffragists employed different representation strategies to propel the public's attention. At first, they promoted the personal stories of respectable, genteel, and determined solitary strikers in their quest to shame the state. As more women joined in, the singular story mushroomed into a shared narrative leavened with personal feelings and details of coercion, mental distress, and bodily agony delivered by the punitive torture of forcible feeding. This systemic clash also tilted scrutiny to prison routines and administration, raising suspicion that they were neither neutral nor necessary. This strategy succeeded by pitching the voices and credibility of the women prisoners over that of the authorities that managed the prison. Beyond the immediate context of their incarceration and treatment, the suffragists framed their defiance as a bodily sacrifice for the cause of gender equality in citizenship. In combination these strategies commanded the public's attention, by dramatizing the immediacy of torturous treatment and by projecting the political symbolism of their struggle for a just nation.

The ferment of first-person narratives changed public understanding and expectations of what a hunger strike is, who does it, what it means, and why it has an impact. It became expected that women dedicated to advancing their political rights would hunger strike. In the early published testimonials, what was emphasized was their steadfast courage and willingness to sacrifice their personal discomfort for their cause. The refusal to eat was detailed with descriptions of rejected foods and meals, long uneventful hours, solitude, and the gnawing anxiety that the authorities would order forcible feeding. Forcible feeding, once imposed, created a dramatic confrontation with orderlies and physicians that was a significant departure from the mundane and uneventful, slow-moving experience of refusing meals. Enraged suffragists' testimonials that filled the pages of the newspaper *Votes for Women* took aim at the authorities' justification of forcible feeding as medical necessity by highlighting the grave medical consequences it caused, including throat lacerations, stomach damage, heart complaints, and septic pneumonia should food accidentally enter the lungs.

As the emotional drama of the force-feeding confrontation captivated media and political interest, it eclipsed the currency of the physical and emotional toll of self-starvation in the public attention. Accordingly, the hunger strike's meaning changed. Rather than focusing on the ambiguity, pain, and self-doubt of the hunger striker's inward-turning violence of self-deprivation of nutrition as a political statement, the media coverage of the strikers' voices focused on narratives and graphic images of external violence imposed on hunger strikers. Prison policy justified the procedure as medical necessity, and so doctors, nurses, and medical orderlies became the main actors while prison wardens and government officials receded, even as they were accountable for enforcing the policy.

SPREADING THE HUNGER STRIKING MESSAGE ACROSS THE ATLANTIC

British suffragists considered their vision of women's fight for the vote as part of a global crusade that spanned the British Empire and included North America. In the nineteenth century, British and American women had crisscrossed the Atlantic sharing enthusiasm, strategies, publications, and fundraising appeals for slavery abolition, temperance, and women's suffrage. With the 1903 establishment of the International Suffrage Alliance, British and American women, predominantly white and wealthy, claimed the right of women to vote as their crusade for the world.

In the fall of 1909, Emmeline Pankhurst was on a six-week U.S. speaking tour, raising funds among respectable and cultured audiences and assuring them of the noble purpose in her followers' public defiance and prison protests. In her speeches and interviews, Pankhurst explained why hunger striking had become an essential weapon in the suffragists' arsenal as they confronted the government's failure to bring legislation to expand the vote to Parliament. She explained to an American reporter that imprisoned suffragists adopted the method of "hunger strike" used by Russian prisoners after being "driven to the last point of resistance." At first, they believed that "going to prison and submitting to prison discipline would have the desired effect in getting the government to act," but its futility drove them to not "submit patiently" anymore, but to "resist as far as [they] could," to the edge of human endurance. She characterized their "agitation" overall as a "game of chess, move and counter move," that required deep concentration, determination, and strategy.[23]

Many of the young women suffragists on the front lines of confrontations with British politicians and police had been inspired by the charismatic leadership of Emmeline Pankhurst and her daughters, and had traveled from across the British Empire and from the United States to join the British suffrage campaign. During the middle of Pankhurst's tour, on November 9, news wires reported that twenty-three-year-old American college graduate Alice Paul had been arrested, along with another American college graduate, thirty-year-old Lucy Burns, as well as several other WSPU activists, for disrupting the Lord Mayor's Banquet at Guildhall. Paul was sentenced to one month at London's all-women Holloway Prison, where more than a thousand female suffrage prisoners would be incarcerated between 1906 and 1914. Pankhurst, in her two final speeches in New York City, raised the subject of Paul's imprisonment as a free-speech issue. She challenged American women to urge U.S. diplomatic pressure to release Paul, noting that Paul was likely to undertake a hunger strike, as she had done in a Dundee, Scotland, prison in September.[24]

American journalists were eager to feature an American angle on the British suffragist imprisonment, hunger striking, and force-feeding story, and they found a compelling subject in Alice Paul, precisely because she was an educated college graduate from a wealthy and distinguished Quaker family in New Jersey. Immediately after Paul was released from Holloway Prison in early December, a *New York Times* reporter tracked her down to interview her. Although she professed to be too weak for an interview, she sent her own account to the journalist through a friend. That account, which was adapted, edited, and published in the *New York Times* on December 10, 1909, provides what we know of her experience a century later.[25]

In her account, Paul delivered on the pattern of suffragist hunger striking. She had demanded that she be treated as a political prisoner, in order to have more frequent and freer communication, to not have to wear prison clothes, and to not be required to do prison labor. When that request was denied, Paul refused to eat.[26]

She then described the coercion and violence of forcible feeding. After five days of refusing to eat, Paul's disobedience put her in direct confrontation with the women guards who staffed the prison and were in daily and intimate contact with the female prisoners, supervising routines, delivering food, and operating and locking the cells. In her account, Paul trained her perspective on her battle with the working-class wardresses who constrained her, wrapped her in blankets or sheets, and escorted her to "another cell to be fed" by force twice daily. "The largest Wardress in Holloway sat astride my knees, holding my shoulders down to keep me from bending forward. Two other wardresses sat on either side and held my arms."[27]

Once she was immobilized, the doctors would intervene; one doctor would place a "towel" around her throat and force her "head back," while a second doctor pushed a five-foot tube down her nostril, sometimes "so hard that it felt as if [the doctor] were driving a stake into the ground." Liquid food and milk were then poured in through a funnel. Frequently, the tube would not reach Paul's stomach on the first try, in which case the tube would be pulled out, greased, and reinserted through her other nostril. Sabotaging the instrument of feeding when inserted in her mouth, Paul would sometimes bite the tube between her teeth. She also managed to work her hands loose and "snatched the tube, tearing it with [her] teeth twice." In response, the attendants and doctors would pry her mouth open and hold it with a clamp. Paul still refused to "give in" to the feeding, so the wardresses adamantly rammed food down her throat.[28]

In a letter to her mother, written two weeks after her account was published in the *New York Times,* Paul described her bodily responses again, relating her bodily distress in even greater detail. She resisted and fought, so the staff bound her to hold her still in order to feed her, but the binding was so tight that it restricted her breathing. After each of the first three feedings caused facial bleeding, the doctors used a smaller tube. Yet Paul's nostrils became inflamed and her throat spasmed, making the force-feeding episodes acutely painful.[29]

The *New York Times* account, reprinted in newspapers across the country, caused a stir. For both journalists and the reading public, Paul's defiance appeared incongruous with descriptions of her as a "delicate, slip of a girl." One American journalist remarked that Paul's "exceedingly feminine appearance" refuted "the popular conception of an agitator" who interrupts public meetings and endures "prison hardships."[30] For Paul and her allies, highlighting the contrast between her genteel femininity and the rough violence she experienced in prison was intended to attract the newspaper reader's sympathy and concern. For newspaper editors, however, it was surely an aspect of the story that could sell papers.

Both class and gender shaped expectations concerning rough prison treatment. Paul believed, like her fellow British suffragists, that the prison wardresses' and doctors' violent approach was all the more harrowing, indecent, and offensive when aimed at elite, genteel, and delicate white women. Male editors, however, might also have wanted to mock these defiant upper-class white women for behaving in an unseemly fashion. More dramatically, the prison clash revealed a spectacular reversal of class behavior: the prisoner was the genteel, educated woman being disciplined into submission by working-class wardresses who usually were expected to handle unruly lower-class prisoners harshly.

A "STARVATION STRIKE" IN SPOKANE

If hunger striking by educated upper-class women evoked solicitous concern in reports by journalists and newspaper editors, it seems this treatment was less likely when the hunger striker was a militant orator of the working class. An article in a Baltimore newspaper reporting on Alice Paul's imprisonment in London paid great attention to her distinguished Quaker heritage and her degree from Swarthmore College, and it quoted her genteel mother's worry for her daughter. On the same page, a column just below the article about Paul reported the early release of a weakened working-class woman prisoner who had been on "starvation strike" along with hundreds of immigrant and white male and female workers in Spokane, Washington.[31]

Agnes Thecla Fair, a twenty-five-year-old poet and street orator, was arrested on November 6 for violating a sweeping ordinance that prohibited public speaking in downtown Spokane, with a belated exception for missionaries. In the midst of an Industrial Workers of the World (IWW) free speech campaign, Fair was arrested for addressing a large crowd and charged with disorderly conduct. Along with more than 130 male and female orators, Fair was imprisoned for fighting for the right to speak freely in the streets, which U.S. cities and towns attempted to regulate by permits and restrictions to control outdoor venues. These regulations were particularly aimed at curtailing organizing and recruiting by IWW labor, suffrage, and civil liberties speakers, particularly in western states.[32] In the first decade of the twentieth century, Spokane, a crossroads railway shipping hub that connected the Upper Midwest and the Pacific Northwest, nearly tripled in population. The number of male transient workers fluctuated throughout the year, surging during the winter months when lumberjacks and farmworkers sojourned in Spokane, looking for temporary work. The IWW was targeted by authorities because its speakers publicly denounced the employment agencies and job sharks for cheating itinerant workers and conspiring with employers to hire and fire work crews capriciously and force workers to pay repetitive fees.

Fair was called lewd and unseemly for her immodest appearance on city streets and her association with transient IWW rabble-rousers, an accusation that haunted her in prison. Imprisoned in a rancid and darkened cell, Fair alone faced down an interrogation by "ten burly brutes" who entered her cell and questioned her about the union. Fair was "too scared" to answer. She described in a letter how one man said, "F—k her and she'll talk," and when another man began to unbutton her dress, she went into spasms and unconsciousness. Later, a male police officer disguised as a drunken woman was admitted to the cell and sexually assaulted her. Fair did not sleep and refused to eat for three days.[33] She joined what the politicians and press labeled a "starvation strike" by the arrested men, who were refusing the punitive bread-and-water diet ordered for them by the police chief after they rejected his demand that they labor on a makeshift rock pile in downtown Spokane.[34]

On November 8, after a doctor recommended her immediate release to a hospital, Fair requested to be carried by stretcher to the courthouse through Spokane's streets, a scene that caused a public commotion. The broader starvation strike ended a few days later, but the prison struggles persisted as confrontations between the IWW and the city continued. The jails of Spokane filled, forcing the city to repurpose an abandoned school and use a federal fort to house prisoners. Over the course of four months, more than five hundred people were jailed, some for two or three months, all for public speaking without a permit.

A week after her imprisonment, Fair published her account of her prison ordeal in the socialist newspaper *The Workingmen's Paper*. The city police confiscated and destroyed copies because of her story's alleged indecency. These accusations of prison sexual abuse and police running a prostitution ring in prison caught the attention of club women and suffragists in the city. Even though workers' speech was curtailed, earlier in the year the Spokane suffragists had enjoyed the benefits of public political organizing when touring East Coast suffragists had stopped in the city to rally support for the Washington state legislative campaign for women's right to vote.

When newspapers across the country reported Spokane's free speech battle and the starvation strike, their scorn for the workers was unmistakable. The articles disparaged the men and women protesters as mostly foreigners and as immoral rabble-rousers who refused hard labor and were undeserving of sympathy. When the men broke their starvation strike, a local newspaper described them as "pathetic" beggars "eating like starved wild creatures."[35] Furthermore, Agnes Fair's account of sexual assault, followed by the jailing of IWW organizer Elizabeth Gurley Flynn and exposure of the police prostitution ring, eclipsed the starvation strike in the media.

The media deployed the term *starvation strike,* like the Russian term for "famine strike," to connote vulnerability to want. A starvation strike was no less a bodily refusal than a hunger strike; however, in usage, *hunger strike* was connected more with an individual's determination, associated with the decisions of the middle and upper classes. Starvation and famine were less a choice and more an endemic condition. Newspaper editors ridiculed Spokane's mass "starvation strike" as pitiful, a desperate effort to neither work nor pay fines. They dismissed the motivation and dignity of the protesting workers, relegating them to the very margins of society and thus undermining the public's sympathy and outrage for their situation while deflecting attention from the IWW's advocacy of free speech.

Class difference was at the core of the media's expression of public alarm and hostility. Suffragists contended with the divergence between the rough treatment they received in prison and the dignity they presumed based on their wealth and status. Not all suffragists were wealthy, but elite and middle-class women played an overwhelming role in shaping the suffragist media narratives. In Britain, even when media exposés revealed the more vicious treatment meted out to working-class suffragist prisoners, it was through elite women's eyes. For example, in 1910, a member of the privileged ruling class, Lady Constance Lytton, disguised herself as a working-class seamstress and suffragist named Jane Warton and was imprisoned. She later related how viciously she was treated by the same warden, matrons, and guards who had previously shown her deference and care, and who had even helped her gain early release from previous prison stints served under her true identity.[36]

AMERICAN NATIONAL CAMPAIGN FOR SUFFRAGE

In the United States in 1910, the American fight for the vote for women was synonymous with neither imprisonment nor the hunger strike weapon. When Alice Paul returned to the United States, she no longer spoke in detail about the emotional and physical distress of forcible feeding upon her release from Holloway Prison just a month earlier. She wanted to leave her prison struggle behind in Britain. In an interview with the *Philadelphia Tribune* in January 1910, Paul tersely recalled the experience of forcible feeding as simply "revolting." When questioned about her plans to apply militant methods to the cause of women's suffrage in the United States, Paul demurred, saying she wanted to return to her home in Moorestown, New Jersey, to recover her health and strength after "her stormy experience" and continue her academic studies.[37] Nevertheless, just a few years later she was deeply involved in the suffrage movement again.

Lucy Burns returned to the United States in 1912, and when she and Alice Paul reunited, they adapted their training under Emmeline Pankhurst for street-corner speaking, organizing parades, and communicating to the media to launch a new chapter in the American campaign for the vote for women.[38] The suffrage movement in the United States had thus far been propelled by victories in the western states. Following the successful grassroots campaign in Washington in 1910, California, Oregon, Kansas, and Arizona granted suffrage to women by 1912, followed by Illinois, Nevada, and Montana in 1914. Paul and Burns took the U.S. suffrage fight to the national stage.

In January 1913, inspired by WSPU pageantry and spectacle, Paul and Burns organized a women's suffrage parade on the day before President Wilson's inauguration that drew eight thousand women marchers, accompanied by bands and floats, on Pennsylvania Avenue. Under the aegis of the National American Woman Suffrage Association (NAWSA), the march nationalized the campaign for women's suffrage, but by welcoming black and brown women, the parade had the potential to inflame opponents, who persisted in suppressing the voting rights of all African American, Native, and Asian American adults. Paul and her fellow white women leaders, fearful that southern white delegations would pull out of the parade and ambivalent about their own prejudices, relegated black women to the back of the procession. Famously, Ida B. Wells, the antilynching crusader who had toured Britain and the United States, flouted these instructions and walked with the Illinois delegation.

Thousands of white male Democratic Party supporters and spectators crowded the parade route, ridiculing and jeering at the female marchers, tripping and assaulting them. The D.C. police, indifferent to the women and sympathetic to the mob, simply countenanced the violence, and more than a hundred marchers were hospitalized. Even as the parade's end was marred by violence, the participation of women from across the United States emboldened Paul and Burns to create a national organization, the Congressional Union, to lobby Congress for a constitutional amendment guaranteeing women's suffrage nationwide.

In 1914 the NAWSA broke off ties with the Congressional Union, distancing itself from Burns and Paul's confrontational approach. Undaunted, Paul and Burns took the fight for nationwide suffrage to congressional districts in the western United States where women had the vote, to pressure reluctant Democrats to support women's suffrage by federal constitutional amendment. In 1916 Paul and Burns formed the National Woman's Party (NWP) to spearhead voter education campaigns and to lobby reluctant Democratic Party politicians to pass a suffrage amendment to the U.S. Constitution. The NWP rebuked the Democratic Party's strategy of blocking national suffrage in favor of state-by-state legislation of suffrage, a strategy to appease conservative and southern Democrats who had effectively curtailed black men's enfranchisement and blocked women's enfranchisement altogether.

By 1917, the NWP numbered fifty thousand members, a tiny organization compared to the two million members claimed by the NAWSA. Yet, under the leadership of Paul and Burns, the NWP's membership actively engaged and effectively commanded the attention of politicians and the public through relentless lobbying, transcontinental auto campaigns, speaking tours, banners, and billboards to spread the urgency of national suffrage. Paul's speaking, charismatic leadership, and fund-raising role dominated the NWP's public face, while Burns trained the nationwide network of volunteers and organized rallies and lobbying campaigns. She also led the publicity operation, publishing a newspaper and commanding the public relations operation that communicated directly with members and supplied two hundred news correspondents with frequent news bulletins. Nearly four years of lobbying, petitioning, and processions, however, had not yielded legislative advances in Congress, although enfranchisement campaigns were gaining traction in midwestern states and New York. So the NWP strategists escalated their campaign and adopted more aggressive tactics.

On January 10, 1917, a dozen women dressed in white marched with pickets in front of the White House, and the picketing continued every day for months thereafter, regardless of the weather. The NWP organizers carefully planned every detail, orchestrating volunteers who were recruited and scheduled for shifts of several hours. Special days were set aside for women

FIGURE 2. Alice Paul, ca. 1920. Photograph by Harris and Ewing studio, Washington, D.C. Courtesy of the Library of Congress.

representing specific states, schools, organizations, and occupations. Nearly two thousand suffragists traveled from thirty states to take turns on the picket line. Banners emblazoned with provocative messages were the medium for embarrassing and pressuring President Wilson into action. Burns and Paul orchestrated a "powerful visual rhetoric on the picket line, one of women standing together as silent nonviolent witnesses to the injustice of denying the vote" to women.[39]

Initially, spectators viewed the marchers with curiosity and some sympathy, and the White House tolerated their presence. When the United States entered World War I in April 1917, however, public mood soured on picketing. Some women resigned from the NWP because they viewed picketing as unpatriotic, besides unwomanly. The tone of the pickets and banners turned to exposing the hypocrisy of the president's advocacy of democracy abroad through war while denying female citizens at home the right to vote.

The suffragists' daily silent picketing began to provoke physical attacks. Crowds of spectators would gather, growing hostile and restive. Male bystanders would tear banners from the picketers' hands. Young men and boys would jeer at, insult, and harass the women, crowding and menacing them "until there was but a foot of smothering, terror-fraught space between them and the pickets" according to suffrage organizer Inez Haynes Irwin.[40] When skirmishes broke out, the police stood by and watched and then arrested the women on charges of obstructing traffic. New recruits replaced them, including socialists, labor organizers, and social welfare workers who were attracted to the campaign's dignified confrontation and persistent demand for justice and the exercise of free speech. In an era when police, militia, and vigilantes violently suppressed union picketing and workers' strikes, the women's bravery stood out.

The government wanted to shut down the protests, and police and prosecutors criminalized free speech pickets with charges of disorderly conduct and obstruction of the sidewalk. In July, police court judges set fines of $25, or three days imprisonment if the arrested woman refused to pay. After serving jail time for three days, the women, emboldened by the arrests, would return to join the pickets again. By September, the police court was sentencing women who refused to pay their fines to thirty days of hard labor at Occoquan Workhouse, established in 1910 by the D.C. government as a prison work farm and reformatory for nonviolent prisoners across the Potomac in Virginia.[41] Throughout that year of civil disobedience picketing, 168 women members of the NWP served prison sentences at Occoquan.

On October 20, Alice Paul and dozens of other picketers were arrested. In the Police Court of the District of Columbia, Judge Alexander Mullowney's notions of respectable women were confounded by the picketing, and he expressed disbelief that "ladies" would persist in disobeying laws. When it came to the sentencing, he claimed that the arrested women's actions forced him "to take the most drastic means in my power to compel you to obey the law." He made a particular example of Paul, "the ringleader," by sentencing her to seven months in jail.[42]

When Paul climbed into the patrol wagon on October 22, she told the press that as a political prisoner, she felt the "deepest indignation against an administration that permits such gross injustice." She explained: "I am imprisoned not because I obstructed traffic but because I pointed out to President Wilson the fact that he is obstructing the progress of democracy and justice at home, while Americans fight for it abroad."[43]

When the government desperately turned to imprisonment to suppress women's voices, the terrain of protest swung from the streets into the recesses of carceral power. At the District of Columbia Jail, Alice Paul and the three women sentenced with her joined Lucy Burns and other imprisoned suffragists who had recently been transferred to the jail from Occoquan Workhouse. The warden ordered all the white suffragists housed together on the third floor, segregating them from the largely black prison population on the second floor. The racial segregation mirrored an unofficial acknowledgment of the suffragists' political prisoner status. Their cells were no different than those of the rest of the prisoners, however, and one and sometimes two prisoners were housed in a dank cement cell, six by nine feet, with an open toilet and hard mattresses on steel cots. The porthole windows were shut from late afternoon until morning, contributing to the stifling atmosphere inside.[44]

Paul led appeals for fresh air, exercise, and privacy. The women's protests netted them solitary confinement, their cells locked day and night, and denial of mail and visitors. The food was barely edible: worm-ridden pork and stale bread. Paul ate little and, like many of the women, grew steadily weaker. After Burns and the other Occoquan transfers were released on November 3, solitary confinement ended for the remaining prisoners and they were given time to exercise in the yard. However, the constant cold and undernourishment had taken its toll. One suffragist prisoner, Rose Winslow, fainted in the exercise yard, and Alice Paul felt too weak to climb out of bed. Both women were removed to the jail hospital in the adjacent building.

There, on November 6, Paul and Winslow began a hunger strike. Concerned prison officials permitted a rare concession: Dr. Cora Smith King, Paul's personal physician, was allowed to visit her in the presence of Dr. James A. Gannon, visiting physician of the District of Columbia Hospital and Asylum. Dr. King was able to give Paul the news that New York voters had approved a state referendum to fully enfranchise women (which had gone down in defeat two years before).[45]

Paul was savvy to the power of her hunger strike on the public; journalists had anticipated it since her sentencing. To Dora Lewis, she sent a secret message with Dr. King: "I had not thought of carrying [the strike] to any great length as I thought no one would know," but with the newspapers picking up the story, "I suppose we are committed to the plan and must go forward!"[46] Paul recognized that her hunger strike, combined with the picket publicity, could leverage the larger goal of making women's suffrage imperative to American democracy, within days of the victory of the New York state referendum to enfranchise women.

In the first seventy-eight hours of her strike, Alice Paul, sequestered and isolated in a medical ward in the prison's hospital, faced down not only the threat of invasive medical treatment but, in a twist to the countermeasures against hunger striking, psychiatric scrutiny as well. Dr. William White, eminent psychiatrist in charge of St. Elizabeth's, the government insane asylum, visited to ascertain her mental state. He skeptically tried to coax verbal communication from Paul, presuming that "these cases frequently will not talk." Paul, at the ready, spoke right up, saying, "Talking is our business . . . we talk to anyone on earth who is willing to listen to our suffrage speeches." She was aware that Dr. White's visit was an attempt to discredit her "as the leader of the agitation, by casting doubt on my sanity or else to intimidate us [into] retreating from the hunger strike."[47]

Paul later described the medical officer in charge, Dr. Gannon, as the "devil incarnate," who "alternatively bullied and hinted" that she would be forcibly fed. In the midst of these continuous threats, Paul said, she exercised self-discipline and "lay perfectly silent on my bed" in spite of her fears.[48]

In her hospital room, Paul met with District Commissioner Gwynne Gardiner, who promised to investigate the jail conditions. However, he refused to treat the suffragists as political prisoners—and she refused to abandon her hunger strike. When he left her room, she overheard him give the order to Dr. Gannon: "Go ahead, take her and feed her." Orderlies came to place her on a stretcher and carry her down the hall into the psychopathic ward.[49] Three times a day for three weeks, doctors and nurses forced a tube down her throat and poured liquids into her stomach that contained as much protein as possible, such as raw eggs mixed with milk.[50]

Paul confronted varied attitudes among the jail hospital's staff, primarily nurses and interns. The doctor had commanded that Paul be observed regularly throughout the night and day. At night, on every hour, a nurse entered loudly and "turned on an electric sharp light" to illumine Paul's face, an "ordeal [of] most terrible torture" that prevented her from sleeping for more than a few minutes at a time. When she did "finally get to sleep it was only to be socked immediately into wide-awakeness with pitiless light."[51] When Paul protested "mildly" to a young medical intern that the blood test he was administering was "unnecessary," he gave a "sneer and supercilious shrug . . . and dismissive retort, 'you know you are not mentally competent to decide such things.'" In contrast to the intern, the nurses, Paul said, were "beautiful in their spirit and offered every kindness." She particularly appreciated one new nurse who would greet her in the morning and reassure her with "I know you are not insane."[52]

This reassurance offered a small counterbalance to the physicians' and psychiatrists' threats that Paul would be "taken to a very unpleasant place if you don't stop this." Their meaning was clear: she would be removed to St. Elizabeth's, the government mental asylum, permanently.[53] Even as she remained outwardly stoic to these threats, she was terrified. The nurses explained to her the carceral power of an insanity diagnosis: after two psychiatrists examine the patient and "sign an order committing the patient to St Elizabeth's Asylum," there is no redress: "No trial, no counsel, no protest from the outside world!"[54] The diagnosis of mental illness was exclusively the prerogative of a physician, who exercised total sovereignty over the prisoner.

Force-feeding and other nonconsensual treatments were routine in mental asylums, and if Paul were committed to the asylum, her isolation would be total. Even in the psychopathic ward of the D.C. Jail hospital, her isolation was severe: "I could not see my family or friends, counsel was denied to me; I saw no other prisoners and heard nothing of them; I could see no papers; I was entirely in the hands of alienist, prison officials and hospital staff. I believe I have never in my life before [so] feared anything or any human being."[55]

LUCY BURNS'S ARREST AND THE TERRORS OF
OCCOQUAN WORKHOUSE

On November 10, just a week after her release from the D.C. Jail, Lucy Burns and thirty-three other suffragists orchestrated a large picket outside the White House. Burns and most of the other women were arrested. Burns's reappearance in the courtroom frustrated Judge Mullowney, and he sentenced her to seven months imprisonment and another twenty-nine women to thirty days or less. Mullowney had ordered their imprisonment in the D.C. Jail, but prison officials feared holding these women in close proximity to Alice Paul, so instead they sent the women across the Potomac to Occoquan Workhouse, where Burns had been imprisoned two months earlier. (She had been arrested on September 4 at the pickets with a dozen women and sentenced to sixty days imprisonment.)[56] During her first time at Occoquan, Lucy Burns and ten other prisoners had petitioned to be recognized as political prisoners and also complained of the guards' rough treatment in the workhouse, as well as the capricious solitary confinement of Burns. As a result of the petition on October 22, Burns and the other prisoners had been transferred to the District Prison.

When the women arrived at Occoquan on November 14, Dora Lewis, speaking for the group, demanded political prisoner status and insisted on seeing the superintendent of the workhouse. When Superintendent Raymond Whittaker arrived, he was furious. Exasperated by the return of repeat offenders like Burns, he was also angered by their damaging accusations of ill-treatment and successful petitions for early release from Occoquan a month earlier. He refused the request for political prisoner status and instead ordered the guards, many of them allegedly ununiformed, to seize the women and place them in solitary confinement. Burns later described what became known as the "Night of Terror," when male guards seized the women from behind, flinging them off their feet, handcuffed them, and dragged them to cells in the men's part of the prison. They threatened Burns with a straitjacket and buckle gag if she did not comply.[57] Detained in her cell, Burns was handcuffed with her hands above her head, even as she continued to shout out and rally the other prisoners. Guards twisted Dorothy Day's arm behind her back, threw Lewis into a dark cell, and slammed both of them against iron benches, knocking Lewis unconscious. Alice Cosu suffered a heart attack and did not receive medical care until the next morning. Yet the women did their best to continue to hold their hands above their head in solidarity with Burns.[58]

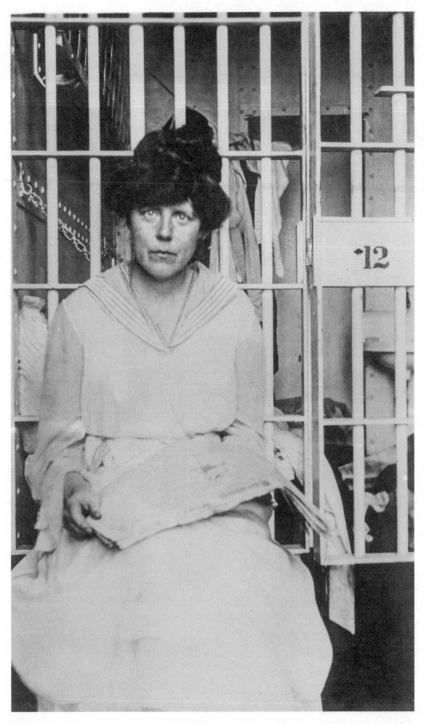

FIGURE 3. Lucy Burns imprisoned in the Occoquan Workhouse in Virginia, November 1917. Photograph by Harris and Ewing studio, Washington, D.C. Courtesy of the Library of Congress.

After enduring this treatment overnight, the women were not brought food until 3 P.M. the next day—at which point they refused to eat. After three days of the women not eating, the guards tried to tempt them with fried chicken. The women viewed this as an insult to their resolve. Burns passed a note to the other women: "I think this riotous feast which has just passed our doors is the last effort of the institution to dislodge all of us who can be dislodged. They think there is nothing in our souls above fried chicken."[59] By November 21, thirty women were hunger striking, and three, Lucy Burns, Kate Heffelfinger, and Dora Lewis, were subjected to forcible feeding. The medical demands of forcible feeding persuaded Whittaker to remove the three to the D.C. Jail hospital ward, where Alice Paul and Rose Winslow were in their fourteenth day of hunger striking and were already being force-fed.

Burns's and Heffelfinger's descriptions of experiencing the same "torture of forcible feeding" endured by Paul and Winslow "three times a day for fourteen days" are preserved in the NWP's records. Their intensely personal and disturbing narratives rebuked their own assumptions that the doctors and their medical technology had therapeutic and beneficial intent. The rubber feeding tube was a particular source of pain and anguish. Burns identified Dr. Gannon as responsible for "forcing the tube through my lips and down my throat." She emphasized the visceral reflexes of "gasping and suffocating from the agony" of the feeding: "I didn't know where to breathe from, and everything turned black." Heffelfinger called the felt experience of it "torture": "the horrible gripping and gagging of swallowing six inches of stiff rubber tubing. Such a strain on the nervous system is not to be imagined." This was followed by "the ordeal of waiting while liquids are poured through" and then the "withdrawal of the tube." The painful tube insertions and feeding caused Heffelfinger to suffer "streaming eyes and parched, burning throat." She wondered "how the people of this nation already tasting blood and pain [of wartime casualties] can let this be done to these women day after day . . . women who are in prison because they ask for liberty."[60]

Two high-profile lawyers working with the National Woman's Party, Dudley Field Malone and Matthew O'Brien, strategized not only to publicize the conditions of the prisoners but to seek their relief and release. Malone concentrated on the case of Alice Paul in the District of Columbia Jail, seeking her release from the psychiatric ward back to the prison hospital wing, while O'Brien developed cases for the prisoners at Occoquan. Forcing their way into these institutions with court orders, both men were outraged at the conditions and treatment of the women.

The prison warden refused to allow Malone to interview Alice Paul, but Malone learned of her condition through the interview he was granted with one of the other prisoners, Rose Winslow. O'Brien obtained a writ of habeas corpus ordering Superintendent Whittaker to produce all his suffragist prisoners for hearings before the U.S. Court of Appeals in Alexandria, Virginia, on November 23 and 24. The hearings were packed with supporters and newspaper reporters. Reviewing the women's affidavits of the brutalities they experienced at Occoquan, Judge Edmund Waddill called the treatment "bloodcurdling" if true. When the women did appear, journalists and supporters were shocked by their haggard, bruised, and disoriented appearance; some were barely able to walk or sit upright. The media coverage of the hearings and the women's affidavits shone a harsh light on the government's extreme tactics to suppress the suffragists. These white upper- and middle-class women, in particular, were seen by the media as undeserving of such brutality. Even though Judge Waddill disallowed testimony about the conditions at Occoquan, he repudiated the women's imprisonment at the workhouse as illegal, "without semblance of authority or legal process," and ordered their immediate transfer to the D.C. Jail, where they were supposed to have been incarcerated. By the evening of Saturday, November 25, the Occoquan prisoners had been moved to the D.C. Jail, where Paul, Winslow, Burns, and Lewis were being force-fed in the adjacent hospital building.[61]

Mounting newspaper coverage and rising public outrage pressured Judge Mullowney to revisit his sentencing of the picketers. On Monday, November 27, 1917, Mullowney asked the D.C. Jail's warden, Louis Zinkham, about the health of the women. Zinkham replied swiftly that there were twenty-two remaining prisoners on hunger strike and they needed to be released. Hours later they were freed. "Greatly relieved" by the judge's order, Zinkham instructed the guards to release the remaining eight prisoners who were not on hunger strike. As a frail Alice Paul left her hospital bed and blinked in the sunlight after five weeks in prison, she declared, "We were out of jail as we were put in—at the whim of the government. They tried to terrorize and suppress us. They could not, so they freed us."[62]

In her 1920 history of the NWP, *Jailed for Freedom*, Doris Stevens wrote of this moment: "With thirty determined women on hunger strike, of whom eight were in a state of almost total collapse, the Administration capitulated. It could not afford to feed thirty women forcibly and risk the social and political consequences, nor could it let thirty women starve themselves to death, and likewise take the consequences."[63]

FIGURE 4. Suffragist Kate Heffelfinger covered in a blanket following her release from the Occoquan Workhouse in Virginia, 1917. Courtesy of the Library of Congress.

NATIONAL WOMAN'S PARTY MEMBERS DEBATE PRISONERS' EXPERIENCES AND STRATEGIES

The NWP followed the lead of the British WSPU in broadcasting the women's own voices as portraying the true life experience of prisoners fighting unjust brutality. As in Britain, official information about the imprisoned suffragists' treatment in prison was tightly controlled, yet the women subverted the secrecy through notes on scraps of paper smuggled out to families and to NWP workers. These bits of information offered public voice to those in prison who had no direct access to journalists, media, and a broad public audience. Testimonial accounts by suffragists after their release from prison were another source of information for what happened within prison walls. The NWP used these firsthand accounts in its publicity campaign, thereby demonstrating that the prisoners' refusal to eat and forcible feeding were not private matters to be dealt with in secrecy. Rather, lifting the veil of secrecy, shame, and isolation from the experience of imprisonment was part of a broad political and public struggle for justice.

To its members the NWP issued telegrams and letters providing details regarding the treatment of its leaders: how and where they were held, moved, and force-fed. During the week in November between her two prison terms, Lucy Burns crafted messages to members that described Alice Paul's "desperate" physical condition as she remained in the D.C. Jail hospital. Burns disputed official suspicions of Paul's sanity and argued that force-feeding was intended to break Paul's will and "endangers not only her health but her life."[64]

The NWP's storytelling strategy followed the WSPU's hunger-striking form in making the treatment of imprisoned suffragists central to its communications with members—underlining the striker's perspective, as well as her courage, tenacity, and "individual sacrifice" for the sake of the broader suffrage crusade. The first-person accounts were intended to inform but also to incite empathy and financial support from the reader who would be shocked by such violent and brutalizing treatment of white middle-class and elite women. They often were sent out in a circular letter, a form letter that appeared as individual correspondence with a request for action and funds— a forerunner to today's mass mailings.[65]

The response among NWP members to the letters and telegrams was polarized. Some quickly telegrammed the government, as the letter requested, to express their outrage about the women's treatment. Others vigorously opposed the picketing and had little sympathy for the imprisoned—views they expressed by either writing their own letters back to the NWP or returning the NWP's appeal with their own commentary written in the margins. The latter are perhaps the most interesting for us, as they are particularly punitive and judgmental, not unlike trolling comments on digital platforms today.

Some of those critical responses vehemently rejected the public spectacle of pickets and arrests. Many of these critics were dismayed by the picketing occurring during wartime mobilization and characterized them as an annoyance and distraction for President Wilson. Responses castigated the women on the picket lines as "unpatriotic" and "fanatical."[66] Cora Howland of Chicago wrote that the arrested women's actions were in "bad taste," "selfish," and "treasonable," and deemed the women "hysterical individualists."[67] Others feared that the controversy would set back both gradual state suffrage and a constitutional amendment. They worried that conservative men might opt to deny suffrage to disruptive women and thereby, as Mrs. Edward Rider wrote, deny it also to "reasonable, thinking women."

Depicting the picketing campaign as "foolish" and "unreasonable," many of these critics approved of the government's treatment of the picketers. Rider wrote that she "heartily applaud[ed] the Administration's method of dealing with such 'inane' women. . . . They might corral the whole bunch and minister similar treatment." Fannie A. Bivans, a lawyer from Decatur, Illinois, wrote, in a letter to Lucy Burns, that Alice Paul "should be let starve to death if she chooses to do so," adding that "I do not doubt you are sincere in your notions of conscience and in thinking that you are martyrs."[68] And a letter by Evelyn Barr Brock and Mrs. Marcus J. Brock said, "Do not picket then you will be not be forcibly fed."[69]

The tenor of the negative responses from these upper- and middle-class white women was consonant with their social responsibilities of ordering the household and training and disciplining children and servants. They had firsthand experience in both exercising discipline and complying with it and understood such submission as proper behavior for their own good and the good of society. They viewed the "disobedient" hunger-striking women through this same lens, infantilizing them and affirming their punishment. The U.S. government likewise dismissed the actions of the women as "hysterical," rendering the very act of refusing food publicly as childish. Political commentators charged hunger striking as domestic blackmail or manipulative.

Paul and the NWP suffragists had reason to worry that their political convictions could be dismissed as a trivial domestic drama, making their cause and tactics not worthy of the realm of politics. Yet the NWP's strategy was radical and militant precisely because it unmade expectations that the suffragists—themselves from the middle and upper classes—were proper, well-mannered women who sublimate their interests for the greater good of husband, family, and nation.

WORLD WAR I AND SUFFRAGE FOR BRITISH AND AMERICAN WOMEN

With the onset of World War I, when the crisis of imperial democracy became enveloped in global conflict, government demands on their citizens and subjects escalated. Proof of loyalty and sacrifice by those citizens and subjects correspondingly shifted the terrain of government's accountability for the lives and treasure it expended. As the war persisted, a new route to expanding suffrage for women and men opened.

In August 1914, within ten days of the British declaration of war on Germany, suffragists of all persuasions suspended political activity, and the WSPU brokered a deal with the government to release all remaining imprisoned suffragists in return for the organization's pledge to back the war effort. Christabel Pankhurst (one of Emmeline's daughters) declared that the WSPU had signed "an armistice with the Government and suspended militancy for the duration of the war."[70] The WSPU thereafter adopted a fervently patriotic campaign, even changing the name of its weekly publication to *Britannia*.

The wartime mobilization and sacrifice had the effect of scrambling the political blockages of class and gender that had impeded universal suffrage. During the war years, women filled more than a million-and-a-half jobs as clerical workers and in ship building and munitions manufacturing. Their contributions to the war effort were publicly visible and valued. Six million men had been mobilized, and their sacrifices of life and limb in combat were enormous, with more than seven hundred thousand soldiers and sailors killed. The upper- and middle-class male stranglehold on suffrage was easing, out of political necessity. With the prospect of millions of soldiers returning from the war, the wartime coalition government chose to reward the returning soldiers and women workers. The events of the 1917 Russian Revolution, which provoked elite fears of working-class upheavals and protests across Europe, also forced the British political parties to find a compromise on voting rights. In February 1918, the Representation of the People Act enfranchised all men over the age of twenty-one, irrespective of property qualifications, and women over the age of thirty who met property qualifications, which was 40 percent of the adult women. The legislation had overwhelmingly passed the House of Commons in June of the previous year. It was not defeated in the House of Lords—as many reform bills had been when the Liberals held power before the war—because Lord Curzon, former Viceroy of India, who led the opposition to women's suffrage, abstained from the vote, persuading other lords to follow suit and not oppose the bill.

After decades of obstruction and legislative stalemate, the right to vote expanded for working men and for women, transforming the electorate. Dropping the age bar for men from thirty to twenty-one (nineteen for men who served in combat) and adding women, even with property and age qualifications, nearly tripled the size of the eligible electorate from 7.7 million to

21.4 million by adding 8.4 million women and 5.6 million men. The British voting system retained class advantage, giving 7 percent of the elite electorate extra votes for their business property (over £10 in a different constituency) and their university degrees. The class and age restrictions for women were intentional, to ensure that women would not be an absolute majority of the electorate after the large losses of men in the war. In 1928, when the Conservative government passed the Representation of the People (Equal Franchise) Act, giving the vote to all women over the age of twenty-one on equal terms with men, that added to the voter rolls five million women aged twenty-one to thirty and an additional two million women over thirty who did not hold enough property to have qualified in 1918.[71]

The 1918 compromise, let alone the 1928 equal suffrage legislation, may not have been plausible if militant women had not waged their own battle with ruling-class men, the government, police, and prisons during the five years prior to the outbreak of World War I. Many supporters of women's suffrage, including Liberal and Labor politicians, discredited the militant protests as delaying women's suffrage. However, the impasse between the political parties and the parliamentary chambers was over whether or not to expand the eligibility of suffrage generally. And the political parties were reluctant to cede voting power to women, whether elite, middle-class, or working women. Without the war, a majority of both houses of Parliament might have remained elusive, and it might have taken longer before giving the vote to women—as a divided Parliament had prevented for a century the granting of the vote to men under the age of thirty and without property.

In the United States, many believed that after the war, obedient, patriotic women would be rewarded for their patriotism with suffrage rights. In the 1916 elections, before the United States entered the war, NAWSA suffragists had secured pledges in both Democratic and Republican political platforms to endorse women's suffrage. The NWP, however, believed these were feeble pledges, since they only maintained the status quo, according to which the power to grant or deny women voting rights was held by individual states. In 1917, when the United States entered the war, all American suffragists were expected to fall in line with patriotic military mobilization, following the example of their British counterparts, a path that the NWP vociferously refused.

After Paul and the other hunger strikers were released from the D.C. Jail, both NWP and NAWSA leaders focused on political lobbying to thaw the legislative stalemate between factions of Democratic and Republican

FIGURE 5. Suffragist Lucy Branham, in a prison uniform, addressing an audience as part of the National Woman's Party "Prison Special" tour in 1919. Courtesy of the Library of Congress.

legislators, and President Wilson, that prevented a vote on the constitutional amendment for nationwide women's suffrage. On January 10, 1918, the same day the British House of Lords gave final passage to women's suffrage in Britain, the U.S. House of Representatives passed the Nineteenth Amendment, endorsed by President Wilson as a "war measure," which would grant women the right to vote. The Senate, however, delayed bringing the bill to a vote until October 1. On September 30, six weeks before the midterm elections, Wilson personally addressed the Senate and pleaded that it "give justice to women." A bipartisan majority voted for the bill the next day, but it fell two votes short of the necessary two-thirds majority to pass. During that fall's election season, coalitions of suffragists waged robust and successful campaigns to elect pro-suffragist Republican and defeat anti-suffragist Democratic senators.

In March 1919, a new Republican majority took their seats in the Senate. After President Wilson called a special session of Congress in May, the Nineteenth Amendment was passed in both the House and Senate and was signed by Wilson. Both the NWP and the NAWSA then rallied their chapters nationwide in a fourteen-month campaign, sending organizers into states to secure ratification by thirty-six states, leading to the amendment's ratification in August 1920.

After the achievement of this monumental goal, an exhausted Lucy Burns declared: "We have done all this for women, and we have sacrificed everything we possessed for them, and now let them fight for it now. I am not going to fight anymore."[72] She retired from political life and devoted herself to the Catholic Church and the care of her orphaned niece. Alice Paul continued to fight for the equality of women and for civil rights and fair employment legislation on the public stage for decades. The NAWSA became the League of Women Voters and worked to inform voters and advocate for welfare programs for women, children, and seniors. The NWP shifted its focus to the Equal Rights Amendment to extend gender equality beyond voting to all aspects of society and the law.

COMMUNICATING THE TRAUMA OF HUNGER STRIKING

Suffragists experimented with the tool of the hunger strike and learned who could wield it effectively and what shape the struggle unleashed by its use would take. They learned that communicating the strikers' voices and their actions to the public was vital. Moreover, the women's courage and determination were crucial to the effectiveness of their demands for full citizenship and the right to vote.

Alice Paul's experience with suffrage agitation and with hunger-striking protest bridged the two sides of the Atlantic across a decade. In that time and across her lifetime, she shaped and reshaped what the hunger striking meant for her political aims. Her 1909 account of her Holloway Prison hunger strike, written right after her release, was remarkable for its candor in describing the visceral and behavioral response while coping with forcible feeding. Subsequently she found sharing the experience with the press vexed and unsettling. Like her fellow British suffragists, she had voiced her experience publicly to draw attention to the government's abusive treatment. But the demand to speak of the trauma repeatedly, and thus to relive it and to have it reverberate ceaselessly in public, was exhausting and unwanted. She resisted having her hunger strike be the defining feature of her work and her legacy.

In 1917, when she and Lucy Burns developed a strategy of U.S. congressional lobbying, public spectacle, and picketing, Paul anticipated that her imprisonment and demands for political prisoner status could lead her to hunger strike and thus to risk being forcibly fed again. She dreaded the possibility of being involuntarily committed to an asylum and the loss of control over her body that would entail. Yet for her the gravest danger may have been the risk of not being heard from again. Involuntary commitment to the asylum would quash her public voice and her ability to lead and strategize the political movement for equality.

During an oral history interview in 1972, Paul, at the age of eighty-seven, played down the physical intensity of her 1917 experience, recalling instead the indifference and isolation: "Oh they just paid no attention to us. You were just locked up and you were in solitary confinement. You never saw anybody. You were not given anything to read. You were just left alone. Nobody paid any attention to you whatsoever." She did curtly declare, "We were forcibly fed you see. We didn't eat anything," evidently not wanting to dwell on those memories. As if to explain the absence of detail about her experience of forcible feeding, she commented on her lack of interest in food: "I still today don't know much about food or think much about it or care much about it. So I don't remember a thing about the food."[73]

The conspicuous absence in her responses of the trauma of hunger striking and forcible feeding may signal her reluctance to dwell upon the trauma itself or her acute disempowerment during that experience, or both. Even at eighty-seven, Paul prized her ability to act, speak, and strategize. During the interview she emphasized her stubborn resolve, her canny political strategy, her command of her faculties, and her steadfast conscience during the suffrage movement. Even as her body was restrained and she was isolated from her fellow prisoners during her 1917 hunger strike, her resolve was unbroken. She tenaciously found ways to communicate with and direct her fellow suffragists outside, and to dodge prison officials' intent to institutionalize her in a mental asylum. Her personal struggle inside the jail hospital ward was always connected strategically to the long game of the political campaign for suffrage on the outside.

The persistent long view and the insistence to communicate were imperative for the suffragist movement and the imprisoned suffragists. Through secret notes, newspapers, telegrams, testimonials, and performance, the suffragists worked to connect the personal agony experienced inside the prison with the political campaign outside it. They leveraged public feelings to build a political movement and to force elite men to capitulate. Their public voices, channeled through suffragist organizations' publicity efforts and the news media, juggled the communication of terror, doubt, suffering, and isolation alongside courage, endurance, and righteousness to maintain their support-ers' confidence in their political strategy.[74]

Even when leaders such as Alice Paul and Sylvia Pankhurst (another of Emmeline's daughters) tried to balance sharing their trauma with maintain-ing their political guidance and leadership, it was the trauma that drew media attention. This raised important questions, relevant now as well as then, about how personal trauma resounds in public. When and how is trauma remembered and for what purpose? And when is it willfully forgotten and suppressed?

Historian Doris Stevens, a friend and ally of Paul, placed the trauma of imprisonment, hunger striking, and forcible feeding at the heart of the para-dox of how the NWP's role in American women's suffrage would be remem-bered: as a "tragic and harrowing tale of martyrdom" or a "ruthless enterprise of compelling a hostile administration to subject women to martyrdom in order to hasten its surrender. The truth is, it has elements of both ruthlessness and martyrdom." Stevens characterized the martyrdom as a "conscious, vol-untary gift of beautiful, strong and young hearts." She added emphatically: "But it was never martyrdom for its own sake. It was martyrdom used for a practical purpose."[75]

WHAT WIELDING THE HUNGER STRIKE WEAPON MEANS

In hunger striking, the suffragists found their weapon to fight back against incarceration. The government found its weapon against hunger striking in forcible feeding. This new battlefield threatened to overwhelm the public's attention, eclipsing both the dramatic visceral impact of hunger striking and the political cause for which the women had been imprisoned.

In both Britain and the United States, the hunger strikes by suffragists were part of a broader picketing, protesting, and persuasion campaign. Suffragists in both countries demonstrated that they were political actors willing to dis-rupt, even violently, the status quo and to draw violence to their bodies to prove the injustice of their exclusion from the electorate.[76] The communica-tion of hunger striking catapulted militant women as political and public participants, despite male condescension and umbrage, into the center of the broader crisis of British and U.S. imperial democracy and accountability.[77]

The prison became a scene of confrontation and battle for the vote, but the struggle was far-reaching and waged on the streets, in the press, and in legislatures. For the suffragists, prison hunger striking was one weapon in an arsenal to combat the injustice of being denied the vote as well as the logjam in the legislative process to gain the vote. British and American suffragists viewed the expansion of the vote as a reform of the existing domestic political system to make the government accountable to women. Its opponents saw it as an upending of the traditional social and political order of an exclusively male and propertied electorate, and saw the women's public disruption and prison disobedience as evidence of their unruly ambitions.

Suffragist agitation in public and in prison became arenas for women to defy conventions through their behavior and bodies, to demand recognition, and to champion their political equality with men. In suffragists' hands, the hunger strike weapon had a precise and unambiguous purpose—to defeat punitive prison practices and win early release. Imprisoned suffragists' voices were intentionally transmitted to expose torture and violence in prison.

The suffragists discovered that representing who the hunger strikers were and who they were not was tricky. First off, to garner a sympathetic response, the convicted women had to wash themselves of the status of "criminal" and "vicious" denizens of prison—the thief, prostitute, murderer, drunkard. Instead they developed a shield of exceptional courage and conscience to remake their imprisonment as an example of the government's injustice and abuse of incarceration to jail their political opponents. They fought back against officials and critics who variously branded them as impudent, disobedient, and misguided, and as inferiors who must be taught a lesson. The government's punitive and infantilizing response won over some of the public, even fellow women's suffrage supporters. Significantly, the government's criminalization of protest found its counterpart in the suffragists' distinction between "criminal" and "political prisoner," a distinction that would reverberate as the hunger-striking tool was taken up in different corners of the globe in subsequent years.

What the suffragist organizations wanted was to influence public opinion to shame and embarrass government authorities. And if imprisonment could do that work, then the hunger strike weapon was effective in directing shame and embarrassment on the government. What was most significant is how the suffragists used their media communication systems to break through prison walls. They turned the hunger strike, a weapon of the weak, into a formidable communicative force.[78]

The suffragists shaped the form of the hunger strike into a political weapon for rights. To do this they needed to narrate not just the actions of the hunger striker but also her voice and feelings. In the women's firsthand accounts, their tone, how they presented themselves, what they emphasized, and what they omitted were critical to how and whether their accounts would be publicly received. They succeeded, in that they developed an expectation among news audiences that the prisoner's voice mattered. They trained the public to assume that when a hunger strike was in the news, they needed to hear or read the voice of the hunger-striking prisoner to understand the motivation for this extreme action. Suffragist publicity made a highly specific personal agony a collectively felt social agony.

The voice of women that was featured was educated, wealthy, calm, and deliberate. It was a voice of intentional and reasoned action, balanced with detailed narration of personal sensory experience of isolation, self-deprivation, and punishment, laced with an unwavering conviction about the women prisoners' inherent human dignity and a confidence that they would be respected within the prison as they would outside. The suffragists were depicted as being not from the margins of society but rather from the center. It was critical that they appear familiar and reputable. And they intentionally drew distinctions between themselves and other prisoners, who were among society's most vulnerable, precarious, and downtrodden. The brutality they experienced in prison was all the more undue and required remedy. As white women of education, embedded in both communities and organizations, they had every reason to believe that when they spoke, they would be heard, at least by their allies, family, and friends, and that their voices would carry to the public square and to the courts through intermediaries.

The hunger strike protest, whether a singular action or taken up by multiple participants, was explicitly a political demand for rights both within the prison walls and in the world outside. In the prison, it was exercised as a fight for political rights to speech and communication—access to newspapers, books, and visitors, and protection from punitive labor regimes. But this demand for political prisoner status was freighted with and linked tightly to the political battle that had landed the women in prison in the first place. For the suffragists, this was a demand for political accountability—the right to vote. For Agnes Fair and the IWW free-speech advocates in Spokane, it was the right to speak, assemble, organize, and fight economic exploitation that was backed by the state's police power.

By 1920, the connection between hunger striking and suffragists had been firmly planted. During 2020 centenary celebrations of British and American women's winning the right to vote, Scotswoman Marion Wallace Dunlop would be heralded as the inventor of the hunger strike. American Alice Paul, who went on hunger strike in both London and Washington, D.C., would be recognized as the defiant and persuasive leader of the victorious fight for a U.S. constitutional amendment giving women the vote.

But a third white woman who in 1909 refused food in prison for political reasons, Agnes Fair, would not receive such accolades. Her starvation strike would be considered an incidental injury of her imprisonment on behalf of itinerant workers. Not unlike her suffragist sisters, Fair created a public spectacle of her march to prison and her release to the hospital. She published the ordeal of her imprisonment in her own daring and bold statement. She spoke of her sexual harassment and assault as "vile" and attempted to maintain her respectable status by parsing her words carefully. It was her endurance of that harassment and violence, not her refusal to eat, that stood out in the news communications about her. Fair even encouraged other women orators to come to Spokane to fill the jails and force the municipal government to renege on its campaign of punitive repression, but to no avail.

Called affectionately a "woman hobo" by the transient community that she supported, Fair continued to fight for worker solidarity and one big union to protect workers. She wrote news articles and published a volume of verse. She worked in kitchens and makeshift clinics giving food and medical aid to indigent workers in Spokane, Portland, San Francisco, Los Angeles, and Reno. At the age of thirty-seven, suffering from failing health that prevented her from continuing her efforts on behalf of the downtrodden, she died after throwing herself in front of an electric streetcar in Portland, Oregon, in 1917. She would become a largely forgotten warrior for workers' rights in the western United States.[79]

Suffragists were not the only ones who employed hunger striking in the 1910s. Many persons confined and caged used the hunger strike as a weapon against the state: Irish republicans, American and British conscientious objectors during the global war, Punjabi immigrants who were refused landing in the Vancouver harbor and were held on board their ship, as well as prisoners around the globe. Their handling of the hunger strike form may have been more challenging or conflicted, and was futile more often than not. Suffragists, however, seized the moment with their hunger striking and made that moment reverberate across time and grow across space. This strategy of bodily self-deprivation protest against state power would evolve, be reshaped, and spread both periodically and persistently. Through its communicative appeal, striking by hunger could jump scale, breaching prison walls into neighborhoods and cities, across nations, oceans, and continents, wherever telegraphic and print communication could reach to make hungering a signal to provoke public demonstration for the prisoners' lives and their cause.

The Medical Ethics of Forcible Feeding
and a Brief History of Four Objects

SUFFRAGISTS WIELDED THE PRISON HUNGER strike and touted it as a new weapon. However, captives and inmates refusing to eat was nothing new. Hence, as prison doctors brandished the counter-weapon of forcible feeding, they experimented with techniques and devices burdened with a long and vexed history for their use in other notorious conditions of unfreedom, including mental asylums and slave ships. The prevailing ideology that negated slaves' and insane persons' knowledge of and control over their bodies, will, and conscience reinforced the perception that food refusal by these people represented a technical but not an ethical problem.

Similarly, when confronted with hunger strikes, prison medical services marshaled the techniques and devices developed in those sister carceral institutions, ignoring the prisoners' political motivations and turning the crisis of refusing to eat into a technical problem of food delivery. The devices most prominently used were the gag, the feeding tube, the liquified feeding substance, and the nutrient enema. Paying attention to the mechanics and development of these four objects, we can see why they were adapted to prison hunger strikes, how they elicited intense emotional and bodily responses in the persons upon whom they were deployed, and how their use became the focus of confrontation between physician and prisoner. Their use instigated medical, ethical, and legal debates that would accompany the hunger strike throughout its history.

DIAGNOSING REASON AND UNREASON FROM
ASYLUM TO PRISON

Being fed against one's will came with a vexing legacy for British and American upper- and middle-class women and girls. Suffragists were aware of how inmates were treated in asylums, where medical treatment was being employed punitively, to coerce rather than to heal, and how women, in particular, faced mental health diagnoses in asylums, which had been used historically to confine, constrain, and silence women. In the first half of the twentieth century, more people were involuntarily confined in asylums and reformatories than were sentenced to jails. In Britain and the United States, women and teenaged girls were confined in asylums and reformatories to remedy the apparent pathologies diagnosed—from hysteria to frigidity, from melancholy to eating disorders.[1]

The suffragist hunger strikers were also haunted by the Victorian-era phenomenon of "fasting girls," who ate irregularly or sparingly and were regarded as either misguided in their piety or pathological. This pathology later mutated into anorexia nervosa, an extreme and "morbid" absence of appetite. Girls and young women in asylums were prescribed treatments of force-feeding, isolation from family, and moral teaching to repair their hysteria and obsessions. By labeling the person mentally ill and placing her in an asylum, force-feeding became an acceptable medical intervention in the eyes of institutional administrators and physicians.[2]

Comparing the asylum and the prison through forcible feeding highlights both similarities and differences between them. In the asylum, the inmate's volition was irrelevant to how the asylum medical service responded. There, refusing to eat was an individual pathology and needed to be dealt with immediately. This is precisely why hunger strikers combated being branded as mentally ill so vociferously. If they were sequestered and isolated in an asylum, their act of hunger striking would never be viewed as a "reasoned choice."

In the prison, no matter how much the prison medical service sought to bend the prisoner to their control, as long as a prisoner was not branded mentally ill, some glimmer of acknowledging the prisoner's reason remained. This wedge of sanity was exactly what striking prisoners and their advocates leveraged in declaring the hunger strike as political, the result of a decision, even if an impulsive one. The physicians sought to deploy asylum rules in the prison to make hunger striking a mental pathology they could then remedy with impunity. The prison hunger strikers vigorously fought off the asylum's carceral logics. The medical authority in carceral domination was unassailable even as the hunger striker tried to make its reach negotiable. The demand for recognition of the prisoner's claim of choice and reason became a necessary feature of the hunger strike. The ethical quandary hinged on the dialectic of reason/unreason and underlying presumptions of who could consent and which institutional setting allowed for that consent's recognition. The capacity to reason was intrinsic to the legal recognition of rights. The physicians' interventions over the prisoner's will was fueled by the perception that prisoners had lost their reason or that their decision-making had been compromised by despair, fanaticism, depression, or pressure from fellow prisoners. The diagnosis of unreason annulled whatever rights one might possess. In prisons and asylums, diagnoses of unreason flourished, disregarding consent and plummeting inmates into a rightless fate.[3]

QUESTIONING THE ETHICS OF FORCE-FEEDING

From the perspective of the hunger striker, hunger itself was not the violence that needed to be quelled. The gnaw of hunger was intense and overwhelming at first, but both physicians and hunger strikers recognized that after a few days of not eating, the physiological sensations of hunger diminish, as does the reflexive impulse to eat. A number of hunger strikers described this paradoxical state of not eating yet not feeling hunger. Often they begin to fathom a spiritual calm that arises from setting aside daily behaviors of eating and digestion. In spiritual traditions of all kinds, fasting is a time of contemplation, slowing down, and reflecting on the relationships among mind, body, and spirit. It is often spoken of as a spiritual and physical cleansing. For hunger strikers who are forcibly fed, whatever serenity they might be experiencing is recklessly shattered.

Richard Michael Fox, a British conscientious objector and antiwar protester still imprisoned in 1919, after World War I had ended, went on a hunger strike, along with fellow imprisoned conscientious objectors, to force his release. In a memoir published more than a decade later, Fox declared that most prisoners would "prefer to starve to death rather than submit to this mauling, especially as after the first two days the ravenous desire for food vanishes."[4]

Mohandas Gandhi strongly condemned the British colonial government's forcible feeding of prisoners "as an undue liberty with the human body, which is sacred to be trifled with, even though it belongs to a prisoner." It was the abusive quality of forcible feeding that troubled Gandhi the most: "No doubt the state had control of the bodies of prisoners but never to the extent of killing their soul. That control has well-defined limits. If a prisoner decides to starve himself to death, he should, in my opinion be allowed to do so. A hunger strike loses its force and its dignity, when it has any, if the striker is forcibly fed. It becomes a mockery if somehow sufficient nourishment is poured down the mouth or nose."[5]

In Fox's rendering, the prison physician was the "front line controller" in wielding instruments to compel prisoner submission. He carefully described "the white-smocked doctor [and] his uniformed assistants" employing the "paraphernalia of rubber tube, gag and funnel, all mobilised to defeat the will of the prisoner—[it] is a horrible business."[6]

Indeed, the physician's role in authorizing and operating forcible feeding was central. And it would be a mistake to believe that the physician's role with the prisoner was the same as with the patient on the outside. The first female inspector of English prisons, Mary Gordon, who at her retirement in 1922 published *Penal Discipline,* had a clear-eyed view of that relationship: the "prisoner does not consult the doctor. The State pays the doctor and consults him about the prisoner," and the doctor shares the prisoner's secrets with the prison governor, the courts, and the state. Gordon recognizes the expansive role of the physician as a "constable" who has "very special powers over the patient's life. . . . He decides on fitness for work, fitness for dietary punishment, fitness for restraint. If corporal punishment is awarded he certifies the punishment and can stay it." The physician's role is not just to "see that [the prisoner] is as little injured as possible" but to authorize and control "all the penal discipline." By virtue of his authority, he possesses the "heaviest hand over the prisoner."[7]

The physician's role in authorizing and operating forcible feeding was thus central, and the physicians apparently had unbridled confidence in their penal discipline techniques to overcome the prisoners' defiance. The nurses, guards, orderlies, attendants, and wardresses who harnessed those techniques onto the resistant prisoners were at the front lines of imposing force and inflicting injury. Prisoners thrashed and cried, but this did not seem to deter the medical staff from experimenting with force-feeding procedures or justifying their actions as in the best interests of the body under their control.

In 1909, when Mary Leigh, who was forcibly fed for a month, brought a suit claiming damages from assault against the prison doctor, the governor of the Winson Green Prison, and Home Secretary Herbert Gladstone, the judge, Lord Alverstone, declared that "it was wicked folly [for Leigh] to attempt to starve herself to death." He ruled that "as a matter of law it was the duty of the prison officials to preserve the health of the prisoners . . . and preserve their lives."[8] This duty came without clarification of limits on either the physician's responsibility or the force exerted on the prisoner's body.[9]

The forcible feeding of suffragists raised a fierce debate in medical circles about the ethics, tools, and consequences of the practice. The debate about responsibility and blame hovered over the "unenviable position" of the prison medical officer caught between government officials and the prisoner.[10]

Some physicians promoted forcible feeding as ordinary treatment used daily in asylums and as a necessity to combat "temporary insanity or criminal suicide of food refusal," reasoning that "if it is lawful to compulsorily feed lunatics and prevent suicide, how can it be contended logically that the suffragettes in prison should not be compulsorily fed?"[11] Some even contended that it might have a therapeutic purpose in hospital and asylum settings—although even there it was under fire as outmoded, brutal, and dangerous.

In fact, the procedures of force-feeding did not heal but instead injured and traumatized prisoners. The WSPU's efforts to document the experiences of imprisoned hunger strikers resulted in a medical database with which sympathetic physicians could dispute the claim that forcible feeding was not dangerous and painful. In 1912, dermatologist Agnes Savill, psychologist Charles Mansell Moullin, and surgeon Victor Horsley published an extensive review of the written statements of 102 suffrage prisoners, ninety of whom had been subjected to forcible feeding. The findings, published in the preeminent British medical journal *The Lancet,* concluded that forcible feeding in prison ignored the medical protocols and precautions used in hospitals. The report documented how rough treatment aggravated injuries of the nose and mouth, and resulted in headaches, earaches, "severe choking, vomiting followed by persistent coughing" and "severe gastric pain." Lasting pain in the chest and digestive system caused insomnia and severe respiratory infections. The authors also identified the mental anguish and trauma of prisoners who heard the cries, choking, and struggles of their friends. The report concluded that force-feeding amounted to "severe physical and mental torture" and should "no longer be carried out in prisons of the twentieth century."[12]

In 1914, in a pamphlet published by the WSPU, Dr. Frank Moxon emphasized the "torture" of forcibly feeding "noble women" and condemned doctors who carried out "this vile order." He argued that it was unconscionable for physicians to "forcibly feed these prisoners until they are either mental wrecks or at death's door." He blasted the prison environment for warping the ethics of prison medical officers, who, he claimed, knew "in their inner consciences" that forcible feeding does not "maintain or prolong life." Instead, its purpose is to "coerce and break the spirit . . . a torture [that] cannot receive the sanction of medical custom."[13]

Dr. Flora Murray, who cared for Emmeline Pankhurst and other women after they experienced force-feeding, emphasized that the "physical agony is great" but the mental suffering is unceasing, replayed in nightmares "night after night and it is months before they recover."[14] Speaking frequently at rallies and marches against forcible feeding, Murray accused the British government of using doctors to crush the women's movement. She branded physicians who participated as "medical accomplices to torture and death." Prisons' forcible feeding policy had turned the medical profession into a "police force whose task it is to break the spirit of the Suffragist women by injuring their bodies" using methods that outstripped the "ordinary police force's" methods.[15]

Dr. Murray laid the blame for the continuation of force-feeding squarely on the shoulders of "medical men . . . willing to take the odious responsibility of watching and measuring the ebbing strength of the starving prisoner, and to perform this same ghoulish task with regard to the same prisoner over and over again during repeated terms of starvation."[16]

APPLYING THE FOUR OBJECTS

In deciding whether to force-feed a hunger striker, Winson Green prison physicians first determined the impact of starvation on the person's body. The British Home Office recommended that prison physicians employ systematic record keeping on which to base any invasive action. Drawing upon care-based and prevailing medical methods, physicians would take pulse and temperature, record weight measurements, note the frequency of urine and stool. They would record meals missed or days without food based on the prisoners' self-disclosure or guards' reports. Based on prevailing medical standards, they would then assess when self-starvation required medical intervention beyond trying to persuade the striker to take food and drink.

Once the decision was made to intervene medically, the first step of medical intervention could be the most ordinary and least invasive: nursing by hand with a feeding cup, a ceramic or metal teacup with a narrow spout, half covered to prevent spills and widely used for "invalids and infants." Dr. E.D. Kirby, who aided in the recovery of released Birmingham prisoners after force-feeding, recommended the feeding cup as the most humane feeding tool.[17]

As the person resisted and continued to resist, the challenges and risks of applying a procedure to feed a captive grew. Resistance could be intentional or spontaneous, as when a foreign instrument like a gag or feeding tube entered the body. In the moment, physicians and orderlies had to struggle and experiment with applying an ensemble of instruments and to react to the prisoners' bodily reflexes and responses. There was a fierce contest between physicians who insisted that they were providing interventionist medical care and prisoners who experienced the same procedures as debasing and torturous.

The Gag

The first refusal was in opening the prisoner's mouth. When the first reports of forcible feeding trickled out to the public, critics focused on the prison's efforts to constrain the women's bodies and pull apart their jaws to feed them. When James Keir Hardie, founder of the Labour Party and longtime friend and ally of Emmeline Pankhurst, challenged Home Secretary Gladstone in Parliament to respond to reports of aggressive and traumatic administration of feeding, he specified prison attendants strapping the prisoners down and using a "screw gag . . . to prise the teeth apart and keep the jaws open." Gladstone denied this directly, saying that "no screw gag was used and the prisoners were not strapped down." Rather, the feeding was a routine medical procedure with instruments commonly used by dentists and anesthesiologists, such as tubes "made of ordinary soft rubber," and an "ordinary wooden mouth-prop was used to keep the mouth open."[18]

Gladstone did acknowledge that carceral instruments were needed to constrain and hold down the prisoner before administering feeding, warranting a team of five attendants, irons, and possibly handcuffs. The intent of his response to Hardie was clearly to defuse a simmering political situation by deflecting accusations by the opposition party that the women were being tortured. However, even as he defended the women's treatment as routine, he could not dislodge their own accounts of being held down and constrained.[19]

The gag, which had its antecedents in dental surgery, was notorious for its use on slave ships.[20] To circumvent a captive's refusal to eat, slave runners had devised a mouth opener called a *speculum oris* for force-feeding.[21] The device, a "wooden instrument shaped like a pair of scissors with a thumbscrew on the side, had prongs placed down a person's throat. A key would be turned to keep the mouth pried open as gruel would be poured down the mouth, often causing gagging and vomiting."[22] The same strategy of bypassing the person's consent and gag reflex appeared in the deployment of mouth openers for force-feeding in other circumstances of captivity.

In 1872, Dr. Thomas Clouston, who treated patients in a mental asylum, published guidance about forcibly feeding the insane in the *Lancet*. He carried a number of crucial tools in his bag, including "a common metallic spoon 'made of German silver,'" a "long, small, stiffish tube for feeding through the esophagus or the nose, a small silver funnel with a tube for feeding through the mouth." To send the tube down through the mouth, an instrument was needed to hold the mouth open. The concept, as Dr. Clouston described it, was to "open the mouth with a simple and safe instrument, place a gag so he cannot close his mouth and [then] introduce the tube, without causing damage or pain, through the patient's jaws."[23]

Despite Dr. Clouston's description of the mouth opener as intended to help avoid "damage and pain," it in fact caused immense pain. Nearly fifty years later, in prison, Richard Fox recalled that each striking conscientious objector "had a wooden gag jammed roughly in his mouth" while a "long rubber tube was threaded through a hole in the gag and pushed down his throat," inducing a "choking, suffocating breath" and a "sickening sensation."[24]

Any choices offered the prisoner were woefully limited. Lady Constance Lytton related how the chief medical officer at Holloway offered her the "choice of a wooden or steel gag" and explained that the "steel gag would hurt and the wooden one not, and he urged me not to force him to use the steel gag." When she refused to speak or open her mouth, the doctor attempted to use the wooden one before taking "recourse to the steel," frustrated at her resistance. He "pressed fearfully on the gum," intensifying the pain as "he got the gag between my teeth, when he proceeded to turn it much more than necessary until my jaws were fastened wide apart."[25]

Sylvia Pankhurst offered a similar assessment of the steel gag. She spoke of the doctor's "fingers trying to press my lips apart,—getting inside," and then "a steel gag running around my gums and feeling for gaps in my teeth." She felt the "steel instrument pressing against [her] gums, cutting into the flesh," and her jaws were "gradually prised" apart "as they turned a screw." She resisted but felt like her teeth were being pulled out. Still, she wrote, she was determined to hold "my poor bleeding gums down on the steel with all my strength."[26]

Pankhurst detailed her experience in a letter to her mother that the British National Archives kept sealed in a file for eighty-five years, even though the details of her forcible feeding had been published in the *Manchester Guardian*

"The Suffragette," January 10th, 1913.   Registered at the G.P.O. as a Newspaper.

The
Suffragette

EDITED BY CHRISTABEL PANKHURST,

The Official Organ of the Women's Social and Political Union.

No. 13.—VOL. 1.   FRIDAY, JANUARY 10, 1913.   Price 1d. Weekly (Post Free 1½d.)

TREATMENT OF POLITICAL PRISONERS UNDER A LIBERAL GOVERNMENT

FEEDING BY VIOLENCE.

The men of Ulster are threatening to resort to violent and lawless insurrection if the Home Rule Bill is carried.

The Prime Minister, speaking in the House of Commons, has said that the attitude of Ulster is a factor which it is no use to ignore or to minimise, which has got to be faced and dealt with. He is even prepared to have a General Election if Ulster will promise to abide by the result, and to renounce militancy should the election endorse the Home Rule Bill.

Why does Mr. Asquith take the threatened Ulster militancy so seriously? It is not because he doubts the power of the police force and the British Army to suppress the insurrection. He is afraid of Ulster militancy because he does not want to be obliged to use violence against the insurrectionists. They are men, and therefore he has, perhaps, a fellow feeling for them. More than that, they are voters and they have friends and brothers in other parts of the Kingdom who are voters too. To deal violently with them will therefore be politically dangerous to Mr. Asquith.

Women Mr. Asquith is perfectly willing to attack by methods of violence. They have no votes so they and their suffering are of no importance politically. The men electors could by their votes punish violence done to the women, but Mr. Asquith trusts to being able to buy them off by giving them something for themselves. Thus he treats women with a brutality that he dares not even to dream of using towards Ulster men.

Feeding by violence is one of the Government's methods of coercing women, and it is a method that they are using even now.

The abominable and reckless cruelty of the Government's action is illustrated by the fact that lately a man died within half an hour of being forcibly fed.

Three of the most distinguished doctors in the country have reported, after careful investigation of the facts, that feeding by violence is dangerous to health and life. They show that it means risk of injury to nose and throat; that it has caused the formation of abscesses in those parts; that it is harmful to the digestion organs; that it puts a severe strain on the nervous system, often leading to sleeplessness, and in some cases to acute delirium; that it involves other most serious consequences. They describe the whole revolting process as "torture," and they point to the fact that in very many cases women put to this torture have had suddenly to be released in order to save their lives.

Another doctor says: "I wonder that medical men can be found to carry out such operations, which I consider to be degrading them to the level of a common executioner!" We too wonder that the medical profession, so many of whose members are now complaining that their own dignity and liberty are being assailed, should be willing to be the tool of the Government, and to do the Government's dirty work of coercing the women of the Suffrage movement.

FIGURE 6. Front page of *The Suffragette* (January 10, 1913), depicting a tube and funnel being used to force-feed a suffragist. Courtesy of the Women's Library, London School of Economics.

newspaper soon after her release from prison—and a more extensive version was published in the American *McClure's Magazine* later that year—as well as being recounted in her memoir published eighteen years later. The bureaucratic sealing of the files was justified as a protection of privacy—often a cover for the state's desire to maintain secrecy about the decisions it sponsored. The notoriety of her treatment in prison, however, did not prevent her frequent imprisonment and force-feedings. Between February 1913 and July 1914, Sylvia Pankhurst was arrested eight times and each time was repeatedly force-fed.[27]

The Feeding Tube

Among the feeding technologies invented, the most important were feeding tubes, inserted through the mouth or nose and intended to move food down the esophagus and into the stomach, that could substitute for the swallowing of food. The feeding tube had broad therapeutic uses that included being a short-term prosthetic esophagus for those who had lost the ability to swallow or chew food, had digestive difficulties, or had diminished capacity to feed themselves.

Physicians also experimented with feeding tubes that could be passed through the nasal passage rather than the mouth. In 1790, the British physician John Hunter created a nasogastric tube of whalebone attached to a probe covered with eel skin and a bladder pump to feed nutrient solutions. In the late nineteenth century, physicians experimented with rubber tubes. In the 1910s, German physician Max Einhorn developed a nasogastric tube that was weighted on one end so that it could pass into the digestive system as far as the duodenum, the first part of the small intestine, where most chemical digestion takes place.[28]

Inserting the tube, whether through the nose or mouth, could have risky consequences. The insertion process could cause acute trauma, including bleeding of the nose and throat. It regularly induced nausea and vomiting. Misplacing the tube in the respiratory tract rather than the esophagus could prompt severe coughing and choking and, in subsequent days and weeks, precipitate infections and pneumonia.

Irish republican soldier Eamon O'Duibhir, who was court-martialed and imprisoned in 1917 for organizing rebellion and for wearing the Irish volunteer uniform, prohibited under British rule, described in an oral history taken decades later the "pipe being passed down through my throat," saying that the "horror of it" far outweighed "any fear of hunger-striking." The palpable dread showed up in nightmares, from which he would awake trembling from the sensation of "this damn pipe or tube going down my neck like a snake." All of the hunger-striking men imprisoned with him at Mountjoy Prison in Dublin suffered this treatment, he reported, and they "vomited terribly." The days of the hunger strike "passed with this as the only relief from the monotony of the cell."[29]

Lady Constance Lytton described the fast speed at which the food was poured through the tube, and that "a few seconds after it was down" she would be violently sick, which made her body writhe and her legs curl up in pain. She recalled the wardresses pressing back her head and the doctor leaning on her knees. She vomited all over both them and herself, saturating her clothes. Despite the "intolerable mess" in which she was then required to lie, "it seemed paradise to be without the suffocating tube, without the liquid food going in and out of my body and without the gag between my teeth."[30]

The technical innovation of the feeding tube continued, motivated by the idea that calibration, in primarily therapeutic settings, could lessen the discomfort and optimize the benefits. In the early twentieth century, the tube became standardized in diameter, rubber material used, and means to adjust the flow of fluids through it. In 1949, polyethylene tubing was first used and the enteral feeding pump was developed. In the 1950s and 1960s, research on surgery patients, severe burn and trauma victims, and premature newborns improved the methods of delivery, which were published in medical journals and adapted for hospital protocols. In the 1970s, improvements in the use of catheters and continuous administration pumps assisted in the uptake of nutrition.[31] In order to reduce the discomfort of inserting and removing the nasal tube at each use, the tube could be left inserted through the nose for a week or more at a time.

Feeding Mixtures

The feeding substances used for forcible feeding changed dramatically over time. In the late eighteenth century and through the nineteenth, they were viscous substances that might include jellies, beaten eggs, sugar, beef broth, and milk mixed with wine or medicinal tonics. Prisons and asylums supplemented their feeding mixtures with tonics such as Valentine's Meat Juice (invented in Richmond, Virginia, in 1870) to address digestive difficulties and the inability to retain nourishment. In Birmingham Prison in 1909, prison medical officers used "milk with Valentine's Meat juice" to forcibly feed Laura Ainsworth, Ellen Barwell, and other hunger-striking suffragists. A two-ounce bottle, holding the concentrated juice from four pounds of beef, was heated with water or milk to make a kind of "bouillon or tea."[32] In the nineteenth and early twentieth centuries, physicians in prisons and asylums employed high-protein and high-caloric regimens of beef broth, eggs, and brandy to force-feed in Britain, Ireland, India, and the United States.

Physicians could adjust the pace of flow and the temperature, consistency, and texture of the feeding substances they experimented with, and sometimes they did so to try to make the force-feeding easier on the prisoner. In the summer of 1912, when medical officer R. G. Dowdall treated veteran suffragist Mary Leigh at Dublin's Mountjoy Prison, he recorded her vitals, urine, and blood before embarking on artificially feeding her. He prescribed a feeding formula of ten ounces of milk mixed with one beaten egg and heated to internal body temperature. When she vomited up this feeding mixture, Dr. Dowdall tried heating it to various temperatures and feeding at different speeds, even purchasing a special chair that allowed Leigh to rest on her back after she was fed, but to no avail. Even as he experimented to find a physically palatable feeding substance, he blamed her "relentless vomiting" on female hysteria while diligently recording that the feeding did not produce other signs of physical distress such as bleeding, pain, weakness, or seizures.[33]

Dr. Dowdall's varying strategies were intended to be responsive to his prisoner-patient. However, historian Ian Miller notes that these adjustments also demonstrated the ways Dr. Dowdall experimented on Mary Leigh's body as an "object that was restrained, observed, manipulated, and tested for its ability to withstand force-feeding."[34] It is telling that her emotions were not recorded in the medical record, even as allusions to her possible mental illness persisted.

In contrast to Dr. Dowdall's efforts to fine tune treatment to a single person's needs, when force-feeding was scaled to treat dozens of prisoners a day, medical staff sometimes resorted to an assembly-line approach that routinized the brutality of the experience and further dehumanized the prisoners. Richard Fox recalled: "They were lined up and put one by one in a big chair where burly men in white overalls gripped their arms and legs, forcing their heads back," and a milk-based liquid "was then poured in through a funnel." One hunger striker commented with grim humor, "Well I've heard o' food queues, but this is the first time I've ever heard of a feeding queue!"[35]

Eamon O'Duibhir recalled a similar scenario in 1917 at Dublin's Mountjoy with the large-scale feeding of forty Irish republican prisoners. Each "man in turn was brought to a large room" and tied into an operating chair, with bands strapped around legs, arms, torso, and neck. Then "into each man's mouth an instrument was passed to keep it open." The same instruments were shared between prisoners and rarely disinfected between uses. O'Duibhir described the equipment of the pump and the tubing of the "forcible feeding outfit" along with "a pint of milk, with an egg broken into it."[36]

In the 1930s, new developments in nutritional science made known the importance of specific nutrients for health and the chemical processes of digestion and absorption. Hospitals and prisons experimented with various liquid substances fortified by nutritional supplements, and the results were circulated among prisons, hospitals, asylums, nursing homes, and military care units in war zones.[37]

The Nutrient Enema

In 1920, O'Duibhir was again imprisoned and on hunger strike, this time in Cork Prison. He had been lying in his prison bed after several days on hunger strike and was "quite weak" when Dr. O'Flaherty, an elderly physician, examined him. O'Duibhir described how Dr. O'Flaherty had him "turned, lying on my face" and "he was doing something he shouldn't be doing in the way of forcible feeding." O'Duibhir exclaimed, "What are you trying to do?" The doctor said, "I am giving you something to keep up your strength." O'Duibhir responded, "Well, my God, . . . if you continue you may overpower me, but I'll tell you this, whenever I get out, or I will get word out somehow, I will have you killed." When Dr. O'Flaherty finally desisted from what O'Duibhir described as "forcible feeding through the posterior passage," the doctor claimed plaintively that he had "only been trying to save your life." He apologized and expressed his own "heartbreak" that O'Duibhir "could die on my hands" if he did not provide nutrients rectally: "Do you suggest I release you and lose my job?"[38]

Imprisoned hunger-striking suffragists were also subjected to nutrient enemas. Fanny Parker, born in New Zealand and a graduate of Cambridge, was a militant suffragist and an organizer of the Women's Social and Political Union in Scotland. She appeared in court in Ayr, Scotland, on July 8, 1914, accused of trying to blow up Burns Cottage in Alloway. While in prison for this offense, Parker refused food or drink for six days. Under prison physician's orders she was wrapped in blankets and taken by car one hundred miles away to Perth Prison. Her account of her experience, titled "Another Prison Infamy," was published in the suffragist newspaper *Votes for Women*.[39]

At Perth Prison, Parker experienced all the force-feeding technologies that had become standard. At first, the prison staff prepared her for tube feeding. Six wardresses held her down and slapped her face, while the assistant doctor gripped her head. The senior physician, Dr. Watson, tried to pry her teeth apart with a steel gag, warning her that "if he broke a tooth it would be my own fault." Thwarted from feeding her through the mouth, Dr. Watson then used a nasal tube. Unable to force it up one nasal passage, he "succeeded in forcing it down the other nostril, and left it hanging there while he went out of the room." Parker pleaded with the assistant doctor to remove it because it was "extremely painful," but "he only laughed." Dr. Watson returned to feed her while the wardresses held her down and the assistant doctor held both hands over her mouth to prevent vomit from spilling out. Parker's resistance to feeding through the mouth or nose invited fierce and violent treatment from the wardresses, including pulling her by the hair, flinging her on the bed, and kneeling on her chest, demanding that she "behave." After struggling for an hour, she was allowed to recuperate with a pillow at her head and a wardress keeping her head immobilized for another hour. Afterward, a wardress kept watch on her through the night.[40]

The following day, the wardresses switched to administering a nutrient enema rectally. Despite her objections "against this indignity," she endured the "unnecessarily painful" procedure, which was not stopped even as she "screamed with agony." The next day, when three wardresses returned, one promised Parker that she would send the others away and do it as "gently and decently as possible" if she stopped resisting. However, Parker regretted consenting when this wardress again attempted to feed her by "the rectum, [which] was done in a cruel way, causing me great pain." The same nurse later administered "a grosser and more indecent outrage" of vaginal feeding, which Parker declared was done for no purpose other than "torture" and resulted in "soreness that lasted for days."[41]

Scholar Jane Purvis notes, in regard to the British suffragists' descriptions of forcible feeding, that "although the word 'rape' is not used in these accounts, the instrumental invasion of the body" was "accompanied by overpowering physical force, great suffering and humiliation . . . especially so for women, such as Fanny Parker, fed through the rectum and vagina."[42] Parker herself noted how tube feeding was continued even as the "stomach rejects everything," and rectal feeding persisted "when the rectum rejects everything and even loses normal control." The patient's actual acceptance of nutrition is made immaterial as physicians and wardresses persist in exacting penal discipline, even as the "patient is becoming weaker every day."[43] She believed that her experience proved the "danger of giving a medical man, who is part of the prison system, full control over the bodies of prisoners." She commented eloquently on how the "refusal to take food, which is a protest against injustice, is made an excuse for forcible feeding, an operation without consent, and that this is punishment not medical treatment is shown by the fact that it is [done] with brutality and every indignity."[44]

Nearly a decade later, prison inspector Mary Gordon echoed Parker's observation in this comment about the prison doctor: "He forcibly feeds the prisoner to prevent his determining his imprisonment, stops when he thinks he has done as much as he dare." Without his command and assistance, "this part of penal discipline would absolutely disappear."[45]

When Parker's family heard rumors about her terrible treatment and declining health, her brother traveled to Scotland to request her release. She was moved to a nursing home pending trial for attempted arson. Her attorney brokered a deal with the Secretary of State for Scotland to delay her trial. She escaped and was on the run when Britain entered World War I in August 1914. Her case never came to trial, and all suffragist prisoners were granted amnesty. During World War I, Parker ran an organization in London that contracted women workers with wartime employers. She later joined the Women's Army Auxiliary Corps and served in France, where she died in January 1924 at the age of forty-nine.

Rectal feeding with nutrient enemas was utilized in the nineteenth and early twentieth centuries in hospitals, asylums, and clinics, most famously to try to revive President James Garfield after his attempted assassination in July 1881.[46] However, by the 1920s, medical studies demonstrated that the lower digestive tract lacks digestive enzymes, so rectal feeding has little or no value in keeping a person alive. Studies and clinical experience also documented the increased chances of internal damage and inflammation from the procedure.[47]

However, rectal feeding, despite its uselessness, still seemed to some people a more compassionate measure than the trauma of the feeding tube. In October 1943, David Dellinger and five other conscientious objectors held at the federal prison in Lewisburg, Pennsylvania, began a hunger strike to protest the censorship of mail and reading material in prison as well as racial segregation in the prison dining hall.[48] Four weeks into the strike, Dellinger's father, Raymond Dellinger, a prominent Boston lawyer, wrote to James Bennett, director of the U.S. Bureau of Prisons, that he and his wife feared that their son and his comrades had "reached a critical stage" and that continuing the hunger strike might "mean death to some of the boys or irreparable injury to their health." Dellinger advocated force-feeding but cautioned against "nasal" feeding as "painful and obsolete" and instead proposed feeding through the "rectum or intravenous" methods.[49] Bennett responded that the Dellingers' son had been moved to a hospital for monitoring and would be "tube fed" once the "doctor considers it necessary."[50] Although David Dellinger held to his convictions, he "cooperate[d] with tube-feeding." His health improved after the hunger strike and he abided by prison rules more readily afterward.[51]

Despite its recognized nutritional ineffectiveness, rectal feeding persisted in the recesses of carceral domination and would reemerge sadistically in the twenty-first century.

AVOIDING FORCIBLE FEEDING BY INTRODUCING "CAT AND MOUSE"

In April 1913, Britain's Liberal Party passed legislation intended to temper the political controversy over the government's force-feeding policy and alleviate fears of fatalities under this procedure. The Prisoners Temporary Discharge for Ill Health Act allowed for the early release of hunger strikers rather than force-feeding them—in some ways a return to the institutional response used with Marion Wallace Dunlop. However, the legislation also required that the prisoner return to prison once she had recovered enough in order to complete her sentence. What the legislators had not anticipated was that once back, she would resume hunger striking and the government would once again be forced to release her. As this became a pattern, the policy was nicknamed "Cat and Mouse."

While the new policy was intended to dodge the optics of physicians imposing force-feeding as a violent assault on the prisoner, Dr. Murray branded it as one of "torture and crimes against the human body." She feared that rearresting strikers after a few days of freedom to "gather up a little renewed strength," then releasing them again when they renewed striking in prison and again grew too weak to continue fasting, created a cycle that would repeat "over and over again until the victim's health is completely deranged, and until as a final outcome, death ensues."[52] For the women the policy was physically debilitating and emotionally draining, while their political grievances were ignored. Both in the press and among legislators, the Cat and Mouse strategy was perceived as futile gamesmanship that heightened the stakes of the confrontation but endlessly deferred resolution.

The state had to confront the results of a prisoner dying from force-feeding. Eamon O'Duibhir and his fellow prisoners began a hunger strike in Dublin's Mountjoy Prison on September 20, 1917, after British prison wardens rebuffed their demands for political prisoner privileges. One of them was Thomas Ashe, a founding member of the Irish Volunteers. The prison guards retaliated by taking away blankets, drinking water, and cots from their cells. After five days of lying on cold stone floors, the prisoners were subjected to forcible feeding. On September 25, at 3 P.M., thirty-two-year-old Ashe was taken by cab from Mountjoy to Mater Misericordiae Hospital, where he died that night. Ashe's death caused outrage among Irish nationalists. O'Duibhir was dismayed, recalling that the previous evening Ashe "was being brought down to the operating chamber for forcible feeding and he was then in first class spirits and health, and now to think he was dead!"[53]

At the inquest, independent medical experts' testimony detailed his punishing mistreatment in jail: "taking away from the cell bed, bedding and boots and allowing him to be on the cold floor for 50 hours, and then subjecting him to forcible feeding in his weak condition." The feeding tube had been wrongly positioned, and the liquid food had accidentally slipped into Ashe's lungs, resulting in congestion and heart failure. The republican political party Sinn Féin published the jury's report, which "condemned the forcible and mechanical feeding as an inhuman and dangerous operation," and urged that the Prison Board and government cease its use.[54]

The British government had previously claimed that forcible feeding safely corresponded with asylum practices of artificial feeding and was not life-threatening, but Ashe's death rebuked these claims. After Ashe died, the British government abandoned force-feeding in Ireland. Yet it was not discontinued in British prisons. British prison commissioners documented 7,734 instances of forcible feeding performed between 1913 and 1940.[55] Forcible feeding continued to be sanctioned during and after World War I for hunger-striking British conscientious objectors, as well as for nonpolitical prisoners throughout the system, sometimes encompassing multiple feedings of the same person over a long period. In 1917, J. W. Illingworth was force-fed with a nasal tube 135 times in Birmingham Prison. Between 1917 and 1918,

Frank Higgins was force-fed twenty-two times at Newcastle Prison and later, over a prolonged period, 188 times.[56]

MEDICAL NECESSITY OR TORTURE?

In early twentieth-century British imperial and U.S. prisons, the government set itself up as the arbiter of whether force-feeding was medical necessity or torture. Wardens authorized physicians to determine "medical necessity" and emphasized the forms of feeding through nose, mouth, and rectum as medical therapy, without malign or torturous intent. As historian Ian Miller explains, commenting on the suffragist hunger strikes in the British prison system, force-feeding became a "closely regulated, technological procedure that incorporated a range of diagnostic and observational medical techniques designed to monitor prisoner health, if only to avoid prisoner fatalities."[57]

Physical violence and punishment of the body in the prison became centralized and backed by medical and psychiatric discourses and practice. Michel Foucault claims that in the eighteenth and nineteenth centuries, disciplinary power emerged that corrects deviance and trains the body and mind through norms, supplants torture and execution as punishment. However, Joe Sim, in his sociological study of the English prison medical service, contends that Foucault's argument that disciplinary power overtakes the sovereign right to punish "overemphasizes the nature of the shift in punishment that has taken place and underestimates the complex and continuous interrelationship between punishment of the body and control of the mind." In prison punishment, torture and violence persist, even if they are less visible to the public. Sim contended that one system did not replace the other, but rather medical and psychological disciplinary training coexisted and were intertwined with physical punishment of the body.[58]

The use of force to repudiate the prisoner's refusal to eat was not a technical problem to overcome but an ethical question: Did the physician and the state have the right to forcibly feed mentally competent prisoners? The clash of wills in this context turned a procedure ostensibly designed to keep a person alive into a weapon against the person's own defiance and resistance. Further, there were structural opportunities and temptations for wardens, officers, and orderlies to use the prison's total authority to control the prisoner and use medical tools to force, humiliate, and assault the prisoner.

Physicians knew the procedures were risky—that both medical error and the prisoner's resistance could exacerbate the likelihood of tearing or puncturing bodily passages, respiratory infection, damage to the digestive system, and even fatality. This situation raises a series of fundamental questions that still haunt us today. Is medical necessity an institutional judgment that can defy a person's conscience? Since medical necessity and medical therapy in prison are susceptible to being used for abuse and torture, what mechanisms short of the fear of fatality can abate their use? If treatment causes vomiting, infection, and rupture, how is it beneficial to a person's health? When prisoners who resist vociferously at first and later comply under threat and constraint, is such compliance under duress understood as consent?

When hunger strikers communicated distress and reflexive revulsion to the treatment of force-feeding, medical professionals and direct observers regarded their defiance as a technical challenge that had to be surmounted, not as a reason to cease. Improvement in the technology may reduce friction in its implementation, but does improved delivery and greater efficiency dampen attention to the prisoners' visceral responses and the original purpose of the hunger strike, which is to protest the state's power to cage and punish?

THREE

Irish Republicans Innovating Hunger Strikes for Anticolonial Rebellion

IN 1920, TERENCE MACSWINEY LANGUISHED in Brixton Prison in London on a hunger strike to the death. His older sister Mary comforted him during his hunger strike. Two years later, Mary embarked on her own hunger strike in Mountjoy Prison in Dublin. Both siblings fought for Irish independence from Britain, and both hunger strikes transpired during armed rebellion and massive political upheaval. In the hands of these devoutly Catholic political prisoners, hunger strikes combined the sacralizing ritual of fasting with the political instrument of a "strike"—the cessation of activities as a demand for concessions.

The two hunger strikes reverberated differently according to their respective political contexts. The differences in age, gender, and marriage status of the two siblings—a forty-one-year-old married brother and a fifty-year-old unmarried sister—also shaped how the two hunger strikes were interpreted. Their adversaries also differed: the British government imprisoned Terence, while the Irish Free State under British dominion imprisoned Mary. Both siblings saw their bodily defiance as an expression of their fight for an independent Ireland, but their differences in gender, in authority, and in the political conditions of their imprisonment influenced how authorities, political allies, and the public saw their prison hunger strike.

Both episodes stretched the form and reach of the prison hunger strike into the realm of anticolonial rebellion. Their actions show how, through news media, the form of hunger striking could mold and transmit the embodied suffering of a local political figure into a spiritual and national project, at times—achieving global reach, reverberating through public mobilization of networks of Irish diaspora, Catholic Church, and eventually other anticolonial rebellions.

THE MACSWINEY SIBLINGS, CATHOLICISM, AND
THE FIGHT AGAINST BRITISH DOMINATION

The MacSwiney family history illustrates the histories of Ireland, of Britain's union, and of the anticolonial rebellion against British rule. The eldest MacSwiney sibling, Mary, was born to an English mother and Irish father in Surrey, England, in 1872. She moved with her family when she was six years old to her father's home in Cork, Ireland, where Terence was born in 1879. After her father's business failed and he emigrated alone to Australia, Mary helped her mother raise her six younger siblings who had survived infancy. In her twenties, Mary taught at a school in England, studied for a teaching diploma at Cambridge, and contemplated becoming a nun. In 1904, when her mother died, she returned to Cork to raise her siblings.

The MacSwineys were a devout family whose Catholic faith motivated the siblings' vocations. Two of their sisters became nuns and worked in missions in the United States and Japan. Mary and her sister Annie taught at Catholic girls' schools. And Terence, both during and after college, wrote poetry and plays that fervently boosted the Irish Catholic cultural revival that imagined Ireland as an independent republic, free from British monarchical and parliamentary rule.

For centuries, British monarchs dominated and colonized Ireland, confiscating lands and depriving Irish Catholics of rights. Through the Irish Parliament, the British monarchy stripped Roman Catholic and dissenting Protestant men of voting rights, forbade their possession of firearms or service in the army, banned Catholic intermarriage with Protestants, and recruited English and Scottish settlers to work in British plantations in Northern Ireland.

Gradually, in the late eighteenth century, the British passed legislation that allowed Roman Catholics to buy land and to practice their religion without fear of civil penalties, and for propertied men to vote in local elections. After successfully suppressing the Irish Rebellion of 1798, the British established the United Kingdom of Great Britain, which abolished the Irish Parliament and consolidated rule over the two islands. Through the nineteenth century, the Irish continued to both wage rebellion and offer political solutions to the disenfranchisement and suppression of Irish Catholics and Protestant dissenters by the Anglo-Irish establishment.

In the late nineteenth century, British imperial reformers proposed Home Rule to provide domestic self-governance for propertied men in "civilized" white settler colonies, while keeping those colonies as dominions under the umbrella of the British Empire and the British Crown. Home Rule was devised to forestall rebellion and demands for full independence from propertied white men. The British Parliament granted Home Rule to Canada (1867), Australia (1900), and South Africa (1909).[1]

Home Rule for Ireland would sever the union of the United Kingdom and restore the Irish Parliament, yet retain the British Crown. It pleased neither unionists nor antimonarchists. The debate over Irish Home Rule was heated, scrambling political alliances and pitting parties and houses of Britain's Parliament against one another. Irish Home Rule attracted Irish Catholics and Protestant dissenters, threatened the power of the Anglo-Irish elite and landlords over Ireland, and agonized Protestant settlers in northeastern Ireland. From the 1880s, successive parliamentary coalitions and governments floundered over the passage of Irish Home Rule legislation. A wing of the British Liberal party sought reforms in governing Ireland, expanding the electorate, and protecting the welfare and rights of workers and tenant farmers. The Conservative Party opposed these initiatives and joined with other Liberals to fight back threats to the status quo of Protestant elite and settler dominance in Ireland. Despite holding a majority in the House of Commons, the Liberal Party in coalition with the Irish Parliamentary Party was unable to overcome the House of Lords' legislative blockade.[2]

Through a series of parliamentary maneuvers in 1911, the Liberal government curtailed the powers of the Conservative-dominated House of Lords to defeat legislation outright and instead delayed it for two years. As passing of Home Rule legislation loomed, regional, sectarian, and political divisions in Ireland grew fierce and violent. In northeastern Ireland, the Unionist Party allied with the British Conservative Party to block Irish Home Rule legislation, for fear of a backlash inflicted upon Irish Anglicans after their centuries of discrimination against Catholics. In 1913, the Unionists organized the paramilitary Ulster Volunteers, along with mass demonstrations, to fight Home Rule in Northern Ireland. In turn, Irish republicans organized and armed the Irish Volunteers to protect Catholics and fight for independence from Britain. Parliament finally passed the Irish Home Rule bill in 1914. However, the outbreak of World War I that year pushed its implementation until after the war, forcing Irish men and women to choose their loyalties. Some Irish Home Rulers urged Ireland's men to join the British army and fight in France. The Irish Volunteers, however, split apart and undermined British enlistment efforts in Ireland.

During the 1910s, both Mary and Terence MacSwiney became strongly committed to a more radical vision of total Irish independence from Britain and rejected the half-measure of Irish Home Rule under the British Crown. Mary's first political crusade was for women's suffrage in parliamentary elections, and she became a founding member of the Munster Women's Franchise League in 1911. As the campaign for Home Rule grew, Mary withdrew from the Unionist-led women's suffrage campaign to fight directly and vigorously for an independent Ireland.[3] She helped found the Cork branch of Cumann na mBan, a women's paramilitary organization to support the male Irish Volunteers, a militia for Irish independence from Britain.[4]

Terence, as a poet and playwright, imagined a free and independent Irish nation. He took arms for his vision in 1913, when he, along with his friend Tomás MacCurtain, organized the Cork Brigade of Irish Volunteers militia. Although miscommunication hampered the Cork Brigade from joining the Easter Rising in 1916—an armed insurrection in Dublin against the British—suspicions of the brigade's role in conspiracy led to British arrests of Terence and, a week later, of Mary.

In the aftermath of the Easter Rising and British repression, both Mary and Terence pursued leadership in nationalist organizations. In 1917, Mary was elected to Cumann na mBan's national leadership and developed strong political networks across Ireland. Terence's political career grew through his leadership in all-male militias, prisons, and internment camps. In 1917, Terence was convicted for wearing an Irish Volunteers military uniform and drilling soldiers and was deported from Ireland to England, where he was imprisoned in internment camps until his release in June 1917. During his exile, he married twenty-five-year-old Muriel Murphy, daughter of an elite Cork distillery-owning family with strong ties to the Catholic leadership. He spent the rest of his life under the constant threat of arrest.

Many Irish Volunteers refused to join the British army to fight in World War I and instead gradually formed the Irish Republican Army (IRA), dedicated to fighting for an independent Irish republic free from British rule. In November 1917, shortly after returning to Cork, Terence was arrested again, this time for wearing an IRA uniform. During his imprisonment, he initiated a hunger strike and drew other men to join him. They were released within four days by British authorities, who feared prisoner deaths in the aftermath of Thomas Ashe's death after force-feeding in September of the same year. In 1918, Terence was arrested yet again and was moved between prisons in Cork, Dublin, Belfast, and Lincoln. While he was in prison, his daughter, Máire, was born.

TERENCE'S HUNGER STRIKE TO DEATH

When Irish Volunteers and republicans were released or escaped prison, they gravitated to Sinn Féin, meaning "we ourselves," which became the political party vehicle to advance the idea of an Irish republic. The Irish Parliamentary Party waned during the war and, particularly after British repression, made the implementation of Home Rule appear elusive, if not impossible. In the December 1918 general election for the British Parliament, Sinn Féin won overwhelmingly, capturing seventy-three of Ireland's 105 seats. Mary had campaigned on behalf of Terence, who was one of thirty-six jailed Sinn Féin candidates who won seats. Their victory repudiated Britain's military repression and foot-dragging on the implementation of Irish Home Rule, and the newly elected took steps to fulfill domestic governance.

In January 1919, the Sinn Féin members of Parliament boycotted the House of Commons and instead unilaterally proclaimed themselves the Dáil Éireann, the Parliament of Ireland. They created a parallel court system and government departments, with Irish republican leader Éamon de Valera as president. When the British government refused to recognize this unilateral resumption of the Irish Parliament, the Irish War of Independence, or Anglo-Irish War, erupted between the IRA and British forces.

The city of Cork—where the strength of the IRA and the Sinn Féin sweep of local political offices had alarmed the British—was under martial law. In January 1920, Terence's ally Tomás MacCurtain, a brigadier commander in the Cork battalion of the IRA, was elected lord mayor of Cork. On March 20, MacCurtain was shot dead by men with blackened faces. The coroners' inquest revealed that they were disguised policemen of the Royal Irish Constabulary. Terence MacSwiney was elected to replace MacCurtain as lord mayor of Cork.[5]

On August 12, 1920, the British military arrested MacSwiney while he was presiding over a meeting of the Cork Battalion council with ten other men in Cork City Hall. He was arrested for the unauthorized possession of a police cipher to relay secret communication.[6] Four days later, he was convicted of sedition and sentenced to two years imprisonment.

Wanting to separate Terence, as the leader, from the other Irish republicans held in prison in Cork, the British decided to remove him from Ireland. In the early morning the day after his conviction, they transported MacSwiney by British naval ship to South Wales, then by night train to London, where they handed him over to the custody of Brixton Prison at 4 A.M on August 18.[7]

Terence's determination was apparent from the outset. At his sentencing hearing, he had declared that he had already begun a hunger strike and would take no food while in detention: "I shall be free, alive or dead, within the month."[8] He had fasted for 107 hours before he was transferred. He is reported to have made the eloquent and prophetic statement: "I am confident that my death will do more to smash the British empire, than my release."[9]

Fasting unto death was a controversial choice for a Roman Catholic. Muriel remembered, in a statement taken in 1951, that while at Brixton, she had heard rumors that the Roman Catholic leadership wanted to "excommunicate" her husband "on the grounds that he was committing suicide," since the Church condemned suicide as a mortal sin. Church leaders, she said, "only desisted because Terry's hunger strike and Ireland's cause were so well put before the whole world."[10]

On August 21, Terence's wife, Muriel, and his sister Mary, accompanied by his chaplain, Friar Dominic O'Connor, arrived at Brixton Prison. Friar Dominic described Terence as "wan, wasted and haggard-looking, but of clear mind, and fully determined" when they greeted him in Brixton's Hospital Wing in a "large, airy" ward that contained six empty beds in addition to the one Terence occupied.[11] Eventually his sister Annie and brothers Seán and Peter also gathered at Brixton Prison. Mary organized a rotating schedule so that family members would be with Terence day and night.

King George V suggested that MacSwiney be released from prison and held under house arrest in England. But the British government and military were determined to stand their ground with MacSwiney. On August 26, Home Secretary Edward Shortt declared that "the release of the Lord Mayor would have disastrous results in Ireland and would probably lead to a mutiny of both military and police in South of Ireland."[12]

The British government's stance regarding Terence MacSwiney in fact helped to spread his story beyond Ireland and the United Kingdom. Terence's political office as Mayor of Cork and the extraordinary number of correspondents, newspapers, and wire services in London ensured that coverage of his hunger strike reverberated globally. Mary MacSwiney worked with Art

O'Brien, editor of the Irish Self-Determination League's paper *Irish Exile* and the Dáil's envoy in London, to shape news coverage to Irish and Catholic supporters worldwide that featured the family's intimate perspective on her brother's condition. The British and the international press adopted the romantic story of the young and frail wife Muriel beside the bedside of her starving husband. O'Brien kept Irish and American press agencies supplied with reports and news items, sending messengers out six or more times a day, feeding news publicity across the globe.[13]

After a visit to MacSwiney's Brixton cell, O'Brien spoke with an *Observer* reporter and raised the political stakes, warning: "If any of the Irish political prisoners die, the Irish people the world over will hold it to be an act of murder on the part of the English government."[14] Sinn Féin and IRA leaders championed MacSwiney's reputation as a sober, rational, and calm man who represented all imprisoned Irish insurgents. By focusing on MacSwiney's slow and solemn dying in Brixton, Irish republicans sought to undercut British accusations of the prisoners' participation in violence, sabotage, and insurrection.

Newspaper coverage across the globe picked up dramatically after MacSwiney's forty-fifth day on hunger strike. Readers were encouraged to write letters and send telegrams to Brixton Prison and to send urgent pleas to free Terence to Prime Minister David Lloyd George. The *New York Times* described MacSwiney's hunger strike as "a gesture of deep tragedy on a stage where all mankind looks on." On this platform the view of an "Irishman willing and glad to die" propelled a worldwide public reckoning of "individual self-immolation" transformed into "the intensity of the national aspiration and demand embodied in it."[15]

The strength of Catholic faith and rituals animated the news coverage and the solidarity of Catholic and diasporic Irish communities worldwide. MacSwiney's spiritual director, Father Dominic, visited him daily in prison to offer communion. Fasting, the short-term abstention from food and/or drink, has biblical roots in the forty-day fasts of Jesus, Elijah, and Moses and in the practices of Lent. Many devout Catholics and Anglicans were familiar with fasting one to three days for purposes such as spiritual purification, repentance, mourning the dead, and seeking God's intervention in crisis and calamity. MacSwiney's abstinence from food, though extreme, and his expression of devout faith in Christ resonated with Catholics and potentially with Protestants. Religious observance melded with Irish nationalist solidarity in vigils and rallies held in Boston, Buenos Aires, New York, Paris,

Melbourne, and Barcelona in support of MacSwiney and other hunger-striking Irish prisoners.

These international gatherings broadcast a collective public vigil to support MacSwiney's devotion to a free Ireland, as a struggle of his life to possible death. The form of hunger striking as anti-imperial rebellion was infused with Catholic community prayer and a global gathering of attention to him and other hunger strikers in Cork. While the purpose of this collective public vigil was to demand the immediate release of the hunger strikers, these public demonstrations carried two other messages as well. First, in their eyes, the British would be blamed for MacSwiney's death if he died. Second and more consequentially, these gatherings joined diasporic Irish, Catholic believers, and their allies worldwide into a solidarity network that would mold the hunger striker into a martyr, a symbol that could pull fierce sympathy, funds, and arms for Irish rebels from around the globe, further wounding British efforts to squash the Irish rebellion.

TERENCE'S FIGHT FOR DIGNITY IN HIS LAST DAYS

Because Terence MacSwiney was later memorialized in the pantheon of Irish heroes who fought for Irish independence, the diary and correspondence of his family members were subsequently collected and archived. These writings provide unique access to their witnessing of his dying. In particular, Annie MacSwiney's diary entries during the last week of her brother's life provide rare insights into the struggles her brother and family waged for the right to die peacefully for his cause.

At the beginning of that week, Annie marveled at how "perfectly conscious" her brother remained after more than sixty-eight days of fasting. She also described how the prison physicians' attempts to treat him disturbed his equanimity. At seventy days on hunger strike, when MacSwiney had survived well past any reasonable expectation of recovery, the prison doctors attempted to introduce both palliatives to reduce his suffering and nutrients to sustain him, administering them, almost sinisterly, in moments when they believed him to be unconscious and incapable of resisting. These efforts to feed him were a last resort both politically and medically to prevent his death. As Terence slipped from consciousness into delirium, his doctors instructed nurses to administer nutrient liquids such as "teaspoonfuls of meat juice in water" or palliatives like "brandy and milk," which resulted in "a dreadful fit of vomiting [up of] . . . green liquid."[16] The attempts to feed him drew Terence violently into conscious recognition of what was happening. He cried out, "They tricked me, they tricked me, how did they do it?" And then he fell back into "delirium, striking out again with his hands at both sides of his bed."

Annie portrayed her brother as a vigilant "soldier of the Irish Republic" to the very end, fighting for his dignity and his conscience, despite the high-handed efforts of prison physicians to delay his imminent death. He became restless and excitable. She described how he threw his arms around her and "began to talk wildly" as he was agitated by the "terror of the doctor's threat" to feed him when he slipped into unconsciousness. His visceral anguish, she recalled, and the "concentrated horror of that two hours of delirium is beyond imagination of anyone who did not witness it."[17]

Mary and Annie MacSwiney sent wires to officials saying the doctor was prolonging her brother's life against his will. Annie questioned the government's purpose in first refusing to release him before he became unconscious and now placing him in purgatory by "administer[ing] doses of food in his unconsciousness—keeping him alive just to let him suffer."[18] By invoking the religious concepts of purgatory and suffering before death, she alluded to martyrdom. Casting the government's policy as the "refinement of cruelty," Annie railed against the medical intervention that he repelled as the infliction of torture.

She recalled that "all the time I was by Terry's side he never once asked for a drink or for anything. When delirious he was always struggling against the enemy; he knew he would attack him, sometime he would lie quietly, looking with unseeing eyes around the room." He sensed betrayal and was vigilant. When "the nurse would put a spoon to his lips, he would close them tightly, as if in his unconsciousness he still knew he was dealing with his enemy."[19]

When Annie confronted the nurse about the misery she was causing her brother, the woman revealed her own ethical crisis. She responded, "You all make me nervous so I can't do my work." She was very aware that she was feeding him "against his will and against your will, but I have to do it and when I feel you are all watching me, I can't do it."

As Terence's condition worsened, the prison would not allow his family—his sisters and wife in particular—to visit for fear that they would interfere further with his care. Annie wrote of the "English doctors' low malice in excluding us from his deathbed."[20] Terence MacSwiney died at age forty-one in Brixton Prison on October 25, 1920, after seventy-four days on hunger strike. His brother Seán was present for his death, and his wife and sisters arrived immediately after.[21]

MacSwiney's hunger strike in London had overshadowed the news coverage of a mass hunger strike in Cork involving sixty IRA volunteers, most of whom were jailed without charge or trial at the time of Terence's arrest. The British had released most of them in August, but among the remaining eleven were two men whose hunger strike duration rivaled MacSwiney's. While international attention was focused on MacSwiney, Michael Fitzgerald died on October 17 at Cork Gaol after hunger striking for sixty-eight days. On October 25, the same day MacSwiney died, the American-born Patrick Joseph Murphy died at Cork Gaol after seventy-six days without food.

As the *New York Times* reported, the prison doctors were amazed that the two men had endured so long without food and credited their longevity to the "devotion and care of nuns" who attended them.[22] After Fitzgerald's and Murphy's deaths, the nine remaining hunger strikers consented to allow prison physicians to administer medical treatment and begin refeeding care.[23]

FUNERAL PROCESSIONS AND THE GLOBAL POLITICAL IMPACT OF TERENCE'S DEATH

After Terence MacSwiney's death, his family spent two days negotiating with the authorities for the release of his body for burial in Ireland. The British government reluctantly gave permission for a procession and funeral in London and transportation of the body for burial in Cork.

While the vigil of Terence's dying had drawn the attention of hundreds of thousands of people worldwide, the death of MacSwiney—and also that of Michael Fitzgerald, who was the first hunger striker to have died on Irish soil since Thomas Ashe, and for whose funerals large crowds gathered in Cork—particularly held international interest. They inspired tributes in Paris, Barcelona, and Buenos Aires. In North America, funeral marches were held in Boston, Newark, New York, Toronto, and Chicago.[24] Diarmuid Lynch, the national secretary of the U.S.-based Friends of Irish Freedom, directed all state and local chapters of the society to hold funeral services in Catholic churches to demonstrate their "indignation and sorrow on the 'murder' of Lord Mayor MacSwiney and Michael Fitzgerald." Invoking public practices used to memorialize fallen soldiers and political leaders, he recommended that funeral processions and masses include "gun carriages, coffins draped, each mourner with a mourning band, societies carrying their banners draped in mourning."[25]

The international media, in print and newsreels, elevated Terence's death by hunger strike despite the fact that few outside of Cork had known of his political career. The Irish diasporic and Catholic networks, through media communication, innovated the form of the hunger strike to inspire collective outdoor tributes, vigils, and funeral processions to publicly memorialize his death in cities across the globe. These translocal echoes were intentionally shaped both by Art O'Brien's publicity machine and by the decisions of Terence's family when they organized the care of the body and conveyance of the casket.

The funeral procession for Terence drew upon earlier spectacles of national public mourning, such as the cavalcades attending the funerals of Irish nationalist leaders Charles Steward Parnell and Thomas Ashe in Dublin. Despite the British government's preference to suppress the use of symbols of Irish independence, the family ensured that MacSwiney's body was dressed in his military uniform in observance of his final wish to be remembered as a soldier. This gesture sacralized his martyrdom for a future independent Irish republic.

In London, the forms of respectful public display reserved for British monarchs and politicians were usurped by an Irish insurgent, guaranteeing that his funeral would endure in public memory. The accompanied casket traveled three and a half miles from Brixton Prison to St. George's Cathedral in Southwark. The Catholic cathedral, built in 1848 to serve the growing population of Irish immigrants in South London, sits directly across the Thames River from the British Parliament, perfectly positioned as a symbolic adversary. Journalists reported that the funeral procession transpired with "impressive solemnity," with "citizens of all classes and creeds" lining the streets to pay tribute as the coffin passed. Instead of being able to condemn the death of a treasonous official, convicted as an accomplice to a terrorist insurgency, the British government had to confront the death of a political and religious martyr on behalf of an independent Ireland.

Terence's body lay in state at St. George's, and from early morning a "continuous procession" of reportedly twenty thousand mourners filed past the coffin to pay their respects. The press described "scenes of deep solemnity" at requiem high mass, with demonstrations of "fervent feeling by many thousands of Irishmen and women from all parts of the kingdom." The cathedral was filled to capacity: people crowded the pews and the side chapels, and long lines extended around the entire building as mourners jostled to find room to stand.[26] During the service, the crowd of mourners outside, unable to gain

FIGURE 7. Women protesting the deaths of Patrick Joseph Murphy, Terence MacSwiney, and Michael Fitzgerald during the MacSwiney memorial parade in December 1920. Image reproduced courtesy of the National Library of Ireland: NPA POLF163.

admission, grew so enormous that police linked arms to hold them back. Inside the cathedral, "the spectacle was [awash in] the white, orange, and green colours of Sinn Fein," amplifying the religious observance of Irish republican bravery.[27]

Fearing large-scale demonstrations in Dublin, British authorities diverted the casket directly to Cork, which journalists described as "a city of mourning" with "blinds lowered . . . shops heavily shuttered," while "white flags on buildings and vessels in the river were at half-mast."[28] The British Pathé newsreel of the event documented images of the Catholic ceremony, including shots of choristers, choirboys, and priests processing into the cathedral and the bishop waving incense over the coffin, while shots of the streets showed armed British soldiers and an armored car vigilantly guarding the streets and crowds of solemn, dark-suited mourners and horse-drawn carriages following the funeral cortège.[29]

On the same day as the funeral in Cork, forty thousand people congregated in Manhattan's Polo Grounds stadium to pay tribute to MacSwiney, with ten thousand more crowded outside the stadium in "an outburst of Irish emotion."[30] In Boston, thirty thousand people, marching to "funeral dirges played by a single band, passed through thronged but silent downtown streets." Police estimated that 250,000 spectators watched the solemn march pass by.[31]

The vigil and funeral processions, while honoring MacSwiney, were simultaneously protests designed to motivate and inspire a national and international audience. Literary studies scholar Paige Reynolds has argued that in the middle of the war for Irish independence, the performative spectacle of "MacSwiney's martyrdom and funerals offered the Irish and international public an alternative mode of revolutionary action . . . by presenting Irish bodies as registers of self-discipline in the face of English oppression."[32] Conjuring the mythic symbols of self-injury and self-starvation to shame the British state, it elevated the insurrection into a struggle of conscience to compel British authority to agree to freedom for Ireland.

Fifteen years earlier, in his play *The King's Threshold*, Irish poet William Yeats had unfurled the Irish custom of protest fasting as a challenge to a monarch's authority and judgment. The court poet, Seanchan, is removed from the council's table and embarks on a hunger strike to restore his place:

> KING: . . . He has chosen death:
> Refusing to eat or drink, that he may bring
> Disgrace upon me; for there is a custom,
> An old and foolish custom, that if a man
> Be wronged, or think that he is wronged, and starve
> Upon another's threshold till he die,
> The Common People, for all time to come,
> Will raise a heavy cry against that threshold,
> Even though it be the King's.[33]

The King rallies the poet's students, friends, and neighbors to "hold" the faster's "mouth from biting on the grave" and "persuade him eat or drink," fearing that the King's "good name in the world" would perish with the protest. The King at last entreats Seanchan to abandon his fast and offers his crown to the poet in humility. After MacSwiney's death, however, Yeats rewrote the play so that the poet dies on hunger strike. His last words are "King! King! Dead faces laugh."[34]

The media coverage of MacSwiney's imprisonment and death—as well as the posthumous publication of his book *Principles of Freedom*—inspired a number of twentieth-century revolutionary leaders to speak of his bravery in the cause of national self-determination.[35] Marcus Garvey, Jamaican-born leader of the Pan-Africanism movement, sent a message expressing sympathy and solidarity: "Hundreds and thousands of Irishmen have died as martyrs to the cause of Irish freedom. . . . They compelled the attention of the world and I believe the death of McSweeney [*sic*] did more for the freedom of Ireland today than probably anything they did for 500 years prior to his death."[36]

A young Vietnamese man working in a kitchen in London, upon hearing the news, burst into tears and declared, "A country with a citizen like this will never surrender." When he returned to Vietnam, he changed his name to Ho Chi Minh and led the Vietnamese struggle against the French, Japanese, and American military for three decades.[37]

While Mahatma Gandhi disagreed with participation in military insurrection, he admired Terence MacSwiney's resolve and believed that Irish independence was won by the "magnitude of the Irish sacrifice which has been the deciding factor."[38]

The long reach of MacSwiney's political influence to anticolonial rebellions worldwide echoed in his words declaring the imperative of independence from colonial rule. In the hands of his sisters and supporters, his prison hunger strike was first shaped as a Catholic and Irish nationalist martyrdom in London, from which journalist and media networks carried the story to the world stage. And then the networks of Irish diasporic and Catholic solidarity transmitted this novel meaning of the hunger strike in public massing and demonstration broadly across the world. This form of the hunger strike resonated beyond ethnic or sectarian boundaries, more so than any other Irish republican hunger strike, and was repurposed in new hands as a geopolitical sign of anticolonial bodily and moral defiance. MacSwiney's death by hunger strike was fashioned by anticolonial leaders and critics as a combined political and spiritual assertion—a national sacrifice worthy of respect and emulation by anticolonial independence movements worldwide.

MARY MACSWINEY CHAMPIONS IRISH INDEPENDENCE

After her brother's death, Mary MacSwiney was determined to communicate his sacrifice as a herald of Irish independence to sympathetic audiences in the United States. She and Terence's widow, Muriel, toured the country, lecturing and fund-raising among Irish American Catholic communities for nine months. They testified before the American Commission on Conditions in Ireland, a body of 150 distinguished politicians and social and cultural leaders, to investigate the Anglo-Irish War and examine political solutions. Their extensive testimony solidified the narrative of Terence's martyrdom as abetted by the cruelty of British authorities. His death thus emboldened the Irish rebellion both materially, through Irish Americans' donations of funds and arms, and symbolically.

When she returned to Ireland in June 1921, Mary ran for election on the Sinn Féin ticket for the Cork Borough constituency, as did her brother Seán. They both won seats in the Dáil Éireann as the British and Irish negotiated Irish Home Rule, which had been legislated and delayed eight years. After a contentious debate in the Dáil in December 1921 and into January 1922, a narrow majority agreed to the terms of the Anglo-Irish Treaty, which concluded the Irish War of Independence and established Home Rule and the Irish Free State. Under the provisions of the Irish Free State's new constitution, full parliamentary franchise was granted to all Irish women over the age of twenty-one—six years in advance of full suffrage for all adult British women. Mary MacSwiney tirelessly fought for universal women's suffrage within the fight for Irish sovereignty. But this victory came at a steep price.

The establishment of the Irish Free State divided the island geographically and politically. Under the terms of the Anglo-Irish Treaty (often called simply "the Treaty"), the six northeast counties, which had majority Protestant populations, could secede from the Irish Free State as Northern Ireland and return to British union. The British conceded the remaining twenty-six counties to the Home Rule governance of the Irish Free State, including power over the police and army, while internationally the Irish Free State remained a dominion of the British Empire. In terms of citizenship, the inhabitants of the Irish Free State were Irish citizens, but to the wider world they remained British subjects and holders of British passports.

Irish republicans split into pro-Treaty and anti-Treaty camps, and the rift was severe and violent. Mary and Seán MacSwiney both strongly opposed the Treaty, which Mary called a "spiritual surrender" because it betrayed the aspiration to full independence and autonomy for the Irish republic. As both vice president of Cumann na mBan and a member of the Dáil, Mary championed the opposition to the Irish Free State regime under British dominion. Along with the other five women members of the Dáil, she was among the minority that voted down the Treaty.[39]

Ireland became wracked by civil war between pro-Treaty and anti-Treaty advocates. Seán MacSwiney served as a military officer and as executive committee leader of the anti-Treaty IRA. He was captured in 1921, sentenced to death, escaped, and continued to fight against Irish Free State forces until he became their captive in November 1923.

MARY'S CAPTURE AND HUNGER STRIKE

On November 4, 1922, Irish Free State soldiers raided a safe house outside Dublin where Mary MacSwiney had taken refuge and arrested her. Under the Emergency Powers Act, the Free State government held Mary in custody, under suspicion that she was fomenting rebellion. Imprisoned in Mountjoy, where dozens of Irish republican prisoners had gone on hunger strike during British rule and where Thomas Ashe had died in 1917, Mary announced a hunger strike to protest her detention without trial and to force her release. She entreated Irish Catholics for their prayers to bolster her, so that she "may be as brave as those who have gone before."

Her hunger strike challenged the resolve of the Irish Free State government to detain its anti-Treaty opponents. While Mary MacSwiney was a high-profile captive, she was, significantly, only "one of 6,000 prisoners." The government feared that if they released her, nothing would "prevent other prisoners going on hunger-strike" in order to gain their release.[40]

Dr. O'Connor, senior medical officer at Mountjoy, who began monitoring her condition near the beginning of her fast, reported to his superiors that Mary was "well-nourished, 45 years of age," and showed "no symptoms attributable to lack of food." Mary had suffered from "headaches, diffuse pain, flushes" for three months prior to the hunger strike, which he attributed to the onset of menopause. Dr. O'Connor speculated that Mary experienced "severe emotional disturbances" aggravated by menopause and that a long hunger strike "may conceivably culminate in unhinging her mind."[41]

Ten days into the hunger strike, Dr. O'Connor reported that Mary was in a "dangerous and weak condition" that necessitated "special nursing, night and day, a waterbed, clothing, [and] a well-ventilated room, constantly kept at an even temperature and free from noise." He worried that "otherwise the loss of sleep or the onset of bedsores" and ensuing "debilitation and confinement" would likely "cause death long before the absence of food alone could do so." Since such facilities and treatment were unavailable at Mountjoy, he recommended her immediate transfer to a private nursing home. However, Mountjoy's governor refused to release her.[42]

Mary MacSwiney's vocal opposition to the Anglo-Irish Treaty and the Irish Free State infuriated the government's leaders, fueling their unwaveringly punitive response in her case. Sinn Féin leader William Cosgrave, an ally of Terence MacSwiney's in the Easter Rising, had advocated for the Irish Free State and was now its first president. In confidential correspondence, he blasted the "prominent and destructive part played by women in the present deplorable revolt." He singled out Mary for her role in bringing about "the prevailing anarchy and crime" and held her responsible for the fact that "too many valuable lives have been murderously taken, too many people's property has been criminally destroyed." Cosgrave and his government insisted that any leniency in her case would be interpreted by opponents and supporters as weakness.[43]

In public, however, Cosgrave was more circumspect. Instead of excoriating Mary's character, he defended the Mountjoy administration as providing "from our hands the greatest care and consideration and the best of food" if Mary should "choose it." The emphasis on the humane care they were ready to offer while she opted for self-starvation was evidently intended to assuage those sympathetic to Mary. He knew that another death like her brother's could be catastrophic and would hamper the battle to unify Ireland.[44]

Mary and her anti-Treaty republican allies, however, sought to deepen the public's distrust of the new government by heralding the message that British rule was continuing in all but name. Her detention and hunger strike under the Irish Free State drew obvious parallels with the detention of prisoners, such as her brother, without trial under the British. Her bodily sacrifice also personalized the stakes of the civil war, which were already felt by many of Ireland's families and communities.

Like her brother's fast, which brought threats of excommunication, Mary's hunger strike challenged Church authority. However, unlike her brother, Mary fenced directly with the Church hierarchy. Cardinal Michael Logue, Archbishop of Armagh and Primate of All Ireland, had advocated for Irish Home Rule and endorsed the Anglo-Irish Treaty. His denunciation of the IRA's extremism lent support to the Free State government's suppression of the insurgents, and he expressed no sympathy for her decision to hunger strike. Catholic theologians debated whether the hunger strike was an exhibition of extreme piety or of suicide. Irish republicans and Catholic supporters claimed that death by hunger strike was martyrdom.

After nearly three weeks on hunger strike, she sent a letter to the *Irish Times* vociferously denouncing Bishop Cohalan, bishop of her hometown of Cork, who had condemned her for "vainly provoking ... an act of self-murder."[45] In a sermon publicized in newspapers throughout Ireland, he had accused Mary of courting suicide, "a mortal sin," and proposed that the Catholic Church should embargo sacramental ritual for her as long as she remained on hunger strike, reproaching her for having already "signed her death warrant."[46] In her letter, Mary pointed out that the very same Bishop Cohalan had demonstrated sympathy for her brother's hunger strike just two years before, conveyed the Pope's blessings at his deathbed, and officiated at his funeral in Cork. "Why, then," she probed, "this extraordinary inconsistence! My protest is for exactly the same purpose as was my brother's."[47] However, the political stage was not the same.

Like the government, members of the Church hierarchy understood the potentially disastrous results of Mary MacSwiney's refusal to eat and proposed contradictory tactics to try to mitigate them. On one hand, in private correspondence Cardinal Logue advised President Cosgrave to refuse the "release of a leader so prominent and so fanatical as Miss MacSwiney" because she would embolden "the young people of both sexes whom she goaded into revolt against both ecclesiastical and constitutional authority."[48] On the other hand, John Clegg, Archbishop of Dublin, predicted that Mary's possible death would have a more "harmful effect than her continued internment" and entreated Cosgrave to allow him to meet with her at Mountjoy. Some Church leaders feared that she and her fellow women prisoners, some of whom were also on hunger strike, "were doing more harm in prison than they were doing outside" and counseled President Cosgrave to release her because allowing her to die in prison would make her a heroine and martyr and frame the Free State government and the Church as her enemies.[49]

Beyond Mountjoy's prison gates, Mary MacSwiney's hunger strike became a windfall of publicity that the Cumann na mBan quickly exploited by organizing rallies and prayer vigils, much as they had against the British incarceration of Irish men during the Anglo-Irish War. Hundreds of women gathered nightly outside Mountjoy for a ritual of public prayer and recitation of the rosary. This peaceful and spiritual prayer by the laity contrasted sharply with the depiction in the *Irish Times* of vicious and abusive Irish Free State soldiers harassing the women and turning water hoses on them.[50]

Although Terence's siblings had been allowed to be present with him during his hunger strike in a British prison, when Mary's sister Annie journeyed from Cork to visit her, prison authorities denied her access. The government was afraid of letting Mary's family intercede and act as her spokespersons to the public.[51] Undeterred, Annie brought a deck chair and screen to camp outside the prison gates, beginning her own sympathy fast. The *Irish Times* reported that she drew public curiosity as she sat in her chair, "wearing a fur coat with a rug about her knees ... supported by small relays of women friends."[52]

Annie was also savvy to the power of shaping media image and narrative. She allowed the British Pathé newsreel crew to film her vigil. The footage features Annie lying in a bed with blankets covering her head and body and wooden screens surrounding the bed for privacy. She sometimes speaks directly to the camera, sometimes writes in a diary. Even without sound or her words in intertitle, viewers could see her calm resolve to offer her sister succor even when blocked by the prison authorities. Women take turns keeping her company, while a nurse monitors her care. The women's public demonstration both communicated the anguish of separated sisters and morally rebuked the Irish Free State's practices of detention without trial.[53] Echoing the unseen hunger strike within the prison, the solidarity fast outside its gates gave a new, visible public dimension to the prison hunger strike.

Because she was denied the privilege of receiving care from her family, Mary drew comfort from the sixteen fellow anti-Treaty republican women imprisoned at Mountjoy for similar allegations of sedition against the Free State government. The women sent letters to newspapers informing the public of Mary's condition. One such letter revealed that after eleven days on hunger strike, Mary experienced a turning point: "Patient and loving, she has struggled to hide her sufferings from us. But to-day a terrible change has come, exhaustion has set in; she is currently scarcely able to speak. . . . [S]he will persist to the end and we know the end is near. Our hearts are breaking, but we are helpless, we can do nothing but pray." The letter berated the public for their "cowardice and inaction" regarding Mary's plight and asked imploringly whether they would "allow Terence MacSwiney's sister to die in an Irish jail." The letter noted that Terence "gave his life willingly, a prisoner in the hands of an English enemy. Mary MacSwiney is a prisoner in the hands of Irishmen." The letter also linked her hunger strike to the political future of Ireland: "As Ireland, physically weak but spiritually unconquerable, withstood the brute force of an empire, so this great woman, imprisoned and helpless," dares "with her dauntless will" to " free Ireland forever" from the "dominion of a foreign Power."[54]

FIGURE 8. Muriel MacSwiney, protesting in Washington, D.C., in support of her sister-in-law Mary MacSwiney's hunger strike at Mountjoy Prison, Dublin, 1922. Courtesy of the Library of Congress.

No one directly claimed that the differences in Terence's and Mary's age, gender, and marriage status mattered. Nevertheless, the claim on political leadership and the cultural symbolism of a hunger strike exercised by a forty-one-year-old married man with a young child was distinct from that of a hunger strike by his fifty-year-old unmarried sister. They both were leaders in Irish independence struggles, but Terence had military experience, won a seat that he refused in the British Parliament, and held ceremonial leadership in Cork. Mary was a leader in Sinn Féin, elected to the Dáil, and internationally known as an outspoken advocate for Irish independence. Yet her social status remained tethered to her brother's name and reputation. Terence could be made to symbolize a united Irish Catholic nation, but Mary was depicted as a partisan in a divided Ireland.

Some of the women who attended Mary recorded what they saw and felt in personal diaries. One of them, Dorothy Macardle,[55] described how Mary's remarkable "vitality during the first 14–15 days" diminished as the days progressed, particularly at night when she was "betrayed by pitiful misery and the exclamations in sleep and the restlessness of the long hours while she lies awake." The following night, Macardle observed the dark room, the fearful deterioration of Mary's "shrinking of the flesh . . . her eyes close, her sweet face hollow and thin . . . so slowly, no monstrously . . . deepening her suffering . . . anguish one can scarcely imagine."[56]

On November 24, the twentieth day of her hunger strike, Mary MacSwiney's condition grew critical. She had a weakened pulse, lowered body temperature, and restless sleep, and she was given the Last Rites by a Catholic priest. Macardle called Sunday night, November 26, "A Night of Fear." Dorothy massaged Mary's wrists and settled her pillows, trying to ease her suffering and provide comfort to help her sleep. "Such horror, and such agonizing. . . . Each moment of this long torture she is inflicting on herself . . . she is crucifying herself . . . for the people of Ireland."[57]

Bearing witness for Mary was steeped in references to supernatural and divine intercession. During what she described as the direst hour of their vigil, Macardle and a companion knelt at an altar "in the landing at the turn of the stairs . . . in the small hours of the morning." She sensed and saw "a presence advance along the corridor from [Mary's] cell, pass between us and disappear down the stairs . . . so serene [the] light—that gave place to a kind of joy. Kept pink and immobile [the presence moved] . . . slowly and stared at me wonderingly."[58] The two women believed that Mary had died and the spectral presence was her spirit as it passed out of her body. They rushed to Mary's cell to discover her still breathing. They pondered, then, if the visitation had been the beneficent spirit of Terence MacSwiney, come to watch over his sister at her time of greatest need, helping to restore her spirit to her fragile body.

Mary's companions agitated for her immediate release, citing the risk of her imminent death. Members of the Free State government fiercely debated how to respond. The political risks of having her die in prison motivated the government to release her before her condition worsened. On Monday, November 27, 1922, Mary MacSwiney was released. She was transported by military ambulance to a private nursing home to recover before returning home to Cork.[59]

A few days after her release, Mary wrote to her women companions, underscoring the authority of devout laywomen who had supported her, in contrast to the Catholic hierarchy, who had abandoned her: "My dear Angels: For that is indeed what you were for the past fortnight especially—Angels of loving kindness and unending prayer and vigil." She made biblical references to the power of prayer in forcing the authorities to release her: "You remember the story of the fall of Jericho . . . the Jews had to walk around seven times praying and singing Psalms . . . Well on Sunday the Women's Procession . . . round Mountjoy seven times—they had done it on every night, saying the Rosary, you did the singing and on Monday the gates fell."[60]

MARY'S POLITICAL FUTURE

Mary MacSwiney persisted in the struggle for an independent Ireland. She was arrested once again in April 1923 and while imprisoned went on a seventeen-day hunger strike. She was reelected to the Dáil in the August 1923 election but refused to take her seat, along with other Sinn Féin members.

In the 1920s, pro-Treaty Irish republicans effectively sidelined Mary MacSwiney and other republican women leaders for repudiating the Treaty and backing the anti-Treaty IRA during the civil war. Many pro-Treaty supporters viewed these anti-Treaty women as unwomanly, and Free State politicians grew increasingly hostile to their demands. In 1924, Free State politician Patrick Sarsfield O' Hegarty, a friend of Terence MacSwiney and the author of his 1922 biography, described anti-Treaty women as "unlovely, destructive, arid begetters of violence, both physical violence and mental violence." They were "hysterical women, living on excitement, enjoying themselves in the ambushes and *stunts*. . . . [T]o them the Truce was nothing but a trick played upon the British, and to them peace was a loveless thing, and no life so good as the life of war. They became practically unsexed, their mother's milk blackened to make gunpowder, their minds working on nothing save hate and blood."[61]

These intense fears of destructive impulses of independent women's political autonomy reinforced conservative politicians' disposition to sideline women politically. To combat this perceived threat, Irish Free State politicians emphasized a domestic role for women, limiting women who ran for office to loyal wives, sisters, and widows; establishing restrictive laws prohibiting married women from taking civil service jobs; and curbing Irish women's freedom in the 1920s and 1930s.[62]

Mary MacSwiney was indefatigable in pursuing the liberation of all Ireland from British rule. She refused to follow Sinn Féin leader Éamon de Valera, who was convinced that abstention and noncooperation were counterproductive. In 1926, de Valera proposed that Sinn Féin members take their seats in the Dáil and govern the Irish Free State. When the vote to do so narrowly failed, he broke away and started a new party, Fianna Fáil, which became one of the two leading political parties in Ireland, holding power in 1932 and dominating Irish government for decades, especially after the transition to an independent Irish republic in 1937.

Sinn Féin's power diminished. Mary MacSwiney lost her seat in 1927 elections and resigned from the party in 1934. Her crusade for a free Ireland pivoted to the struggle in Northern Ireland. Until her death in 1942, Mary wholeheartedly supported the IRA, including the violent campaign of assassination and bombings in England, to reunite all of Ireland and sever all ties to Britain.

HUNGER STRIKING AND THE BATTLE AGAINST BRITISH IMPERIAL RULE OVER IRELAND

Because Terence and Mary MacSwiney's hunger strikes were informed by their Catholic faith and invested with the goal of Irish independence, they presented a moral as well as political challenge to the state's power to isolate, punish, and dehumanize political insurgents. However, their status as political leaders allowed them better treatment than most Irish republican prisoners received, with more opportunities for visits and care from their family and fellow prisoners. In both cases the prison held back from imposing forcible feeding, and so there was an opportunity for intimate observation of the siblings' prolonged fasting and spiritual journey toward dying by family and friends. It is the diaries and letters of those people that offer us today such a profound perspective on the witnessing of a hunger striker's suffering and approach toward death.

The MacSwiney hunger strikes were twin gambits at symbolizing individual personal agony against imperial state power in two distinct forms: the Union of Britain and Ireland in Terence's case and the new Irish Free State under British dominion in Mary's. In both instances the imprisoned striker's individual defiance became reshaped on a nationalist register of an Ireland steeped in Catholic Christian rituals and meanings of martyrdom. Among the many concurrent hunger strikes, it was each individual MacSwiney's personal hungering that was projected symbolically and that demanded public vigil, picket, and ceremony.

Terence's hunger strike became immortalized as a model of anticolonial selfless sacrifice. His dying and death forged his international and Irish national reputations. By contrast, Mary's strike was tossed into the chasm of the Irish Civil War, where partisans faced off to win the Irish Catholic polity to their respective sides. She was recognized as keeper of the public memory of her brother's death while also forging her own indomitable political leadership for Irish independence, both in her oratory in the Dáil and on the international stage.

The vigils in prison for both siblings reinforced gender expectations that women provide care and solace to the ill and dying and can communicate their intimate witnessing of the agony of others, whether male or female. They testify, through their letters and private diaries, to the private bravery of men and women when they are most feeble and weak. In early twentieth-century Ireland, that weakness on the part of a man could be restored in death by the insurrectionist's military uniform. The prayerful women surrounding Mary MacSwiney sought divine mercy and intercession for the dying hunger striker, despite the disapproval of male priests. However, women as hunger strikers, no matter how brave or obstinate, were liable to be publicly and privately disparaged.

In Terence's funeral procession and in the women's vigils for Mary, Catholic suffering and national martyrdom reverberated personally in the lives of hundreds of thousands of Irish women and men. The tumultuous years encompassing the Easter Rising, the Anglo-Irish War, and the Irish Civil War brought injury, deprivation, and death into Ireland's communities and homes. Both the British government in Ireland and the Irish Free State exacted punishment, widespread wounding, and death. In this context, Irish prisoners of all kinds went on hunger strike. Their families and friends agonized over whether they would live or die. The vigil for hunger strikers was both personal and experienced broadly in Irish society. The publicity of the MacSwineys' hunger strikes anchored the meanings of this sacrifice of one's life for the nation. Irish sociologist Michael Biggs estimates that nearly ten thousand Irish republican prisoners went on hunger strike between 1916 and 1923.

The largest number of strikes occurred in October 1923, when approximately seventy-eight hundred anti-Treaty IRA prisoners in Mountjoy and in ten prison camps went on hunger strike.[63] Beginning at midnight, October 14, at Mountjoy, prisoners signed a printed statement: "I pledge myself in the name of the living Republic to the lives of my comrades, that I will not take food or drink anything except water until I am unconditionally released. What I am about to suffer I offer to the glory of God and for the freedom of Ireland."[64] Most struck for a few days or at most a couple of weeks. Weakened and despairing, most of the hunger strikers quit in mid-November, but nearly two hundred continued, and two died on November 20 and 22, respectively. The following day, after forty-one days of hunger striking, the remaining hunger strikes ceased, pressured by Catholic Church and anti-Treaty leaders. The Irish Free State, allegedly fearing influenza outbreaks in overcrowded prisons, granted amnesty to three thousand prisoners, including all the women, before Christmas on condition that they pledge loyalty to the Irish Free State.

In the hands of the suffragists, prison hunger striking was a demand for rights within the prevailing system of British imperial democracy. In Ireland, the hunger strike form of protest expanded into a weapon used to face Britain's political obstinance. The British government, by cunning and calculation, had deferred and denied domestic self-governance to British imperial subjects in Ireland for more than a half century. In the hands of the MacSwiney family and their supporters, the carceral power that enveloped the hunger striker's body was shaken. It crumbled in unexpected ways, revealing ordeals of resistance in mind, body, and spirit that eluded the prison's and the state's total sovereign dominion.

The nationalist symbolism of these two prison hunger strikes manifested a new geopolitical form of anticolonial rebellion in the hands of the Irish diaspora and Catholic faith communities and inspired anticolonial upheaval in Asia, Africa, and the Americas.

FOUR

Gandhi's Fasts, Prisoner Hunger Strikes, and Indian Independence

ACROSS THE GLOBE FROM IRELAND, another crisis in the British Empire over the demand for democracy churned in the first decades of the twentieth century as the people of India demanded to govern themselves. Confrontations with the British rulers led to bodily defiance on the streets and in prisons.

In India, the hunger strike was not the only form of political refusal to eat. The public protest fast developed by Mohandas Gandhi became a signature tool of nonviolent civil disobedience. With the protest fast, Gandhi enlarged the scope of the traditional spiritual fast, recasting its purpose as a public demonstration of spiritual self-discipline and also, by his own example, rousing his followers' ethical consciousness to forsake violence as a means to political independence. The British government in India responded to Gandhi's public fasts quizzically and saw them as a strange brew of religious fervency and political miscalculation. Indeed, the British saw them much as Indian militants did, as a self-inflicted wounding of India's nationalist political movement.

In the 1920s and 1930s, when Indian prisoners convicted of insurrection and sabotage deployed the hunger strike weapon in prison to gain release or accelerate parole, this conflicted with Gandhi's ethos for public fasting. While he recognized hunger striking as politically potent and, like his protest fasting, as a means to reach a mass audience and impel mass action, he censured it on both moral and strategic grounds. Gandhi's intent was to preserve that political transformative power for the protest fast. But the prison hunger strike was not so easily deterred; anticolonial rebels persisted in deploying it in prisons on the Indian subcontinent and in the penal colony on the Andaman Islands. These prison hunger strikes stoked public outrage, making them impossible to ignore.

In the first two decades of the twentieth century, the political opposition to British rule in India transformed from an accommodationist and reform approach of educated and wealthy urban Indian elites to uniting students, workers, and rural farmers into a mass movement for a new nation. The Indian National Congress Party, founded in 1885, was a British-authorized platform for college-educated Indians to consult with the government on civil and social reform. For two decades, its meetings drew a small group of elite Indians jockeying for power and devising declarations for a social reform agenda. However, by 1905, militants who agitated for greater independence from Britain cleaved away from moderates who favored legislative consultation. When public agitation against the British imperial partition of Bengal led to the *swadeshi* movement, an independence movement that championed the economic boycott of British manufactured goods and the revival of Indian crafts and industry as a measure of self-reliance, militants energized the movement's urban and international arm.

This movement connected with other regional movements in Maharashtra and Punjab and awakened Indian demands for home rule and domestic autonomy during World War I. During the 1910s, militant urban strategies of insurrection, bombing, and assassination of British authorities also erupted. The British government successfully arrested, tried, and imprisoned a number of rebels, who mounted challenges to British authority in prison. Hunger strikes erupted among a handful of these prisoners. Prison wardens treated these occurrences as routine instances of prisoner disorder, using corporal punishment to put down prison "mutiny." News of these prison hunger strikes was suppressed, being reported only through rumor or in appeals for government inquiry. They drew the immediate concern only of fellow prisoners, prisoners' families, and local allies.

One of the earliest recorded hunger strikes, in 1912, was by Nani Gopal Mukherjee, a young Bengali imprisoned for throwing a bomb at the motorcar of a high-ranking police official in Calcutta.[1] At the notorious Cellular Jail in the Andaman Islands, eight hundred miles off the coast in the Bay of Bengal, after weeks of escalating confrontations with prison guards, Nani Gopal demanded to be treated as a "political prisoner," arguing that the prisoners were "not thieves, robbers and dacoits." After a vicious caning, he was isolated to a smaller jail on Viper Island, where he began his hunger strike.

For three days he lay on his cell floor without speaking or eating. He was returned to the Cellular Jail, where fellow prisoners tried to coax him to eat, but to no avail. After six days of Nani Gopal's fasting, the prison physician forced a tube up his nose and he "was made to inhale milk through the nose." Even with the daily administration of milk, he was "reduced to skin and bones," but he refused to relent even when he was forced to stand for a week with his hands and feet in chains. His suffering led six or seven fellow prisoners to go on a sympathy hunger strike, but they too were subjected to chains and similar punishment.[2]

During World War I, the British feared alliances between Germany and Indian exiles and migrants in the Ghadar Party, which was fomenting anticolonial insurrection in North America and in British military installations in Singapore and Hong Kong. In 1915 the British government in India passed the Defence of India Act, which suspended rules regarding trials, evidence, and legal defense and authorized local governments to create special tribunals to try and convict suspects of conspiracy and sedition, enhance sentences, and deny appeal. These provisions were used against Ghadar revolutionaries for launching mutiny among Sikh Indian soldiers stationed in Singapore and Hong Kong, and for running arms and fomenting rebellion in the Punjab. Imprisoned Ghadar rebels turned to hunger striking to protest not being allowed access to religious texts, gain dietary privileges, and otherwise retain the elements of their Sikh faith.[3]

British administrators worried that the strategy of hunger strikes and demands for political prisoner status used by suffragists and Irish republicans would travel across the empire. Indeed, the *Times of India* published accounts of legal and political debate over wardens' force-feeding suffragists in Birmingham in 1909.[4] The English-language Indian press further sharpened its readership's awareness of prison hunger strikes by printing accounts of the release of Irish hunger strikers following Thomas Ashe's death in 1917, as well as reports of Indian prisoners, convicted of political insurrection, going on hunger strike to secure their release, which even received international wire coverage.[5]

World War I had deep ramifications for British India, intensifying the reach of British rule. The demand for military recruitment drove the British even more deeply into towns and rural regions, particularly the Punjab and northern India. The British Indian Army grew threefold during World War I, from a standing army of 155,000 in 1914 to 573,000 in November 1918. When the war was over, India was wracked by high taxation, trade disruptions, high inflation, and a devastating death toll from the influenza pandemic. The British also now had a larger military and surveillance force in India with which to suppress opposition. Further, Indian nationalists expected that the British would reward dominion status to India for its wartime service and sacrifice, as it had granted in the nineteenth and early twentieth centuries to Australia, New Zealand, Canada, and South Africa. Instead, the British government in India, beset by fears of insurrection, prolonged the wartime repression of civil liberties, seeking to squelch the growing movement for home rule and self-determination.

GANDHI'S PUBLIC FASTING

Mohandas Gandhi had returned from South Africa in 1915, after his success in fighting racial discrimination there. Since writing *Hind Swaraj* in 1909, he had backed a wide-ranging transformation of Indian society in order to obtain *swaraj,* or self-rule, which he argued was preferable to the replacement of the British by Indian rulers overseeing a British-designed government, economy, and society that would crush rather than benefit the mass of the Indian people. He remained on the edges of Indian politics for the first few years, but by 1919 he was leading the Indian National Congress party.

In February 1919, the British government in India passed the Rowlatt Act, which extended the arrests without warrants, juryless trials, curfews, preventive indefinite detentions, and measures to suppress free speech put in place during the war. When the act became law, Gandhi proposed a countrywide day of prayer, fasting, and abstention from work as a peaceful protest against the act's injustice. Without directly calling for a general strike, Gandhi made mass use of public fasting serve the same purpose. His plea generated an overwhelming response as, on April 6, millions of Indians in Bombay, Karachi, Patna, Madras, Dacca, Calcutta, and Amritsar closed shops, stayed home, prayed, and fasted.

In response, the British government shut down Gandhi's ability to travel. Gandhi boarded a train in Ahmedabad on April 8, headed northward, but when it stopped at a station more than fifty miles outside of Delhi, the police served Gandhi with an order prohibiting him from entering the region around Delhi or the Punjab, his destination, and restricted his movements in his home region of the Bombay Presidency. His temporary detention provoked protests in the streets of India's cities, including Ahmedabad itself. Millhands torched government buildings, looted homes of officials, and attacked Europeans. Gandhi returned to Ahmedabad on April 13, and he repudiated the violence at a gathering at Sabarmati Ashram, where he lived and worked, the following day. He called off the campaign and vowed to undertake a seventy-two-hour fast, joined during the first twenty-four hours by his followers gathered at the ashram, as atonement for the violence. As a result, demonstrations in Bombay Presidency stopped completely.

Meanwhile, in Amritsar, capital of the Punjab, news of Gandhi's detention inflamed unrest that continued for several days. The local civilian authority put Amritsar under martial law and summoned Brigadier-General Reginald Dyer to restore order. Dyer prohibited all public meetings, closed temples and mosques to worshippers, and ordered public flogging of rebels. Despite the severity of martial law, on April 13 a crowd of several thousand, augmented by pilgrims leaving kirtan services at the Sikh Golden Temple, gathered at a walled public garden, Jallianwala Bagh. Dyer responded by bringing fifty armed troops, blocked the garden's single entrance, and opened fire without warning.

More than four hundred died in the carnage that became known as the Amritsar Massacre. Despite British censorship, rumors of the tragedy circulated across India. The authorities in London eventually condemned Dyer's conduct, forcing him to resign in disgrace. The massacre profoundly impacted the course of Indian independence as more moderate politicians, like Gandhi, now began to wholeheartedly support the idea.

In 1920, Gandhi and the Congress Party committed themselves to India's *swaraj* and employed *swadeshi* (economic self-reliance) to achieve it. This political, economic, and social campaign challenged Britain's guiding presumption that Indians were incapable of ruling themselves and required British rule and tutelage. Gandhi and Congress specifically deferred the question of whether India would remain within the British Empire or leave it completely, figuring it would be answered by the response of the British.

In September 1920, Gandhi launched a noncooperation movement—promoting self-reliance, boycotts of foreign goods, and nonparticipation in legal, educational, and governing institutions—that spread broadly across urban India and reached parts of rural India. Gandhi also orchestrated the reorganization of the Indian National Congress's governance. By 1921, the Congress Party had shifted from an elite metropolitan organization to a grassroots, nonviolent, noncooperation movement as Congress volunteers coached and organized tens of thousands of young men in local chapters across the subcontinent.

The Congress Party vigilantly tried to prevent their newly trained volunteers from instigating violence in the evitable confrontations with British police, who had a long history of suppressing what they called "unruly mobs" to maintain law, peace, and order. The optics of these confrontations were striking: Indians made up the nearly three hundred thousand constables and lower-level officers in the Imperial Indian police force that patrolled a population of three hundred million across the subcontinent. The commanders, however, were exclusively British men until 1920, when qualifying examinations were opened to Indians.

The tensions between Congress volunteers and police exploded in February 1922 in Chauri Chaura, a small town in present-day Uttar Pradesh, in the wake of the police beating Congress volunteers during a demonstration and jailing local leaders. When crowds gathered outside the police station to demand release of a local leader, police fired warning shots into the air, inflaming the crowd, who responded by pelting the police with stones. Police then opened fire on the advancing crowd, killing three. In the ensuing chaos, the heavily outnumbered police fell back to the shelter of the station. The crowd set the station ablaze, killing all twenty-three of the Indian policemen and messengers trapped inside.[6]

Even as the British crowed that civil disobedience was thinly disguised violent rebellion, Gandhi found the breakdown of self-restraint among his followers distressing. He feared that the movement had veered off course and could spiral into a deadly cycle of recriminations and revenge. To atone for the violence, Gandhi fasted for three weeks, appealing to the Indian public for an end to violence and calling off the noncooperation movement. Gandhi was perhaps the only person who could single-handedly stop the very movement he had launched.

At the conclusion of his fast the government arrested Gandhi. He was convicted of sedition and served two years of a six-year term. He was released in February 1924 after an emergency operation for appendicitis. By the time of Gandhi's release from prison, his fame as an ascetic and saint had spread.

Many Indians as well as revolutionary observers across the globe criticized Gandhi for abandoning the civil disobedience campaign at the height of its mobilization. For Gandhi, however, it was not British guns alone that kept the Indian people subjugated. The mass movement he led was for the social and political transformation of India's people to become capable of self-governing ethically and equitably. He labored against violent revolution because he distrusted the kind of society that insurrection, sabotage, and assassination would create. For him, fasting was necessary to confront the possibility of such a society.

GANDHI'S PUBLIC FASTING AS PHILOSOPHY
AND AGENT FOR CHANGE

Mohandas Gandhi undertook seventeen long-term fasts, the first in South Africa in 1913 and the last in Delhi in January 1948. The fasts were for varied purposes, many of them public, of timed duration, often for three to five days, although several went for twenty-one days. Four were intended to be until death if need be.

His first public fast in India—in Ahmedabad in 1918—he examined in his autobiography, wanting to explain the necessity of nonviolent self-restraint in the face of provocation.[7] While Gandhi intended his fast to calm the mill workers' "rowdyism"—indeed, many volunteered to join his fast or substitute for him—his fast provoked fury among the mill owners, who were Gandhi's friends and donors to the Congress Party, for forcing them to settle an industrial labor dispute.[8] Gandhi had sowed dissension among his followers instead of effectively training their behavior. Thereafter, while a number of his subsequent fasts targeted Hindu customs and inequality, their more common target was training his followers to create an equitable and independent India to supplant British rule.

Gandhi's public fasting was a penitent practice that tapped into self-purification practices of the Hindu, Jain, and Muslim traditions familiar to the people of India. Believing that his followers' emotions were volatile and easily provoked, he fasted to atone for any part he might have played in the eruption of negative emotions as well as to redirect his followers' rage, which could erupt into retaliation, to concern for his health or possible death.

In his writings about his experiments with *satyagraha*, literally "truth force," including his practice of fasting, after his release from Yerawada Central Prison in Poona in 1924,[9] Gandhi reflected on the differences between hunger striking and his practice of public fasting. If hunger striking was understood as a political weapon, he envisioned fasting as a bodily epistemology, a way of knowing and perceiving. For him, fasting was both a self-purification and an instrument to clarify truth, involving rigorous self-scrutiny to gain a true observation of an unjust situation as well as one's own motivations. Gandhi recognized that the visceral and emotional communication involved in his public fasting was not unlike that of a hunger strike. However, he reckoned with emotions that public fasting could provoke as a training of self-discipline that modeled for his followers how to cleanse themselves of aggressiveness, selfishness, and sensory impulses and convert negative emotions into spiritual strength and potentially a "mode of revelation and visionary experience" that scholar Parama Roy claims that Gandhi experienced as an "elemental, even a somatic need." For this "bodily and philosophical" training to be effective, Gandhi advocated short-term fasting for himself and his followers as a regular practice. He promoted a method of managing visceral feelings to his grassroots followers as a pathway to forsake violence and advance national renewal and independence from British rule.[10]

The setting of Gandhi's fasts, usually at his ashram home and sometimes at the homes of supporters, was another factor that set his experience apart from those of prisoners undertaking hunger strikes. He was able to shape his day and his activities, and the kind of care he received, since family, friends, and his own doctors could attend to him. Even when he fasted under imprisonment, the British allowed him access to companions and to his doctors.

In keeping with the *satyagraha* principle of transparency, Gandhi announced his fasts publicly with the intent to persuade his opponent to have a "change of heart." Gandhi considered fasting a persuasive and personal strategy of communication between people who share compassion and respect. At its best, the outcome of such a struggle for truth would be neither defeat nor victory but the creation of a new harmony between the two parties in the revelation of immorality or injustice. In a letter to *satyagrahis* in Travancore who were fasting on the road to a Shiva temple that was barred to low-caste Hindus, Gandhi explained that "fasting can only be resorted to against a lover [by which Gandhi meant 'one you love'] not to extort rights but to reform him, as when a son fasts for a parent who drinks." On the other hand, he told them, "You cannot fast against a tyrant." He believed it was impossible to fast to reform "say, General Dyer who not only does not love me, but who regards himself as my enemy."[11]

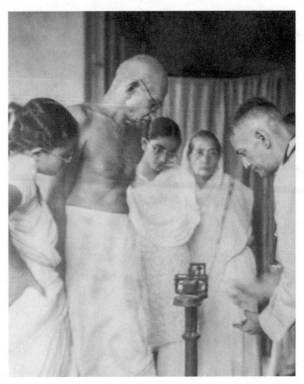

FIGURE 9. Mahatma Gandhi weighed during his hunger strike for Hindu and Muslim unity, Khadi Pratishthan, November 5, 1946. Credit: Kanu Gandhi/GandhiServe.

Gandhi used his principled approach to fasting as a measuring stick against which to assess not only his opponents but also prison hunger strikers, most often finding them morally wanting because they were motivated to fast for material or self-centered ends, such as access to media, political prisoner status, or release. Most often he expressed empathy for their moral failure in his columns and speeches, although sometimes he expressed his frustration publicly.

SAVARKAR'S REJOINDER TO PRISON HUNGER STRIKES

Gandhi's revolutionary and intellectual rival Vinayak Savarkar, as a law student in London, was given a life sentence for sedition—for leading a London secret society, a member of which assassinated Sir Curzon Wyllie, political aide-de-camp of the Secretary of State for India, in 1909—and was incarcerated in the Andaman Islands.[12] The 1912 hunger strike of Nani Gopal Mukherjee and subsequent hunger strikes in the Cellular Jail were known in India largely as rumors until 1925, when Savarkar began publishing his narratives of the malicious abuse, torture, and brave resistance occurring in the Cellular Jail. These became known to the public in conjunction with the large-scale incarceration of Congress members as political prisoners during both the 1920s noncooperation and the 1930s civil disobedience movements.

Savarkar admired Mukherjee's courage and endurance in fighting the British. However, he decried hunger striking. During his time at the Cellular Jail, Savarkar led prison strikes, organized the use of work stoppages, and petitioned British Indian authorities in Delhi and London to protest prison administration policies—but he also worked to dissuade his friends from hunger striking. However, he could not persuade Mukherjee, so he took "an extreme measure to overcome his resistance," going on a hunger strike himself to convince Mukherjee to stop hunger striking. Mukherjee, who by this time was gravely ill, was "stricken with grief" when he learned of Savarkar's three days of hunger striking. Savarkar deftly used Mukherjee's grief as emotional currency to persuade the warden to allow him to visit Mukherjee and then to sway Mukherjee to end his strike. Savarkar whispered in Nani Gopal's ear, "Do not die like a woman; if you must need die, die fighting like a hero. Kill your enemy and then take leave of this world."[13] This pointed gendering of heroism found its target. After seventy-two days on hunger strike, Mukherjee agreed to break his fast on December 6, 1912.[14]

In his memoir, Savarkar narrated several instances of convincing other fellow prisoners in the Cellular Jail to cease their hunger strikes, persuading the "proud men," without "unduly deprecating their action," of the "utter folly . . . to throw away their lives by fast unto death." Venerating heroic warrior manhood, he took every opportunity to write about the political miscalculation and immorality of hunger striking: "One was not right in giving up his precious life without exacting full price for it. If one resolved to die, he must die fighting. Patriotic service meant heroism. . . . Not the death of a man by hunger and in a lonely cell like a rat. If one killed himself in the name of his country in this fashion, one was harming and not helping the cause of his country."[15]

Savarkar deployed the intensity of his fellow prisoners' suffering to make a case to the Indian public for a more seasoned and aggressive political strategy against British rule than that of Gandhi and Congress leaders. He believed in inflicting violence and harm directly on the British and, like many militant nationalists, feared that Gandhi's nonviolence and civil disobedience were passive, feminine, and too easily co-opted by British force. Savarkar explained with great satisfaction the strength of his life-saving approach: "Today some of those whom I had drawn from the jaws of death were doing great national work" in advancing an independent India.[16]

MILITANCY AND JATIN DAS'S HUNGER STRIKE TO THE DEATH

In the 1920s, the goals of Gandhi and the Congress Party remained moderate: an increase in Indians' democratic participation in the government of India, an expansion of the exercise of civil liberties, and a pathway to domestic self-government under dominion status in the British Empire. However, Gandhi's curtailment of the noncooperation campaign in 1922 dismayed militant young men who had come into the movement. Concerned that a demobilized movement would make civil disobedience campaigners and militants more vulnerable to British repression, many favored escalating militancy to keep the British off their guard. They joined groups such as the Hindustan Socialist Republican Association (HSRA), which was founded in October 1924 with an agenda for armed revolution.

A member of the HSRA, Bhagat Singh, had been implicated by government investigators in the murder of two police officers, John Saunders and Chanan Singh, in December 1928 in Lahore. Bolting from the scene of the shooting, Bhagat Singh fled to Calcutta, where he met, through a militant network, Jatindra Nath Das. Das agreed to help manufacture gun cotton, or nitrocellulose, a standard early twentieth-century explosive, for firearms and artillery ammunition. Das then traveled to Agra in February 1929 to teach militants how to make gun cotton and assemble bombs.

Singh remained on the run for months but finally surfaced in April 1929, when he and another extremist detonated bombs in the empty corridors of the New Delhi Central Assembly. Although the bombing neither killed nor injured anyone, the two were sentenced to life imprisonment. After being sent to separate prisons in the Punjab, the two men each began a hunger strike independently to demand treatment as a political prisoner.

Meanwhile, police investigating the bomb-manufacturing network arrested two dozen young men who possessed live bombs, chemicals, empty bombshells, revolvers, and revolutionary books. Prosecutors gathered evidence linking the bombing and police murders through a wide-ranging "Lahore Conspiracy" that charged Singh and twenty-seven other men with conspiracy to wage revolution against the Crown. The impending trial and his physical deterioration by hunger strike led to Bhagat Singh's transfer to Borstal Jail in Lahore, where he was kept separated from the other arrested men.

At the conspiracy trial hearing on July 10, when all the arraigned were assembled in the Lahore courtroom, Bhagat Singh was brought in on a stretcher, weakened by his three-week hunger strike. His appearance shocked his alleged co-conspirators, and on July 13 they joined Singh for a fast unto death.[17]

Among these new hunger-striking prisoners was explosives expert Jatindra Das, arrested on June 11 and held in Borstal Jail. Das was no stranger to imprisonment and hunger strikes. While imprisoned for a 1925 robbery of a railway treasury train, Das had gone on a twenty-day hunger strike to protest the mistreatment of prisoners.[18] Das eventually resumed eating, served out the rest of his term, and upon his release had returned to Calcutta in September 1928 and joined a paramilitary organization, the Bengal Volunteers.

A fellow prisoner in Lahore, Shiv Verma, recalled that Jatin Das warned the other prisoners of the rigors of hunger striking: "It is far easier to die of a police bullet or by going to the gallows then perishing away 'iota by iota' in a hunger strike." Das advised them to first fast for twenty-four hours to test their "capacity to carry it to its logical end."[19] Das himself did endure. Two weeks into the hunger strike, the Lahore prison physician, with the assistance of a half-dozen guards, tried to force-feed Das and other hunger strikers. Das fiercely resisted, and the tube punctured a lung. Fellow prisoners observed Das being overcome with violent fits and bouts of severe coughing, and suffering from a shooting temperature. A team of physicians intervened, injecting stimulants and attempting to clear up the congestion in Das's lungs. The physicians discontinued artificial feeding of all the prisoners because of the intensity of their resistance, but Das became gravely ill.[20]

Even though Gandhi and the Congress Party repudiated Singh's bombing of the Assembly, media reports of the hunger strikers inflamed demonstrations and pressured Congress leaders to negotiate bail for Das and release him to the care of his family. As the weeks passed and Das's condition worsened, the government offered to release him on bail pending his trial. However, both Das and his younger brother, who was advocating for him, refused, demanding instead his unconditional release.[21]

By the end of August, all of the hunger strikers were being cared for in the prison hospital. On September 2 the government yielded and, to forestall further countrywide protests, appointed a Punjab jails inquiry committee to investigate prison conditions and the hunger strikers' treatment. That day, Bhagat Singh, after seventy-nine days, and the rest of the hunger strikers, after fifty-one days, abandoned the strike. But Jatin Das did not. Two days later, after the government both refused to release Das unconditionally and reneged on the hunger strikers' political prisoner demands, Singh and the others resumed their hunger strike.

By September 10, Das's condition had become perilous. His father and brother stayed at his side. By the morning of September 12, his heart had become weak, his body was paralyzed, he had lost the ability to speak, and his extremities were "cold as ice." On September 13, 1929, at 5 A.M., he died after sixty-three days on hunger strike. He was twenty-four.

Terence MacSwiney, who had fasted to death as a political protest nine years before Das, had been valorized for his martyrdom in India as well as Ireland, and now Jatin Das became known as the "Indian Terence MacSwiney." The media coverage of Das's funeral procession to the train station in Lahore and later in Calcutta echoed the solemn public witnessing of MacSwiney's coffin passing through the streets of London and then Cork. The connection was underscored when Mary MacSwiney sent a cable expressing her solidarity with "patriotic Indians in grief and pride in the death of Jatindra Nath Das. Freedom will come."[22]

Durgawati Devi, an Indian woman revolutionary who had helped Bhagat Singh escape in 1928, led the procession accompanying Das's body to the Lahore train station. Crowds lined the streets to observe the procession of mostly men dressed in white accompanying the garland-draped coffin. In a British Pathé newsreel of the procession, the opening intertitle expressed the British Empire's fear of the power of martyrdom: "India ... the Empire's greatest problem today: Fanatical hordes 'martyrise' Jotindra Nath Das, agitator who died after hunger strike of 61 days!" Despite the incendiary framing of the crowd as "fanatical hordes," the two-minute film showed an orderly and solemn procession with respectful crowds on the sides of the streets.[23]

As in Terence MacSwiney's case, the people and the news media observed the martyr's body returned to his home. The transit of Jatin Das's body by train the one thousand miles from Lahore to Calcutta became a historic event. Thousands gathered at stations en route to pay homage, throwing flowers and wreaths on the train as it passed. As the train approached Calcutta's Howrah Station, people gathered in crowds along the railway, and large numbers could be seen in the tops of trees, on bridges, and on roofs of houses. As the train passed by, the crowd raised cries of "Bande Mataram" ("Hail to Mother India") and "Long Live Jatin Das." Tens of thousands had gathered at Howrah Station. The Bengal Volunteers, commanded by Subhas Chandra Bose, accompanied Das's casket for a six-hour, mile-long procession through the streets to the cremation grounds. An unprecedented crowd, estimated at six hundred thousand, followed his coffin. The lord mayor of Calcutta, J. M. Sen Gupta, declared Jatin Das a local son who had become a national hero and said that "the cause for which he gave his young life gallantly in a last full measure of sacrifice" had made him "the Indian Martyr."[24]

Jatin Das's biographer, C. S. Venu, wrote that the "hunger strike has no tongue: it speaks for itself."[25] In Das's case, his dead body spoke volumes more than he had been able to directly communicate. The eulogies Das received from Indian leaders transformed him from an unknown, headstrong militant into a symbolic sacrifice for the nation of India. Muhammad Ali Jinnah, head of the All-India Muslim League, in the very Delhi assembly hall where Singh had detonated bombs in April, offered a tribute to Das, commending his courage and determination to "go on starving himself to death. Try it for a little while and you will see. . . . The man who goes on hunger strike has a soul. He is moved by that soul and he believes in the justice of his cause" and bravely challenges "this damnable system of government, which is resented by the people."[26] Subhas Chandra Bose, too, admired Das's perseverance: "As the days rolled by, one by one the hunger-strikers dropped off but young Jatin was invincible. He never hesitated, never faltered for one small second—but marched straight on towards death and freedom."[27]

Gandhi kept public silence but privately disapproved of Das's wielding the moral authority of a hunger strike to the death, branding it as "self-immolation." His choice of words was pointed, as it invoked the practice of *sati*, the North Indian high-caste Hindu custom of widows being burned on top of their husband's funeral pyre—a practice that Hindu moral reformers,

British missionaries, and the British government all repudiated and prohibited as barbaric.[28] Bose challenged Gandhi's "inexplicable" public silence on "the martyrdom of Jatin Das which had stirred the heart of the country."[29] Gandhi responded to his critics in his newspaper, *Young India,* saying that his silence was in the "national interest," since he believed that his "opinion was likely to do more harm than good to the cause for which brave Jatindra fasted unto death."[30]

NEW CAMPAIGN FOR THE DEMOCRATIC
RULE OF INDIA

The fight for full independence swelled. The same year that Jatin Das died, a political struggle was underway in the Congress Party. Gandhi influenced the selection of Jawaharlal Nehru as Congress Party president, rebuffing his rival Subhas Chandra Bose. Both Nehru and Bose were frustrated by the tepid British response to Congress's proposal of gradual self-government under British dominion status. Gandhi had sought this gradual process, but when Viceroy Lord Irwin spurned a clear pathway to dominion status in the upcoming negotiations in London, Gandhi and other moderates reassessed their position.

When Congress convened in Lahore in December 1929, past compromises and gradual approaches were thrown out. Congress voted to declare full independence and sever all ties to Britain: "The British government in India has not only deprived the Indian people of their freedom but has based itself on the exploitation of the masses, and has ruined India economically, politically, culturally and spiritually. . . . Therefore . . . India must sever the British connection and attain *Purna Swaraj* or complete independence."[31] At midnight on New Year's Eve, President Jawaharlal Nehru hoisted the tricolor flag of India upon the banks of the Ravi in Lahore.

The stage was now set for Gandhi's leadership of Congress's massive new national civil disobedience campaign, which launched on March 12, 1930, with the 241-mile Salt Satyagraha march to the sea in protest of the British monopoly on salt. The scale of civil disobedience, which continued for two years, forced the British to fully reckon with Gandhi's leadership and with Congress's demands to turn over power.

Through the 1930s, the British administration in India continued their strategy of delay, obfuscation, and sowing of division, even while attempting "to ward off future rebellion by bringing Indian political leaders into government." Under the 1935 Government of India Act, which authorized limited self-rule, thirty million literate, property-holding Indian men and women were allowed to vote in provincial assemblies that would govern domestic policy under the supervision of British governors.[32] This limited provincial self-government was a double-edged sword. Congress leaders were troubled by the absence of a plan for dominion status and by the inequity of British-appointed governors supervising Indian-elected ministers, but they stood for election nevertheless, seeking electoral dominance.

In the provincial elections held in the winter of 1936–37, Congress took power in seven provincial governments, though notably they did not claim majorities in two religiously diverse provinces, Bengal and Punjab, which were run by coalitions. Even so, Congress remained a political force in these two provinces because of its substantial role in the provincial assemblies and its capability to mobilize across India. Committed to Indian independence, the Congress Party at its March 1937 meeting in Delhi authorized the elected Congress legislators to take office and form provincial governments, as long as they pledged an oath of national independence and allegiance to the people. The British colonial government was now less able to chip away at the dominance of the Congress Party, the overall momentum of its broad membership, and its ability to quickly mobilize targeted demonstrations. However, the British government in London continued to sidestep any commitment to full independence for India.

ANDAMAN PRISONERS' HUNGER STRIKE INSURGENCY

During the 1936–37 elections, Congress had publicly renewed its commitment to see that the notorious Andaman Islands Cellular Jail would be closed and its prisoners transferred to the mainland and set free. Once in power, whether as the majority in most provinces or the minority in others, Congress began fresh negotiations with the colonial government to close the prison. However, 225 political prisoners in the Cellular Jail, most of them from Bengal, took the matter in their own hands in July and August 1937, going on hunger strike to seek their immediate release and repatriation and the repeal of all sedition laws. The Congress Party, now running provincial governments, could neither turn their back on the protests nor fully support the disorder the strikes created.[33]

The mass prison hunger strikes stirred up youth activists in Bengal to secure the release of all political prisoners not only in the Andamans but throughout India. Public meetings outside the Calcutta town hall sought to pressure the Bengal Assembly to respond to the strikers' demands. Political prisoners at Alipore Central Jail and at Presidency Jail in Calcutta resorted to sympathy hunger strikes, and political supporters organized an All Bengal Andaman Prisoners' Day on August 9.

Despite his categorical repudiation of the terrorist methods that had resulted in these prisoners' convictions, Gandhi negotiated with Viceroy Lord Linlithgow for the prisoners' transfer, pleading the wisdom of taking swift action to avoid unnecessary deaths. Over the course of seven weeks, Gandhi also mediated the crisis by telegram, wiring personal appeals to the prisoners to abandon their hunger strike and "end the national anxiety." His negotiations—and the British government in India's political and bureaucratic calculations—resulted in a new policy to repatriate the men to jails in their home provinces.[34] The government also issued guidelines for individual case reviews for probationary release of political prisoners in mainland jails, including the returned Andaman convicts. In Bengal alone, some three thousand detainees and political convicts were released.

By January 1938, however, the releases slowed. The Bengal government held the remaining 387 political prisoners, who were convicted of politically motivated violent crimes of murder, robbery, and gun-running, as too dangerous to set free.[35] Hunger strikes for additional prisoner releases erupted across India, but the British refused to give in, while Congress leaders declared that the hunger strikes were undermining their negotiations with the government. Eventually, Gandhi and Bengal's provincial government negotiated a gradual release plan for the remaining 242 prisoners.

In July 1939, thirty-six of the fifty remaining Andaman transfer prisoners held at Calcutta's Dum Dum prison went on hunger strike to pressure the government to release them. Within three days, thirty-two were being artificially fed in prison and one was released to the hospital. Simultaneously, prisons across India reported political prisoners undertaking sympathy hunger strikes.[36]

These hunger strikes precipitated a governing crisis on national and regional levels. Congress leaders at the national level sought gradual probation and release of the prisoners, while provincial Congress leaders favored public demonstrations to intimidate the prison administration into releasing more prisoners. While the British government feared agitation erupting in

Calcutta, the military, the police, and prison bureaucrats, some of whom were Indian, advised "crushing such attempts" by suppressing the "ringleaders before such agitation gains momentum."[37] Meanwhile, the Bengal government cut off prisoners' communication by denying them visits, interviews, and access to mail; prohibited lawyers from mediating between the prisoners and the government; and censored hunger strike information in the media. In response, Subhas Chandra Bose, then Bengal home minister, threatened direct action and large-scale protests in Calcutta to press for the immediate and unconditional release of all political prisoners.

Gandhi wrote in his newspaper *Harijan* that women were "inundating" him with telegrams and letters about hunger-striking prisoners in Bengal, begging him to undertake a sympathy fast or advocate the prisoners' release. Instead, Gandhi encouraged his correspondents to persuade the "hunger-strikers to give up their fast," and to "not mislead the public" by expecting him to "do the impossible." He told them to pursue the "legitimate method" of rallying public opinion to pressure the government instead. At the same time, Gandhi urged the Bengal administration to release the prisoners on a different principle: voters had expected the liberation of the Andaman transfer prisoners once the new provincial legislature was established.[38]

Gandhi was irritated that the message of fasting he had cultivated was being hijacked for purposes he believed were unethical. He disapproved of prisoners going on a hunger strike simply to accelerate their own release, which for him was directly contrary to enduring suffering for the expiation of one's errors. Further, he could not ignore that the men had been sentenced for participation in violence, not civil disobedience, and he was adamant that the end of independence and democratic self-rule could not be justified by violent means. He argued that the women and other advocates pleading with him were "damaging the Nationalist cause."

In another newspaper article, Gandhi implored the prisoners to view him not as a heroic leader who has the capacity to lobby the highest British rulers for their release, but as simply "an expert in fasting." In the name of "the science of political prisonership," he pleaded with them to cease putting their bodies on the line to demand their freedom. He urged them instead to accept his counsel and allow the Congress intermediaries to negotiate for their gradual release. Echoing the concerns of prison administrators, Gandhi commented: "Such hunger-strikers, if they are largely copied, will break all discipline to pieces and make orderly government impossible."[39] He bemoaned that the "Hunger Strike has positively become a plague. On the slightest pretext some people want to resort to hunger-strikes."[40] Ironically, the same criticism had been frequently made of his own use of fasting.

Rival politicians, in media coverage and at rallies on behalf of hunger strikers, implored Gandhi to intervene to support the hunger strikers. He held firmly, however, to advocating his philosophy of public fasting being used as atonement and penance only and distinguishing it from hunger striking, which he saw as a much-abused weapon against prison authority and for personal advantage.

THE "QUIT INDIA" CAMPAIGN AND GANDHI'S PRISON HUNGER STRIKE

In 1942, with Japanese forces overrunning the British in Singapore, capturing Burma, and on the verge of invading India, Gandhi and Congress launched the "Quit India" movement, demanding that Britain leave India voluntarily, taking special care to insist that free India would join the Allies. Gandhi launched the Quit India campaign in a speech delivered in Hindi at a Congress meeting on August 8, 1942, in Bombay: "You may imprint it on your hearts and let every breath of yours give expression to it. The mantra is 'Do or Die.' We shall either free India or die in the attempt; we shall not live to see the perpetuation of our slavery."[41] Congress resolved that Gandhi should lead another nonviolent mass movement and passed the "Quit India" resolution for India's independence, which also launched the plan for a provisional government on August 8. At 5:00 the next morning, British authorities arrested Gandhi and other Congress leaders, preempting Gandhi's public address the next day. Gandhi and his wife, Kasturba, were imprisoned at the Aga Khan Palace in Pune, which the Bombay government had specially acquired and outfitted to detain Gandhi and his party in luxurious surroundings that would receive favorable publicity when the international press came for interviews.[42]

The Indian press was forbidden to publish Gandhi's speech and Congress's resolution or to report on British measures to suppress the movement. In a speech broadcast from London and widely reprinted in Indian newspapers, Secretary of State for India Leopold Amery, while justifying the government's detention of Gandhi and Congress leaders for fomenting rebellion, unwittingly provided a blueprint for precisely that. He spoke of "strikes, not only in industry and commerce, but in the administration and law courts, schools and colleges, the interruption of traffic and public utility services, the cutting of telegraph and telephone wires, the picketing of troops and recruiting stations." He then commented: "The success of the proposed campaign would paralyze not only the ordinary civil administration of India but her whole war effort. It would stop the output of munitions, the construction of aerodromes, and, above all, shelters against air attack; it would put an end to recruiting; it would immobilize the forces."[43]

Amery's speech backfired. As historian Paul Greenough writes, "The chief irony of 1942 in India was that the awesome power of the press to inspire united action was unleashed by the British government; the radicalizing text was the composition of Leopold Amery, not Mahatma Gandhi . . . the self-consciously rebellious underground press was never able to duplicate the impact or achieve the degree of mass coordination which Amery's speech had provoked."[44]

Gandhi's mantra of "Do or die," promoted in the underground press, became a rallying cry for a civil disobedience campaign across India that lasted from August 1942 to September 1944. Civilians attacked railway stations and post offices, fought police officers, and rioted. Trade unionists struck at textile factories and steel plants essential for wartime production, disrupting Britain's military defense of India to the east, against the Japanese military poised to invade from Burma; and to the west, fighting Germany in the Middle East. The police and the British Army in India led a violent crackdown on the rioters, arresting over one hundred thousand people, while civilian deaths totaled more than a thousand.

Quit India brought together unlikely and reluctant allies. Even though Muslim participation in the movement was less than that of other groups, supporters of the Muslim League offered shelter to activists. Indians employed by the British government as police officers and administrative officials turned on their employer. Historian Bipan Chandra wrote that these employees "gave shelter, provided information and helped monetarily. In fact, the erosion of loyalty to the British Government of its own officers was one of the most striking aspects of the Quit India struggle."[45]

In December 1942, Gandhi declared in a letter to Viceroy Linlithgow that if he was not released from his detention at the Aga Khan's palace by February, he intended to fast. He had patiently waited for the British authorities to release him, he wrote, but the viceroy continued to blame him for fomenting violence. Gandhi expressed regret over the violence that had followed his arrest. But his solution was to ratchet up the pressure on the British government by fasting even at the age of seventy-three, taking command of the confrontation in a characteristically Gandhian way.

Fusing New Testament imagery with his philosophy of fasting, Gandhi wrote: "The law of Satyagraha, as I know it, prescribes a remedy in such moments of trial . . . 'crucify the flesh by fasting'—used as a last resort."[46] He promised to "fast according to capacity" and outlined the dates and times his fast would begin and end. He even laid out the protocol he would follow regarding drinking water: "Usually, during my fasts, I take water with the addition of salts. Nowadays my system refuses water. This time, therefore I propose to add juices of citrus fruits to make water drinkable. For, my wish is not to fast unto death but to survive the ordeal, if God so wills. This fast can be ended sooner by the government giving the needed relief."[47]

In an article published during his fast in *The Hindu* newspaper, Gandhi explained this modification of his fasting protocol: "I had to choose between death on the one hand and sweet-lime juice on the other. I had promised to live; I must try to live and hence mixed sweet-lime juice with water on Sunday to enable me to drink water and get over nausea."[48]

Through his regular penitent fasting, Gandhi had trained his body to withstand the deprivation of food. He had learned to sip water regularly to avoid the bloating that comes with consuming large quantities of water without food. He acknowledged the grave muscular pain that fasting exacted on him. He would use spiritual chanting to calm his mind and also to manage his impulses of hunger and the visceral impact of fasting on his body.[49]

On February 12, 1943, Gandhi announced that he was undertaking a twenty-one-day fast to protest the British allegations that the Congress Party leadership was responsible for slayings and train wrecks. He demanded the unconditional release of all Congress leaders in prison. Although this was his ninth fast in twenty-five years, it was one of his few fasts while imprisoned. In a letter to Gandhi distributed to the news media, Viceroy Linlithgow advised him against undertaking a fast out of concern for his health but then added bluntly that the fast would constitute "political blackmail for which there can be no moral justification."[50]

This fast of Gandhi's while in detention differed from the hunger strikes of other political prisoners in multiple ways, partially because of his political stature and his age. The government was prepared to set him at liberty for the duration of his fast so that he might have access to "his own medical attendants and also receive visits from friends with permission of the government

... [therefore,] if he fasts while in detention he does so solely on his own responsibility and at his own risk." However, Gandhi refused such a cat-and-mouse half measure.[51] An English doctor offered unsolicited advice to the Secretary of State for India that Gandhi be forcibly fed, commenting: "Personally I have found this method successful and there is a precedent, for the suffragettes, who also were political prisoners, were forcibly fed when on hunger strike." In response, the secretary noted that while forcible feeding is used in India, Gandhi's "age and physical conditions" precludes its use in his case.[52]

Gandhi broke his fast at 9 A.M. on March 2, 1943, as he had promised. Witnessed by doctors and other prisoners held at the Aga Khan Palace, Kasturba handed him a glass containing six ounces of orange juice. Gandhi, in a feeble voice, thanked the doctors for the care, "love and affection" that had "saved his life."[53] Tragedy struck shortly afterward when Kasturba, who had suffered several heart attacks while in detention, developed bronchitis; she died there just a month before Gandhi was released in May 1944.

Until the weeks right before his assassination in January 1948, Gandhi continued to use public fasting, no longer directed at British rule but now to secure peace between Hindus and Muslims during and after independence and the partition of India. When people's rage and vengeance were at fever pitch, he fasted to confront and expunge "all kinds of fear—fear of death, fear of bodily injury, fear of hunger, fear of insults, fear of public disapproba-tion, fear of ghosts and evil spirits, fear of anyone's anger. Freedom from all these and other such fears constitute fearlessness."[54] He sought to focus the attention of followers, adversaries, and detractors alike on his bodily self-destruction and then shape that attention into an ethical political conscious-ness that would forsake violence as a means to a goal.

PUBLIC SUFFERING AND CREATING
THE NATION OF INDIA

Internationally and over time, Gandhi became known for his "hunger strikes," despite his insistence that he engaged in another form of alimentary protest: public fasting. This characterization arose from the resemblance of his fasting to the hunger strike form in its visceral and emotional communicative power: Gandhi's fasting electrified his followers while antagonizing British imperial rule, forging an anticolonial weapon of mass mobilized upheaval. The protest fast became associated with Gandhian nonviolent civil disobedience and would be perpetuated after independence in the hands of many.

Meanwhile, political prisoners in jails across India readily claimed the hunger strike as their weapon against British carceral power. It was a hunger strike to the death that made indicted prisoner Jatin Das into a national martyr. And for many hundreds of prisoners in Andaman and other jails across India, the hunger strike weapon was a strategic tool to coerce early parole. However, while many Indian leaders hailed the conscience and endurance of Das that earned him martyrdom, they were more interested in harnessing his death as a prelude to the robust civil disobedience movement they were launching. For them, other large-scale prisoner strikes unleashed unwelcome attention to the prisoners' violent records and were inconvenient during delicate negotiations with the British about turning over power. For militant nationalists such as Savarkar, the hunger strike was a misguided weapon that failed to exact harm on the British, and thereby was a waste of martial sacrifice. The hunger strike embodied anticolonial rebellion, but outside the prison, nationalist leaders preferred to employ a mobilization strategy with a larger political goal.

Through the news media and oral storytelling they triggered, these acts of self-deprivation created a national public in India that could bear witness to the suffering body and, in the hands of Indian nationalist leaders, reflect, grieve, and agitate. In India, the detailed visceral suffering of the hunger striker was rarely expressed in the media as it was in the British, Irish, and American contexts we have seen in earlier chapters. Instead, the focus was on rousing public emotion and action on behalf of seeking moral justice for the hunger striker. For the Indian nationalists, what mattered was the feelings—rage, fear, anxiety, despair, disgust—triggered in the public by Gandhi's suffering during protest fasting and by prison hunger strikes, and the harnessing of these feelings to inspire mass demonstrations to achieve the goal of independence from Britain.

PART TWO

Hunger Striking and Democratic Upheavals

FIVE

Solidarity and Survival in the Tule Lake Stockade

CARCERAL INSTITUTIONS HAVE MANY FORMS—prisons, reformatories, asylums, detention centers, and camps. One of the more notorious forms is camps where targeted populations are gathered and contained during war. During World War II, these included, of course, the Nazi concentration camps but also the so-called internment camps for U.S. residents of Japanese descent once the United States had entered the war.

On New Year's Eve 1943, more than two hundred Japanese and Japanese American men and boys incarcerated at the Tule Lake Segregation Center, a detainment camp in remote northeastern California, went on indefinite hunger strike. They were protesting their detention of more than a month without formal charges or trials in a makeshift stockade within the camp, following demonstrations over labor conditions and food shortages in November.

Information about the hunger strike was scarce. The War Relocation Authority (WRA) and the military had allowed press coverage of the Tule Lake camp protests in November, but once martial law was imposed, news of the incarceration of hundreds of men in the stockade and the hunger strike that followed was tightly suppressed. Even family and friends in the camp had only scant information and no contact with the prisoners in the stockade. Even so, enough information eventually leaked out to send shockwaves throughout the camp, reverberating from one sector of the institution to the entire system.

How does the hunger strike change in practice or meaning when the protest is marooned from means of communicative amplification to the public? How do the strikers communicate their protest to authorities? How do they test, maneuver, and push back against them? How do they console, encourage, and sometimes judge their fellow prisoners to keep the strike going?

Seventy-five years later, we have access to two remarkable diaries by prisoners in the stockade. The diaries, alongside interrogation records accessed through University of California social science research on the internment camps, reveal how the stockade prisoners handled the challenges of maintaining group solidarity through a mass hunger strike and how feelings of fear and pain, shame and pride, hunger and distress were negotiated in the uncertainty of their detention. These accounts are rife with cultural contests over masculinity, courage, and character as the two men confronted the hostility and indifference of their military captors and their isolation from their families and the outside world. Drawing on these diaries and the interrogation records, the hunger strike is fashioned as a symbol of integrity and honor for both their peers and adversaries. In the intimate revelations of these diaries we can see how hunger striking can be reshaped by two men in captivity at the junction of two cultures: one perceives the hunger strike as a martial strategy while the other sees it as a plea for nursing and care.

THE MAKING OF THE TULE LAKE STOCKADE

The Tule Lake protests were the result of the WRA's efforts to separate "loyal" and "disloyal" Japanese camp prisoners and to create a pool of draftable men through a mass registration and questionnaire distributed in the camps in 1943.[1] Questions 25 through 28 asked whether an individual's birth had been registered in Japan, if the individual had renounced his Japanese citizenship, if the individual would serve in combat duty wherever ordered, and finally if he would declare loyalty to the United States and renounce allegiance to the emperor of Japan. The infamous questions 27 and 28, which demanded an oath of allegiance to the United States and repudiation of allegiance to Japan, split camps into "yes-yes" and "no-no"—or loyal and disloyal—populations. Among the seventy-eight thousand camp prisoners imprisoned at the ten camps who were seventeen and older, those who answered "no" to both questions 27 and 28 comprised 17 percent of all registrants and approximately 20 percent of all Nisei—those born in the United States to Japan-born parents and thus citizens of the United States.

To the surprise of WRA administrators, the questions intended to identify military recruits provoked a sharp rise in applications for expatriation from the United States and repatriation by Japan. By the end of 1943, the number of requests had surpassed nine thousand, and most new applicants were Nisei. Through 1944, the number of requests topped out at nearly twenty thousand, or 16 percent of the total incarcerated population.[2]

Many who responded "no" were disillusioned Issei, first-generation Japan-born immigrants, who, because of the U.S. immigration legislation of 1924, were unilaterally denied the opportunity to become U.S. citizens. Others were angered by their treatment as second-class citizens and used their "no-no" responses to the loyalty questions as a nonviolent protest. Many families feared that the young adult men would be drafted and deployed overseas while their families could plausibly be deported to Japan, after having been forcibly moved already at least twice, once to assembly centers, hastily assembled on race tracks and fairgrounds, and then to one of ten relocation camps within one year.

The questionnaire reinforced the no-way-out carceral logic of internment. In March 1942, four months after the United States declared war on Japan, ethnic Japanese, both immigrants and American citizens, were evicted from their homes and their civil liberties were suspended because of white American racist suspicions of all Japanese Americans, irrespective of citizenship, as enemy aliens. The U.S. government branded all the Japanese on the Pacific Coast as enemies—even as only a few thousand, handpicked Japanese Hawaiians were incarcerated and both citizens and noncitizens of German and Italian heritage were recruited to fight as Americans. The Japanese left behind their businesses, homes, and possessions quietly and obediently as a way to demonstrate their loyalty to a government and society that doubted their allegiance and to neighbors who blatantly harassed them. Incarcerated in camps located across the United States, they found themselves living in harsh, isolated conditions with no official clarity about whether they would return to their homes or be summarily deported to Japan at war's end. The questionnaire a year later offered an opportunity to protest against an imperious U.S. policy. As historian Richard Drinnon has explained, the results of the questionnaire cannot fully reveal the damage it inflicted as intimate family disputes on how to respond to the questions "blasted marriages, . . . estranged parents and children, fueled deadly enmities, . . . and sliced the already vulnerable Japanese American community into warring majorities and minorities, with only victims of the oath on both sides."[3]

The loyalty test results, publicized during congressional hearings, sowed anew the vehement, reactionary anti-Japanese rhetoric in the press and by politicians that had bolstered the forcible removal and confinement of Pacific

Coast Japanese Americans to begin with. For some, it confirmed the "military necessity" of the program of unilateral imprisonment.[4]

Resistance to question 28 was higher at Tule Lake than at any other camp, with 42 percent of the men responding "no," in sharp contrast to other camps such as Manzanar in California (26 percent), Topaz in Utah (15 percent), and Granada in Colorado (2 percent). Evidently wanting to contain all the "disloyal" camp prisoners in one place, in July 1943, WRA Director Dillon S. Myer directed that all "disloyal" prisoners from the nine other campuses be brought to Tule Lake, now renamed Tule Lake Segregation Center. During September, some 6,250 Tule Lake prisoners who were deemed loyal were transferred to other relocation camps, while trainloads of "disloyals" from other camps arrived—adding more than 8,600 to the remaining 6,000 Tule Lake camp prisoners who had responded similarly. With more than 18,700 people crowded into a camp built for 15,000, Tule Lake became the largest camp in the archipelago of WRA incarceration sites.[5]

Making Tule Lake a segregation center resulted in its rapid architectural and spatial transformation into a militarily secured carceral institution. A lighted seven-foot-high perimeter fence topped with barbed wire was installed around the entire camp, with another warning fence fifty feet inside it. Ten more camp residential blocks were added, for a total of sixty-six. The guard towers around the camp's perimeter were tripled, from six to nineteen. Adjacent to the secure entrance, a fully functioning military police compound was built to house twelve hundred U.S. Army soldiers, providing the structural and practical ability to enforce martial rule and ensure that the "disloyal" Japanese Americans were securely corralled.[6] During this time, a number of white WRA personnel, many of them active in building democratic and reform processes with the camp prisoners, resigned in protest.[7]

Squalid and crowded housing, poor sanitation, inadequate food and medical care, and unsafe working conditions at food-harvesting sites outside the camp, where many camp prisoners worked, sharpened dissatisfaction within the camp. In October and into November 1943, eight hundred of the camp's farmworkers went on strike following the death of one farmworker in a trucking accident. Camp prisoners held a large funeral in defiance of prohibitions against sizable public gatherings. Work stoppages and demonstrations protesting dangerous work conditions, lack of jobs, poor pay, and meager food rations continued.

On November 1, 1943, the Daihyo Sha Kai, a democratically elected community organization of prisoners, formed a fourteen-member Negotiating

Committee and requested a meeting with national WRA director Myer and camp director Raymond Best. A crowd estimated at more than five thousand gathered near the administration area during the meeting. The mass gathering alarmed the white WRA workers and administrators, who ordered the construction of a barbed wire fence around the WRA administration offices the following day, while the army lined up eight tanks outside the camp as a display of force.[8]

On November 4, camp prisoners (numbering 150–200) prevented trucks from leaving the camp as rumors spread that the trucks were transporting food to strikebreakers brought from other camps and housed in tents outside the camp, to replace protesting Tule Lake farm laborers. They confronted WRA security police, and a brawl ensued. Director Best panicked and called in army troops from the military compound. At 10 P.M. that evening, tanks and armed soldiers took over the camp. Camp police dragged several Japanese American men into the administration building to interrogate them. Some young men suspected of leading the disturbances were taken to a room in the military compound barracks, where they were interrogated and beaten with fists, rubber hoses, and baseball bats, as well as choked and kicked.[9] Several had to be hospitalized, and one suffered permanent brain damage. After being released from the camp hospital, these men were herded into tents in a heavily guarded area—the beginning of the "stockade."[10]

On the morning of November 5, the army ordered camp prisoners assembling for work back to their barracks. They began to comply, but when the dispersal slowed as curious residents from nearby barracks came out, the soldiers teargassed the crowd—an act that further enraged the camp prisoners. Over the next eight days, a committee of Daihyo Sha Kai leaders tried to negotiate with the administration to restore jobs, the army and WRA refused. Instead, the army used a "work or starve" policy to punish prisoner mess workers who engaged in sit-down strikes and work stoppages, denying the prisoners food rations and coal for a day or two.[11]

On November 13, the camp administration called an assembly meeting of all camp prisoners. Army Lieutenant Colonel Verne Austin, commander of the military compound, mounted an outdoor stage—and delivered his address to an empty field. As a WRA representative from Washington, D.C., reported: "At 2 o'clock nobody came and there was no sign of anyone coming to hear his speech. Like an Army man, true to his tradition, Austin began his speech. No one was there. Not a single soul. Colonel Austin spoke to the air . . . [I]t was a pitiful sight which I cannot forget."[12]

Thereafter the administration declared martial law and arrested Daihyo Sha Kai leaders and others whom they called "troublemakers." Tom Yoshiyama, author of one of the two diaries discussed below, recalls four armed soldiers seizing him at 8:30 P.M., strip searching him in the army compound, and then depositing him in the stockade.[13]

The army had corralled the first arrested men into a tent camp on the Tule Lake camp grounds, surrounding the 250-by-350-foot area with fences and four guard towers. However, in a matter of weeks, the army constructed a makeshift compound of five barracks, a mess hall, and a latrine. This new fenced-off, high-security area, separated from the regular camp residential housing by a six-hundred-foot firebreak and another eight hundred feet of administrative area, became known as the stockade, a "jail within a jail" that quickly became the Tule Lake Segregation Center's most infamous feature.

Inside the stockade, the army conducted regular "roll calls" and disciplined "troublemakers" by placing them in the "bull pen"—a group of flimsy, unheated tents placed directly on the frozen ground where prisoners were forced to bunk with no extra clothing and only one or two blankets to cover them. Tokio Yamane, a stockade inmate, recalled nights in the "bull pen" as "a life and death struggle for survival."[14]

The Tule Lake stockade became a consolidation imprisonment site for the larger Japanese American carceral system, processing inmates from WRA prisons and "troublemakers" who led protests in other camps.

On December 9, the WRA recorded the stockade population as 233. Of that number, sixteen were Issei and thus Japanese citizens, and 217 were Nisei, U.S. citizens. Among the Nisei, 151 were Kibei—born in the United States but educated in Japan and then returned to the United States. The Kibei numbered approximately eleven thousand across all the camps. Their fluency in the Japanese language and educational and cultural training in 1930s Japan drew the suspicion of the WRA. They were often viewed with ambivalence by their Nisei peers, who had not been educated in Japan and were anxious to prove their loyalty to the United States.[15]

In *Race for Empire*, Takashi Fujitani argues that, at first glance, the ten internment camps seem intended to distance their 120,000 ethnic Japanese prisoners from an American identity, framing them as other and enemy; however, the everyday life in the camps operated through a suppression of Japanese culture, traditions, and language. "All-American" activities like baseball, swing dances, and scouting were promoted to reform and assimilate the U.S.-born second-generation Nisei and their Issei immigrant-generation elders. The

WRA also implemented self-governance committees to administer activities and consult with officials. However, the transformation of Tule Lake into a "segregation center" for the disloyal supplanted the Americanization reforms and rehabilitation projects, suspended self-governance, and represented a martial-law departure from the U.S. government's liberal, democratic vision of WRA camps.[16]

The practice of Japanese internment already flouted the 1929 Geneva Convention relative to the Treatment of Prisoners of War, which limited incarceration to noncitizens politically allied with a war enemy. The Tule Lake stockade's "administrative separation" flagrantly ignored the Geneva Convention's prohibition on placing persons in a stockade for more than thirty days or isolating them from their families without due process of law. Indeed, beyond leveling accusations of insurrection against the prisoners held in the stockade, camp administrators did not charge them or hold trials. The WRA brazenly attempted to suppress dissent by applying indefinite detention without legal appeal, depriving the U.S. citizen stockade prisoners of rights considered a universal guarantee of U.S democracy.[17]

Colonel Austin, as camp commander under martial law, justified not only the imposition of martial law to restore camp order but also raids and surveillance to protect peaceful camp prisoners from harassment by "hoodlums and goon squads."[18] On November 26, the army initiated a massive search-and-seizure campaign throughout the camp. Three groups of 150 soldiers each, armed with gas masks, sidearms, and grenades, searched all the barracks. The contraband they seized included five hundred knives, four hundred clubs, and explosives.[19] They also confiscated all means of independent communication, including a Japanese-language press, two public address systems, and five hundred radio receivers that prisoners used to receive news from and communicate with the outside.

In addition, they confiscated food. The Tule Lake camp was like a small city, with over eighteen thousand inhabitants, split into seventy-four residential blocks, each containing fourteen barracks, each of which typically housed three hundred people. Families lived in a single room furnished with a single lightbulb hung from the ceiling, a coal-burning pot-bellied stove, and up to eight cots. Each block was arranged with lavatories and laundry in the middle and a common mess hall and recreation building at one end. Camp prisoners were required to take all communally prepared meals in their block's dining hall at enforced meal times. Prisoners complained bitterly about the quality and monotony of the menu choices. Thus, families cherished the food and drink they were able to collect and prepare for themselves in their barracks, which the WRA opposed but tolerated. This made the military's food confiscation a bracing and effectively punitive measure. Within two weeks, soldiers and guards confiscated twenty-five tons of rice and other grains, twenty-two barrels of sake, four hundred boxes of canned goods, twenty crates of dried fruit, twenty cartons of cereal, and two sake stills.[20]

DEFIANCE AND THE "SINCERITY" OF THE FIRST MASS HUNGER STRIKE

The capricious imprisonment of hundreds of men, many of them leaders of the camp's barrack blocks, compounded by regular military sweeps and food confiscation, made the stockade a bitter flashpoint for grievances and anxiety among Tule Lake camp prisoners. Since November, the camp inmates had been on a work-stoppage strike as a protest against the martial-law suppression and the incarceration of their leaders, while army administration dismissed every appeal they made. Unemployment and impoverishment were taking a heavy toll on the camp. WRA Camp Director Best commanded his administrators to find new camp leaders who were critical of Daihyo Sha Kai representatives. Many of these leaders were eager to cooperate with administrators to improve the miserable conditions in the camp and end martial law. In late December and January, almost daily meetings and discussions were focused on breaking down the impasse. In the meantime, the army stepped up arrests of Daihyo Sha Kai supporters in the camp, while, in the stockade, guards dragged prisoners out during midnight raids and made them stand in the snow in their underwear for several hours with a machine gun pointed at them.[21]

As December progressed, the treatment of the stockade prisoners grew harsher. Interrogators were frustrated that prisoners had no organized conspiracy to confess, and the prisoners were anxious and angry that military officials refused to either charge or release them. On December 31, 1943, at the daily roll call at noon, the men in the stockade, exasperated by the late-night ransacking, abuse, and punishments, refused to step outside. That morning, on a sanitary inspection, Lieutenant Shaner, the stockade warden, had criticized the unsanitary conditions of the latrine, shower, and barracks. Tom Yoshiyama describes in his diary how he had spoken up, saying that the problem was the lack of buckets, brooms, and mops. He and two other men,

FIGURE 10. Tule Lake raid, ca. 1944. Photograph by Robert H. Ross, courtesy of the Tule Lake Committee.

who had responded similarly to criticisms of the dirty condition in the mess hall, were punished for their insolence and placed in the "bull pen." Later that afternoon, soldiers pulled men from the barracks, forcing them to line up for roll call. Lieutenant Shaner reprimanded the men for the incident earlier that morning and taunted them, asking "if any else wanted to join those men in the bull pen, step out." One of the stockade leaders, Koji Todorki, "boldly and defiantly stepped out," and other prisoners joined him. Shaner said, "I was just waiting for that." Addressing all of the men, he said, "You men will be put on bread and water for 24 hours. You men will have to learn that we mean business and we will not tolerate such a demonstration."[22]

Over the two months of the stockade's existence, the army had delivered institutional food rations, and the stockade prisoners had parceled out among themselves the work of food preparation, meal service, and cleanup. Shaner's orders now set in motion a reversal of the food delivery system. Two military trucks rolled into the stockade, and prisoners were ordered to remove any food from their cells. When some hesitated, soldiers kicked and prodded them with bayonets and confiscated their food supplies.[23] Soldiers searched the inmates' belongings, removed food from the mess hall, and confiscated holiday presents of apples, oranges, nuts, cigarette cartons, cakes, and pies.

The seizure of the presents and the soldiers' threats and humiliations inflamed the prisoners' resolve. That night, two hundred of them signed a petition and vowed to hunger strike until all were unconditionally released from the stockade.[24]

After the twenty-four hours on bread and water, for several days the army resumed placing the day's rations in the stockade mess hall. The rations went untouched. Soldiers then promised the prisoners more appetizing and additional rations if they stopped their fast.[25] As seen in other hunger strikes, the withholding and then promising of food was a way for the wardens and guards to crank the screws on their power over the prisoners' subsistence and survival—sometimes accompanied by accusations of surreptitious eating by taunting them with candy wrappers and food debris they found.

Ironically, as the hunger strike progressed, pastoral care of the prisoners increased. Japanese camp prisoners who were doctors and nurses were introduced into the stockade to monitor the hunger strikers' vital signs.[26] Instead of the rhythm of grocery delivery, meal preparation, and food service in the stockade kitchen and mess, protocols of medical monitoring and care were imposed on the stockade schedule.

On January 5, 1944, six days into the hunger strike, one of the strike leaders, Hiroyoshi Tsuda, who requested the meeting, met with seven white camp military and police administrators led by Sergeant Sam Yeramian and Captain B. M. Hartman.[27] The typed meeting transcript reveals the struggle between the hunger strikers and the prison administration over the meaning and import of the strike. Even though the hunger strike had erupted over humiliating treatment by the warden and guards, Tsuda explained, the protest was squarely aimed at the indefinite administrative detention without charge or trial. He spoke of the strikers' "sincerity" and "resolve," which he believed would vindicate their humanity, ensure respect, and disprove the accusations that had led to their unjust incarceration.[28]

Tsuda's claims, however, were met with denial, umbrage, and diversion. The meeting became an interrogation and a dressing down of Tsuda and the strikers he represented. Sergeant Yeramian said that the army refused to "bargain with you people," since they were "using their bodies as hostages." He denounced the rebellion and belittled the prisoners' demands for unconditional release, mocking their "self-interested" demands and their "sincerity." The administration thus refused to acknowledge the strike as a claim for due process rights; instead he shamed the strikers as "willful," irrational delinquents. What Tsuda experienced was characteristic of being rightless: whatever grievances and claims he made about the experience and motivation of the stockade prisoners were dismissed as not credible.

Legitimate claims to the American system of legal protection for the accused were summarily dismissed for the stockade hunger strikers. They were so rightless that by virtue of the military's targeting them, they lost any right to hear the charges against them or to defend themselves in a court. They would suffer the punishment of isolation and caging in the stockade without any recourse. Their status had slipped from neither "internee" nor "prisoner of war" into some abyss of rightlessness, where they were required to be obedient to the caprice of U.S. Army authority and where their claims did not matter, because there was no accountability for the army's stockade incarceration. Scholar Naomi Paik describes rightlessness as both the deprivation of rights for the politically excluded and the conditions that justify the compounding of state violence of removal, detention, surveillance, interrogations, coercion, and vulnerability to physical and emotional punishment that Japanese Americans endured.[29]

An index of the felt experience of rightlessness emerged in the emotions that punctuated the otherwise dry transcription of the interrogation. The interrogation transcriber described Tsuda as being in a "very depressed, melancholy mood, speaking very slowly and deliberately," his gloom no doubt compounded by the effects of six days of fasting. At times during the interrogation, he would drop his head on his chest and pant and gasp for breath as if in misery or pain. The administrators dismissed his "emotion" as a disingenuous display—while evidently believing that their own anger, frustration, injured honor, and sense of what they insisted was their "victimization" at the hands of the prisoners were justified. Tsuda was obliged to apologize for the prisoners' behavior and solicitously appreciate the "anger" of the administrators, possibly a familiar survival strategy of supplicating to the white men's power and to their sense of injury as a means to evade further punishment.[30]

Tsuda returned to the stockade empty-handed, and his report back dismayed and demoralized the hunger strikers. The administration's refusal to negotiate their release as long as the hunger strike continued led the stockade prisoners to take another vote. One hundred and fifty-two voted to end the hunger strike and to negotiate with the army and camp administrators, while fifty supported the continuation of the fast.

Divisions among the hunger strikers erupted after a week of hunger striking, and the breakdown in solidarity is captured in the Japanese-language diary that Tatsuo Ryusei Inouye, a Kibei and a judo instructor from East Los Angeles, managed to hide from the guards. First interned with his wife and daughters at Poston, Arizona, Inouye and his family were transferred to Tule Lake in the tumultuous days of November 1943. Within days of their arrival, Inouye was rounded up and held in the stockade.

His handwritten diary, translated in 2015 by a Japanese-language scholar commissioned by Inouye's by-then-elderly daughter, reveals the complex last days of the January 1944 hunger strike. In particular, his diary entries show how some prisoners understood the hunger strike as a collective performance of heroic masculinity and drew on Japanese cultural and ethical codes that emphasize group loyalty, perseverance, and sacrifice of individual needs for a higher cause.

Writing about the stockade debates that led up to Tsuda's negotiation attempt, Inouye expresses fear that some prisoners, having become "completely irrational from hunger," irritable, and impossible to calm, would capitulate to the army's demands. After the vote to end the hunger strike, the men agreed to a ceremonial resumption of eating together on the morning of January 7. At midnight, Inouye wrote a mournful poem expressing how the pangs of hunger and the inability to control bodily instincts had overwhelmed the prisoners' earlier resolve.

> Total defeat of the hunger strike. Oh, what a shame.

> After the defeat of our hunger strike, I could only lament and cry. We surrendered and we
> ate. Food won us over. How shameful.

> As the Japanese army we marched together, but some gave up
> As an avalanche in a snowy valley, they all suddenly collapsed
> Alas, these small fry, so charged in the beginning
> Their war cries were wasted, their voices are now pitiful
> Living on American soil and sky
> Gutless losers
> I wish those in our homeland will all believe this to be untrue.[31]

Inouye had expected that the camp officials would respect their unwavering commitment to fasting as evidence of their martial honor. He expresses humiliation and dismay that the "hunger strike was fought in vain" because personal weakness resulted in the collapse of stockade prisoners' solidarity. Being forced to end the strike was a "trap set by the administration" to eliminate the hunger strikers' moral standing, he argues, making it impossible for them to "negotiate any further." By giving up the fight, he bemoans, they "would be branded publicly as thugs."[32]

Referring to eighteenth-century legends of the Samurai warriors' code of honor, Inouye portrays the inmates as sharing in warriors' honor if they can withstand adversity and endure pain for a just cause. He invokes Samurai values when he critiques their behavior, saying: "One should commit ritual suicide (*seppuku* or *hara kiri*) if one was truly Japanese. How can they return to Japan after their disgracing conduct? It is outrageous. It is even more offensive that they are now trying to come up with excuses."[33]

Inouye refers to another East Asian cultural concept, the "hungry ghost," a tormented spirit overwhelmed by insatiable hunger and unquenchable thirst. These pitiable, restless, animalistic figures are depicted with freakishly distended stomachs, pinhole mouths, and necks so thin they cannot swallow, denying them the sustenance they desperately seek. Beings are reborn as hungry ghosts because of their greed, envy, and jealousy. In colloquial Japanese, the word for hungry ghost, *gaki,* also refers to misbehaving children who suck one's energy and never seem to be satisfied with what they are offered.[34]

Inouye derides the behavior of one young man, Kawano, saying he acted in "the way of hungry ghosts." During the fast, Kawano was "a boastful talker and a foolhardy warrior," but he was overcome by his own physical urges immediately after the vote. Unable to wait until they collectively and honorably broke the fast the next morning, Kawano cravenly went to the kitchen to gather food. The fellow prisoners who served as kitchen staff and guarded the rations from use "threw five pieces of bread at him, saying, 'You can take these, too!'" Kawano responded by bowing, expressing gratitude, and disregarding their insults. Inouye attributes the weak resolve and "mental relapse" of this "desperate warrior" to his being a Kibei who had only partially digested the education and character training he received in Japan. If the young Kibei men were true warriors, Inouye reasons, they would display impassive visages that would not betray their hunger, fear, doubt, and physical needs.[35]

Inouye argues that the strikers' capitulation was based on both an incapacity for self-restraint and a tragic misreading of the Tule Lake commanders' indifference to the strikers' plight. Inouye believed the U.S. Army would not allow the hunger strikers to die in their custody.[36] He was correct; records reveal that the army had called an emergency meeting of the Japanese American doctors and nurses at the camp hospital with instructions to save the lives of the prisoners if they reached the point of dying.[37]

WITHDRAWING MARTIAL LAW

Six days after the conclusion of the hunger strike, the WRA and the army orchestrated a referendum of all adult camp prisoners, excluding the stockade prisoners, on whether their protests in support of the imprisoned men would continue. Since December, camp prisoners had refused to cooperate with army orders and had held work strikes. However, this meant losing their desperately needed $16 monthly wage. Conflicts among camp prisoners increased as internal divisions between "loyals" and "disloyals" widened. On January 11, 1944, weary prisoners voted by secret ballot, with soldiers present at every polling station. The result was a narrow margin of 473 votes in favor of restoring "normalcy" as opposed to the current work strikes and protests. Then, on January 15, a second referendum vote empowered seven new block leaders, who had already rallied support for the normalcy referendum choice and now became the publicly acknowledged negotiating members in talks with the WRA. Simultaneously, the army lifted martial law at the camp, restoring the WRA's civilian command but keeping the stockade under army command.

The government leveraged its victory in achieving the end of martial law to restore at least the appearance of ordinary life at the camp. Carl Mydans, a photojournalist, visited Tule Lake for *Life* magazine and wrote a photostory that included his famous pictures of the stockade's "pressure boys" obediently lining up for roll call and a young man "killing time" by playing the guitar. The article both revealed and erased the boundary between the camp and stockade for the reading public. Nothing was said about these men being held in indefinite detention without arrest charges or trial. These pictures belied the reality that, although the crisis of martial law had been lifted in the camp, and journalists like Mydans could visit (by invitation), the indefinite detention stockade within Tule Lake Segregation Center was a pernicious amalgam of detention center, expatriation holding pen, and prisoner of war camp—ubiquitous during World War II.

With martial law lifted, people in the stockade could now communicate with people in the camp, and camp prisoners could send mail to the outside

FIGURE 11. "Pressure boys" at roll call, Tule Lake stockade. *Life* magazine, March 20, 1944. Photograph by Carl Mydans/The LIFE Picture Collection via Getty Images.

world. As a few prisoners were released from the stockade, some information was passed along to stockade prisoners' families. These developments opened an avenue to reach outside the camp for support for the interned prisoners, even though the army retained a firm grip over the stockade.

On the same day in January when Tsuda met with the army and WRA administrators, underground activists in the Tule Lake camp had written for help to the neutral Spanish Embassy, which at the time represented Japanese citizens' interests in the United States. The Spanish emissaries reported the situation to the Japanese government, which lodged a protest with the U.S. State Department on April 18 that got results. The State Department pressured the army to free 276 stockade prisoners by April 29, leaving only two dozen men in the "jail within a jail." A month later, on May 23, the army withdrew from the stockade, and the WRA took control.[38]

Through the released men, the remaining stockade prisoners conveyed requests to relatives in the camp to seek outside lawyers. A recent transfer to Tule Lake from the Heart Mountain Relocation Center in Wyoming advised contacting the American Civil Liberties Union (ACLU), which had begun a defense for Heart Mountain draft resisters.

In response to letters received by the ACLU, Ernest Besig, director of the San Francisco office of the ACLU, spent July 10 and 11, 1944, at Tule Lake. In a report of his visit, Besig expressed shock at the lengthy imprisonment of the two dozen men still in the stockade. He decried the Tule Lake administration's capricious and cavalier imprisonment of the men, especially holding them in isolation from their families and friends and refusing them due process of law or clear charges for their detention. Although Director Best attempted to thwart him, Besig was ultimately allowed to interview a few prisoners who requested to speak with him. They reported being humiliated and brutally beaten, which white WRA employees speaking to Besig confidentially corroborated.[39]

Only after the release of almost all the stockade prisoners did the WRA provide a statement outlining its procedures of "administrative separation" of the prisoners from the rest of the camp. Published as a manual on April 25, 1944, the statement explained that to secure "peaceful and orderly administration," the camp director had wide discretion in designating suspect individuals, empowering a fact-finding committee, and reviewing evidence or hearing appeals. In the isolation area all mail was censored, and visiting with camp prisoners was not permitted except in specially designated rooms and under surveillance. The manual said nothing about due process claims for formal charges or hearings for the prisoners and did not provide a time limit for isolation in the stockade.[40]

THE SECOND HUNGER STRIKE AND TOM YOSHIYAMA'S DIARY

One of the men Besig interviewed was Tom Yoshiyama, a U.S. citizen who had been held in the stockade for eight months and was being pressured by the WRA to renounce his citizenship. Born in San Juan Batista, California, Yoshiyama spent eight years of his education in Japan. He returned to the United States in 1938, enrolled in San Francisco Junior College, and in 1941 began the degree program in economics at San Francisco State University, while his parents returned to Japan. Transferred from another camp to Tule Lake in September 1943, he was elected as a block representative. Tom described to Besig the night of November 13, 1943, when he was arrested by four soldiers carrying flashlights and bayonets who searched the barrack room he shared with other single men. He served as the first spokesman for the stockade prisoners until the end of December.[41]

On July 18, 1944, less than a week after Besig's visit, the remaining sixteen prisoners in the stockade resolved to go on an indefinite hunger strike. Their grievances included the suspension of due process; the lack of evidence that justified detention; the denial of visiting privileges with their "wives, children, fiancées or anyone else"; abusive treatment by the stockade's Internal Security staff; and denial of medical care, first aid, and service in the camp hospital. Fresh grievances were detailed that since July 2, they were denied packages with cigarettes and toiletry materials.[42]

Yoshiyama kept a diary, a portion of which was later typed up in English as part of the records collected by the University of California research team. The typed portion includes the summer 1944 hunger strike and offers a unique record of the physical, emotional, and psychological effects of refusing food on these sixteen men. Because this hunger strike lasted longer than the weeklong strike in January, it required the strikers' hospitalization. Thus, it also offers the hunger strikers' perspective on their hospital treatment and refeeding care.

In his entries during the first several days of the hunger strike, Yoshiyama notes the timetable of his habitual activities, remarking on brushing his teeth, taking showers, doing laundry by hand, and attending the daily roll call. He speaks of difficulties sleeping and experiencing some dizziness. After nine days of hunger striking, he writes that his head is clearer but his "legs are very wobbly." He has difficulty walking during the daytime but can move better in the evening and early morning. However, he fears falling if he visits the toilet alone.[43]

The WRA released two of the men from the stockade soon after the hunger strike began—a decision made, they argued, not because of the men's "hunger demonstration" but in light of completion of an administrative review. Unlike the army during the January hunger strike, the WRA administrators did not order daily medical checks of the fourteen remaining men, though they had frequent interactions and interviews with the stockade's internal security officers. On July 25 one prisoner fainted and was taken to the Tule Lake camp hospital, and two more were taken for treatment and then returned to the stockade. On July 27 Yoshiyama was denied his request that four ailing prisoners be taken to the hospital and be allowed to stay there if they complied with measures to feed them.[44]

In the camp, relatives and close friends sent frantic appeals to WRA officials in Washington, D.C., and sought advice from camp resident leaders to bring the strike to an end. One group of leaders, who called themselves the "resegregationists"—they were pro-Japanese and preferred the Japanese way of life—believed that the camp should be physically divided between collaborators with the WRA and those, like themselves, who were branded "disloyal" and were considering repatriation to Japan. On July 28 they circulated a petition, said to be signed by eight thousand camp prisoners, that appealed to Director Best "for the lives of our racial brothers. Already several persons have collapsed from hunger. If any or several of our racial brothers should die on account of the Hunger Strike, we all would feel deeply grieved. Reverse the case: suppose Americans in an internment camp in Japan should die on Hunger Strike, how would you feel? Would not the American people be deeply grieved? So will we if our racial brothers die of Hunger Strike."[45]

On July 29, after eleven days of self-starvation by the hunger strikers, Internal Security escorted all fourteen of them to the hospital for physical checkups by Japanese American physician Dr. Ikuta, and they were all admitted to the hospital. Besig arrived at the camp the following day but was refused permission to interview the men.[46]

Tom Yoshiyama's diary describes how, when he first settled onto his hospital cot, he was given a substance that he describes as a "(stimulant, presumably whiskey)."[47] In the mornings and again in the evenings, Japanese nurses took his temperature and pulse, and he was given milk to drink and "an alcohol rub down by the nurse." His stomach ached and "made noises all night like thunder," and he could not sleep. The rehydration and nourishment regimen began with liquid foods such as milk, orange juice, chicken broth, Jell-O, tomato juice, and later coffee and pudding. By the third day of refeeding, the prisoners were eating soft-boiled eggs, toast, sliced carrots, soft rice, hamburger, and string beans. Yoshiyama reported that all of them experienced severe constipation and could not physically get out of bed for several days. On his fourth day of refeeding, Yoshiyama noted that his appetite had improved and the Japanese nurses were treating them to candy and ice cream, along with a more normal solid diet of fish, rice, carrots, "macaroni, soup, milk, and a custard." As the diet normalized, the routine of baths and alcohol rubdowns before sleeping became more relaxing. Yoshiyama relished the routine of care from the nurses after more than eight months of isolation and punishment in the stockade.

On August 4, after taking showers, shaving, and eating breakfast, the fourteen men received word that they would not be released but instead would be returned to the stockade. They chose to resume their hunger strike. They were allowed to see family before returning to the stockade. In a brief, timed afternoon visit at the hospital, Yoshiyama saw his fiancée for the first time since his confinement in November. Combining the symbolic with the ordinary, the men returned vitamin pills given by the doctor and laundered their underwear before returning to the stockade. Evidently not wanting to coax the men to prepare meals, the WRA did not deliver foodstuffs to the stockade.[48]

Yoshiyama describes a greater number of emotions and bodily sensations during the second hunger strike than he does during the first. On August 6, he writes that he has dizzy spells every time he leaves his bed and that he "nearly fainted" when he reached the toilet. The foreboding and despair he felt with the resumption of the hunger strike was a "miserable experience both mentally and physically [that] could not be expressed in writings." He describes his eyes as looking "like those of [an] animal, far in deep. My cheek has fallen in. When trying to drink I must hang on to some support." He adds how lethargic and disoriented he feels being confined to "bed all day," and reports feeling "very dizzy" as well as a derangement in his digestive system and the resumption of chronic constipation.[49]

The gravity of Yoshiyama's physical condition amplified the despair of his isolation from the care and comfort he had received from the Japanese American hospital staff, who were denied access to the stockade. On August 9, he writes that it "seems like we are a forgotten soul." The following day he describes the experience as "unbearable" and wishes to be released from conscious awareness of such "misery." By August 11, the seventh day of the second hunger strike, he expresses alarm that stockade officials have refused to recommend rehospitalization for the prisoners. When he tried to get up that evening, his "head and face became very hot and everything became dark." The following day the dizziness increased. He notes that conversation among the prisoners has ceased. "Everybody is trying to force a smile. They all have a sad looking face and I never felt sorrier before."[50]

Meanwhile, two Daihyo Sha Kai leaders from the camp had been negotiating with the WRA for the men's release if they commenced eating. As part of this negotiation, on August 12, a doctor from outside the camp, Dr. Jack Sleath from the Newell Community Hospital, visited to check on the men's physical condition. He recommended that eight of the prisoners be immediately taken to the hospital, that they were "on edge and . . . probably . . . will not last another day." The administration still refused to hospitalize the hunger strikers, so at 1:30 A.M. on August 13, Dr. Sleath "brought the men warm milk and a baby's mush," which ended Yoshiyama's additional nine days of hunger strike. On August 23, after more than nine months in detention, Yoshiyama was finally released from the stockade.[51]

After his visit to Tule Lake in July, Besig enlisted the assistance of civil rights lawyer Wayne Collins. In a stormy meeting with National WRA Director Myer and Tule Lake Director Best, Collins threatened a series of habeas corpus suits, and Besig promised a full-scale exposé of the violation of the constitutional rights of U.S. citizens imprisoned in the stockade without trial.

Largely because these threats might lead to a federal court case and national publicity, on August 24, 1944, the WRA released the last of the stockade prisoners. These prisoners, along with more than three hundred others from Tule Lake who were labeled as troublemakers and had renounced U.S. citizenship, were transferred to a repurposed Civilian Conservation Corps camp in Santa Fe, New Mexico. The transfers were intended to further isolate these men, as the outside scrutiny on Tule Lake Segregation Center and the stockade had grown too intense for the WRA. When Collins visited Tule Lake just days after winning the inmates' "freedom" to confirm that they had been liberated, he discovered that the stockade had been demolished without a trace.[52] The camp administrators preferred to expel the remaining "troublemakers" to an isolated carceral center, twelve hundred miles away, before camp discontent grew into rebellion.

REMEMBERING TULE LAKE

The government order during World War II to forcibly incarcerate Japanese Americans in relocation camps has haunted both the people imprisoned and their descendants. In the first few decades that followed, the experiences of dislocation, violence, and coerced repatriation were repressed by both Japanese Americans and U.S. society and government in an attempt to move past the tragedy. However, in the 1970s the imperative of sharing suppressed family histories and conflicts grew within the Japanese American community. From July to December 1981, more than 750 witnesses, many of them Japanese American survivors and their descendants, testified to the Commission on Wartime Relocation and Internment of Civilians. The commission report led to congressional legislation resulting in the Civil Liberties Act of 1988, which granted redress and reparations.

Decades later, Nancy Oda, Tatsuo Ryusei Inouye's daughter, gained the agreement of her siblings to share her father's story, including what was viewed as his "disloyalty" by family members and people in the Japanese American community who judged each other's actions through the lens of loyalty to the United States. It took decades for her to make the diary public. She commissioned its English translation through the Suyama Project, sponsored by UCLA's Asian American Studies Center.[53]

In his diary, Inouye cast the hunger strike as a form of battle-hardened military prowess engaged in a timeless struggle—and he was deeply troubled by the human frailty and fickleness of his fellow prisoners. Invoking the masculine stoicism of heroic samurai in epic battle under overwhelming odds, beleaguered by doubt and hunger but enduring in unanimity, he despaired that the courage of at least fifty resolute warriors was undermined by "gutless" boasters, who brought ruin upon their reputation in the eyes of their captors, their families, and even the commanders in Japan. In the waning days and aftermath of the first strike, Inouye crusaded for the strikers to forge a united dignity to fend off the U.S. commanders' disdain that the men were weak and could be bought off. He feared that their surrender to hunger and indiscipline diminished their future if they survived to be repatriated to Japan.

By contrast, Tom Yoshiyama's diary, written in English and full of American colloquial expressions, reveals the hunger strike as an entreaty for caregiving and a return to everyday habits and pleasures. Yoshiyama did not reach for the extraordinary; rather, he savored hospitalization after nineteen days of hunger striking, the solicitous care and touch of the Japanese American nurses, and the mundane pleasures of consuming ordinary American food. The hunger strike here takes on a quality of yearning for a homecoming. This fleeting hope, experienced for less than a week, reflects the optimistic, utopian quality of the hunger strike that Yoshiyama communicates in diary entries addressed both to himself and to advocates. The contrast of hope and despair is explicit when the men, sent back to the stockade and honor-bound to continue their hunger strike, are broken and suffer a cascade of visceral despair. After nine months in detention, Yoshiyama expected little from the obstinate white American administrators. After his interview with Besig, he could perhaps hope only that the administrators would be publicly shamed into releasing the dozen remaining prisoners. In both striking and recuperation, his recitation of human fragility and feeling is intended to reach an American audience.

The diaries of Inouye and Yoshiyama reveal different strategies of bearing witness to the rightless condition imposed on them by the state, expressing different values and shaping different aims for their hunger strike. While neither disavowed the state's implicit accusation of rebellion, both of them pleaded in words and deeds for the military and civilian leaders to recognize them as men. Did their actions warrant perpetual isolation and punishment? Their strikes were a rebuke to the U.S. military and civilian command's power play to make the camp prisoners docile and to undermine their leadership. The stockade prisoners were punished to put the camp into obedience and order.

Both men reckoned with the narrow opportunity available to them to use self-starvation as a means to resist being cast as helpless and to destabilize the impasse concerning their indefinite and unaccountable incarceration. Their hopes rested with their friends, family, caregivers, and allies, both Japanese and American, outside the stockade's barbed wire. They yearned to touch their minds and hearts and to enlist them to speak on behalf of the prisoners' dogged endurance against their rightless predicament.

Tule Lake was not the only instance of race erupting in upheavals that triggered hunger strikes as the global war raged. In numerous episodes in U.S. prisons from 1943 to 1946, both white and black conscientious objectors, most famously David Dellinger and Bayard Rustin, protested prison rules and rejected the racial segregation of prisons.[54] Yet another example, at the naval base in Port Hueneme, California, a thousand African American naval construction workers staged a two-day hunger strike in March 1945 to protest systemic discrimination in awarding naval promotions.[55] But it wasn't only U.S. prisons that saw racially or ethnically charged hunger strikes in this era. In 1946, at the Italian port of La Spezia, 1,046 Eastern European Jewish survivors of the Holocaust went on hunger strike when, about to embark on a ship, they were refused passage to their destination in the British Empire's Palestine Mandate. Their sixty-five-hour strike and sympathy strikes in Tel Aviv and New York forced concessions from the British government as part of a larger campaign to disobey immigration controls and ensure the Zionist settlement.[56] Before the war, hunger strikes were also used by Jewish Polish students to protest discriminatory bans on admissions to higher education throughout the 1930s.[57] Outside Geneva's Palais de Nations in 1954, a Vietnamese man pitched a tent and fasted to protest diplomats' partition of his homeland. In the 1960s, protest fasts were used both in public and in prison to fight racial segregation, economic inequities, and war taxes by U.S. civil rights activist students and pacifists.[58] Many of these achieved notoriety and their goals through widespread media coverage and political pressure. In Tule Lake camp, however, the prisoners endured in a vacuum of media attention.

SIX

South African Anti-apartheid
Hunger Strikes

PRISONER HUNGER STRIKES ARE IDIOSYNCRATIC and desperate protests. Sometimes they fail. Sometimes they succeed in changing conditions or practices in a particular prison. Yet other strikes have a broader impact—challenging detention policies, leading to prisoner releases, thawing political stalemates, or galvanizing broad-based political change. The question of how and why some hunger strikes motivate broad political change while others fail to do so is particularly salient in the case of hunger strikes under South Africa's apartheid regime. Two hunger strikes in the 1960s, one by detained white women activists and the other by prisoners on Robben Island, and a succession of hunger strikes in the late 1980s allow us to examine a range of results and the reasons for them. In every instance, the clash between anti-apartheid rebels and an intractable apartheid regime shaped the terrain of power struggles and the context of hunger strike protests.

We can glean the strikers' ambitions from the published memoirs and diaries of prisoners held in Johannesburg's Old Fort prison and on Robben Island. In their determination to fast, they reveal a confidence that they can outwit and outmaneuver authorities. By collectively wresting control over their bodies from the authorities, they seek a shield of prisoner solidarity against the guards and wardens. And, under this shield, they can organize, strategize, and heave their defiant bodies onto a shared platform to collectively demand justice and freedom in the world outside.

Hunger strikes might be the catalyst for more far-ranging political transformation months and years down the line. Outcomes are ongoing as political forces and fortunes toss and lurch into the future. Regimes rupture in unanticipated ways, and change reveals itself in political landscapes seemingly frozen solid.

In 1948, when the Afrikaner nationalist National Party unexpectedly won the national election, defeating the more moderate Union Party, the policy of racial segregation and inequity—sanctioned by law and widely practiced in South Africa since the nineteenth century—spread, hardened, and was named apartheid.[1] In the decades that followed, the government of apartheid South Africa elaborated laws, bureaucracy, and police to enforce a system that curbed the movements of nonwhites and subordinated them to white rule.[2] The Group Areas Act of 1950 divided residential and business sections by race: white, black, Indian, and Coloured. In 1952, the government updated "pass laws" to control black South Africans' mobility and labor, requiring all black men over the age of sixteen to carry a passbook that detailed their personal identity.[3]

The government criminalized protest, deploying armed force and detention to suppress its challengers. The Public Safety Act, passed in 1953, empowered the government to declare a state of emergency and to imprison or whip people for protesting or advocating for the repeal of a law. Nevertheless, people did continue to protest, first with the Defiance Campaign from 1952 to 1954, followed in 1956 by a massive march in Pretoria by an estimated twenty thousand women of all races. Early in 1959, the government extended the pass laws to apply to black women and escalated the laws' enforcement. The African National Congress (ANC), founded in 1912 to defend the rights and freedoms of Africans and the organization that spearheaded anti-apartheid actions in the 1950s, responded by planning a nationwide anti-pass campaign on March 31, 1960.

As government repression intensified, stark cleavages over strategy erupted among anti-apartheid activists. In contrast to the nonracial egalitarian democracy promoted by the ANC, some black Africans believed that true freedom would be possible only in an exclusively African-led society. In April 1959, many disaffected ANC Youth League members broke away to form the Pan Africanist Congress (PAC).

The PAC marshaled the physical power of African mobilization on March 21, 1960, with a demonstration by seven thousand nonviolent black anti-pass protesters in the black township of Sharpeville. The PAC urged the demonstrators to leave their passes at home and incite police officers to arrest them. Like Gandhi's strategy in the fight against passes for South African Indians in 1913, the PAC strategy was to fill the jails and bring the economy to a grinding halt. When the demonstrators converged on the Sharpeville police station, the white South African police opened fire on the crowd, killing sixty-nine people and injuring 180, including twenty-nine children. The Sharpeville massacre unleashed protest marches, labor strikes, boycotts, and riots throughout the country. On March 30, nine days after the massacre, similar pass demonstrations of tens of thousands in Cape Town and Durban alarmed the government and triggered another state of emergency, making all protests illegal. A week later, the government implemented the Unlawful Organizations Act, which banned the PAC and ANC immediately. Both organizations were forced underground and into exile, prompting both to spin off military wings that eventually launched campaigns to sabotage government facilities.

Within two months, the security forces had arrested and detained eighteen thousand persons, holding them without access to lawyers or family and, in many cases, in solitary confinement. Among these predominantly black African detainees was a group of white women being held in the women's prison in Johannesburg's Old Fort prison complex for critiquing the regime and espousing egalitarian, socialist, and communist views.

On May 2, 1960—for some, nearly a month after their arrest—twenty-one "European women detainees," as they called themselves, petitioned South Africa's minister for justice, Colin Steyn. After days of discussion and debate, the women had composed and signed a petition that enumerated their complaints of being held in custody without charges or access to legal counsel and newspapers. They did not include the complaints about prison food and sanitary conditions they had made in the weeks before. Instead they focused on their unjust custody. As women, they noted the vulnerability of their children. "Seven of us, whose husbands are also detained, have left outside 19 parentless children. The other women detainees between them have 15 children, and we do not know how many other children of all races have been similarly deprived of one or both of their parents." They demanded their immediate release on or before May 12 or they would "exert the only pressure within our means—namely, to engage in a hunger-strike."[4]

The hunger strike plan had grown from the solidarity the women developed during their month of imprisonment. In the Old Fort prison, white and black women were separated, and white women had many more privileges of socializing together, receiving limited visitors, and communicating once a week by mail. When not locked in their cells, they could gather in a communal area, where they organized classes in Zulu, Afrikaans, French, and shorthand, and coached each other in physical exercise.[5]

Their demand for release was not met, and so, keeping their word, the women initiated a hunger strike. One of them, Hilda Bernstein, kept a prison diary that she concealed by cutting a hole in the underarm of her overcoat lining.[6] She and her husband, Lionel, were members of the South African Communist Party, and from 1943 to 1946 she served on the Johannesburg City Council as the only communist elected to public office by Johannesburg's whites-only electorate. In the 1950s, Hilda focused on organizing women for campaigns for both gender and racial equality. Her husband worked closely with ANC leaders Nelson Mandela, Walter Sisulu, and Oliver Tambo. He is credited with drafting the Freedom Charter that became a rallying call for the overthrow of apartheid. Both Bernsteins were subjected to bans and restrictions and were arrested frequently for campaigning for the rights of black people.

In 2019, Bernstein's daughter Toni Strasburg published a family memoir that drew partially upon her mother's diaries. In Toni's memoir, the dreadful prison food takes on greater significance in motivating the hunger strike than in the published version of her mother's diaries. The first complaint listed in an April 30 memo the women submitted to the prison's administration was "FOOD: Continues to be revolting, inedible. We want something better than mealie meal and bread for lunch, and white bread. Curry soup was disgusting. This is not the exception as the Colonel said but the rule." The second complaint was about the need for "plates, knives and forks"; the fourth was "Special diets—have not been satisfactorily provided for our ulcer and fat-free cases." It is also on April 30 that Bernstein wrote about receiving the "inspiration of inspirations" to go on a hunger strike and that "everyone delighted [in] this."[7] They agreed to give the administration one week to change their prison diet before launching this strike.

We learn from Bernstein's diary that on May 6, in the middle of the night, the women were moved from the Old Fort to a prison in Pretoria, forty miles away. Their new quarters were "two, enormous barn-like rooms, cold and gloomy, with high barred and meshed windows." Despite the gloomy facilities, however, there was more access for communal support and socializing here, as they were "provided with tables and chairs, crockery, cutlery, a stove." In her daughter's memoir, she notes that the food quality and social conditions for eating improved in Pretoria: "Our porridge is brought up in new utensils and sugar, jam and fat rations are served in little dishes for each of us. We sit at the long tables with the unaccustomed cloths and crockery." And for lunch: "We are astounded at the food, really tasty stew, mashed potato and beans. I enjoyed a cooked dinner for the first time in four weeks."[8] It appears that the government's response to the women's petitions was to improve their conditions while further distancing them from their families and ignoring their demand for release.

The women did relish the opportunities for communal activity and building solidarity. They continued their classes, lectures, and poetry readings. They also prepared for their hunger strike and discussed how to respond to possible "deprivations or solitary confinement." The night before beginning their strike, the women engaged in vigorous exercises before their final supper, where they shared their "private stocks of chocolate, cheese or biscuits," a Christmas-like evening.

During the first days of fasting, the women drank cups of hot water and went to sleep early with the "icy wind blow[ing] in the night." One of them daily monitored and recorded the women's pulses, bowel movements, and symptoms of starvation. In her diary entry on the third day, Bernstein complained that they were experiencing persistent headaches. Even the previously soothing "hot water taste[d] so horrible" that they drank cold water.[9] The following day, she reported that her most odious pangs of hunger had receded.

The prison warden threatened to separate them, sending some to prisons eighty miles away, if the hunger strike persisted. On the fifth day, May 17, South African security police set up an interrogation cell to question the women individually, without legal counsel, about their political views and contacts. The women were then locked inside "tiny, dark and very cold and unpleasant cells" in pairs before being allowed to return to the communal room the following day.[10]

At first the women had continued their classes in Zulu and shorthand, but after several days of fasting, weakness made reading, concentrating, or even playing Scrabble difficult. On the seventh day of the hunger strike, Bernstein wrote: "Every day is a triumph for us. We are a lot weaker, and everything is an effort, but we are surprised that on the whole we have kept well—we expected to feel much worse than we do."[11]

Bernstein astutely observed how their fasting upended "the whole social ceremony of eating, particularly in the evenings." During the few days prior to the hunger strike in this new setting, they had prepared and eaten meals together. Now, the "day becomes endless without the preparations for a meal, sitting and eating, sitting over our cups of coffee and cigarettes—always the most pleasant time of the day—and cleaning up afterwards." The day now lacked a "middle," instead "merg[ing] into one long, cold, never-ending procession of hours." Late afternoon was the "worst time of all," when they retreated "to the great, grey and gloomy rooms. We walk slowly. . . . There is nothing at all between us and bed-time but hours and hours and hours."[12]

On the seventh day of the hunger strike, May 19, the prison superintendent visited the women with Captain Cilliers from the Special Branch, who had orders to expedite investigations. The prisoners' initial optimism for release was dashed by the warden and staff, who issued warrants for each woman and threatened to detain them for a year. They were shocked by their "re-arrest within a prison," Bernstein wrote. "In silence we hear this; our hearts feel as though they have collapsed inside us." The women were fingerprinted, and the prison superintendent announced that eight of them would be transferred to another prison the following morning. "We greet this with bitter indignation," wrote Bernstein, "and find after eight days without food that we cry very easily." The prison doctor diagnosed one woman as quite ill and advised her to "cease [her] hunger strike immediately" or it would worsen her heart condition. Two other women were failing as well.

On the eighth day, May 20, at 8:30 P.M., the women ended their hunger strike on "medical grounds," in solidarity with the women whose health was compromised.[13] Bernstein wrote, "We all had fruit juice or weak tea with Marie biscuits soaked in it. I believe I have never enjoyed food less. We always imagined that the end of the hunger strike would be a happy celebration, but this was ashes, with sawdust."[14] In the women's eyes, the eight-day hunger strike was a failure because it ended with their goal of release unmet—in fact, the carceral grip had tightened.

On June 28, five weeks after the hunger strike ended, Bernstein and the other twenty women were released from prison. Bernstein later transcribed and augmented her diary and smuggled it out of South Africa to Ronald Segal, an influential, exiled Jewish South African editor in London, who published diary excerpts in his journal, *Africa South in Exile*. Segal's editorial choices shaped what diary excerpts made it to publication and eventually circulated underground in South Africa.

HUNGER STRIKING ON ROBBEN ISLAND

In October 1962, Nelson Mandela, after raising funds overseas and mustering international support for the ANC, was convicted of leaving the country without a passport, as well as inciting a strike, and he began a five-year prison sentence. In July 1963, Special Forces raided an isolated farm in Rivonia and arrested ANC leaders, including Lionel Bernstein. The subsequent Rivonia trial in 1964 charged Bernstein and nine other ANC leaders, including Mandela, with sabotage and conspiracy. Mandela, Walter Sisulu, Govan Mbeki, and Ahmed Kathrada were convicted and incarcerated on Robben Island. Lionel Bernstein was the sole accused who was acquitted; shortly afterward, the Bernsteins and their children fled to exile in London.

A hunger strike could be deliberately planned and carefully prepared, like the one by the women in Pretoria detention, but it was just as likely triggered by escalating grievances that exploded in a singular moment, then crystallized into concerted action. The July 1966 hunger strike on Robben Island was one such event. Once the refusal to eat was sparked, prisoners had to swiftly and secretively marshal their resources and communicate across political and racial divides. The hunger strike could falter at any moment, at any scheduled meal. Decades after the event, the memoirs of ANC leader Nelson Mandela and PAC leader Moses Dlamini, as well as the recollections of Indian ANC liberation army soldier Indres Naidoo, offer bracing insight into the communication and strategy that made the hunger strike a success.

Located six miles off the coast of Cape Town, Robben Island was first used as a place of incarceration in the seventeenth century, when the Dutch held captured leaders from the Cape region and the islands of Indonesia there. In the nineteenth century, the British isolated lepers and the mentally ill in asylums on the island. Before and during World War II, the island had served as a military outpost. It reopened in 1962 as a maximum-security prison for nonwhite male prisoners and was quickly filled with political prisoners charged with "security" and political crimes such as sabotage, sedition, and conspiracy. Initially, most of the prisoners were black PAC members imprisoned after the 1960 demonstrations, in addition to prisoners charged with violent crimes. As anti-apartheid sabotage and security raids netted convictions, black, Coloured, and Indian ANC prisoners filled Robben Island. When Indres Naidoo arrived in December 1963, the island had a thousand political prisoners but only thirty-five ANC members; by 1965, there were five hundred PAC members, while ANC members topped a thousand. White political prisoners were incarcerated in Pretoria.

The prison authorities' manipulation of food quantity, quality, and distribution was a daily feature of their "constant brutalities and humiliations," with guards frequently punishing prisoners by forcing them to "starve for a day."[15] The 1966 hunger strike, Naidoo recalled, was precipitated by Head

Warden Delport's order, in response to a shortage of food in the kitchen, to reduce rations for Africans and keep the rations for Coloured and Indian prisoners the same. This racially punitive decision backfired. When the men returned from the quarry at lunchtime, "a long, grim" line of Coloured and Indian prisoners walked right past the outdoor tables where the food was being ladled out, refusing the food. Black, Coloured, and Indian prisoners gathered to grouse about their hunger and to discuss their determination to hunger strike until the punitive treatment ceased.[16]

The spontaneous solidarity upended the warden's strategy of fomenting racial division and political rivalry among the prisoners. The following day, as the hunger strike continued, an exasperated Delport yelled, "It's your bloody business if you don't want to eat." Another prisoner, PAC member Moses Dlamini, recalled that the prison authorities expected the hunger strike to be over within a day. Lieutenant Bosch, who led the kitchen and meal distribution, disparaged the prisoners' capacity for self-restraint: "I know the Bantus [pejorative term for black Africans], that's how they behave when their stomachs are full. As soon as they become hungry, they'll outrun each other to collect their porridge."[17] Determined to prove him wrong, the prisoners threatened that their hunger strike would "drag on indefinitely until prisoners started to collapse."[18]

Naidoo describes the prisoners' fears at the outset of the hunger strike. They feared that the censorship of news from Robben Island would make it impossible to "get word to the outside world" about the strike. They feared that the guards would engage in retaliatory violence, including "baton charges and ... mass assaults," and that they would be subjected to abusive forcible feeding. They were also wary that as the strike persisted and the physical toll on the strikers grew dire, the newly established solidarity might splinter and break.[19]

As the hunger strike began, the quarry work continued. The men's resolute conviction meant that when they returned to the quarry after lunch break, their "plates remained on the table; the food on them cold ... [but] the pace [of work] did not slacken at all." The guards taunted the prisoners saying that "kaffirs and coolies" were motivated only by their empty stomachs and instinct for self-preservation.[20] The prisoners remained impassive and did not react to the guards' taunts. They conducted themselves as if they had eaten, following all the regular procedures, including, as Dlamini described, doing the expected "tauza [a degrading strip-search dance]" in front of guards allegedly to recover contraband items but in practice a ritual of humiliation and racial subordination. After the strip search, the hungry prisoners would be paraded "past the kitchen to sit on our haunches or flat on our buttocks waiting to go to our cells and be counted in."[21]

On the third day, in Naidoo's memory, most strikers supported continuing the strike, feeling that they could endure since their hunger had by now dissipated. Prison authorities sought to weaken the strikers' will by improving the food quality and quantity. The jailers set out "plates [that were] piled high with mealies, beans and mealie rice, looking tasty and covered with appetizing fat."[22] Despite the tempting food and the arduous days of labor in the quarry, the prisoners resisted.

The strike began among the cadres of ANC and PAC prisoners who were housed with general criminal prisoners in H-Block cells and labored daily in the quarries. The Robben Island administration made it nearly impossible for these regular prisoners to communicate directly with ANC and PAC political leaders, who were sequestered in small, stark individual cells, all in one building cordoned off from the rest of the prison campus. Into this void, the guards spread "disinformation" to aggravate the striking prisoners' feelings of isolation and despair. They said that leaders such as Mandela were not "participating in the strike" and were in fact "gorging... on gourmet meals." Mandela, in his autobiography, described this tactic as "standard operating procedure" intended to aggravate divisions between political party factions and ethnic groups.[23]

In fact, prisoners had established a clandestine communications network between buildings through the food delivery and dishwashing systems, with the prisoners working in the kitchen at the center, wrapping notes in plastic and hiding them at the bottom of food delivery drums. News of the hunger strike eventually came to Nelson Mandela through these notes. Through the same system, the general prisoners learned that the political leaders, including Mandela, had joined the hunger strike. Naidoo recalled that the general prisoners were "thrilled" by news of Mandela's participation "and sang with even more intensity" that night.[24]

By the sixth day, the hunger strike was taking its toll. The general prisoners "shuffled" to the quarry "at a snail's pace." When a number of prisoners collapsed, they were taken to the isolation block and detained there for refusing to work.[25] As the strike wore on, prisoners began to lose heart. Dlamini describes how one lamented, "We are in a mess," and exclaimed, "God knows how we're going to get out of it alive." Another despaired, "Young and old, by next week, we'll all be dead ... and of all things to die such a slow, miserable and painful death."[26] Naidoo recalled the prisoners' fear that "the authorities would let [them] go on endlessly" and that news of the hunger strike had not reached the world beyond the prison.[27]

In his autobiography, Mandela declared that hunger strikes were not his preferred route of political action. They were "altogether too passive," and they also redoubled the misery of already-suffering prisoners, imperiling their health and life. He "always favored a more active, militant style of protest such as work strikes" and "go-slow strikes" that "distressed and exasperated" the authorities. He also worried that the guards "secretly enjoyed watching [the prisoners] go hungry."[28]

Yet Mandela steadfastly claimed solidarity with the striking prisoners. When Robben Island's commanding officer, Colonel Wessels, ordered Mandela to his office to explain why the political-leader prisoners had joined the strike, Mandela said, "As political prisoners we saw protest to alter prison conditions as an extension of the anti-apartheid struggle." Wessels replied, "But you don't even know why they are striking in [Sections] F and G." Mandela responded that it "did not matter, that the men in F and G were our brothers and that our struggle was indivisible."[29]

An unusual byproduct of the 1966 hunger strike was that the white junior and bachelor prison guards embarked on a hunger strike of their own, protesting the quality of their meals compared to the diet served to married guards and senior officers. The combination of the prisoners' and the guards' hunger strikes overwhelmed the authorities, who settled with the guards first. Mandela recalled that the prison-wide hunger strike was resolved not because of the prisoners' physical collapse but as a result of the guards' going "on their own food boycott, refusing to go to their own cafeteria ... [and] demanding better food and improved living conditions" for themselves.[30]

One day, Major Kellerman, the prison administrator, was ready to negotiate with the general prisoners—it was the day after resolving the guards' boycott, Naidoo surmised—and he visited the quarry. He first expressed disdain: "I don't care two hoots if you eat or not," adding, "It is your stomachs that are going hungry and you won't achieve anything by your stupid action." Yet he then asked to negotiate. He met with six representatives from the general section and eventually agreed to investigate their complaints. At that point, the ANC and PAC "general prisoners declared victory and called off the hunger strike," with the leaders of the political prisoners following a day later.[31]

The substance of the hunger strikers' victory was improvements in food quality, clothing, hygiene, and for the ANC and PAC cadres to be housed separately from the criminal prisoners, who they believed had been placed with them to intimidate and assault them. The improvements lasted only a short while, but the political consequences were durable. Naidoo recalled that the prisoners had not expected the gains to last, but their conviction ensured that, no matter what retaliatory measures the guards might inflict, "they could never take away our sense of victory or our sense of power."[32]

The hunger strike also reinvigorated political organizing in the prison as alliances were forged between rival organizations. Natoo Babenia, a South African Indian National Congress member and journalist who joined the ANC armed struggle, observed that the hunger strike emboldened the prisoners to get "back to conducting political struggle."[33] The organizational effort required to conduct, communicate about, and negotiate a mass hunger strike forged a "nascent political order on Robben Island," ensuring that the hunger strike's success was not fleeting but part of a broader process in which prisoners, as historian Fran Buntman phrased it, "consciously and intentionally remade the political environment. . . . The men on Robben Island used resistance as a baseline for a more far-reaching project, namely, fundamentally reshaping existing power relations within the prison and the society outside the prison."[34]

THE STATE WIELDING THE HUNGER STRIKE

The South African government not only faced the hunger strike weapon; it also wielded it to excuse brutality under police interrogation. When Black Consciousness Movement leader Steve Biko died in police custody in Pretoria on September 12, 1977, South Africa's minister of justice and the police, James Kruger, claimed that Biko had died from a hunger strike. The chain of events leading to his death, Kruger alleged, began on September 5, when "Mr. Biko refused his meals and threatened to go on a hunger strike." He denied the government's responsibility for Biko's fate by contending that Biko had been "regularly supplied with meals and water" and regularly monitored by the district surgeon.[35]

However, the government's claim of death by hunger strike was suspect. Kruger's report beggared belief, concluding that a man in good health and of normal weight could have died solely from refusing to eat after six days. There was national and international outrage and immediate suspicion of the government's cynical subterfuge meant to shift the responsibility for death onto the detainee himself.

Steve Biko, a medical student at the University of Natal in the late 1960s, was founder and first president of the South African Students' Organisation. He advocated Black Consciousness, a black liberationist ideology that promoted physical and psychological liberation from white dominance. The popularity of his ideas and his leadership in uniting South Africa's black liberationist groups posed a threat to the government, which placed him under a "banning order" in 1973 that prohibited him from speaking in public, to the media, or to more than one person at a time, and from leaving his home in King William's Town. In August 1977, Biko broke his banning order by secretly driving to Cape Town to meet a political leader. On his way back, on August 18, police intercepted him and took him to the Walmer police station for interrogation.

The postmortem and the inquest investigation revealed that Biko had been kept naked and manacled in a cell in the Walmer police station for twenty days, after which he had been transferred to the security police headquarters in Port Elizabeth. Through the night of September 6, Biko was tortured. He sustained massive head injuries. On September 7, the police called in Dr. Ivor Lang, who alleged that Biko was "shamming," despite finding him in a daze with a badly swollen face, hands, and feet. His senior colleague, Dr. Benjamin Tucker, the next day recommended that Biko be transferred to a hospital, but withdrew his recommendation over police objections.

By September 10, Steve Biko's injuries had still not been treated, and his condition had deteriorated alarmingly. On September 11, the police put Biko in the back of a Land Rover and took him to the prison hospital at Pretoria—a drive of more than 740 miles that took twelve hours. Here is how Barney Pityana described his friend's last hours: "On the night of 11 September Biko, evidently a seriously ill patient, was driven to Pretoria, naked and manacled to the floor of a Land Rover. Eleven hours later he was carried into the hospital at Pretoria Central Prison and left on the floor of a cell. Several hours later he was given an intravenous drip by a newly qualified doctor who had no information about him other than that he was refusing to eat." Biko died on the night of September 12.[36] The postmortem investigation revealed that Biko suffered massive brain injuries, and major abrasions and bruising of his scalp, lip, and ribs.

Ten days later, Minister Kruger addressed the Afrikaner National Party Congress and exclaimed, evidently to laughter: "I am not saddened by Biko's death and I am not mad. His death leaves me cold."[37] Kruger's callous remarks reverberated around the world in a torrent of skeptical press and outraged protests.[38] His death became emblematic of the brutality of apartheid. He was the twenty-first person to die in prison within twelve months and the forty-sixth political detainee to die during interrogation since the government had permitted ninety-day detention without charge or trial in 1963.[39] The apartheid regime had seized the prisoner hunger strike and twisted the prisoner's resistance into a hackneyed accusation of suicide. At the heart of their deception and flimsy pretext was a menacing portent of the security state's unbridled carceral power to exonerate torture while disavowing responsibility for death as its result.

Decades later, at the time of Mandela's death, a music critic reckoned with Biko's legacy as expressed by songwriters across the world: "It was Steve Biko, not Mandela, who became the first anti-apartheid icon. When the young leader of the radical black consciousness movement died in police custody in 1977, he inspired songs by the folksinger Tom Paxton, the prog-rock star Peter Hammill, the reggae artists Steel Pulse and Tappa Zukie, and, tardily but most famously, Peter Gabriel."[40] At the anniversary of Biko's death, Mandela himself called Biko "the spark that lit a veld fire across South Africa," and said that the apartheid government "had to kill him to prolong the life of apartheid."[41]

Many South African physicians spoke out against the appalling ethical and medical conduct of the physicians involved in Biko's case. They challenged the Medical Association of South Africa (MASA) and medical licensing boards to discipline them for their collusion in police brutality and prison torture.[42] In December 1982, five years after Biko's death, when MASA had still not taken these steps, fifty-two South African physicians and dentists formed the National Medical and Dental Association (NAMDA) as the progressive, independent, multiracial anti-apartheid alternative to the professional medical and dental associations that collaborated with the South African government and military. NAMDA would play a vital role in the anti-apartheid movement over the next decade.[43]

HUNGER STRIKES UNDER EMERGENCY RULE

In the early 1980s, new anti-apartheid coalitions emerged in black townships and Indian and Coloured areas, and in August 1983, the United Democratic Front (UDF) was launched, comprising more than six hundred civic, church, student, and worker anti-apartheid organizations. Initially, the UDF came together to oppose the 1983 South African Constitution, which put in place a new and controversial tricameral parliament, with chambers for Coloured and Indian communities and a white-dominated electoral college to elect the state president, while excluding black Africans from voting and citizenship. During the 1980s, this umbrella organization, allied with trade unions, became the country's leading liberation movement.

On September 3, 1984, when the Tricameral Parliament opened in Cape Town, UDF organizations launched school boycotts, work stoppages, and demonstrations in Transvaal black townships. The marches led to clashes with police and left thirty dead, a wreckage of looted shops, and rampant arson. By the end of the year, almost 150 people had been killed in political violence. This marked the beginning of the longest and most widespread period of black resistance to white rule.[44]

In response, on July 25, 1985, State President P. W. Botha declared yet another state of emergency and the South African Defense Force moved to quash the township rebellions, killing hundreds and injuring and detaining thousands. Emergency rule authorized the banning of organizations, prohibited meetings, censored media coverage of the police and military suppression, and enabled detention with no disclosure of the detainees' names or location. New emergency regulations severely restricted political funerals, banned indoor gatherings, and prohibited television news crews from filming in areas where there was political unrest.

Despite the bans, beginning in 1985, UDF affiliates used "media campaigns, protest marches, political funerals, and staged public events" to resist political repression, recruit new supporters, and amplify a vision of a nonracial democratic South Africa. Reaching beyond South Africa's borders, they campaigned to pressure governments, sports competitors, institutions, endowments, and corporations to boycott, isolate, and divest from apartheid South Africa. UDF's allies abroad harnessed activism and marshaled international television and print media "to inspire, mobilize and educate politically large numbers of people."[45]

At the height of emergency rule, more than thirty thousand young students and trade union members were corralled in indefinite detention without recourse to judicial charges or trial, some for weeks and some as long as three years. South African academic researchers called the apartheid government's use of detention a brazen political strategy to "quell, contain and eradicate democratic political opposition."[46]

The toll of indefinite, secretive detention and being denied legal recourse led some detainees to "resort to the one weapon they have: denying themselves food."[47] Hunger striking began to spread. As it did, NGO support groups and religious organizations organized to publicize the injustice of the detainees' plight.

Despite the government's enforced tight censorship of the news media and media blackouts on detainee names, locations, and conditions, news of the hunger strikes did seep out from prisons and detention centers. Some of the first hunger strikes were reported out by Christian leaders and UDF-affiliated NGOs. Lawyers were able to relay accounts of individual prisoners' failing health and the consequences of the government's refusal to respond. In 1987, the advocacy organization Lawyers for Detainees shared details of the hospitalization of Thapelo Seoka, who had lost consciousness after twenty-one days without food, and Robert Masasu, who had lost consciousness after thirty-three days without food. It was through these limited announcements that family members and friends learned even a few details about loved ones languishing in detention.

The Detainees' Parents Support Committee stated in a press release on February 4, 1986, that thirty-five to fifty teenaged youths and men were on hunger strike in Soweto's Diepkloof Prison. The press release announced a day of nationwide fasting and prayer to demand the unconditional release of the detainees and other "prisoners of apartheid."[48] On February 25, seventy-two detainees at Modderbee Prison in Benoni, east of Johannesburg, commenced hunger strikes. The South African Human Rights Commission faxed press releases about the hunger strike to media organizations, human rights allies, religious charities, and sympathetic legislators in Western Europe and North America.[49] The hunger strike dissipated without a long-term outcome.

Six months later, in August, a letter smuggled out of Modderbee Prison announced that 601 detainees had begun another hunger strike. Prison spokesmen vehemently denied that the number of hunger strikers was so high but admitted to "occasional and isolated" instances of prisoners refusing food for short periods. News of the Modderbee hunger strike fomented solidarity rallies at South African universities. International reporting, however, was sketchy, being constrained by government censorship. In a brief news report about the strike in the New York Times, an editor's note alerted readers that the news dispatch was "written under press restrictions imposed as part of the emergency decree. The restrictions prohibit reporters from referring without official authorization to the movements and actions of security forces and from reporting statements deemed to be subversive."[50]

Human rights organizations documented thirty-seven hunger strikes from 1985 to 1988, involving hundreds of detainees in prisons across South Africa. They also conjectured that, across the archipelago of South Africa's official and unofficial detention sites, more than ten thousand detainees were being held, and many detainee hunger strikes, particularly in remote rural areas, "never reached the public eye."[51]

In larger cities, religious organizations ventured into the contentious territory of political support of hunger strikers, speaking of detainee hunger strikes in their sermons and conducting sympathy fasts. In November 1985, after a weeklong hunger strike by a hundred Johannesburg prison detainees, Anglican Bishop Desmond Tutu and Catholic Father Smangaliso Mkhatshwa held a morning-to-sunset solidarity fast to direct prayers and witness the "human peril" of prolonged prisoner strikes with the wider goal of ending the state of emergency and releasing all detainees.[52]

NAMDA became a crucial medical advocate for detainees during this period, establishing clinics to examine released detainees, and arranging for their follow-up medical care and counseling. Through interviews with released detainees, NAMDA documented crucial evidence that the overwhelming majority of detainees had been beaten, tortured with electrical shocks, subjected to partial suffocation, burned with acid, or held in solitary confinement. More than half of the released detainees testified to the lack of medical care while in detention. Among those who did receive medical attention, 65 percent claimed that prison physicians performed cursory physical examinations and provided inadequate treatment.[53]

Secretive detention intensified between June 1986 and June 1987. During that time, an estimated twenty-five thousand people were imprisoned and hunger strikes continued.[54] Even as advocacy organizations did their best to circulate information about hunger strikes, the South African censorship apparatus remained mercilessly efficient. Publishers and reporters feared harassment, police violence, and imprisonment. However, UDF advocacy organizations were rapidly developing their own communication infrastructure that within two years would take advantage of cracks in the censorship regime to spotlight the brutality of detention on young black men.

For the twenty young men at Diepkloof Prison who began a hunger strike on January 23, 1989, there was little hope that their strike would be any more successful than the thirty-six documented hunger strikes that preceded it. Yet within weeks, this hunger strike sparked a "national wave of hunger strikes" involving an estimated three hundred detainees in Transvaal, Natal, and the Cape provinces, as well as solidarity rallies and sympathy fasts across South African cities and in Western Europe and the United States, leading to the successful negotiation for a large-scale release of detainees. A number of factors contributed to this hunger strike's broad influence, including successful coordination of mass striking within one prison; transmission of news between prisons; a media-savvy campaign run by local and national legal, medical, human rights, and religious advocates; the ramping up of attention from international media, particularly U.S. television; and capitalizing on the South African regime's obsessive interest in amplifying scandals concerning Nelson Mandela's wife, Winnie Mandela, which created an unexpected opening in media censorship.

This hunger strike began with a strong, clear statement by the twenty Diepkloof hunger strikers that they were making a "conscious, deliberate and voluntary personal choice" to hunger strike while fully aware of the "risks and dangers involved." Many of the strikers had languished in detention for as long as two years; they had gained experience mounting protests within prison in that time, and had established networks for communicating outside prison through family, advocates, and lawyers, who had tracked them down over the years. Even though the government had "tighten[ed] up every knot and closed whatever existing legal channel there was to secure [their] release," their words were smuggled out of the prison by lawyers and advocates, who were able (through fax and telex) to quickly transmit the information to sympathetic organizations and individuals. Within forty-eight hours, the South African Human Rights Commission publicized the Diepkloof hunger strike both nationally and internationally. The commission's statement refuted government propaganda that the detainees were criminals and terrorists by emphasizing that they "came from all walks of life: workers, students, youth, teachers, trade unionists, Christians, parents . . . breadwinners . . . and students whose future is deliberately wasted here."[55]

Within Diepkloof Prison, solidarity for the hunger strike built, escalating its size and scale. Each successive wave of strikers was publicized along with news of the health and conditions of previous waves. On January 30, fifty-three more Diepkloof detainees joined the hunger strike. Seven days later, the remaining 118 detainees joined the hunger strike, and the prisoners issued another statement to the local press, saying that "this hunger strike is a life and death issue" that they were "prepared to take to its logical conclusion."[56] By this time, the initial group of hunger strikers was experiencing "deteriorating health," to which the authorities responded with "insensitivity and intransigence."[57]

In a February 6 press statement, a fresh group of Diepkloof prisoners joined the strike. The press release charged authorities with abusing fellow hunger strikers by moving them to "extremely cold parts of the prison where they are not even provided hot water." It also disputed the assumption that only adults were imprisoned, revealing that twenty-three teenagers, mostly aged fifteen and sixteen, were among the detainees, a source of outrage among the prisoners.[58]

The Diepkloof strikes gained early support from medical and legal organizations. On February 8, the Faculty of Medicine at the University of Witwatersrand released a statement condemning detention without trial as "injust," "inhumane," "an abuse of fundamental human rights," and "a serious threat to the health of the detainee."[59] Despite the official blackout of verifiable information concerning detainees, Lawyers for Human Rights, using scraps of news from lawyers, regional support committees, and the testimony of released detainees, assembled a census of detained hunger strikers, including their locations and conditions, eventually documenting the identities of 610 of them in dozens of prisons and detention centers across South Africa from February to April 1989.[60]

THE STRIKE SNOWBALLS

The weekly waves of fresh Diepkloof hunger strikers generated a momentum that radiated to other prisons and detention sites, inspiring other prisoners to join the strike. When 105 prisoners in St. Albans Prison in Port Elizabeth began their hunger strike on February 6, their supporters emphasized that the prisoners had vowed the "total end of all food consumption (liquid and solid)." Their previous hunger strikes, targeted at improving prison diet, recreation, and access to books, visitors, and mail, had failed to bring change or even normal judicial review, so now they would continue this "final action" until all detainees were released unconditionally. The advocates championed the resolve of the detainees, who claimed they had "no alternative but to take our lives into our own hands."[61]

The New Africa, an alternative news magazine, published an account by one of the hunger strikers at St. Albans: a fellow journalist, Brian Sokutu, age twenty-six. He described how gossip from the hunger strike at Diepkloof Prison had prompted discussions among the St. Albans detainees, during which they decided unanimously to join the fast. When the strike began, the warden sent prisoners in the hospital ward who joined the strike back to their regular cells. By the third day, the strikers shared complaints of pain and weakness. They "walked around in small groups and spoke to each other in low voices," deciding to stop all of their usual activities such as playing sports and chess and engaging in political discussions.[62]

Medical attention was haphazard. No physician appeared on the first day of the hunger strike. When the prison physician did come, he read aloud from the World Medical Association's Declaration of Tokyo, an international physicians' set of guidelines on the ethical care of prison hunger strikers. Mostly it was delivered to warn the strikers, since he mentioned the death of Irish Republican Army soldier Bobby Sands in 1981 as a caution. The physician's manner was arrogant and defensive; he tested the prisoners' urine but refused to give "medicines or treatment" to alleviate discomfort. On the fifth day, two hunger strikers collapsed and were whisked by stretcher and wheelchair to the prison hospital, but the doctor still refused to treat them.[63]

On the sixth day, the security police visited the prison, asked for the detainees' lawyers' information, and promised their release if they stopped the hunger strike. The strikers decided to persevere. They were buoyed by news of "support from the community, the prayer services, the fast by journalists, international pressure," and negotiations. For Sokutu, these signs demonstrated that the apartheid state was "cracking" and that the minister of law and order, Adriaan Vlok, was buckling to demands despite his vow that the government would not be "blackmailed to release."[64]

In vain, the South African government attempted to suppress information about the hunger strikes, banning all public gatherings that called for the release of detainees or expressed solidarity with the hunger strikers. By February 9, 1989, the news had exploded across the South African and international press. Newspapers in Johannesburg and Cape Town reported that seven of the original twenty Diepkloof hunger strikers had been hospitalized for kidney damage and failure, as the total number of hunger strikers across South African prisons multiplied.[65]

But the information flow was not restricted to newspapers. The UDF affiliates mobilized their capacity for information dissemination, developed over six years, creating press releases and media events, and enlisting high-profile figures such as Archbishop Desmond Tutu. The use of "clerical robes" and "biblical civil rights sound bites" imparted a Christian moral righteousness to UDF messaging to European and North American media. Meanwhile, the alternative anti-apartheid press spread the news through its own networks, inflaming State President Botha's suspicions of conspiracy and accusations that journalists were "media terrorists."[66]

The robust communication network from below created opportunities for UDF affiliates and church organizations to orchestrate letter-writing campaigns and public vigils, picketing, and solidarity fasts, an especially resonant form of public fasting, to amplify attention for the invisible hunger-striking detainees.[67] The solidarity fasts proliferated in the cities. NAMDA doctors and dentists participated in a thirty-six-hour solidarity fast, joined by parents, families, and friends of the detainees. In Durban, members of twenty organizations joined in a sympathy fast, defying the government's prohibition against meetings and publicity. On February 10, forty-two lawyers conducted a two-day sympathy fast in four cities in support of more than three hundred hunger strikers in detention in Transvaal, Cape, and Natal provinces. Solidarity fasting, vigils, and interdenominational services drew together white, black, and Indian faith congregants, as well as students and faculty.[68]

PUNCTURING MEDIA CENSORSHIP

Since November 2, 1985, when the South African government banned photographic and sound recordings of political demonstrations—and of military crackdowns on protesters—as part of its emergency rule, news coverage of detentions and hunger strikes had been tightly censored. In January 1987, the government had even barred international newspapers from having staff correspondents in the country. However, in June 1988, the government responded favorably to requests from U.S. and European newspapers and television networks to establish bureaus in South Africa. Rapidly, in 1988 and early 1989, European and U.S. media hired correspondents, photographers, and videographers, and learned how to navigate the government censorship and surveillance machinery.[69]

As the mass hunger strike escalated through the first months of 1989, the South African government diverted the attention of international media to the erupting national scandal surrounding criminal allegations against Winnie Mandela's bodyguards. Reporting on the scandal, however, gave U.S. and British journalists a credible cover under which to test the government's censorship by producing short reports on the hunger strike. On February 9, during ABC's continued coverage of the Mandela investigation, Johannesburg correspondent Richard Sergay reported on the hunger strikes, outlining the government's policy of indefinite detention without trial under emergency rule and referring to the detainees as "political prisoners." Sergay also interviewed attorney Kathleen Satchwell and Mary Nzwe, mother of one of the hunger-striking detainees.[70]

On February 9, in a press conference, Minister Vlok called the hunger strikes "coordinated" political blackmail that undermined the government's review of individual prisoners. Vlok justified the use of emergency regulations to detain but not try prisoners in court, arguing that he had "enough evidence" that the detainees were "busy" in undisclosed "activities [that] were detrimental to the safety of the public or to the maintenance of law and order." However, he lacked evidence necessary to convict them under "normal law."[71]

On February 13, as the hunger strike crises spilled over into hospitals, international news coverage of the strike intensified, eclipsing coverage of the Winnie Mandela story. That day, CBS correspondent Martha Teichner's report included a recorded audio message of a hunger striker recovering in a hospital. It also featured Reverend Allan Boesak, president of the World Alliance of Reformed Churches, who said there was growing sympathy for the hunger strikers among South African Christians of all races.[72]

The next day, Tuesday, February 14, the South African hunger strikes were the lead story on U.S. news broadcasts. ABC News reported that Archbishop Desmond Tutu had called on all Anglicans in South Africa to fast in support of the hunger strikers. Richard Sergay personalized his report by interviewing Aaron and Rosina Ingunzulu, parents of a detainee. Coverage was rounded out by reporting on solidarity fasts being held in the United States.[73]

That same day saw increased pressure on the government from South African Christian churches. The South African Catholic Bishop's Conference called upon state authorities "to terminate the cruel and unchristian treatment of detainees" and to cease interfering with Christian believers' free speech rights and rights to assembly, undercutting their exercise of "religious and civil liberties."[74]

Also that day, three weeks into the widespread hunger strike, NAMDA reported to the press that the hunger strikers were in grave physical danger and many had been transferred to hospitals. Prisoners were under armed guard in public hospitals, where the government expected that physicians would implement intravenous feeding. However, physicians and nurses were ignoring security officials, providing any treatment the "detainee-patient may request" and stalling hospital release for recovering prisoners to prevent their return to detention. NAMDA invoked the Declaration of Tokyo guidelines to insist that doctors cannot pressure prisoners to eat " against a patient's will." Instead, NAMDA stipulated that doctors directly observe the hunger strikers' physical condition and respect their "willingness" to "face the real prospect of dying."[75]

NEGOTIATIONS AND RELEASES

The international publicity, in addition to the solidarity campaigns by UDF and the Congress of South African Trade Unions (COSATU), and by human rights organizations, churches, and mosques, along with the scale and tenacity of the hunger strike itself, pushed the South African government to negotiations. Newspapers reported on February 14 and 15 that Minister Vlok had begun an unusual round of meetings with lawyers and relatives of detainees.[76] On February 16, he met for two and a half hours with Archbishop Desmond Tutu and Reverend Allan Boesak, who succeeded in negotiating for large-scale releases of detainees from both hospitals and prisons. The cleric reported that Vlok wanted a peaceful end to the strike before "the death of a hunger striker would have consequences too ghastly to contemplate." In a news conference after the meeting, Desmond Tutu told reporters, "I don't want to speak of victory, but it does give our people hope. . . . It shows that success can be achieved by negotiation and nonviolent action."[77]

That day, Minster Vlok issued a public announcement in which he pledged to "release a 'substantial' number of [the estimated thousand] detainees" by March 2.[78] While reports of the negotiations suggested that as many as 90 percent of the detainees could be eligible for release, Vlok's announcement declared that only those who had ended their strike and were "rehabilitated and declared medically fit" would be released. Thus, hospital treatment became pivotal for a detainee hunger striker to be set free.[79]

Vlok's announcement was met with both jubilation and caution. A *Los Angeles Times* journalist noted that the "hunger strike fell short of its ultimate aim—the abolition of detentions altogether. Yet, anti-apartheid leaders were encouraged that the Government yielded." Oliver Tambo, president of the outlawed ANC, said that the outcome of the negotiations proved that the hunger strike was "a jolly good idea." And Sheena Duncan, leader of the white women's anti-apartheid group Black Sash, claimed that the "strike showed that the government doesn't have absolute power over anyone. . . . It put the government on the defensive."[80] Desmond Tutu remarked that the "burden is on the shoulders of Mr. Vlok. Our goal is to get all the detainees released and then we will carry on to change the total structure of apartheid."[81]

On Friday, February 17, the original Diepkloof detainees suspended their hunger strike until March 2, waiting to see if Vlok would deliver on his pledge.[82] However, not all of the hunger strikes stopped. In fact, new ones began. Buoyed by the success of the Diepkloof hunger strikers and skeptical that Vlok would release others without further pressure, three hundred detainees in Natal and Eastern Cape provinces began hunger strikes in the weeks that followed.[83] The Pietermaritzburg Detainees Aid Committee documented that within a week, forty of the new hundred hunger strikers in Natal province were suffering from dizziness, headaches, problems with their joints, and difficulty in urinating. Eight days into the hunger strike, police split up the hunger strikers, moving them to various police stations in the region. By February 28, twenty of these detainees had been dispatched to hospitals.[84]

In fact, not one detainee was released on March 2. On that day, to keep up pressure on the government, anti-apartheid activists held vigils and forty-eight-hour solidarity fasts at churches, mosques, and university campuses across the nation.[85] Five days later, the government slowly began to set detainees free. The government attributed the slow pace and timing of the releases to the sheer numbers of detainees and the challenges of the bureaucratic review process. However, anti-apartheid activists saw the delays as further evidence of the government's manipulation and obfuscation.

Declaring March 10 National Detainees Day, detainee aid committees organized rallies and vigils for that day in cities across South Africa. Local groups organized a roster of prominent community members willing to undertake twenty-four-hour sympathy fasts, and had group members distrib-

FIGURE 12. Dorothy Boesak (center), wife of Reverend Allan Boesak, at a demonstration in support of the release of hunger-striking detainees in Cape Town, March 14, 1989. Courtesy of African News Agency/ANA.

ute yellow ribbons at church services. There were also rallies outside prisons and fresh hunger strikes initiated within the prisons to increase pressure on the government.[86]

In North America and Western Europe, Amnesty International, interfaith organizations, and anti-apartheid university student groups organized protests and prayer services, study sit-ins and petition drives for the same day. In the United States, solidarity fasts and rallies were held at university and high school campuses and sit-ins were held in front of South African embassies and consulates.[87]

On March 10, human rights organizations reported that two-thirds of the initial Diepkloof detainees had been set free. However, the government, in what detainee advocates branded an act of "extreme cynicism and cruelty," imposed harsh restriction orders on 90 percent of the released detainees, in effect imprisoning them in their homes and denying them access to their former occupations and the "right to live a normal life." Students were denied readmission to schools and universities.[88]

Furthermore, the additional detainees were being set free at a much slower pace, which bred impatience and distrust. The slow churn of bureaucracy, some feared, was again subterfuge by the government to renege on its promise to free the detainees. Since hunger striking had proved that actions by detainees were capable of grabbing government and international attention, impatient detainees escalated more crises and standoffs, wedging themselves between European nations and the South African government. On March 20, four black male detainees recuperating from a hunger strike escaped their guarded rooms in Johannesburg's Hillbrow Hospital and traveled by taxi to the German Embassy forty miles away in Pretoria. All four were in their twenties, were active in Transvaal township Youth Congress chapters, and had been held in detention for eight months to nearly two years.[89] They were granted asylum by the West German Embassy. The detainees said they had spent five weeks in the hospital and were suffering "severe depression and psychological stress due to our continual detention." Their escape from the hospital was intended to recapture the "attention of the international community to the plight of hundreds of detainees still kept behind in apartheid dungeons," and to undermine Minister Vlok's claims that "substantial numbers" of prisoners would be released.[90]

Vlok's administration ridiculed the four detainees' escape as "stupid" and a "propaganda ploy" that undermined the negotiating process and bureaucratic review of their cases.[91] The escape, however, emboldened other recovering hunger strikers to flee hospital beds and seek refuge in U.S. consulates and the British embassy in late March.

The number of hospital escapes suggested that sympathetic hospital staff were aiding detainees' getaways. Brigadier Leon Mellet, spokesman for Vlok, announced that all the remaining hunger-striking prisoners, possibly numbering hundreds, instead of being taken to nearby public hospitals, would be confined at Grootvlei Prison near the city of Bloemfontein, a conservative Afrikaner stronghold some 400 kilometers south of Johannesburg and 650 kilometers west of Durban.[92] Vlok's office evidently forecast that Afrikaner medical staff would be less likely to undermine government authority than the white, Indian, and Coloured medical workers in other urban centers.[93]

Meanwhile, public support for the hunger strike was proliferating in urban public demonstrations that wove together Christian and human rights messages. On Good Friday, March 24, in central Durban, traffic came to a standstill when Archbishop Denis Hurley led a procession of marchers carrying crosses in silence preceding Good Friday services. Applying crucifixation analogies to the hunger strikers, Bishop Wilfrid Napier preached that "the detainee, the political prisoner, the prisoner of conscience, no less than

FIGURE 13. Moulana Faried Esack, Reverend Allan Boesak, Archbishop Desmond Tutu, and Reverend Colin Jones at a service for detainees, ca. 1989. Courtesy of African News Agency/ANA.

was Lord Jesus, is attacked in the very depths of his or her being. They are reduced to the status of nonpersons, by being stripped of their fundamental rights—the right to freedom, the right to their good name, their integrity, their dignity." He explained that they were marching for those who "are suffering for the truth, some like (seriously ill hunger striker) Sandile Thusi, to the extreme limit. Truly they are being crucified for the truth."[94]

Thusi was a charismatic and well-known Durban South African Youth Congress leader and university researcher whom many U.S. and South African media featured in their coverage. Church leaders negotiated for Thusi's release from the hospital. When an agreement was reached, Thusi ate for the first time in over five weeks on Easter Monday, March 27: "Thusi, a devout Lutheran, symbolically broke his fast Easter Monday with a bedside communion service led by two Lutheran priests."[95]

The government and human rights organizations estimated that more than a thousand people were being held in detention nationwide. By the end of March, more than seven hundred of them were on hunger strike. By

April 5, the Human Rights Committee documented, only 302 detainees had been freed, while the remaining seven hundred languished either in the hospital or in detention. In protest of the sluggish pace of releases, that same day, Reverend Allan Boesak joined twenty other clergymen in Cape Town, and vowed to undertake a sympathy strike again, this time indefinitely, if the government did not pick up the pace of releases.[96] Further detainee hunger strikes and sympathy fasts pressured the government to continue to discharge recovering hunger strikers and other detainees, until approximately eight hundred detainees were given their liberty. Even so, these detainees had to live under modified house arrest as well as under strict banning orders that limited their communication with the media, allies, and the public.

BROADCASTING THE STRIKES AND SPREADING COLLECTIVE REBELLION

The hunger strikes in 1989 succeeded where the dozens of earlier ones during the latest Emergency Rule had failed. Their success was specific. Bolstered by broad public pressure nationally and internationally, they had forced the government to negotiate the liberty of eight hundred detainees. The previous strikes had not ended with prisoner releases. The government's "law and order" justifications would persist, but its moral authority was under siege. Christian leadership—black, Coloured, and white—intervened and reshaped the register of the righteousness for the prisoner's cause. The government could still select whom to negotiate with, and it chose religious leaders—Tutu and Boesak—instead of the hunger strikers themselves or the political leaders of UDF, COSATU, and human rights organizations. Behind the scenes, prisoner lawyers were involved, but publicly Vlok needed to invest his policy pivot with a Christian humanitarian aura, not an open concession to the political opposition or to the hunger strikers directly.

Publicity and harnessing networks of solidarity in South Africa and globally were critical. In his memoir, Nelson Mandela told the world of his own hunger strike and wrote: "In order for a hunger strike to succeed, the outside world must learn of it. Otherwise prisoners will simply starve themselves to death and no one will know."[97]

However, advocacy and public pressure on the government were impossible without information. Sometimes the public learned about a hunger strike weeks, months, or even decades afterward, once secreted missives and diaries were published. Today, we know about South Africa's 1960s strikes largely through autobiographical writings, retrospectively reporting events largely unknown to the public at the time. These accounts describe organizing for a hunger strike, how solidarity built and dissipated, and strategies of survival. A number of these memoirs later circulated underground in South Africa, and some, in being read and retold, inspired subsequent strikes.

Mandela's imperative for publicity was in play in the 1980s hunger strikes. Once word of a hunger strike breached the walls of any prison or detention site, other factors could impact how swiftly and effectively it inspired public demonstration, media communication, and government concession. Pithy, exigent press releases—containing prisoner numbers, health status, and brief testimonials—were sources of information for local, national, and international news accounts and rallied public support and advocacy for the detainees' well-being and for their freedom. Delivering the information that was most urgent, news reports and press releases featured prisoners' numbers, names, detention locations, and potential fatality.

Since strict government censorship provided few avenues for even basic information to spread, the intimate details of prisoners' bodily experiences and feelings are few and far between, unlike in the British suffragist and Irish hunger strikes. In the South African context, the most detailed personal telling is from a politically prominent South African white woman's diary, which was published in London a year after her strike. It was through this publication that the black, Indian, and Coloured men incarcerated at Robben Island in the 1960s were aware of her experience. The 1966 hunger strikers wrote their own memoirs, published in the 1980s and 1990s, which could have inspired subsequent detainees while informing the world that at Robben Island, they too endured hunger striking in their long game for freedom.

However, the detainees in the 1980s strikes, mostly young black men, were local activists, students and workers. Most undoubtedly became active in government and society in the new South Africa. Their political and prison struggles were a mark of their endurance and fortitude in the fight for an egalitarian South Africa. Few became recognized national figures. Political leaders, educated professionals, and journalists determined which detainee voices were amplified and which were obscured. When journalists, advocates, and religious and political leaders spoke for the 1980s hunger-striking detainees, just a few names were known and publicized. Detainees had been set free before, but secretively and under banning orders that severely limited public information.

The shape of hunger striking changed in the hands of 1989 South African detainees and their anti-apartheid advocates nationally and globally. South Africans had experimented with massification of the hunger strike from dozens in one prison, building up weekly with scores of fresh strikers, and then it caught velocity by hundreds more prisoners picking up the strike in prisons across South Africa. Publicity for the Diepkloof strikes accelerated once those hunger strikers' declining health overwhelmed the prison's rudimentary care facilities. The transfer of strikers to public hospitals and university medical centers created a new front in the hunger-striking crisis, pulling care regimens and the strikers closer to public view. Doctors and nurses who serve the public now were on the front lines caring for hunger strikers and preventing their further punishment. The massification and persistence of the Diepkloof strikers compelled a medical emergency, forcing the state's hand and denying the prison's quest for total control.

The striking also went public in another arena. Hunger striking in secretive detention breached the walls by the reverberating public impact of twenty-four-hour and forty-eight-hour sympathy strikes by lawyers, family, doctors, and religious leaders and their congregations, with international demonstrations and vigils spreading through the networks of global anti-apartheid organizing. By testing and breaking the injunctions against public assembly, public demonstrations scrambled the clamps of media censorship and control over the plight of the detainees in the carceral web.

The hunger strikers at Diepkloof had, through their planning and communicating, precipitated a mass political movement. They had found a way to snowball their hunger strike, adding new strikers week by week at Diepkloof, and by rumor the inspiration spread to detention sites across the country. The long-term detainees had established communication strategies within the prison, as well as to the public beyond the prison walls through lawyers and UDF organizations. These organizations had improved strategies of communicating the experiences of the hunger strikers to domestic and international sympathizers who put pressure on the South African government to release detainees. These networks also fed information across the detention centers and jails. The advocacy organizations and media coordination made it possible for lawyers, physicians, nurses, clerics, detainee family members, students, and sympathetic congregants to all play roles in a mass public movement. Yet the hunger strikers themselves remained abstract, rarely seen and heard from, and under strict banning and censorship orders once they were released.

What changed in 1989, compared to previous South African strikes, is how frequently and freely common South Africans could speak of and for the hunger strikers. They could act in their capacities as doctors, nurses, lawyers, students, and fellow believers—Christians, Muslims, Jews, and Hindus—naming the hunger striker into a field of common humanity and challenging the state's dispossession of detainees' rights and personhood. Speaking up for detainees had certainly occurred before, but at the cost of police harassment and imprisonment. High-profile religious leaders could intervene and negotiate with the government on behalf of the hunger strikers, which in turn generated fresh opportunities to keep the story in the international press. Vlok's negotiations with the clerics and lawyers fomented additional public pressure through vigils, processions, and sympathy strikes to push for detainees' releases.

Religion became a timely vehicle to press political aims. The symbolism of Christ's crucifixion and resurrection, employed during the advent of Easter that year, dramatized the righteous solidarity mobilized for the predominantly black and Coloured anti-apartheid prisoners on hunger strike. This public culture of sympathy protest addressed the rightlessness of detainees in the communities of the rightful. The city streets and churches became sites of a coalescing of communal, multiracial moral authority that harnessed vigil, biblical narratives, and public ritual to pose a powerful weapon against the South African government's tactics of repression and indefinite detention.

The use of punitive violence on detainees, rumored and speculated upon during the years of secretive detention, came to light when the solidarity campaigns pierced state censorship regarding the detainees' conditions in 1989. The civil infrastructure to make the government accountable and to break the cloaks of secrecy blossomed as UDF umbrella of anti-apartheid organizations set up parallel operations to track, assist, and treat the detainees whom the state had denied legal protections or recourse. They transformed the "terrorists" and "threats" into individual persons with lives and families shattered by indefinite incarceration.

The success hit limits. The state of emergency persisted and the structures of capricious detention, censorship, and banning orders remained in place.

The global news coverage of the 1989 anti-apartheid hunger strikes set off two trajectories—the mass public strike and the mass prisoner strike—that influenced protests against unaccountable and repressive governments globally.

The public strike resonated with hundreds of thousands of students gathered in Tiananmen Square in Beijing that same spring of 1989 to rebel against autocratic rule. After weeks of student sit-in protests, boycotts, and demonstrations across eighty cities, momentum grew to two hundred thousand student protesters converging on the square. On May 13, a dozen students began a public hunger strike in Tiananmen Square, demanding negotiations with Chinese Communist leadership for democratic reforms. Three thousand students joined the hunger strike, and a million workers, teachers, students, and intellectuals demonstrated across China. Despite meetings with the hunger strikers, Premier Li Peng ousted reformers, consolidated power with the hard-liners, and imposed martial law on Beijing. The student hunger strikes waned. Military force tightened, culminating in the June 4 military massacre of an estimated seven hundred to one thousand unarmed people during the forcible evacuation of the square, with thousands jailed in the reprisals that followed. The weeklong public hunger strike at a critical point had galvanized public support and wedged the demand for democratic accountability into public discourse. Nonetheless, in the wake of military repression, the democracy movement was driven underground.[98]

Mass prisoner hunger strikes erupted in late June 1989 in Turkey, led by leftist prisoners and outlawed Kurdish labor party members. After two Kurdish strikers died, the protests spread to twelve other prisons as over two thousand hunger strikers protested the deaths, systemic prison brutality, and deprivation. Violent and lethal repression persisted, prolonging the strikes for two months. International human rights organizations investigated, and international and domestic pressure as well as the Turkish government's desire to join the European Union pressured Prime Minister Turgut Özal to pledge to reform prison conditions, punish guards who engaged in torture, and improve prisoner access to lawyers, which led to the end of the two-month-long mass hunger strike. Investigations after the fact, however, showed that conditions had not improved. In the following decades, large-scale political-prisoner hunger strikes in Turkish prisons erupted frequently.[99]

TIPPING THE TRANSFORMATION OF SOUTH AFRICA

The 1989 hunger strikes were a stepping-stone to revolutionary change in South Africa. Retrospectively, the solidarity movement for the hunger strikers was both spontaneous and ripening on an arbor of progressive civil society institutions and communication networks. Historians and political observers considered it the prelude to the national defiance campaign organized that August and September to boycott and protest the 1989 tricameral parliamentary elections. These actions echoed the agitation that blossomed in 1984, but this time the anti-apartheid organizing was more expansive, seasoned, and confident that the apartheid police state could be ruptured.

At every key moment of the 1989 solidarity movement and negotiations to free the detainees, a struggle in political leadership at the highest levels of the government was underway, and the leadership was distracted by its own power struggles. On January 18, 1989, State President Botha suffered a stroke, and on February 2 he resigned as leader of the National Party. Yet he refused to yield the presidency when the governing party elected F. W. de Klerk in March. In a compromise etched out in early April, Botha agreed to relinquish the presidency to de Klerk after the September parliamentary elections.

It turns out that Botha's regime had begun secret negotiations with Nelson Mandela and the ANC, and these talks hastened in 1988 and through 1989, when de Klerk expanded their scope. On February 2, 1990, de Klerk announced the repeal of the ban on the ANC and other organizations as well as Mandela's release after twenty-seven years in prison. Mandela's walk to freedom was televised across the globe on February 11, 1990. The negotiations for Mandela's release were the beginning of protracted consultations to set free ANC and PAC leaders from Robben Island and to work toward a post-apartheid South Africa.[100]

While leadership at the very top was changing, the machinery of governance in South Africa continued its political suppression and incarceration. Before, during, and after the 1989 defiance campaign, security forces arrested and detained more political opponents. Finally, in June 1990 the state of emergency was rescinded everywhere except Natal province, where it was lifted in October.

The hunger strikes in this chapter offer insight into both how difficult and how instructive it can be to measure success and failure. To begin with, point of view matters. The very terms of justice and achievement may appear strikingly different from the perspective of a hunger striker, advocates, physicians, and opponents. In the political arena, as communicated in the media, opponents and supporters of hunger strikers can steer the yardstick of success, declaring the hunger strike to be alternately perilous self-destruction, futile protest, desperation, martyrdom, or blackmail. The hunger strikers' own insights are often overwhelmed in the political crossfire.

A hunger strike's failure is measured by the ferocity of the prison authorities in clamping down to halt the fast and demoralize the strikers. Its success can be viewed through the prism of the authorities' perspective as well, measured by the prison administration's recognizing the strikers' grievances, negotiating with them, and conceding improvements in conditions. However, if we measure success by the prison administration's actions alone, we are denying the very power that the hunger strikers seized from the prison authorities when claiming control of their own bodies. Making the gauge of a successful hunger strike a return to the status quo of prison confinement and domination makes us complicit spectators in the system of rule and unwitting allies to the prison authorities' project of exerting dominion over the prisoners.

The 1989 hunger strikes bolstered prisoners' confidence in the power of the mass hunger strike. After 1989, the South African government continued to cage its opponents, and from 1989 to 1994, South African prisoners of all kinds used the hunger strike to force the government to set them free. However, the imprisoned fasting body had transformed the terrain, the goals, and the agents of politics in South Africa. The mass hunger strikes, global publicity, and public demonstrations emboldened the dismantling of the apartheid regime. They inspired agitation, both in prison and in public, against authoritarian regimes and state-sponsored repression in other corners of the globe. The detainees' demand to be heard reverberated as both a message of a particular injustice and a collective crusade for democracy and a just future.

SEVEN

Controversies of Medical Intervention in Northern Ireland

HALF A CENTURY AFTER THE PARTITION of Ireland in 1921, civil strife erupted in Northern Ireland, escalating into armed clashes and insurrection. Northern Irish men and women employed violence in their struggle to expel British military and rule from Northern Ireland. Once detained in camps and prisons, the Irish Catholic prisoners documented their experiences of bodily humiliation and the militancy of their defiance to prison rules and to the guards' brutality. They turned violence on their own bodies by hunger striking to fight for political prisoner status. These claims for prisoner rights reverberated internationally with inquiries of abuse and the violation of human rights. In this context of violence both inside and outside the prisons, prisoners and their families coped with the dilemmas of living and dying, survival and sacrifice.

The role of prison physicians in medical monitoring and intervention received renewed public and professional scrutiny in the context of these hunger strikes. From the outset, questions reverberated beyond Northern Ireland about which institutional and medical responses are ethical, and which are abuse and even torture. Debates about whether to respond to hunger strikers by force-feeding versus non-intervention erupted anew as the British government revised prison policies in Northern Ireland and England. As the policy directives were switched and power impasses between strikers and the state became intractable, the stakes over injury and trauma, life and death, advanced in ways that made both of the responses unworkable and unbearable.

The partition of Ireland in 1921, which placed the six northeastern counties, as Northern Ireland, under direct rule of Britain, fomented divisions and inequality between Protestant unionists, who favored remaining in the United Kingdom, and Irish Catholics, who supported reunification with the Republic of Ireland. For decades, the Protestant unionist government systematically maintained dominance by electoral gerrymandering and by tipping the scales of local electoral power through excluding non–property owners from voting.

In the late 1960s, a broad coalition of trade unionists, socialists, and republicans forged the Northern Ireland civil rights movement, which in 1968 initiated peaceful civil rights marches against anti-Catholic discrimination regarding housing, jobs, and voting in Derry and Belfast. The Northern Irish government responded by repeatedly blocking and banning march routes through Protestant areas. Marchers were ambushed by Protestant loyalists and by the police, who refused to defend the Catholics' right to protest. In August 1969, when police raided Catholic neighborhoods in Derry, residents set up barricades and pelted the police with rocks and petrol bombs during three days of fierce clashes. In Belfast the bloodiest clashes left seven dead and hundreds wounded.

The era named, in weary understatement, the "Troubles" erupted. The violent police repression provoked IRA and unionist militias to retaliate with terrorist bombings and political assassinations. Northern Ireland's cities were turned into battle zones, and terrorist bombings struck England and the Republic of Ireland. In mid-1969, the unrest toppled the Northern Irish government, and the new government trying to secure peace announced the end of plural voting, which unfairly advantaged property holders and university graduates with more than one ballot in elections. The civil rights movement nevertheless persisted, demanding the disarming of the police, the disbanding of government paramilitary forces, and the end of state practices of detention and repression. As paramilitaries fought back against the police, the Northern Irish government requested that British Army troops be sent into Catholic neighborhoods.

Confrontations between the British Army and the Catholic population escalated in frequency and militarized intensity. IRA traditionalists favored political agitation over military action to defend Catholic areas and broke with the Provisional IRA (PIRA), which promoted rioting and retaliation.

Both IRA and Protestant loyalist militias counter-retaliated by planting bombs. Civil disobedience and street politics became increasingly unstable.[1]

The conflict escalated. In August 1971, at the Northern Irish government's request, armed British soldiers launched dawn raids throughout Northern Ireland, sparking four days of violence during which two PIRA members, two British soldiers, and twenty civilians were killed. Activating the controversial 1922 Irish Partition-era Special Powers Act to suppress Protestant-Catholic paramilitary conflicts, the British Army conducted mass arrests and interned 342 suspected PIRA members.

In response to the raids, the British Army came under sustained attack from Irish Catholic rioters, who assaulted British soldiers, hijacked vehicles, and burned factories in Belfast. Residents blocked roads with burning barricades to stop the British Army from entering their neighborhoods. Northern Ireland's Ulster loyalist paramilitaries retaliated with violence against Catholics.

The conflict escalated further in early 1972, when British soldiers attacked a peaceful but unauthorized demonstration in Derry on Sunday, January 30. The demonstration, organized by the Northern Ireland Civil Rights Association, was to protest the interning of hundreds of suspected IRA members without trial. Fourteen civilians were killed on what became known as "Bloody Sunday."

The clashes continued to escalate. In March 1972, British Prime Minister Edward Heath suspended the constitution and parliament of Northern Ireland, ending a half century of Home Rule and restoring direct rule from London. In response, peaceful civil disobedience was sidelined and the PIRA dominated, promoting militancy and violence to accelerate their goal of ousting the British military and reuniting the northern counties with the Republic of Ireland. The British Army troops' suppression of the rebellion grew.

INQUIRY INTO BRITISH ARMY TORTURE

In 1969 at the World Medical Association (WMA) meeting in Paris, a delegate representing the Republic of Ireland presented evidence and charged the British Army with acts of torture in Northern Ireland.[2] The controversy escalated after the raids in August 1971, with accusations publicized in the press that the men arrested were beaten, deprived of sleep, and tortured by British soldiers in the detention camps. Some reported being kept naked, burned with cigarettes, harassed by dogs, forced to run barefoot over barbed wire and broken glass, threatened by a rope bound around their necks or gun barrel pressed against their heads, or hooded and thrown from helicopters that they were told they were hundreds of feet in the air but were actually only a few feet from the ground.[3] These allegations became known as the British military's "five techniques" of torture: placing prisoners in stress positions; exposing them to loud or interminable noises; and restricting their sight, their sleep, and their food or water.[4]

The British Parliament sent a parliamentary inquiry group, the Compton Inquiry, to Northern Ireland to investigate these claims of abuse and torture. Because the inquiry group lacked international members and because of the inquiry's limited scope, the prisoners boycotted the inquiry. The Compton Report, made public on November 16, 1971, determined that Irish prisoners had been exposed to "a measure of ill-treatment" but stopped short of calling it brutality.[5] The public outrage this caused in Northern Ireland, Ireland, and Britain led to the Parker Inquiry, which released its report on March 2, 1972. The panel members were split over whether the "five techniques" of torture could be exercised in moderation, the position of the majority report authored by Lord Parker of Waddington, Chief Justice of England, or were illegal under domestic and international law and should be abandoned, the minority position of Lord Gerald Gardiner. The British government followed the minority report and banned the use of the "five techniques."[6]

However, according to WMA Secretary General André Wynen, the Compton Report had established an unsettling linkage between interrogation, torturous methods, and physician participation. It stated that if, in the course of interrogation, "torture had become inevitable," then the British military would "humanize" the torture by requiring an "attending physician to moderate it, and even to stop it if, in his medical opinion, it became physically dangerous!"[7] The report did not specify that military physicians directly participated in moderating the five techniques in Northern Ireland in 1971, but suspicions of their role grew, particularly since the Parker majority report affirmed that the same ruthless interrogation techniques had been widely used and condoned in preceding decades by British forces while suppressing insurrections of colonized people in Palestine, Aden, Kenya, Malaysia, British Cameroons, Brunei, Cyprus, and the Persian Gulf.[8]

The public disclosure of these colonial counter-insurgency techniques and their use in Northern Ireland alarmed members of the British Medical Association (BMA) who feared that the taint of complicity with torture in the British colonies implicated physicians in Britain. The BMA prohibited its members from participating in established British military interrogation procedures or torture, for which they were roundly criticized domestically, and therefore appealed to the WMA for guidance. The WMA condemned the British military's depriving Irish prisoners of food and water and expressed concern that doctors might contribute to the practice of physical and mental torture of prisoners. Yet the controversy also revealed that the British military's use of torture was not condemned in all quarters; in fact, many believed that combating terrorist insurrection demanded a counter-force of merciless methods.

BARGAINING FOR SPECIAL CATEGORY STATUS THROUGH HUNGER STRIKES

As the civil war grew fiercer, the British military detained both PIRA members and unionist paramilitary members suspected of violence. In 1972 the uptick in detentions led to PIRA prisoners demanding political prisoner status for the men and women interned at Belfast Prison (Crumlin Road), Armagh Prison, and the camps at Long Kesh.

On May 15, 1972, five PIRA male prisoners in Crumlin Road, led by Billy McKee, started a hunger strike. They had carefully planned the strike and informed the IRA of their intention five days earlier. Prisoners later recalled the strike as coordinated and well organized, with a clear focus on five demands for political prisoner status and treatment in the prison: the right to wear their own clothes, segregation from criminal prisoners, freedom from doing prison work, permission to receive food parcels, and extra visits by family.[9]

Sinn Féin used its publicity tools, particularly its publication *Republican News* ("The Voice of Republican Ulster") and press releases to international correspondents, to inform a restive public of the strike and put pressure on the Northern Irish government. The *Republican News,* a four-page tabloid established in 1970 and published biweekly, provided news of PIRA actions and provided health updates of men on hunger strike.

Participation in the hunger strike widened. On May 25, Susan Loughran began a hunger strike and, one by one, all eight women held in Armagh Prison joined the strike. An estimated forty to eighty internees at Long Kesh joined the protest in solidarity. This swelling prison hunger strike resounded in widespread solidarity fasts in other prisons and in public. The following weekend, sympathetic groups staged twenty-four-hour and thirty-six-hour sympathy fasts in various towns and cities in Ireland, Britain, and the United States in solidarity with those at Crumlin Road.[10]

On June 6, striker Robert Campbell was removed to Mater Hospital while Billy McKee was confined to his cell. As McKee's physical condition worsened, the British government's minister responsible for direct rule, William Whitelaw, began clandestine negotiations indirectly with the IRA.

When false rumors spread that Billy McKee had died, causing rioting to erupt in Belfast, Whitelaw agreed to meet the IRA's precondition for talks by promising to consider what he termed "special category status" for detainees in Northern Ireland who saw themselves as political prisoners. At the prison at Crumlin Road, prisoners debated whether Whitelaw's promise was sufficient to meet their demands through the night and into the morning of June 20, when they decided to end their hunger strike. The strike had lasted thirty-five days. Billy McKee was moved to a hospital that day.

In July 1972, Whitelaw granted special category status to both PIRA and union loyalist paramilitary prisoners, granting them the privileges of prisoner of war status enumerated in the Geneva Convention and their five demands, including being allowed to freely associate with other PIRA members in prison.

The PIRA's victory in being granted special category status was no triumph for civil liberties—in fact, it was the opposite. New policies slashed safeguards of civilian rights against unjust arrest, and administrative detention mushroomed. In 1973 the British Parliament passed an emergency provisions act that authorized detention for any suspected involvement with terrorism. New administrative procedures made it possible to detain someone indefinitely without a jury trial. Legal protections for accused terrorists were squashed, and evidence previously considered inadmissible, such as hearsay, confessions under interrogation, and forensic evidence without corroboration, could be used in a summary prosecution to justify detention.[11] As a result, the prison population swelled, with more than 1,100 special category prisoners and 553 regular detainees in Northern Ireland's prisons by 1975.[12] At the same time, the open association and access to media for political prisoners who had special category status allowed PIRA prisoners to educate each other in the Gaelic language, Irish political history, and revolutionary ideas, as well as to self-govern and to spread political strategies and dissent in the prison.[13]

THE PRICE SISTERS, MICHAEL GAUGHAN, AND
BRITAIN'S SHIFT IN POLICY REGARDING
FORCE-FEEDING

Two years after the military torture inquiry, the British government confronted the question of physicians' participation in torture again, in the force-feeding of two Northern Irish sisters implicated in bombings in Britain. Marian and Dolours Price were sentenced on November 15, 1973, to life imprisonment for participating in a car bombing of the Old Bailey in London on March 8, in which over two hundred people were injured. Both sisters began hunger strikes in Winchester Prison because they wished to be repatriated to Northern Ireland, where they would have special category status. Instead, they were transferred a week later to Brixton Prison hospital in London, where Terence MacSwiney had been imprisoned in 1920.

Three weeks into the sisters' hunger strike, the prison physicians reported that each had lost 20 percent of her body weight and was in "very poor condition" and "extremely ill." They were dehydrated, had low blood pressure, and their urine tested for high levels of toxins that could damage the liver. By force-feeding them 1,600 calories a day, the doctors planned to avert further weight loss and clear out toxins.

One of the physicians, Dr. Blyth, believed that the "girls could have gone longer without force-feeding if they were confined to bed." But the sisters were in a "good routine, associating with other prisoners and carrying out small daily tasks," and waiting might increase the risk that the two would "decline into [a] moribund state." Delaying might have led to "more fainting and lethargy" and disruption of their electrolytic balance, which could have proved difficult to correct.

Hoping it would provide a psychological advantage, the doctors began feeding Dolours first, on December 3, because they considered her the "dominant sister." Marian was first force-fed on December 5. They reported that the sisters struggled "initially against the first feeding," making their experience "more unpleasant and difficult." However, on December 10, the doctors reported that "both girls [were] now accepting the feeding by means of tube without a struggle." In addition, the women were seen every two weeks by a psychiatrist, who continued to assess them as "not insane and quite responsible for their actions."[14]

Although Dolours and Marian physically succumbed to the process, they instructed their attorneys to file suit against the forcible feeding. The attorneys challenged the government's stance, claiming that the women were "in sound mind and body and have conscientious reasons for refusing food," so the government must either "let them die" or "move them to a place at which they are prepared to eat."[15]

Their hunger strike lasted for two hundred days, until June 1974, and they were force-fed on 167 days. Two white male British physicians, Dr. Blyth and Dr. Turner, assisted by three male Indian doctors and a British woman doctor, all took part in supervising the force-feeding.

Marian Price, in an interview in 2004, recounted the experience of force-feeding as a daily experience of forcible constraint: "Four male prison officers tie you into the chair so tightly with sheets you can't struggle."[16] Dr. Blyth elaborated that the prisoner is "placed in a chair and one person holds the head steady by means of a towel round the prisoner's forehead. Another person pins the prisoner's arms and two more hold the prisoner's legs" and then inserts a dental gag.[17]

Marian described the use of a "metal spring device around your jaw to prise it open" despite her efforts to clench her mouth closed. "They force a wooden clamp with a hole in the middle into your mouth. Then, they insert a big rubber tube down that. They hold your head back. You can't move. They throw whatever they like into the food mixer—orange juice, soup, or cartons of cream if they want to beef up the calories. They take jugs of this gruel from the food mixer and pour it into a funnel attached to the tube."[18] Her description is reminiscent of the force-feeding tools and substances used on suffragists, conscientious objectors, and Irish republicans in British prisons fifty years earlier, replete with the ad hoc feeding substances that strikingly contradicted the physician's documentation of the same substance being used every time.

The director of prison services recognized that the repetition of the unpleasant experience produced submission: "in the far majority of cases . . . the prisoner finds the passing of the tube . . . so unpleasant that after one or two days the struggling stops and the tube is passed easily and without discomfort." He explained that the "unpleasant part of this is when the tube touches the throat at the back which may cause vomiting and other unpleasant reactions," while downplaying as a "slight risk" the danger of "the tube going down the windpipe" and emphasizing how distilled water was run down the tube first to prevent food from entering the lungs.[19]

Marian described how the feeding tube was once mistakenly inserted into her lung. "I felt like I was drowning. I passed out. They carried me back to my cell. The doctors were standing over me when I came around. If it had been food, not water in the tube, it would have killed me." Both Price sisters suffered mouth sores and permanent loosening of their teeth after months of force-feeding.[20]

The force-feeding of the Price sisters, extending over months, drove the British Home Office and Parliament to wrestle with the ethics and legality of the practice. Not wanting to appear politically biased or as exacting punitive treatment, Home Office bureaucrats opted to defer the decision of whether and when to begin "compulsory artificial feeding" to medical professionals and their assessment of the prisoner's condition, thus equating forcible feeding with the necessary treatment of a "hospital patient."[21] Yet the medical profession was conflicted about their responsibilities and legal liability for prisoners' lives. Some doctors saw force-feeding as a palliative necessity, and others saw it as an assault. Some were wary of being perceived as "instruments of political pressure" while also fearing that by not taking action they could "let the prisoner die of starvation." Many prison doctors preferred to send debilitated prisoners to a public hospital, where they could be fed intravenously.[22]

Among the options for artificially feeding the sisters, a suggestion of intravenous feeding was raised, but the physicians responded that it required a "cooperative or comatose" patient and at least three hours to complete. Furthermore, it could not substitute for feeding through the nose and mouth over the long term, since it was not an effective means to "feed protein," and it required frequent blood and urine testing, which the sisters resisted.[23]

At the same time, long-term feeding through the nose or mouth overburdened the prison medical staff and battered their morale. Dr. Blyth warned that Brixton Prison's medical service was ill-equipped for the daily, time-consuming demands of ongoing force-feeding. It was damaging the medical "staff more than it does the girls, which was a repugnant and difficult situation" causing crippling "emotional drain."[24]

Marian Price sympathized with the physicians' dilemma. In a letter to her father, excerpted in an IRA pamphlet, she commented that her abstinence from food "must be frustrating to the dedicated doctor" after receiving so much "training to counter diseases, [and] psychiatric illnesses." Yet, she said, her real malady was having an "incurable" political conscience. She reaffirmed that the two sisters' hunger strike was a battle against the British government's refusal to either transfer them to prison in Northern Ireland or grant them special category status while in England.[25]

The British government found the options before it—to release the Price sisters until their health improved, transfer them to Northern Ireland, or keep them in England and grant them political prisoner status—all unappealing for political reasons. Regarding the last option, the British government was already frustrated with the special category status policy in Northern Ireland and wanted to end it, not prolong it. The government lawyers counseled the Home Minister not to capitulate to "political blackmail" by giving in to the Price sisters' demands, which would reward insubordination and spiral into more hunger strikers making similar demands.

Seeking a resolution despite his qualms, Home Secretary Roy Jenkins announced to Parliament on May 23, 1974, that the British government would end the Price sisters' forcible feeding because of their lack of cooperation. However, before his statement could lead to changes in policy, Michael Gaughan—who, along with six other PIRA prisoners, had gone on a sympathy hunger strike to support the Price sisters on March 31, 1974—died.

Gaughan had already served nine months in prison for possession of two revolvers and conspiracy to rob a London bank. When Gaughan and his six fellow prisoners were moved to the high-security Parkhurst Prison on the Isle of Wight, they demanded an end to solitary confinement, education while in prison instead of doing prison work, and a date for transfer to a prison in Northern Ireland. Gaughan began being forcibly fed on April 22 and was force-fed seventeen times until June 2. After hunger striking for sixty-four days, he died on Monday, June 3, 1974. He was twenty-four.

The cause of death was disputed. Although his family "insisted that [his] death must have been caused by a feeding tube either rupturing Gaughan's stomach or piercing a lung," prison authorities attributed his death to pneumonia and malnutrition as a result of his self-starvation. Gaughan's death added pressure to the British government to transfer the Price sisters and other PIRA prisoners to Northern Irish prisons and to placate the PIRA, who vowed to step up terrorist reprisals unless the transfers were made.

In July 1974, government authorities formally discontinued all force-feeding, stating that the hunger strikers' resistance to force-feeding could have life-endangering consequences.[26] Even as Jenkins upheld the British state's preference to use the "distasteful and objectionable" procedure of force-feeding to control the prisoners' life and health, he declared that the government would no longer require prison physicians and nurses to "resort to artificial feeding (whether by tube or intravenously)" and would respect the prisoner's decision to fast and to not accept feeding irrespective of "inevitable deterioration in his health ... without medical intervention."[27] Also in 1974, the newly elected British Labor government's strategy in Northern Ireland shifted away from military suppression of the Catholic insurrection, aiming to reduce the number of British troops in Northern Ireland and return responsibility for civil order to local policing, positioning the British government as a neutral referee.

The widespread media coverage of the Price sisters' force-feeding and Gaughan's death pressed the British medical profession to likewise take a clear ethical position on force-feeding in prisons. Earlier that year, at an Irish Civil Rights Association meeting in Dublin, psychiatrist Dr. Brian Laverty had declared that the effect of force-feeding on the Price sisters had been "similar to multiple rape" and that its "inhuman, degrading" nature violated the European Human Rights' Convention and the UN Declaration on Human Rights.[28] Members of the British and Irish medical associations agreed to draft a joint statement on medical ethics, force-feeding, and torture and would present it in September 1974 at a WMA meeting. Independently, the BMA ethics committee repudiated the British military's policy of force-feeding hunger strikers but left the decision of whether to participate or not to the individual physician's conscience.[29]

These developments gathered momentum for far-reaching policy. In 1975 the WMA issued the Declaration of Tokyo, which prohibited any physician from participation in torture, either actively or by passive complicity. Regarding the practice of force-feeding, the document advised: "Where a prisoner refuses nourishment and is considered by the physician as capable of forming an unimpaired and rational judgment concerning the consequences of such a voluntary refusal of nourishment, he or she shall not be fed artificially."[30] The declaration offered physicians a script for how to respond to hunger-striking prisoners ethically. It obligated doctors to explain the consequences of long-term fasting to the prisoners. It also affirmed the autonomy of the physician's medical judgment, independent of state or political pressures. It did not, however, provide guidance on problematic issues surrounding force-feeding: how a physician should balance the prisoner's expressed wishes with the physician's role "to alleviate the distress of his or her fellow human beings," how the physician should judge whether the patient's judgment was impaired or not after days or weeks of hunger striking, and under what circumstances a physician should override the prisoner's will and prescribe artificial feeding by force.[31]

The British government's decision to end use of forcible feeding had new consequences, however. In February 1976, hunger striker Frank Stagg, a member of PIRA, was allowed to die without medical intervention. Historian Ian Miller notes that the political message of Stagg's hunger strike and death by starvation "ultimately attracted less humanitarian concern than the fate of force-fed prisoners," perhaps because it was his own conscious decision, rather than one perpetrated by prison doctors.[32] The new policy was also in force in March 1981 when the British government ordered prison administrators and medical officers at Long Kesh prison to monitor hunger strikers' deteriorating conditions but not to forcibly feed them.

MAKING BODIES INTO WEAPONS AT LONG KESH

In January 1975 the Gardiner Parliamentary Committee, led by the same Lord Gardiner who had authored the minority Parker report condemning use of the five techniques of torture, published the results of its recent inquiry into terrorism in Northern Ireland. The committee's report maintained that the British military acted legitimately in the abrogation of civil liberties during civil strife, and recommended that there be no amnesty for convicted prisoners. It also recommended that special category status be terminated because it undermined prison authorities' ability to maintain discipline and order. The British military and counterintelligence wanted to phase out special category status in an effort to break the PIRA's ability to organize within prisons, as well as to undercut the legitimacy of the PIRA's struggle.[33] Instead, the government returned to "criminalization" of PIRA prisoners for participating in terroristic violence and weapons possession. Ultimately, the British government aimed to deter the recruitment of young men and women into paramilitaries and to cleave away PIRA insurgents from the sympathy and support of Northern Irish Catholics.[34]

Thus, two major policy shifts in the treatment of PIRA prisoners—the discontinuation of force-feeding and the end of special category status—preceded the prisoner protests that took place at Long Kesh prison beginning in 1976 and built to a crisis in 1980–81.

The Long Kesh prison compound had opened in 1971 to accommodate the increasing numbers of prisoners interned after the military raids in August of that year.[35] Situated in a disused Royal Air Force station nine miles southwest of Belfast, at the time it consisted of large huts that could accommodate up to eighty men. The revocation of special category status in March 1976 coincided with the opening of eight new "H-Blocks," providing eight hundred additional cells, at Long Kesh, now officially named Her Majesty's Prison Maze. The initial hut compound system, called the "Cages," had formerly held both detainees and special category prisoners. From March 1976 onward, those convicted of "terrorist offences" were housed exclusively in the H-Blocks, bifurcating the prison into two distinct architectural spaces and carceral regimens. Political prisoners already at Long Kesh remained in the Cages and retained their special category status, while new detainees were denied special category status and were housed in the H-Blocks.[36]

The denial of special category status—which, among other things, had meant not having to wear prison uniforms—for new prisoners triggered a rebellion. In September, six months after the revocation of special category status, a new prisoner, Kieran Nugent, refused to wear the prison uniform. He was held for several days in solitary confinement before being given a blanket to wrap himself in. Other incoming prisoners followed his example, and the "blanket protest," protesting the loss of special category status for new PIRA paramilitary convicts, grew. Prison guards tried to break the prisoners' resistance by confining them to their cells for twenty-three hours a day, reducing access to toilets, and stepping up cell searches and harassment. In April 1978 the prisoners escalated their protests into what was called the "dirty protest" by refusing to shower and by collecting feces and urine in pails in their cells and smearing the mixture on the walls. By July 1978, nearly three hundred prisoners were participating. The administration retaliated with forced bathing and haircuts. Prison guards also conducted invasive and humiliating searches, using mirrors in the showers to examine prisoners' rectums, ostensibly to curtail contraband.

Allen Feldman, writing about the crisis of the prisoner body, comments that the guards' violence and "counter defilements of the prisoners" were intended "to divorce the prisoner from what little sense of somatic mastery he had managed to retain in prison."[37] Both commentators at the time and scholars later on commented that the "blanket men" had launched a military campaign of "insurrectionary violence" within the prison that deployed "their bodies as weapons." The prisoners expected these acts of "self-directed violence" to trigger "mass insurrectionary violence outside the prison."[38]

Among the blanket men was twenty-five-year-old Bobby Sands, who described his first days in the H-Blocks in an account published in the *Republican News*. He found himself "sitting on the cold floor, naked, with only a blanket around me, in an empty cell" and experiencing the "sudden and total deprivation of such basic human necessities as exercise and fresh air, association with other people, my own clothes, and things like newspapers, radio, cigarettes, and books." He suffered from daily blinding migraine headaches and muscular pains, the consequence of his isolation and lack of exercise. As days passed, his appearance and his health deteriorated from the toil of the dirty protest: Sands described his "eyes, glassy, piercing, sunken and surrounded by pale, yellowish skin," his beard unkempt, and how he "resembled a living corpse."[39]

Sands's experience in the H-Blocks was in stark contrast to his first time at Long Kesh in 1973, when he was in the Cages and allowed free association with other PIRA prisoners as part of special category status. He had cherished the opportunity to read, learn Gaelic, and debate with his fellow prisoners. By the time he was released in April 1976, Belfast had become a war zone of barricades, security checks, bombings, and militia confrontations. In 1977, when he returned to Long Kesh after being convicted of a weapons possession charge, the prison had been transformed into a high-security H-Block isolation facility.

On October 27, 1980, the first coordinated hunger strike at Long Kesh began, with seven detainees selected to represent different counties in Northern Ireland. When they began their fast, the prisoners were individually informed that the government would not intervene to force-feed them.[40] Bobby Sands served as commanding officer during these hunger strikes but did not participate. On December 1, three women in nearby Armagh Prison joined the hunger strike in solidarity with the men. In mid-December, more than two dozen male prisoners joined the strike.

Before the hunger strike even began, the British government was keenly aware of the insurrection forming at Maze and Armagh prisons. Britain's secretary of state for Northern Ireland, Humphrey Atkins, wrote in a communication to Prime Minister Margaret Thatcher: "A hunger strike would be a deliberate and ruthlessly determined act to achieve political status for terrorist prisoners. This is the objective of the dirty protest itself, and it is an indication of the failure that a hunger strike is being considered." He added: "[We] must not give in, or do anything that can be used as a sign that we are not resolute."[41]

Thatcher refused to yield on the issue of "political status for terrorist criminals" or relent on the no-force-feeding policy. And the British government, determined to carry out its 1974 policy not to initiate medical intervention in further hunger strikes, was prepared to allow the "inevitable deterioration— and consequent death—of a hunger striker to take place unless the prisoner specifically asks for medical intervention." It was also "unlikely that any prison medical officer in Northern Ireland would resort to forced feeding" for fear of reprisals.[42] The European Commission on Human Rights also vindicated the government's refusal of special category status for the prisoners and rejected the prisoners' claims of ill treatment by prison officials.

On December 18, 1980, the hunger strikers at Maze ended their fifty-three-day fast upon the condition that an agreement on improving prison conditions would be hammered out between the PIRA and the British government. The prisoners were then outraged when the prison authorities changed their position, refusing to reinstate special category status or to cease the brutal treatment in the H-Blocks. The prisoners regrouped and developed a new, disciplined strategy of successive individual hunger strikes to the death.

On March 1, 1981—the five-year anniversary of the removal of special category status—a second hunger strike began, in which Bobby Sands was the first to refuse his meals. The next day, all the remaining prisoners—in a "tactical move" to demonstrate their willingness to cooperate and also to spotlight the hunger strike—ended the dirty protest by showering and receiving haircuts.[43] The strike strategy, designed to capture the attention of the public and keep up pressure on the authorities, was to stagger nine additional hunger strikers to follow Sands. Two weeks later, Sands was joined on hunger strike by Raymond McCreesh and Patsy O'Hara, and a week later by a fourth, Francis Harris. Five more prisoners began hunger strikes in the weeks that followed.

Sinn Féin and the PIRA, bypassing British and Irish government-managed television and radio, publicized news and personal stories of the Long Kesh hunger strikers and their families through the combined periodical *An Phoblacht/Republican News*. The newspaper's sales soon reached up to sixty thousand copies per week. Some issues quadrupled in size, running up to forty-eight pages long. The paper featured the prisoners' voices, publishing their written notes smuggled out of Long Kesh. In turn, miniature versions of the paper were smuggled into and circulated among prisoners in Long Kesh, Portlaoise, and Armagh prisons.

Twelve days into his hunger strike, on March 12, Sands in his diary connected his strike with those of earlier famous Irish republicans, referring to the "awful fate and torture endured to the very bitter end by Frank Stagg and Michael Gaughan" and to Terence MacSwiney, whose death "stirred" his own "heart and mind." In contrast to the deaths of those men at the "unmerciful ugly hands of a vindictive heartless enemy" in Britain, Sands appreciated that he was imprisoned in Northern Ireland, with his comrades near and his family able to visit him.

The struggle for Sands was keeping conscious, mindful, and resolute, "holding the slowly creeping weariness" at bay while he amassed his "energy and thoughts into consolidating . . . [his] resistance." He describes struggling daily against temptation, noting that the "fight" was an internal battle, since "the body doesn't accept the lack of food, and it suffers from the temptation of food . . . [that] gnaw[s] at it perpetually. The body fights back sure enough, but at the end of the day everything returns to the primary consideration, that is, the mind." He describes how one day after returning to his cell after attending St. Patrick's Mass, the orderlies were handing out trays of food to the prisoners, and one put a plate of food "in front of my face"—Sands ignored it as if "nobody was there."[44]

Sands projected his internal struggle outward as resolute confidence directed against the United Kingdom political system through parliamentary elections. During the hunger strike, Northern Ireland Member of Parliament Frank Maguire had died of a heart attack, resulting in a special election being held in the Fermanagh and South Tyrone constituency. From his prison bed, Sands campaigned for Parliament as an "Anti-H-Block/ Armagh Jail Political Prisoner." He won the seat on April 9, 1981, his victory unifying Northern Irish Catholic support for Sands and bolstering national and international publicity for the hunger strike at Long Kesh.

A week later, Sands and the four other hunger strikers were moved to the prison hospital for monitoring. Senior medical staff reported to Northern Irish and British authorities that Sands had lost 25 percent of his body weight, had developed a distaste for water, was experiencing constant headaches, and found even daylight aggravating. It had become difficult for him to read, listen to the radio, or watch TV. He was in danger of cardiac arrest and might be in a coma within a week. Daily visits by his close relatives were authorized, and the chief medical officer stipulated a clear policy of medical action: they would intervene if Sands agreed to treatment. If he refused but became comatose, they would intervene if his relatives requested it. However, if both Sands and his relatives refused, they would not intervene. Asked if she would authorize treatment if he fell into a coma, his mother, Rosaleen Sands, quietly said to reporters and news cameras, "It is a sad thing to say. . . . I love my son just like any other mother does. . . . He asked me not to and I promised him not to."[45]

Bobby Sands died of starvation on May 5, 1981, at the age of twenty-seven, after sixty-six days of hunger striking. The public's emotional response to his

FIGURE 14. Members of the Lenadoon Action Committee protesting in support of the demands of Irish republican hunger strikers. *Andersonstown News,* July 25, 1981. Courtesy of the Bobby Sands Trust.

death unleashed violent rioting and bus burning in Northern Ireland's Catholic neighborhoods. Enormous crowds, estimated at one hundred thousand, lined the route of his funeral procession in Belfast. Demonstrations and vigils were held in the United States, Germany, Italy, Greece, France, and Australia. Delivering the funeral oration, his election agent, Owen Carron, spoke of Sands's mother's suffering and sacrifice: "It is hard to be a hero's mother and nobody knows this better than Mrs. Rosaleen Sands who watched her son being daily crucified and tortured for sixty-six long days and eventually killed. Mrs. Sands epitomizes the Irish mothers who in every generation watch their children go out to fight and die for freedom."[46]

In the weeks that followed, three more Long Kesh hunger strikers died. Other prisoners took their places, and the hunger strike persisted through the summer, with six additional hunger strikers dying.

The deaths at the Maze Prison sparked international outrage and reanimated the debate over the ethics of allowing hunger-striking prisoners to die versus feeding them against their will. These deaths also jolted physicians and human rights advocates to reconsider the protocols for consent and intervention of medical treatment of hunger strikers.[47]

In the British and the American press, there was sympathy, but also outright hostility to the way Sands wielded the hunger strike as a weapon, in comparison to other practitioners. One critical author compared Sands unfavorably to Gandhi. A *Chicago Tribune* editorial written a week before his death commented: "Mahatma Gandhi used the hunger strike to move his countrymen to abstain from fratricide. Bobby Sands' deliberate slow suicide is intended to precipitate civil war. The former deserved veneration and influence. The latter would be viewed, in a reasonable world, not as a charismatic martyr but as a fanatical suicide, whose regrettable death provides no sufficient occasion for killing others."[48]

It is true that, by Gandhi's moral measuring stick regarding the purpose of fasting, Sands's use of the hunger strike was tainted by his association with violent insurgency and civil war. Gandhi fasted in order to purify himself and persuade his followers to disavow violence and retaliation, whereas Sands ostensibly used the hunger strike as an insurrectionary weapon. Since Sands's purpose was to bring insurrection into the prison, perhaps it would be accurate to say that, in contrast to Gandhi, he and his fellow striking prisoners turned violence on their own bodies to communicate their refusal to be crushed by the prison's brutality. They renounced first clothing, then bathing, and finally food to vent their rebellion against the prison's power to subjugate and control them.

Leveraging public motivation for the uprising against British rule was central to the prison hunger strike that Sands and his fellow IRA strikers waged. Politically, there was calculation in selecting strikers as "emissaries" of distinct localities and sending them "one by one to their deaths as the prison collective waited for the political effect of each death."[49] Many have remarked on how Bobby Sands marshaled an image of the suffering Irish nationalist who is prepared for martyrdom in an epic struggle against an obstinate British power. Sands righteously and reverently invoked the heroes of Ireland's independence in his own hunger strike protest, claiming his legacy in the pantheon of "separatist and insurrectionary Ireland."[50] This legacy was performatively instantiated in the way each of the ten men was remembered in his death. Pulling at both the religious and paramilitary strands of Irish nationalism, the funeral processions featured the casket draped in the Irish tricolor flag, gun salutes, and crucifixes accompanied by family, neighbors, and masked IRA soldiers.

The message of Sands's hunger strike had an immense communicative reach. His struggle to the death reached beyond his constituency of IRA members and sympathizers to Irish Catholics worldwide, to people of a variety of faiths and political aspirations, to other prisoners worldwide, and to medical professions and prison administrators. The death of Bobby Sands by hunger strike would endure in symbol, myth, and memory.[51]

A MOTHER'S DILEMMA

On May 12, a week after Sands's death, his fellow hunger striker Frank Hughes died of starvation. Meanwhile, Raymond MacCreesh and Patsy O'Hara were on death watch. O'Hara, born into a multigenerational Irish republican family, had joined the youth wing of the IRA at thirteen. In May 1979 he was arrested for being linked to the possession of Soviet-made grenades. On January 15, 1980, he was sentenced to eight years imprisonment and taken to Long Kesh, where he immediately went on a blanket protest. He was scheduled as a replacement during the first hunger strike and chose to lead as a principal hunger striker in the second campaign.[52]

Once he was on hunger strike, his mother, Peggy O'Hara, moved from Derry to Belfast to be close to her son and to intervene in case he took a turn for the worse. In an essay written and published retrospectively in *An Phoblacht/Republican News,* she offered her perspective on his dying days and on her own moral conflict as she held a "lonely vigil watching my son's life ebb away." She recounted his determination to fast even when "every day a meal was brought to O'Hara and left there all day on show ... even though he was unable to take a sip of water and the smell of the dinner made him vomit." She comforted her son by "wetting his lips and tongue with moistened cotton wool" since he could no longer endure drinking water. "His eyes were open but he could not see." He was "very weak and seemed unable to speak," but she "held his hand that he was still conscious." Soon after her move to Belfast, Patsy had a heart attack.[53]

She had to grapple with her son's "resolute" determination and her own: "In my mind I was determined that my Patsy was not going to die." She had decided that when her son slipped into a coma, she would authorize the use of medication to save his life—though, at his bedside, she was "very careful to avoid making any promise to Patsy, so as not to be bound as the other families were to their sons." Still, she was "consumed by grief and torn by this dilemma" between following his wishes and keeping him alive. One day, she recalled, "as if he was reading my mind, he suddenly turned to me and spoke loudly and firmly. He said, 'I'm sorry we didn't win but please, mammy, let the fight go on.' Those words gripped my heart like a vice, and only then did the reality of his dying hit me."[54]

As a devout Catholic mother, she compared her sorrow to how "Mary felt when Jesus told her: I must be about my Father's business. I prayed for strength, I prayed for help, it was so lonely." Her loneliness in her grieving was compounded by the sadistic policy of the guards, who kept her husband away from her and refused to let her sit and seek solace with the McCreesh family. Peggy O'Hara exemplified the ways that some family members turned to Catholic spiritual imagery and language to express the dilemmas of conscience, the sorrow of witnessing a loved one's dying, and to make sense of the hunger striker's battle with the government. Like the family vigils earlier in the century for Terence and Mary MacSwiney, her vigil poignantly revealed a mother's grief as her words and image circulated globally in print and on television.

She speculated on the value of medical intervention, although she did not indicate that she spoke with the doctors or even saw them as allies. She feared that medication would "only prolong his agony and his suffering" and that by saving him, she might make him available to greater pain and violence in prison. She confessed that she wanted him to outlive her even if "he hates me for the rest of my life." Yet, she wrote, "each time I wanted to cry out loud I want to save my son, his last words gripped my mind and I froze."[55]

As the mother of another hunger striker reflected in an interview years later: "It was traumatic for mothers because it's a reversal of all what it means to be a mother. . . . You have struggled all your life to put food in their bellies, sometimes at the expense of yourself, and [then] to watch them die of starvation."[56]

Peggy described her son's final hours: "His eyes have rolled back in his head and showed only the blood-shot whites of his eyes. There was an unbearable smell of death in the over-heated cell . . ., [and] Patsy was blue in the face and moaning with pain." In the taut sensorial agony she felt at her dying son's bedside, Peggy expressed relief that he was liberated from the prison's vortex of violence. Yet despite his maddening cries, she resolved that "Patsy was unbreakable, either by me or anybody else, but at least now was free from all the beatings, the torture, the degrading naked body searches which brought the prisoners to the desperation of the hunger strike in the first place."[57]

On May 19, within hours of each other, Patsy O'Hara and Raymond McCreesh died. Other prisoners took their places as hunger strikers, and a

FIGURE 15. Youth supporters stand behind photographs of the Maze Prison hunger strikers, Andersonstown, West Belfast, Northern Ireland, August 9, 1981. Credit: AP Photo/Chuck Zoeller.

total of ten men died in the long summer as negotiations between the IRA and the British broke down. Michael Devine, who died on August 20, 1981, was the last hunger striker to die. The families of the last four hunger strikers took matters into their own hands. As those young men lapsed into unconsciousness, their families gave permission for medical intervention.[58]

Once the prisoners realized that their family members were going to continue to intervene, prolonging the hunger strike was no longer tenable. The remaining hunger strikers negotiated to end the strike and for concession to just one of their demands: to not wear prison clothing.

One of the hunger strikers was Laurence McKeown, who had joined the IRA in 1973 at the age of seventeen. In April 1977 he was sentenced to life imprisonment for setting explosives and for the attempted murder of a policeman. He participated in the protests in Long Kesh for four and half years. McKeown began his hunger strike on June 29, 1981, with the intention of continuing to the end. However, his family intervened when he fell into a coma after his seventieth day on hunger strike and permitted intravenous feeding.

After the hunger strike, McKeown enrolled in education programs at Long Kesh and received his bachelor's degree. After his release in 1992, he wrote a doctoral thesis on the Irish republican prisoner community. McKeown notes, in his book *Out of Time,* that prison life became ordinary again in the months that followed the hunger strike. "For the first time in five years we could get out of our cells, eat in the canteen, go to the yard for exercise, watch television during association time, listen to the radio, get access to the library and have weekly visits." However, the PIRA prisoners continued to protest the conditions of their incarceration, and they were prone to losing access to these improvements as a result. "For me personally the ending of the hunger strike prompted a mixture of emotions," McKeown writes. "Relief that it was all over and that no more comrades would die was probably uppermost but that was tinged with the sorrow and anger that so many had died."[59]

THE ENDURING SHADOW OF LONG KESH

The Long Kesh standoff, resulting in the deaths of ten men, cast a long shadow. As Sands's death reverberated internationally, it elicited sympathy from Catholics in the United States, Europe, and South America. The voluminous news coverage, journalists' books, and the IRA's own memorialization of the crisis further spread the words of Bobby Sands and the experiences of the hunger strikers across the globe. Governments and prisons feared that the widespread notoriety of Sands's hunger strike to the death would inspire prisoners to imitate the practice. People heard far less about the nine men other than Sands who had died hunger striking. And they likely knew even less about the other prisoners who decided to persist, prolonging the hunger strike for five months after Sands's death.

The 1981 strike could be viewed as a failure, since people perished without concessions being made regarding the treatment of prisoners or prisoner release. On the other hand, both the British government in Northern Ireland and Sinn Féin believed that the strike's outcome vindicated their stance. Margaret Thatcher and the Conservative Party believed they had won on principle with the breaking of the Long Kesh hunger strike. They had proved their steadfast resolve to not be cowed by emotional blackmail by PIRA prisoners and to not concede to the prisoners' demands, even if it meant the deaths of ten men. And they remained confident that they could manage the public uproar and protests both in Northern Ireland and across the globe. Meanwhile, the extended hunger strike helped Sinn Féin achieve its objective of mobilizing the Irish Catholic public in Northern Ireland, the Republic of Ireland, and the diasporic Irish Catholic community, particularly in the United States. As a result, from the 1970s into the 2000s, Sinn Féin consolidated electoral power and influence in both Northern Ireland and the Republic of Ireland. In the mid-1990s, Sinn Féin was vital to the protracted negotiations, the cease-fires, and the eventual Good Friday Peace Agreement on April 10, 1998, as well as to the subsequent successful referendum votes in both the Republic of Ireland and Northern Ireland.[60]

The crossfire of political success and failure, however, was not taken from the perspective of prisoners. The very terms of justice and achievement may appear strikingly different from the perspectives of a hunger striker, advocates, physicians, and opponents. Nowhere was this more vexed than in the institution's clamping down on the hunger strikers' protest by imposing forcible feeding. The crisis in Northern Ireland had produced a policy shift in the British government's stance on force-feeding in 1974. The experiences of the Price sisters, and later of Sands and O'Hara, had exposed physicians' ethical quandaries regarding applying the state's weapon of forcible feeding and whether inaction and non-intervention could make them responsible for the death of a hunger-striking prisoner. The Price sisters, their father, and supporters all reshaped the hunger strike form to emphasize the torture and pain of forcible feeding. Also in 1974, a broader public debate arose, in particular among international medical professionals, about what kinds of bodily constraint and control, justified as medical therapy, could be considered torturous. This debate made the physicians and authorities acutely sensitive to those accusations. It exposed the dark side of medical responsibility for preserving life at all cost. And it raised forcefully a question that had stalked forcible feeding of hunger strikers since the 1910s: whether unwanted treatment forcibly imposed was torture.

The new British non-intervention policy challenged prison doctors to only observe, monitor, and manage hunger-striking prisoners. It also brought family members into the personal scene of the hunger-striking prisoner, giving them a new role. In 1981 the hunger strike was distilled—in the hands of the strikers and their mothers—into the agony of wasting away to the death. In the funeral processions of the ten men who died, in the demonstrations of their photographs, remade into murals and posters, IRA allies, Catholics, and artists worldwide molded the hunger strike into political martyrdom of young men and into somber collective reckoning of injustice. With neither the hunger strikers nor the government backing down, the government's new policy of non-intervention culminated in the decision to permit medical assistance to be provided by the families once the strikers were no longer able to object.

Yet, even as Northern Ireland's Department of Health embraced the protocols and ethics of the new policy, there was still "so much that was unknown," as historian Ian Miller explains. "Physiological knowledge of human starvation was relatively uninformed . . . lacking a full understanding of how the human body wastes away without food or intricate matters of under-nutrition."[61] After seventy years of prison hunger strikes in Ireland and Britain, with robust use of medical monitoring and invasive intervention, how was it possible that the medical knowledge of human starvation and its consequences was so limited and underdeveloped?

EIGHT

Biomedical Technologies, Medical Ethics, and the Management of Hunger Strikers

IN THE LAST DECADE OF THE TWENTIETH CENTURY, the century-long medical implementation of instruments and substances that cast forcible feeding as the carceral protocol to hunger striking was torqued and calibrated in the service of human metabolic research and then implemented in medical management protocols. While caring for hunger-striking prisoners who had been transferred to hospitals in 1989, South African university physicians documented clinical research of adult male metabolism under prolonged starvation and recovery. The metabolic functioning and care protocols they developed for managing individual bodies could also be applied more broadly and abstractly as population-wide norms. From their research, prosthetic devices, technologies, and artificial nutrition became combined into standardized protocols in a process called *biopolitics* or *biopower* by renowned philosopher and historian Michel Foucault. With these terms he draws attention to a rationality of governing modern society that "endeavors to administer, optimize and multiply" life and is dispersed across society through networks of professionals intervening in every institution to foster life and health.[1]

When this life-extending medical knowledge and protocols migrated from the hospital to the prison setting, however, they were expanded into new ways to deprive the prisoner of human dignity in the context of artificial feeding. This dehumanization in the guise of life preservation was implemented in many carceral locations in the twenty-first century, including sites in Israel and India, U.S. prisons, immigration detention, and the detention camp at U.S. Naval Station Guantánamo Bay (hereafter "Guantánamo").

In this chapter, we will see how, in the twenty-first century, the physician's responsibility becomes positioned in the battle between prison power and the prisoner's voice in a double-edged manner. On one hand, the physician's responsibility in patient-centered care and ethics could benefit the prisoner. On the other hand, the prison's power became even more ruthless in harnessing biomedical technology for its own purposes, keeping the striker alive through force-feeding and maintaining unmistakable authority over the prisoner.

Prison power in its most intensive forms suppresses the prisoners' voices, making them bereft of the social and political recognition necessary for human dignity. Prisoners repeatedly express how they are being treated as less than human, as an animal, or as the "living dead." In expressing what they perceive and feel, they show their aliveness, their sentience, as an assurance to themselves, to each other, and to the agents of the prison's power, even as they recognize that their bodies are made into objects to fit biomedical technologies and protocols.

These experiences were heightened after the late twentieth century, when administrative detention flourished as states captured and held those who threatened their security, branding them as enemies, threats, and terrorists whose incarceration did not require a judicial hearing. State security demands snaked into the protocols of punitive capture and control over the body and life of detainees, irrespective of their claims for human rights. These experiences raised the fundamental question of what civil liberties and rights noncitizens had if the security state branded them a threat. Moreover, if the justification for incarceration was protection of citizens, could the people rise and demand another way, an alternative to the coercive force being used in their name?

Also in the twenty-first century, as digital and visual media proliferated, journalists, artists, and activists used these media to explore the biomedicalization of hunger striking and force-feeding. The hunger strike form was repurposed to show the objectification of humans in prison and gain the attention of the public. Commissioned by media companies and human rights organizations, video artists, animators, graphic artists, and photographers animated the prisoners' resistance, finding new ways to convey the prisoner's agony in a visceral punch that ricocheted ceaselessly in the media, provoking viewers and listeners worldwide to reckon with the inhumanity of the prisoner's battle with the biomedical management of feeding. When these public feelings turned into outrage and protest on behalf of the force-fed hunger-striking prisoner, the public uprisings confronted the imperatives of security states head on.

During the 1989 mass hunger strike in South Africa, as striking detainees were sent to urban and university hospitals for care, physicians had the opportunity to study long-term fasting and its effects, as well as develop new medical protocols of ethics and care to manage that condition, modeled after the World Medical Association's (WMA) Declaration of Tokyo. The first step was to remove the shackles from detainees who were chained to their beds and guarded by police, thereby recognizing them as patients in a hospital, not prisoners in detention. The second step was to cultivate the patients' trust and confidentiality. The third step was to keep the patients informed of their health and care options, respecting their choices. The WMA guidelines encouraged medical staff to tend to the patients' expressed care needs without prioritizing forcible feeding or pressuring them to stop fasting. Rather, persuading patients to eat on their own was the goal.[2]

As the hunger striking persisted for years after 1989, the South African government became obliged to negotiate with the physicians at hospitals and university medical centers, rather than unilaterally dumping hunger-striking prisoners into hospitals when their health deteriorated dangerously, marking an abrupt change from the government's culture of secrecy and total authority over prisoners. The university physicians sought to apply standard care protocols and definitions for assessing a hunger-striking patient. The regime in prison changed as well. No longer would a prisoner's verbal declaration—smuggled out to the public—or vague records of guards' observations be sufficient. These gave way to a systematic and normative accounting of the number of missed meals, the number of days without food, the amount of food intake, the amount of weight lost, and an inventory of symptoms of bodily distress or metabolic derangement. Before 1989, South African prison authorities would report a hunger strike only after the person had not eaten for five days. Now Dr. William Kalk, a university physician and leader in ethical treatment protocols, recommended that a 10 percent loss of body weight should trigger hospitalization and medical monitoring, and that a 15 percent loss of body weight necessitated transferring the patient, with consent, to a high-care hospital.[3]

In the 1990s, with the hospitalization over time of multiple fresh groups of hunger strikers, physicians had the opportunity to gather medical data to better understand the physiological and psychological effects of prolonged fasting. Because many prisoners were transferred to the hospital after only a few days of hunger striking, the physicians could study even the early phases of fasting. In one of the first peer-reviewed clinical studies of the physiology and psychology of hunger striking, Dr. Kalk and his colleague Yosuf Veriava documented, with patient consent, the medical histories of thirty-three hunger strikers. Their study offered a more acute medical understanding of the bodily processes of starvation and renourishment than had previously been available.[4]

Kalk and Veriava's study documented how, during the first few days of a fast, the body consumes its stores of glycogen in the liver and muscle, causing substantial weight loss. As the fasting continues, the body conserves muscle and breaks down fat, releasing ketones as the main energy source. After the second week, the body enters "starvation mode" and then "mines" nutrients from the muscles, bone marrow, and vital organs, impairing their function. During these two weeks, hunger strikers report feeling "faint and dizzy" and are often confined to bed.[5] Documenting the prisoners' metabolic deficiencies resulted in data about mineral depletion, impaired thyroid function, and suppressed insulin secretion accompanied by weakness, feeling cold, abdominal pain, and dehydration.

The research reaffirmed that thirst and hunger are diminished during prolonged fasting. It also quantified the extent of clinical depression and post-traumatic stress after prolonged fasting, with 77 percent of the prisoners exhibiting symptoms measured by independent psychiatrists. Processes that could prolong life both during fasting and afterward received scientific scrutiny, such as the experiential knowledge of fasters that they must continue to take fluids with added salt. This informal knowledge became converted into medical guidance that recommended the consumption of 1.5 liters of water per day, supplemented by half a teaspoon of salt.[6]

Kalk and Veriava's research also advanced the understanding of the hazards involved in refeeding. An inappropriate pace and type of refeeding can precipitate potentially lethal physiological conditions, the worst being cardiac failure, convulsions, or coma. Kalk recommended that patients who stop fasting should remain under hospital care for a full week, with close monitoring of their blood biochemistry, while taking oral supplements of key vitamins and minerals. Patients who have been starved for some time often experience gastrointestinal disturbance during refeeding, in particular abdominal pain, reflux symptoms, nausea, and diarrhea.[7]

This data set on metabolic functioning during and after fasting aided in the establishment of biomedical management procedures for hunger strikers across the globe. However, these protocols would be implemented differently in prison settings than in hospitals.

In 1975 the World Medical Association issued professional guidance to help physicians under pressure from their governments refuse to participate in practices construed as "cruel, inhuman and degrading treatment." The WMA's Declaration of Tokyo offered three interrelated principles clarifying the physician's role when treating a hunger striker: first, the physician has exclusive authority to appraise the prisoner's state of mind; second, the fasting prisoner's capacity to form "an unimpaired and rational judgement concerning the consequences . . . of a voluntary refusal of nourishment" should be assessed; and third, if the criteria for unimpaired judgment are met, the physician should not artificially feed the prisoner.[8]

Fourteen years later, in 1989, the WMA again took up the topic of physicians managing hunger-striking prisoners, drawing in part upon the research by South African and European medical leaders. Over two years of meetings, the WMA drafted another declaration focused specifically on the ethics of managing hunger strikers, which was approved by the World Medical General Assembly in Malta in November 1991. The Malta Declaration defined a hunger striker as a "mentally competent person who has indicated that he has decided to embark on a hunger strike and has refused to take food and/or liquids for a significant interval." Both competency and intention distinguished a hunger striker from a case of suicide or anorexia, a point the WMA had debated. The declaration's preamble framed the values conflict between the physician's oath to preserve the sanctity of life and exercise "skills to save life," and his or her duty to respect a patient's autonomy.[9]

Yet the WMA's care guidelines also placed squarely on the shoulders of the physician the choice of what to do when a "hunger striker who has issued clear instructions not to be resuscitated lapses into a coma and is about to die." The WMA left this decision up to the doctor's exclusive judgment, prevailing over the authority of government officials and pulling that authority away from the patient: "When the hunger striker has become confused and is unable to make an unimpaired decision or has lapsed into a coma, the doctor shall be free to make the decision for his patient as to the further treatment which he considers to be in the best interest of that patient, always taking into account the decision he has arrived at during his preceding care of the patient during the hunger strike."[10]

The medical authority to make that decision was to be backed by regular patient exams and the patient's medical history. Physicians were advised to maintain clear communication with the hunger striker, using an interpreter's services when necessary. A daily checklist for meeting with patients included inquiring about the patient's health and the status of his or her strike, informing the patient about the health consequences of continuing to fast, and confidentially recording all decisions. The declaration forbade physicians from pressuring a patient or withholding treatment to make the patient suspend his or her strike. And patient care was defined beyond force-feeding to include treating infections, advising increased water intake, and administering a saline drip as a "respectful" medical intervention if undertaken with "patient approval."

Although both declarations insisted that the physician should respect the hunger striker's wishes, the Malta Declaration's allowance for feeding unconscious hunger strikers exposed physicians to greater pressure from prison authorities, governments, and public criticism. The British Medical Association submitted to the WMA concerns about the Turkish government punishing doctors who refused to force-feed prisoners based on "the erroneous perception that the WMA Declaration of Malta (unlike its Tokyo Declaration) permits force-feeding once the prisoner is unconscious." The Declaration of Malta softened the earlier declaration's hard-line stance against force-feeding and, in so doing, increased prison authorities' pressure on physicians to intervene.[11]

Fifteen years later, in October 2006, following international condemnation of U.S. military force-feeding in Guantánamo, the WMA revised the 1991 Declaration of Malta to unequivocally protect both hunger strikers and physicians from government coercion: "Forcible feeding is never ethically acceptable. Even if intended to benefit, feeding accompanied by threats, coercion, force or use of physical restraints is a form of inhuman and degrading treatment. Equally unacceptable is the forced feeding of some detainees in order to intimidate or coerce other hunger strikers to stop fasting."[12]

SUSPENDING RIGHTS IN U.S. PRISONS

As an international umbrella organization of national medical associations, the WMA could expect that its guidance would apply to all settings where a physician would be involved—hospitals, prisons, the military, and detention centers. However, the WMA had no power to dictate or implement, so nation-states could choose to evade its guidelines. As early as the 1980s, the Federal Bureau of Prisons interpreted the Declaration of Tokyo as inapplicable, according to a Northern Ireland prison official who toured U.S. federal prisons in 1984. He wrote that "a prisoner has . . . *forfeited the right of a citizen at liberty* to refuse medical treatment where he is deliberately putting his own life at risk, particularly where the purpose of the refusal of food is to put pressure on the authorities."[13] Administrative procedure, backed by law, could extract rights from the prisoners, making them relatively rightless persons.

The U.S. federal prison system's 1980s regulations determined who a hunger striker was and what punitive and control measures could be taken on the striker's body. A hunger striker was defined as a prisoner who either self-declared that he or she had not eaten, or was observed by guards not to have eaten, for seventy-two hours, a description that triggered a medical evaluation. Medical professionals were instructed to regularly weigh the hunger striker, monitor vital signs, test blood and urine, and perform psychological exams. A hunger striker could be consigned to solitary detention to break the person's resolve and foil attempts "to gain attention" or foment emulation. Surveillance of their eating increased. Guards confiscated any personal food items in the prisoner's cell, and served the prisoner three meal trays per day, inspecting the contents afterward for any evidence of consumption.[14]

In June 1994, the Bureau of Prisons amended its protocols to specify the conditions for "forced medical treatment," championing the physician's sovereign decision-making after the Malta Declaration. A physician who determined that a prisoner's health or life is in jeopardy should persuade the prisoner to receive artificial feeding, and should document efforts to explain the risks involved if the prisoner refuses. Physicians alone were authorized to treat prisoners without their consent.[15]

A decade later, the purview of these rules was expanded into every jurisdiction of federal prison power. On July 29, 2005, Bureau of Prisons Director Harley Lappin issued a memorandum that expanded the "medical and administrative management of inmates who engage in hunger strikes" to include "pretrial and holdover inmates and ICE Detainees" as well as prisoners held at Guantánamo. The guidance to administer "involuntary medical treatment" was both medical and legal under federal authority. The memorandum detailed the procedure for inserting a nasogastric tube for feeding and also the authorizations required for various procedures—medical authorization for an intravenous drip; a court order review and hospitalization for tube feeding through the stomach; and, in all cases, prior to medical intervention, contacting the regional prison counsel, who would communicate with the U.S. attorney.[16] Hunger striking in the federal prison system now triggered a repertoire of biomedical management that required legal notification.

MANAGING HUNGER STRIKERS AT GUANTÁNAMO

On February 27, 2002, ten weeks after the Guantánamo Bay naval base was authorized as the new detention center for prisoners of the U.S. War on Terror, the first coordinated hunger strike by prisoners at Guantánamo began. The hunger strike followed two incidents: on the Muslim holy day of Eid al-Adha, a prisoner accused a guard of kicking his copy of the Koran, and some days later, a guard forcefully removed a prisoner's makeshift turban during midday prayers. Within days, the guards tallied hundreds of missed meals. Marine Corps Brigadier General Michael Lehnert, who was in command, found the hunger strikes "unnerving." He recalled years later, in an interview, "You don't want to give it too much attention . . . because then it will cause everyone to go on hunger strike . . . but at the same time I was very concerned about the physical aspects of it." He visited the hunger strikers and acceded to their demands for allowing makeshift head coverings when praying, supplying prisoners with prayer caps, and disciplining abusive guards. He persuaded most of the strikers to halt within fourteen days.[17]

In mid-June 2005, prisoners began another hunger strike to call for better living conditions in the prison, more respectful treatment of the Koran by guards, and fair trials. Unlike in 2002, there was now an avenue for the prisoners to filter their experiences to the public through their attorneys. In 2004, the U.S. Supreme Court in *Rasul v. Bush* had granted Guantánamo detainees habeas corpus rights, which allowed lawyers to visit and represent prisoners and for their detention to be legally reviewed.

In August 2005, Bisher al-Rawi, an Iraqi-British prisoner who had been detained by the CIA while on a business trip to Gambia, sent a communication securely to his attorney, Clive Stafford Smith, who received it a month later. Since the communication was sent via Guantánamo officials, al-Rawi very likely believed that it would be read by U.S. military officials and be censored before reaching his attorney.

In the document, al-Rawi relates his experiences while enduring the monthlong hunger strike. In the middle of the night he was "always wide awake going through memories, some happy, some sad. It all flows back to this dismal and depressing reality ... this new existence [that] is the food strike. It has me live in the shadows where one can't quite feel alive, but one does not die. It is a very strange existence." In this limbo between living and dying, al-Rawi wrote of his empathy for the "feelings and emotions of the poor and millions of human beings who are starving through the world. Pictures in mind of the starving men, women and children which I have seen through the years, now all make sense. Now I understand what deprivation really means, why people fight and kill each other over food." Al-Rawi's reflections bolstered his spiritual strength. "Despite my weakness and the helplessness that I feel during the days, I am determined to survive this and think this is my biggest struggle in jail. Just like the whole experience has been a self-discovery full of pain and sadness, full of desperation and hope." Raising his struggle in prison to a transcendent plane, he beseeched "God that this last episode will not break me but will help me be the best and most I can both be here and when I get out. It'll be a valid and precious asset that will always be by my side."[18]

As the hunger strikers grew in number, significant demands were put on the Guantánamo medical staff. As they began to tube-feed the hunger strikers, additional military nurses, psychologists, and orderlies were flown in from Florida and Missouri. According to Captain John S. Edmondson, an emergency physician and commander of the medical group that administered the prisoners' care, the additional staff were "screened" before arriving "to ensure that they [did] not have ethical objections to assisted feeding."[19]

By September 11, the four-year anniversary of the 9/11 attacks, 131 prisoners had refused meals for at least three days and a core group had been fasting for months. By the end of September, nearly two hundred prisoners were on hunger strike, and more than twenty were being force-fed. Guantánamo medical authorities attempted to placate the detainees, as well as lawyers, physicians, and critics outside the camp, by saying that "involuntary feeding" was authorized by "lawful order of a higher military authority" and that the procedure followed protocols developed by the Bureau of Prisons.[20] One detainee, Yussef al-Shihri, began his hunger strike on August 11 and was fed enterally beginning on August 25. On October 1, after meeting with his lawyer earlier in the day, he removed his feeding tube, which was ordinarily implanted for the week. He incited seven other detainees to do the same, saying that his lawyer had advised that the government does not have the right to force-feed them. When he returned to his cell block without his feeding tube, he was offered food and water, which he refused. After two days of still refusing to eat, al-Shihri was returned to the feeding block to be rehydrated intravenously and to resume enteral feeding.

The protocols of the Bureau of Prisons allowed medical staff to experiment with the technologies of force-feeding. Captain Edmondson confirmed that the staff had used larger nasal tubes, 4.8 millimeters in diameter, which were permitted for higher-volume feeding to shorten feeding times and reduce the number of feedings per person by feeding more per session. After two days of prisoners protesting acute pain from the larger tubes, they returned to using three-millimeter tubes, which "are soft and flexible, and are in common use as nasogastric tubes in hospitals throughout the United States."[21]

In January 2006, a new device was introduced to facilitate forcible feeding: the safety restraint chair. The chair is described by its inventor, a former Iowa sheriff whose jailer had been injured by a prisoner, as a "padded cell on wheels."[22] The naval base ordered at least twenty-five of these chairs. The prisoner is strapped into the chair with a six-point restraint system—head, torso, hands, and feet. The chair had been designed to transport a resisting prisoner, not for medical treatment or for punishment. However, the record of the chairs' use in U.S. prisons was littered with controversy and litigation regarding abuse and fatality. Even so, the U.S. military was ready to deploy them at Guantánamo to immobilize prisoners during force-feeding.[23]

Detainee Emad Hassan's description of the chair made its way through his lawyer to the New York Times: "The head is immobilized by a strap so it can't be moved, their hands are cuffed to the chair and the legs are shackled." The medical orderlies then question the hunger striker: "'Are you going to eat or not?' and if not, they insert the tube." Hassan stressed the callous and gloating behavior of the orderlies and the vicious spiral of humiliation and infantilization that the hunger strikers experienced daily: "People have been urinating and defecating on themselves in these feedings and vomiting and bleeding. They ask to be allowed to go to the bathroom, but they will not let them go. They have sometimes put diapers on them."[24]

One anonymous official disclosed to a reporter that Guantánamo officials regarded force-feeding as a precaution to avoid the notoriety of a prisoner death. "We don't want a Bobby Sands," the official said. "The worst case would be to have someone go from zero to hero."[25] Resurrecting the analogy of hunger striking to intentional suicide, which the WMA had debated, Dr. William Winkenwerder Jr., then assistant director of defense for health affairs, justified the use of both bodily restraint and forcible feeding at Guantánamo as a "moral question": "Do you allow a person to commit suicide? Or do you take steps to protect their health and preserve their life?"[26]

Being force-fed to be kept alive overrides an individual's capacity to persevere in his or her being—an imperative that the philosopher Spinoza recognized all conscious beings as having, even under the harshest constraints.[27] Hunger strikers at Guantánamo continued their effort to reclaim that imperative by finding new ways to fight back. By 2007 they were using force-feeding itself as a territory for protest, finding ways to suck on their feeding tubes to siphon the contents from their stomach or simply to vomit after being fed. On February 27, Yemeni hunger striker Adnan Farhan Abdul Latif reportedly told his lawyer: "My wish is to die. We are living in a dying situation." In a poem, he described the prison guards as "artists of torture, pain, fatigue, insults and humiliation." Even so, the strikers understood that their protest was symbolic, given that they clearly would not be allowed to die.[28]

THE REEMERGENCE OF RECTAL FEEDING IN CIA BLACK SITES

Beginning in March 2009, the U.S. Senate Intelligence Committee inquired into the torture treatments across the archipelago of top-secret "black sites" run across the globe from 2002 to 2006, where the CIA interrogated captives of the War on Terror. Released in December 2014, after years of delay and secrecy, the committee's more than six-thousand-page report, disputed by CIA leaders and heavily redacted, received wide international press coverage. It revealed the widespread use of notorious torture techniques to combat hunger strikes, including rectal feeding.

This objectifying technology took on new, euphemistic names in this new context. In 2003, the chief of interrogations at Detention Site Cobalt ordered the "rectal rehydration" of Khalid Sheikh Mohammed, an alleged suspect in the September 11 attacks, "without a determination of medical need." This procedure was among an extensive range of "enhanced interrogation techniques" that Mohammed experienced even after being subjected to facial and abdominal slaps, facial grabs, stress positions, standing sleep deprivation (with his hands at or above head level), nudity and water dousing, and being waterboarded 183 times.[29]

According to the report, CIA officers opted for rectal feeding for its leverage in behavior control over "safe and effective" intravenous feeding for emergency hydration when a prisoner refused water as well as food. One said the best way to insert the "rectal tube" was to "place it and open up the IV tubing" so that the "flow will self-regulate, sloshing up the large intestines. . . . No need to squeeze the bag—let gravity do the work."[30]

The report revealed that in March 2004 Majid Khan, a Pakistani detainee and legal U.S. resident, was also subjected to this indignity. Khan had gone on hunger strike several times during interrogations at various secret detention centers in the Middle East and Europe, and was later transferred to Guantánamo. CIA records showed that Khan cooperated with the tube and intravenous feedings and willingly took Ensure (a brand of nutritional shake) to rehydrate. However, after three weeks, the CIA implemented "a more aggressive treatment regimen," subjecting Khan "to involuntary rectal feeding and rectal hydration." Later the same day, interrogation officers administered a "lunch tray" enema to Khan that consisted "of hummus, pasta with sauce, nuts and raisins [that were] pureed and rectally infused." The Senate report concluded that this treatment was intentional humiliation and torture. An unnamed CIA officer quoted in the report said the enemas helped to "clear a person's head," suggesting that the detainee was more amenable to cooperating afterward, while a chief of interrogation characterized the procedure as a demonstration of "total control over the detainee."[31]

Responding to the report, Dr. Vincent Iacopino, senior medical advisor for Physicians for Human Rights, stated that the procedure was medically unjustifiable: "There is no clinical indication to use rectal rehydration and feeding over oral or intravenous administration of fluids and nutrients."[32] After CIA Director Michael Hayden declared on CNN that rectal feeding was an authorized medical procedure, Senator Dianne Feinstein, as chair of the Senate Intelligence Committee, disputed his claims, arguing that that ample evidence showed it was intended to violate detainees. She concluded that it was neither a "medical procedure" nor approved by the "Justice Department's Office of Legal Counsel as an authorized interrogation technique." Dr. Iacopino bluntly concluded that "this is a form of sexual assault masquerading as medical treatment. In the absence of medical necessity, it is clear that the only purpose behind this humiliating and invasive procedure is to inflict physical and mental pain."[33]

The U.S. Senate committee waited years to release the redacted report, and the Department of Justice investigation ended without any prosecutions.

In January 2009, President Obama signed an executive order banning the operation of "black sites" and withdrew permission for "enhanced interrogation techniques." However, neither the Senate report nor subsequent congressional legislation made the practices illegal or put decisive restraints on CIA, FBI, and military operatives or executive branch authorities using them in the future.

BROADCASTING PERSONAL AGONY FROM GUANTÁNAMO

In April 2013 news leaked out, again through attorneys—this time through the London-based legal assistance charity Reprieve—that more than half of the prisoners still at Guantánamo were on hunger strike. Despite denying it at first, military spokespersons admitted that 104 of the 166 detainees were on hunger strike, and 44 of the strikers were being force-fed. Attorney Clive Stafford Smith, director and founder of Reprieve, after learning of the hunger strike, had started visiting his Guantánamo clients regularly. Interviews were tightly regulated, and audio recording was not allowed, so Smith scribbled down notes once he had left the base. His notes from conversations with two prisoners were transcribed, translated, and edited to appear as editorials authored by the prisoners themselves—the one by Shaker Aamer in the UK *Observer* and the one by Samir Naji al Hasan Moqbel in the *New York Times*.

Aamer had lived in the United States in his late teens and had served as a U.S. Army translator in the Gulf War in 1991. In 1996 he moved to Britain, where he married and had four children. By December 2001 he had moved his family to Afghanistan and was working for an Islamic charity. The U.S. military, alleging that Aamer was an Al Qaeda recruiter and financier, captured and remanded him to Guantánamo in 2002. His translation skills enabled him to serve as an unofficial spokesman for other prisoners. Aamer had participated in the 2005 hunger strike, negotiating with camp commanders for improved conditions and treatment. He had also participated in several subsequent hunger strikes. His editorial was titled "I Want to Hug My Children and Watch Them as They Grow."[34]

In the editorial, Aamer said he had been on "hunger strike for more than 60 days now. I have lost nearly a quarter of my body weight. I barely notice all of my medical ailments any more—the back pain from the beatings

I have taken, the rheumatism from the frigid air conditioning, the asthma exacerbated by the toxic sprays they use to abuse us. There is an endless list. And now, 24/7 (as the Americans say), I have the ache of hunger." He asked, "Have you ever tried going without food for 24 hours? Today, I am on my 68th day. But a man in my block has been on strike since 2005. Can you imagine it? He's only alive today because the Americans force-feed him, preventing him from making that ultimate statement of principle, the same one they have on their New Hampshire license plates: 'Give me freedom, or give me death.'"[35]

In his article, "Gitmo Is Killing Me," Moqbel, a Yemeni man imprisoned at Guantánamo since 2002, commented that he had spent over a decade in detention without a charge. He had been on hunger strike since February 2013 and had lost over thirty pounds. "I will not eat until they restore my dignity," he said. He painted a vivid, detailed description of the dystopic "care" he received. He would "never forget the first time they passed the feeding tube up my nose." As the tube was "thrust in, it made me feel like throwing up. I wanted to vomit, but I couldn't. There was agony in my chest, throat and stomach. I had never experienced such pain before. I would not wish this cruel punishment upon anyone." He explained how his body was constrained: "Two times a day they tie me to a chair in my cell. My arms, legs, and head are strapped down. I never know when they will come. Sometimes they come during the night, as late as 11 P.M., when I'm sleeping." The scale of the mass hunger strike had outstripped the capacity of the nursing personnel at Guantánamo: "There are so many of us on hunger strike now that there aren't enough qualified medical staff members to carry out the force-feedings; nothing is happening at regular intervals. They are feeding people around the clock just to keep up."[36]

While doctors and nurses supervised, the feedings were generally carried out by navy corpsmen—enlisted sailors who are specialized medical assistants—once guards had brought the hunger striker from his cell and shackled him into a restraint chair. In the weeks after the testimonials were published, the U.S. military sent dozens more navy nurses and corpsmen to Guantánamo, increasing the prison's military medical staff to nearly 140—a nearly one-to-one ratio of prisoners to health providers. Meanwhile, professional medical associations persisted in disputing the ethics of force-feeding prisoners. Dr. Jeremy Lazarus, president of the American Medical Association, advised in a letter to Defense Secretary Chuck Hagel that "every

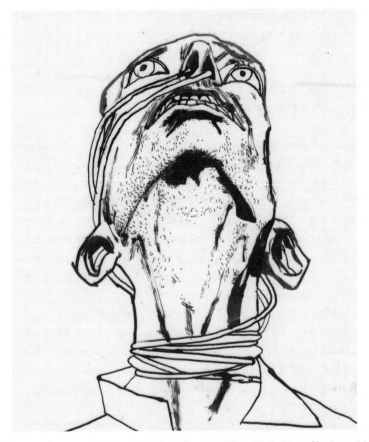

FIGURE 16. Illustration by Matt Rota for "Gitmo Is Killing Me," an op-ed by Samir Naji al Hasan Moqbel, *New York Times,* April 14, 2013. Courtesy of Matt Rota.

competent patient has the right to refuse medical intervention, including life-sustaining interventions."[37]

From the 1970s onward, the importance of patient rights and patient consent had been promoted by patients and their advocates for all kinds of medical treatments and research. However, government inquiries continued to expose how physicians' ethics and responsibility for the patient had been manipulatable, selective, and not responsive to patient care preferences. In the WMA protocols and national medical associations, physicians carved out their authority and sovereignty over patient well-being. Prison regimes were no less cunning in dictating protocols for medical personnel that bypassed the feelings and needs of the prisoner to ensure order and control over the prisoners in their custody.

THE "STANDARD OPERATING PROCEDURE" AND THE RISE OF BIOPOLITICAL ALGORITHMS

During the wave of hunger strikes at Guantánamo in 2013, the procedure manual for force-feeding detainees used at Guantánamo was leaked to the press, perhaps purposively to demonstrate, to a doubting public, the professionalism of the U.S. military's medical procedures. The document, titled "Standard Operating Procedure: Medical Management of Detainees on Hunger Strike" (SOP), drawing from policy used in U.S. federal and military prisons, delineated protocols for diagnosing hunger strikes and for administering enteral feeding. The Department of Defense and the Joint Task Force Guantánamo Bay coauthored the SOP to "protect, preserve, and promote life" and specifically to prevent "any serious adverse health effects and death from hunger strikes." It directed the Joint Medical Group staff at Guantánamo to make "reasonable efforts to obtain [a prisoner's] voluntary consent for medical treatment." However, diagnostic and treatment protocols outlined enteral feeding exclusively as the necessary response to the refusal to eat and as imperative to "preserve health and life," irrespective of "consent from the detainee."[38]

Michel Foucault coined the word *biopower* to account for the shift in modern power toward administering "life" at the level of the population: "to ensure, sustain, and multiply life, to put this life in order" through a mesh of material coercions to either "foster life or disallow it to the point of death."[39] German sociologist Thomas Lemke concurred that "'life' has become an independent, objective, and measurable factor."[40] In the case of hunger striking, medical management measures how long the average adult human body can survive without food, and then calibrates techniques and volume of refeeding to restore nutrients necessary for metabolic functioning and to forestall damage to organs and vital systems. "Life" is thus extracted and externalized as a metabolic functionality that can be measured, calculated, made workable, and remedied. And "life preservation" develops as technologies of discipline and control that can be externalized and manipulated to ensure the extension of life at the behest of the state, despite the patient's will.[41]

The SOP exemplified biopolitical practice par excellence. It offered an "algorithm" for distinguishing between someone refusing food occasionally and someone on a hunger strike by calibrating the number of meals missed and the person's caloric intake and bodily measurements. Refusing nine consecutive meals (each meal defined as the consumption of 500 calories) constituted a hunger strike. Two eight-fluid-ounce containers of Ensure could substitute for a regular meal. The SOP included a form called the "Medical Management and Evaluation of Hunger Striker" to inventory missed meals and record "intake (food/fluids) history," alongside documentation of the person's vital signs, weight, and ideal body weight (calculated based on general population averages). The loss of 15 percent of ideal body weight could trigger "involuntary medical treatment."[42]

The algorithmic approach shifted the ground of treatment for hunger strikers from the ethical guidelines expressed in the Tokyo and Malta declarations to a system of institutional logics. This approach emptied the prisoner's protest of its political purpose and ignored its context: prison coercion and denial of legal process. It was an attempt to reframe hunger striking and force-feeding in biomedical terms rather than as a political decision that requires an ethical response from physicians and nurses.

The SOP recommended initiating, three to five days after enteral feeding had begun, daily urinalysis and a blood serum basic metabolic profile, as well as lab tests for liver function and magnesium, phosphate, and calcium levels. After receiving "sufficient caloric intake" for three days, the detainee was removed from the hunger strike list and transferred from the detention hospital to a "feeding" block for further regular feeding and monitoring.[43]

The SOP's menu for enteral nutrition recommended Pulmocare, an Abbott Labs product that is "halal, kosher, gluten-free," and designed to provide high-calorie nutrition to people with chronic obstructive pulmonary disease, cystic fibrosis, or respiratory failure. Daily increases in Pulmocare were supplemented with Morton's salt substitute in order to provide 2,300 milligrams (mg) of potassium, 2,000 mg of chloride, and 2,300 mg of sodium. Over the next several days, the recommended dosage, water mixture, and pace of infusion were increased in order to steadily increase the person's caloric intake to 1,500 calories per day (the equivalent of four cans of Ensure Plus or Nestlé's Boost Plus with nutrient supplements). Liquid Centrum was added to meet minimum requirements for vitamins and minerals. A repertoire of over-the-counter medications and dosage was recommended to combat possible symptoms during the feeding, including pain, headache, indigestion, heartburn, postnasal drip, and nausea.[44]

The detainees' strategies of questioning, interrupting, or disrupting the standardized procedures by attempting to slow the flow of the feeding solution, direct the order of ingredients, use the toilet during feeding, or express pain and nausea were met with tailored responses designed to ensure that the staff was responding in a "safe, humane and consistent manner" while preventing the detainees from gaining a "measure of control over an involuntary process."[45] The person being fed was thus rendered apolitical and incompetent, as someone upon whom care regimens must be imposed.

Force-feeding dozens of resistant prisoners a day posed a massive challenge for the medical staff. Instances of staff members refusing participation were rarely publicized. However, in 2014, an unnamed navy nurse who had eighteen years of active-duty service as a sailor, nurse, and commissioned officer, refused to force-feed Guantánamo prisoners.[46] He was relieved of his duties and faced disciplinary hearings.[47]

His refusal drew national attention and garnered professional, political, and ethical support. One nurse, reflecting on the International Council of Nurses code of ethics, declared: "The force-feeding at Guantanamo is not in the interest of the patient, but of the imprisoning state. Reading the ICN code, I cannot find anything about nurses having a responsibility to protect the interests of the state."[48] The American Nursing Association and Senator Feinstein backed the nurse's refusal and called for ending the "unnecessary force-feedings of detainees at Guantánamo Bay."[49]

In a rare interview with a Guantánamo staff person, Daniel Lakemacher, a former mental health technician assigned to the behavioral health unit at Guantánamo, commented that repeated force-feeding sessions were "far and away the most dehumanizing thing I've actually seen with my own eyes in my entire life."[50]

VIEWING FORCIBLE FEEDING IN DIGITAL MEDIA

From the time of the British suffragists in 1909, prisons and governments had prohibited the photographic depiction of an actual tube feeding of an imprisoned hunger striker. Visual representations were available to the public only through imagined depictions in drawings or as dramatized in films about the British and American suffragists or the Irish Republicans. The U.S.

government, however, introduced the possibility of videotape documentation, as recommended in the Lappin memorandum. The purpose was to document both refusals to comply with feeding and the benevolent use of force, as in forcible cell extractions, in which a specially trained team used body shields, tasers, and other chemical and nonlethal weapons to remove a restive prisoner from his cell, often for medical treatment.

These videotapes remained unknown to the public until the 2014 federal court case of Guantánamo hunger striker Abu Wa'el Dhiab, a Syrian national who was still detained despite being cleared for release in 2009, to block his being force-fed during the Ramadan holiday. During Dhiab's trial, the U.S. government revealed that it had extensive videotape evidence of Dhiab's being forcibly extracted from his cell and then force-fed. At the defense attorneys' insistence, the court had acquired the tapes, which Judge Gladys Kessler, along with federal prosecutors and defense attorneys, viewed in closed session. These twenty-eight videos of Dhiab were filmed at the height of the mass hunger strike in April 2013, when nearly a hundred prisoners were receiving the same treatment.

In June 2014, a coalition of sixteen news media organizations requested that the videotapes be unsealed and made public under the First Amendment. In October 2015, Judge Kessler ruled that the U.S. government must release redacted versions of the tapes. Her ruling championed public oversight of government action while rejecting the government's "fears and speculations" that releasing the videos would incite extremist groups to violence against U.S. personnel and lead detainees to develop countermeasures to forcible cell extractions, resulting in more frequent forcible extractions.[51]

Ironically, it was the international outcry over medical ethics violations that had encouraged the secret digital documentation of cell extractions and forcible feeding; the military had expected that these recordings would monitor the consistent use of "safe" and "humane" procedures in Guantánamo. The government had no intention of sharing them publicly, but it complied in releasing them for secretive viewing in federal court, and likely in closed-door congressional hearings.

However, the Obama administration feared that making the videotapes' contents, specifically the forcible extractions, public would undermine the government's claims of humane treatment. In January 2016 the U.S. government appealed Judge Kessler's ruling, and in March 2017 a three-judge U.S. appeals court ruled in favor of the government's position that releasing the videotapes posed a national security risk. Judge A. Raymond Randolph wrote

FIGURE 17. Activists participating in Witness Against Torture's "Fast for Justice," Washington, D.C., January 2013. Protester Molly Kafka reads a poem by Sudanese journalist and Guantánamo detainee Sami al-Hajj. Photograph by Justin Norman. Credit: Flickr/Witness Against Torture.

that the "images [were] more provocative than written or verbal descriptions." Jon Eisenberg, Dhiab's attorney, was dismayed, saying it was a "loss to the American people that they will never see the shocking images of force-feeding at Guantánamo Bay that a handful of lawyers have seen behind closed doors."[52] Cori Crider, attorney and strategic director for Reprieve, who had viewed the tapes of her clients being force-fed but otherwise forgotten in Guantánamo's carceral tomb, remarked that the detainees persisted in painful force-feeding out of desperation to "remind the world that they still exist and they're still human."[53]

While the question of sharing the videos publicly was ensnared in a four-year legal limbo, media companies and human rights organizations commissioned artists to reenact the experience of force-feeding, drawing from the communication of Guantánamo hunger strikers with their lawyers published in 2013. Director Asif Kapadia and Reprieve worked together to create one such video featuring the music artist Yasiin Bey (also known as Mos Def).

On camera, Bey first appears in a white room. He is dressed in a black leather jacket and jeans, and the camera roams, focusing eventually on his black designer shoes and a turquoise ring on his finger. He greets the viewer

FIGURE 18. Mos Def (Yasiin Bey) force-fed in a film shared on the *Guardian* newspaper's *YouTube* channel in 2013. Image courtesy of director Asif Kapadia.

with "Peace" and explains that he will demonstrate the experience of Guantánamo's forcible feeding as outlined in the leaked SOP document. Bey then appears in an orange jump suit and shackled. He walks to the restraint chair, and two attendants in green scrubs with blue-gloved hands restrain his hands, bare feet, and head. One attendant prepares the nasogastric tube and shoves it repeatedly up his right nostril. Bey gasps, moans, yells, and hyperventilates as tears stream down his cheeks. The attendants wrestle his head down, and another man dashes in to help hold him down. The tube is removed and reapplied. Bey turns his head away and screams, "Please, please, please! Don't, don't!" and sobs. They try again and he pleads, "No, please. Stop, stop!" and then: "This is me, please stop." We hear someone out of view say, "Stop. Stop. Stop," and the attendants stop. One puts a consoling hand on Bey's forehead, and Bey holds his face in his hands and wails, while an attendant gently rubs Bey's back. The camera fades and we are left with text: "In Guantanamo Bay, the full procedure is carried out twice a day. It takes two hours."

We see Bey next in the orange jump suit, visibly trying to recover. He thanks the crew for their work. Anguished, he says he "really didn't know what to expect" and then proceeds to explain that the tube produced a burning sensation in his nasal passages and then "it gets to be unbearable as it goes down the throat. . . . I really couldn't take it." The camera pans out to reveal the lights, a medical tray, and Bey seated in the restraint chair in the center of the antiseptic white room.[54] The entire demonstration takes less than three minutes.

A second project was even more ambitious. The *Guardian* newspaper's multimedia editor Mustafa Khalili and video producer Guy Grandjean worked with artists and journalists to create an animated video, *Guantánamo Bay: The Hunger Strikes*. Using the prisoner narratives gathered by the attorneys at Reprieve, a team of animators and sound artists created animated sequences that depicted the isolation and despair of the prison, the decision to hunger strike, and the forcible feeding, including cell extraction and the brutality of prison guards and doctors.[55] The sound design and music included the "nocturnal marching of sentries . . . used to torment detainees" and sampled Mos Def's "agonised gasps" from his video.[56] The animated video was distributed digitally on October 2013 on the *Guardian*'s website and *YouTube*.[57]

ALWAYS-VISIBLE PROSTHETICS OF FEEDING

The medical trappings of force-feeding were also made publicly visible as signifying a long-term protest hunger strike in photographs of Irom Sharmila in Imphal, the capital of the Indian state of Manipur. Photojournalists depicted Sharmila's endurance in being force-fed for a decade and a half by the mundane depiction of her wearing the permanently installed feeding tube when she appeared in public.

Sharmila's protest began with the massacre of ten civilians in the village of Malom on November 2, 2000, when Indian paramilitary opened fire in retaliation for a bomb explosion that occurred as a military convoy passed a village bus stop. Three days later, twenty-eight-year-old Sharmila, an activist and intern with Human Rights Alert who was documenting alleged abuse by Indian soldiers, began a fast outdoors near the Malom bus stop. Her purpose, beyond the tragic incident, was to denounce India's Armed Forces Special Powers Act (AFSPA) of 1958, which permitted the Indian army and paramilitary groups to search and enter homes, make arrests, and shoot on sight in order to quash antigovernment insurgencies in India's Northeast States and Kashmir. For decades Manipur activists had protested massacres by the military, as well as extrajudicial executions, tortures, rapes, and disappearances that occurred with impunity.[58]

After six days of fasting, Sharmila collapsed and was hospitalized and put on a saline drip. As she decided to persist in her hunger strike, the government arrested her, charging her with attempted suicide, an imprisonable offense in India. The arrest, intended to discourage her, only bolstered her resolve, and she vowed to fast until AFSPA was repealed. The police then threatened to force-feed her, and Sharmila's family and allies persuaded her to accept artificial feeding. Ten days later, she was "affixed with a Ryles tube used to funnel a boiled slurry of rice, lentils, and vegetables—fortified with vitamins, minerals, and medicine—through her nose and directly into her stomach. When Irom would periodically rip the tube out, she was put on an intravenous glucose drip until doctors could convince her to accept the Ryles tube again. The exact composition of her diet shifted constantly, as a medical team monitored her vitals and adjusted their dosages to keep her gastrointestinal health fair, and her weight steady at around 112 pounds."[59]

For sixteen years, Sharmila was held in isolation in the security ward of Jawaharlal Nehru Institute of Medical Sciences in Imphal and tube-fed three times a day. The authorities controlled her meetings with visitors. Once every year, the police would release her and promptly rearrest her on the same charge—a strategy that allowed them to circumvent a law against holding a prisoner before trial for over a year. The court would reimpose the yearlong sentence, and Sharmila would return to detention in the hospital, where she would again declare her hunger strike and be fed artificially.

Sharmila's nasal feeding tube became "a permanent fixture," publicly evident during her annual visits to the court. Her image while wearing this biomedical device became well known in Indian media. The Indian government allowed the feeding tube to be seen as a demonstration of the state's therapeutic and life-sustaining care of a person on suicide watch. For Sharmila, however, it offered "a visible symbol of her fight as . . . part of her identity," even as it marked the state's control over her body and life. It brought her notoriety, and through press coverage and interviews she could communicate her agenda to end the AFSPA.[60] Rather than feeding her, Sharmila wanted the Indian government to engage in dialogue with her. Journalists and supporters described Irom Sharmila as having "fielded her body as a weapon," saying that "by fasting without end, she is asserting her right to deploy her body as she sees fit."[61]

Indian journalist Minnie Vaid, interviewing Sharmila in the judge's chambers, asked if she missed food. Sharmila reframed the question into an affirmation of the sustenance she received from her faith. "God's will, I feel no appetite. Always I feel satisfied by the choice because we're not living just to eat. I just want to ask myself, 'why, how am I living here'? I feel contented."[62]

FIGURE 19. Irom Sharmila escorted by two prison guards ahead of her May 11, 2007, court appearance in New Delhi. Credit: STRDEL/AFP via Getty Images.

She acknowledged the impact of her protest on her connections with family; she had met her mother only once during her fast, fearing that seeing her mother's anguish might break her resolve. She added: "The day AFSPA is repealed I will eat rice from my mother's hand." She contrasted social and familial eating with the mechanized, calibrated biomedical feeding that the government required. "Why do they feed me? They are not my mother and father." Her rebuke was clear and simple: it was the parents' role to feed their child, not the role of the state.[63]

One doctor who attended her assured the public, in an article in the *Hindustan Times*, that Sharmila was "getting the healthiest and most balanced of diets that even the richest Indian probably is not getting." A team of five doctors, two nurses, three police women, and two medical supervisors were responsible for her care. They regularly assessed her blood, stool, and urine and adjusted her nutrient dosage if her weight changed dramatically. Though she cooperated, at times she "would pull out the nasal tube and [have] to be put on intravenous glucose drip," and doctors and prison officials would need to persuade her to continue her nose tube feeding.[64]

Because of her capacity to endure so long on force-feeding, admirers and followers came to see her as an avatar or saint.[65] Fifteen years into her hunger strike, she expressed fatigue at continuing, commenting that local Manipuris "want me to remain a deity" or a "symbol of the resistance," but she was after all "a human being who has all desires of life." She scolded the international human rights organizations for perceiving her as "if I am demanding for my right to death" and therefore "campaigning for my release without condition." To her frustration, the government, rather than considering her cause, was simply keeping her alive. "They don't bother to touch on my cause, my real hopes, which is to repeal AFSPA. [What] I really want from the world is their voice against this draconian law."[66]

Eventually the law did change. In July 2016, the Indian Supreme Court issued an interim ruling for the police and military to release details of 1,528 cases of alleged extrajudicial killings in Manipur between May 1979 and May 2012 for investigation by the government.[67] A month later, after 5,574 days of fasting, Sharmila licked a smudge of honey off her hand under the gaze of reporters, photographers, and news cameras. She ate normally, free of the biomedical trappings.

Her purpose accomplished, Irom Sharmila confessed that she ached to return to life outside the hospital ward. In particular, she wanted to marry her fiancé: "[I] can't escape human love, human emotion, and him demonstrating his love, his care for me." She wanted to lead a "normal" life—to continue her work to bring about change, but as a free person.[68]

PROTESTS IN ISRAEL

In Israel, as elsewhere, videography and photography were prohibited in prisons, so activist artists turned to graphic media to represent hunger striking to the public. One prisoner, Palestinian Khader Adnan, a member of Islamic Jihad, began a hunger strike on December 18, 2011, that was one of the longest on record, ending it after sixty-six days.[69] A Beirut-based data and media organization, Visualizing Palestine, decided to use Adnan's story to publicize the hazards of hunger strikes. Using the state's biomedical language of measurement as a tool of protest, they combined it with graphics and data about the duration and consequences of well-known hunger strikes globally to put Adnan's plight and prognosis into context.[70]

The poster, titled "Hunger Strikes," deploys a calendar that inventories symptoms, intensifying after day 14, and the daily breakdown of physiological processes of someone on an extended fast, using norms and averages

FIGURE 20. "Hunger Strikes" poster (2012), designed by Naji El Mir for Visualizing Palestine to commemorate the end of Khader Adnan's sixty-six-day hunger strike. Image courtesy of VisualizingPalestine.org.

gleaned from medical research and medical counsel. The countdown of days and consequential bodily disruption imposes a time-based sense of distress and fatality that is otherwise glossed over in verbal descriptions in the press.

The interplay in the poster between physiological symptoms and the durations of hunger strikes by world political figures, including Bobby Sands and his infamous fast unto death, offers a shared biometric scale with hunger strikes through history. The comparisons are meant to heighten Adnan's notoriety, the nobility of the Palestinians' fight against administrative detention, and the dire urgency of action by solidarity social movements and the Israeli government to avert Adnan's death.

For five decades, hunger striking was a recurrent protest strategy for imprisoned and detained Palestinians, and Israel's government was repeatedly obliged to reconsider its policies. In the 1970s and early 1980s, after several Palestinian prisoners died as a result of force-feeding practices, the Israeli government abstained from forcible feeding in its prisons and detention centers. This policy persisted even though prisoner hunger strikes flared when the government intensively used administration detention in 1996, 2004, 2008, and 2012.[71] In June 2014, however, with more than a hundred Palestinian detainees on hunger strike, Israel's Knesset took up legislation to allow forcible feeding again. In July 2015 the legislation narrowly passed. Opposing this legislation, the Israel Medical Association (IMA) published a guide in which it laid out the bioethical issues of force-feeding and the international conventions prohibiting it, and presented a model for monitoring and treating hunger strikers without using it.[72] The guide was distributed to physicians at internal medicine wards, where dozens of hunger-striking Palestinian prisoners were treated without force-feeding, some for as long as fifty days.

The Supreme Court of Israel rejected the IMA's petitions claiming that the law was in violation of the UN's Convention against Torture (1984) and Israel's Basic Law: Human Dignity and Liberty (1992), which forbids "violation of the life, body, or dignity of any person."[73] The court ruled that a hunger striker "is not an ordinary patient but a person who knowingly and willingly places himself in a dangerous situation as a protest or a means of attaining a personal or public goal." A member of the Knesset, Tamar Zandberg, scorned the court's decision: "One doesn't need the High Court in order to realize that this law is cruel, immoral, unethical, and will not be carried out by any doctor. Force-feeding is defined as abuse and is contrary to the Hippocratic Oath. The law is intended to be defiant and intimidating," to both hunger strikers and doctors. As Zandberg and Dr. Leonid Eidelman of the IMA predicted, Israeli physicians subsequently refused to undertake the medical examinations required for judges to approve force-feeding for several Palestinian hunger strikers.[74]

"Force-feeding is not an act to save detainees whose lives are in danger," wrote Zvi Bar'el, a historian and columnist of the Israeli daily *Haaretz;* it only hides the justification for administrative detention behind a "political bulletproof vest."[75] While saving the prisoner from dying of self-starvation, the state diverts attention from how it has suspended the prisoner's legal right to trial and is keeping the prisoner in custody indefinitely. The government obfuscates the purpose of the hunger strike, overrides the physician's professional ethics, and undermines legal protections for human dignity in order to uphold the abstract goal of life preservation for the rightless—a perfect illustration of the complex wrangle of biopolitics.

THE WRANGLE OF BIOPOLITICS IN U.S. COURTS

The battle between the state's biopolitical imperative and the striker's claim for dignity was fought in courts in the United States as well. While federal judges could require the release of prisoner information and diagnostic data, judicial authority could be disturbingly circumscribed when confronted with prison power buttressed by medical authority. If the courts were expected to pay attention to the prisoners' rights and consent, their decisions were in fact often decided on the basis of carceral and medical experts' definition of preserving life, despite every prisoner plea and petition to prevent the imposition of force-feeding tools.

In the summer of 2013, prisoners of all kinds in California's penitentiary system coordinated a massive hunger strike involving some thirty thousand out of a total of 133,000 inmates. Their protest was to raise awareness of the severe psychological and medical effects of long-term solitary confinement. After the initial large-scale fast, forty-five hunger strikers at the maximum-security Pelican Bay State Prison continued hunger striking for nearly six weeks. More than two thousand were in solitary confinement in Pelican Bay's notorious Security Housing Unit (SHU) for suspected gang associations. In 2011 the California Department of Corrections and Rehabilitation estimated that five hundred of these prisoners had spent ten or more years in the SHU, more than two hundred had spent over fifteen years, and seventy-eight more than twenty years.

Prison policy allowed inmates to starve to death if they signed legally binding do-not-resuscitate (DNR) requests. However, California corrections officials and a federal receiver who controlled inmate medical care had received blanket authority from U.S. District Judge Thelton Henderson to feed inmates who were in failing health. The prisons sought this authority, especially with prisoners who had lost consciousness or whom they suspected may have been coerced to sign DNR forms. Henderson obliged, while other judges turned back prisoner petitions to not be force-fed. The biopolitical purpose of tube feeding "to sustain their life" was the imperative through the thicket of ethical quandaries.[76]

A similar dynamic emerged when a federal court in Florida addressed the prison administration's petition for forcible feeding related to refugee hunger strikers. In December 2015, after as much as a year in detention, ten Bangladeshi asylum seekers went on hunger strike in Florida's Krome Immigration Detention Center. After two weeks, all ten men were brought in wheelchairs into the federal district courtroom in Miami, where U.S. District Judge Cecilia Altonaga ordered that their health be monitored with routine medical examinations as their hunger strike continued. After three weeks, physicians testified that the strikers had lost an average 15 percent of their body weight, which prompted an emergency judicial order to force-feed them. In her determination Judge Altonaga followed the prison doctors' medical guidance that force-feeding in prison would be more efficient and effective than gaining the men's informed consent for hospitalization.[77] From the perspective of one of the detainees, Mahmudul Hasan, it appeared that the prison administrators, prison physicians, and courts were a unified system that both incarcerated detainees against their will and kept them alive in limbo: "We came here to escape violence and danger in our country. But it seems like this place is like Guantánamo. ICE would rather force-feed hunger-strikers than listen to our basic demands for freedom."[78]

Detainees and their attorneys may have perceived the courts as able to intercede on behalf of hunger strikers, but in court only the timing of treatment protocols could be challenged. The issue was not whether the prisoner could refuse forcible feeding but whether it could be delayed or must begin right away, depending on the physician's judgment backed by biomedical diagnostics.

The experts convene to extend the prisoner's life, against the prisoner's will, based on the biopolitical power to, in Foucault's terms, "qualify, measure, appraise, and hierarchize" an individual life in relation to population norms.[79] The state's advocacy of "life-saving" technologies against the will of the prisoner selectively championed the physiological minimum life of the body over the choice of the person whose body it is.

The sectors of the state—courts, prison authorities, and prison physicians—are working in concert. The physician's wedge is diagnosis and biomedical care under the ethical mandate to save life, and both the courts and the prison rely on that authority to govern how they control the prisoner. Physicians and nurses may resent how they are used by the state as tools, yet their intervention to mitigate the pain and suffering of the prisoner does not actually overtake the state's authority over the prisoner's body. Anthropologist Corinna Howland argues that force-feeding is a "violent reconfiguration of the physical body in line with state politics of life perpetuation" that drives an ethos of "save the body and the mind will follow."[80] This presumes that the conscious mind will relent and accept feeding once the saving of the body is under way. However, it is just as likely that saving the body by these violent means results in shattering of the spirit. As the power of care is handed off from prison administrators to physicians, the prisoners' autonomy dims and their voices are subverted.

THE LIFE-PRESERVING COUNTERPOINT
TO FEEDING BY FORCE

While prisoners resist force-feeding, they sometimes present another vision of how they would welcome the experience of eating again, in contrast to ingesting a biomedical feeding substance that has been calculated and measured. In the hollows of self-denial, strikers remembered the meals they savored, the hands that created them, and who fed them or broke bread with them.

For some hunger-striking prisoners, the social fabric of eating was vital to reimagine. Eating is not just about biological survival; it also engages the social sustenance of comfort, familiarity, and care by family and friends. When Khader Adnan was incarcerated in administrative detention a second time, he went on another hunger strike beginning on May 6, 2015. An international solidarity campaign and the Israeli state's fears that he could die in detention led to his release on June 29 after fifty-five days—a release he called a triumph in "the battle of empty stomachs."[81] Israeli officials, as a condition of his release, expected him to demonstrate to the international public that he had eaten something to break his strike. Reminiscent of Irom Sharmila, Adnan insisted that only his seventy-five-year-old mother, Nawal Mousa, could feed him. She brought him a bowl of soup. She said in a telephone interview to a reporter, "He ate a little from my hands. . . . He said 'Mother, I want you to make my favorite meal, I want stuffed vegetables from your hands, Mama.'"[82] Adnan reclaimed authority over his body by choosing what and from whom he would eat again.

At Guantánamo for a decade, the counterpoint to prisoner isolation, starvation, and forcible feeding was when prisoners shared food with their lawyers. After the U.S. Supreme Court granted prisoners habeas corpus rights and visits from lawyers in 2004, lawyers would sometimes bring food to meetings with prisoners, creating a cultural practice of food sharing, gifting, hospitality, and care. Attorney Alka Pradhan of Reprieve commented that the prisoners were relieved to accept their lawyers' food but still suspicious that "a guard had spit or mixed pork into the food." Even lawyers of prisoners on hunger strike brought nourishment to their clients. Guantánamo detainee Abu Wa'el Dhiab reported that his lawyers "brought fruit juice to meetings that he would sometimes sip for strength at the height of his hunger strike."[83]

In 2015 Guantánamo's military commander, Rear Admiral Kyle Cozad, put a stop to this practice of sharing food: "Food of any kind, other than that provided by guard force personnel for Detainee consumption, is prohibited within meeting spaces."[84] Alka Pradhan, who had brought "everything from Egg McMuffins and traditional Middle East sweets to fresh fruit and granola bars" for her imprisoned clients called the new rule "petty and nasty." The purpose was clear: to exact total control over the prisoners' food intake and undermine the social sustenance gained by sharing food with the only advocates allowed to visit them.[85]

TO LET LIVE, BUT IN LIMBO

In the early twenty-first century, as hunger strike protests shook the authority, discipline, and order of carceral institutions around the globe, biopolitical management as a strategy of prison governance increased, strengthening the prison's material and psychological coercion of prisoners—even as prisoners pushed back in a "battle of empty stomachs." Through the hunger strikers' lawyers and journalists, and through the work of media artists, we learn of this grab for power as detainees seize some measure of sovereignty over their bodies. Strikingly, some prisoners' anguish was relieved momentarily in rare occasions of eating with lawyers or by the dream of eating with family, which lifted the prisoners' isolation onto the plane of mutual humanity. The hunger strike form had, by imagining and remembering the desire of eating, placed the isolated prisoner in a social and familial setting.

The prisoners' agenda was most often overridden by the prison's power and the physician's responsibility. Prisons and detention centers, armed with biomedical knowledge and protocols, could prevent a hunger strike from continuing to the death by pursuing life extension via straps, tubes, and packages of Ensure. Physicians and nurses, tasked to diagnose, calibrate doses, and supervise forcible feeding, were themselves trapped in the carceral system. When confronted with medical intervention to feed them, the prisoners could only say "yes." Their rightlessness is fully revealed in the impossibility of their saying "no." The biomedical regime cloaked the rightlessness of the prisoners with a kind of beneficence in the eyes of those who supported the government's right to control the lives of those it caged.

Prison guards could not prevent all prisoner deaths. Some prisoners died from overdose or suicide, inviting critique of the prison surveillance and monitoring systems for failing to prevent these deaths. By contrast, a hunger strike summoned heightened surveillance and monitoring, and often hospitalization and medical intervention, irrespective of the prisoner's consent. The biomedical arsenal encased the prisoner as patient, under the state's sovereign power, to let the person live, but barely and in limbo.

NINE

Australian Refugee Detention, Trauma, and Mental Health Crisis

IN THE 1980S AND 1990S, Australia and the United States developed new regimes of capture, mandatory detention, and deferred administrative review to hold unauthorized refugees arriving by boat. This was in sharp contrast to the United Nations–led humanitarian programs for refugees from Vietnam, Cambodia, and Laos that both nations had applied from the mid-1970s to the mid-1980s. Further, beginning in the 1990s and into the twenty-first century, wars in the Middle East, North Africa, and South Asia pushed millions across borders and oceans to seek refuge. Australia as well as the United States and Western Europe imposed mandatory detention for Asian, Middle Eastern, African, and Latin American persons who reach their shores. Incarceration only aggravated the precarity and insecurity of these refugees.

The UN defines a refugee as someone who has been forced to flee his or her country because of war, violence, or persecution for reasons of race, religion, nationality, political opinion, or membership in a particular social group. As Australian scholar Lucy Fiske contends, a person is made a *refugee* by events in their home country, not by the decisions of the receiving nation. By contrast, the term *asylum seeker,* a recent invention of Australian, European, and North American governments, turns the refugee into a suspect supplicant to the receiving nation. This term refers to the "status of applying to government for protection," and migration scholars have argued that it "creates a label of suspicion" that "enables governments to cast the arrival of refugees as a security threat" and thereby to justify "policies employed by Western governments to deter and repel refugees from their nations."[1]

This predicament reinforces Hannah Arendt's observation, made more than a half century earlier, that the "stateless person" is a rightless person, cast outside the international political order of nation-states. The losses reverberate. "The first loss which the rightless suffered was the loss of their homes," making them vulnerable to losing the "entire social texture into which they were born." Arendt eloquently prophesized that "the calamity of the rightless is not that they are deprived of life, liberty and the pursuit of happiness, or equality under the law or freedom of opinion—formulas that were designed to solve problems *within* given communities—but they no longer belong to any community whatsoever." From her perspective, criminals have more rights than asylum seekers and other noncitizens because they can still claim their rights as members of a political community, while the latter are stripped of the very "right to have rights."[2]

Beginning in the 1980s, Australia corralled refugees in detention in ever more remote locations, some offshore. The refugees' isolation and invisibility propelled camp protests, riots, hunger strikes, and self-mutilation. Mental harm and illness became an index of their experiences even as their access to Australian lawyers, refugee assistance agencies, and immigrant communities declined. The advocates and media who persisted to overcome these barriers generated publicity over the refugees' experiences that challenged the state's justification for mandatory and prolonged detention and inspired humanitarian intervention. The hunger strike form mutated in this setting to communicate how the harms of detention were bodily and psychically expressed and to overcome the physical barriers separating refugees and their advocates.

AUSTRALIAN MANDATORY DETENTION

In 1973 Australia abolished the White Australia policy that had restricted immigration and citizenship to Europeans for more than seventy years, and accepted the terms of the UN's *Protocol Relating to the Status of Refugees* (1967). However, in the 1990s, after a decade and a half of policies that welcomed refugees from Asia, the former Soviet Union, and Eastern Europe, the Australian government, hoping to repel the influx of Somali and Southeast Asian asylum seekers arriving by boat from across the Arafura and Timor seas, aggressively pursued increasingly restrictive deterrence strategies.

The number of refugee maritime arrivals in Australia was not constant but fluctuated considerably between 1973 and 2013, ranging from zero to several thousand per year. The numbers increased sharply between 1999 and 2002, declined precipitously from 2003 to 2007, and after 2008 rose once again.

The government reported twenty-five arrivals in fiscal year 2007–8; 7,983 in 2011–12; and 25,173 in 2012–13.[3] When boat arrivals swelled, controversy flared, and when the numbers fell, the debates over policy dissipated.

Since 1958, the detention of unauthorized migrants in Australia had been discretionary, but by the end of the century it was mandatory. The government's approach shifted from providing protection and refuge to deterring "illegal entrants." This shift began with legislation in 1989 that stiffened fines and penalties for detainees in response to fears of large waves of refugees arriving after the Tiananmen Square massacre and repression in the People's Republic of China and after the collapse of the Soviet Union.[4] The Migration Amendment Act of 1992 created mandatory detention of 273 days or less; but by 1994, when the number of boat arrivals and asylum requests grew, the government removed the time limit on detention and imposed mandatory detention on all persons who arrived without a visa or overstayed their visa.

This deterrence policy corralled all unauthorized migrants into detention, severely curtailing the immigration minister's discretionary use of parole pending review of a migrant's application. Under the UN's 1951 Refugee Convention and 1967 Protocol, a speedy application review process would establish an asylum seeker's credible fear of persecution and result in a temporary protection visa and parole. The refugee could then live, work, and go to school in Australia while awaiting the final decision on his or her application. The new policy, however, criminalized unauthorized migrant entry and ballooned into a punitive bureaucratic culture that downplayed the assessment of an individual's vulnerability, instead casting overwhelming suspicion on the person's lawful or unlawful arrival and origins. Review processes were stiffened, and detention facilities were set up in remote places. Criminalization corroded the "rights" of refuge seekers who arrived uninvited.

These ad hoc policies culminated in the "Pacific Solution" policy established in 2001. Boats carrying unauthorized asylum seekers originally from the Middle East, Northeast Africa, and Sri Lanka were intercepted, and the migrants were detained and processed in islands north of Australia. Offshoring the asylum seekers, often in the custody of private prison companies and weaker client nations, intentionally diminished Australia's accountability for their care and outcome. With no incentive to expedite asylum proceedings and appeals, the government ignored or dragged them out. The hope was that after protracted detention the refugees would return to their home countries or go elsewhere and that their treatment would deter future asylum seekers.

This and similar policies enacted in Western Europe and the United States undermined UN refugee treaties and protocols written to ensure that all signatory nations provide humane reception and speedy review of applications for asylum seekers, and prevent forcible repatriation and further persecution. Governments justified these policies on the grounds of the security needs of the state and its citizens.[5]

TRAUMA AND MENTAL ILLNESS AMONG DETAINEES

Hundreds of Vietnamese, Cambodian, Chinese, Somali, Iranian, Iraqi, Sri Lankan, and Indian "boat people" arrived on Australia's shores from 1989 to 1993 seeking refugee status. Of the 650 who applied, only 116 were accepted, and 56 of those experienced lengthy detentions before receiving refugee status. The other 400 or more remain incarcerated while fighting in court to stay. A few escaped from detention camps, while others were either deported or left the country voluntarily, seeking more welcoming prospects elsewhere.

Facing indefinite detention and the threat of deportation, the detained refugees began to protest. In June 1991, at a detention center in Villawood, twenty-five kilometers west of Sydney, six Somali men starved themselves for thirteen days to protest delays in processing their applications. After two were granted temporary refugee status, all the men resumed eating. Nine months later, in March 1992, 270 Cambodian and Vietnamese detainees split between Villawood and the Port Hedland detention center in Western Australia went on hunger strike after their refugee applications were rejected.[6]

In August 1992, rumors of imminent extradition provoked three Cambodian women at Villawood to refuse to eat. The women had been among 118 Cambodians crammed aboard a fishing boat that braved its way across the Timor Sea in early 1990. The Australian coast guard had intercepted them along the desolate northwestern Australia coast. They endured nearly three years of detention while awaiting the outcomes of their requests for asylum. In their applications, the women had testified to the intense brutality their families had experienced during the civil war in Cambodia. Each had had a close relative killed by the Khmer Rouge and feared persecution and possible death if she returned to Cambodia.[7]

The first hunger striker, Gek Bouy Mok, was found by guards catatonic in her cell and subsequently hospitalized. The two other women, Ung Bun Nat and Ly Muy Heng, began their strikes three weeks after Mok's.[8] Their prolonged hunger strikes—for up to seven weeks—resulted in hospitalization for severe dehydration. The hospitalizations provoked media attention, and the scrutiny plunged the Australian government into a political and legal crisis.

The causes and manifestations of the women's trauma were multifaceted. One woman refused to talk, and instead wrote long letters about her suffering before and during her hunger strike. She eventually abandoned the hunger strike because she believed that the guards would allow her to die. When she got her strength back, she attempted suicide. She heard voices and feared that she was being spied upon, leading the prison's psychologist to diagnose her with depression. When she was transferred to the hospital, she was diagnosed as a danger to herself and kept in a locked ward. Despite her horrific stories of her experience in Cambodia, government officials would not recognize her as a refugee. Instead, they insisted that a UN-brokered peace accord between warring factions in Cambodia would make it safe for her to return there.[9]

Another woman went on hunger strike to protect the future of her young son, with whom she had escaped from Cambodia after government forces killed her husband. In detention, she attempted suicide by overdosing on tablets. Believing the refugee application process was futile, she then planned to fast to death, expecting that the Australian state, though unwilling to let her into the country, would accept responsibility for her orphan child. She asked Andrew Biro, who worked for a year as an immigration welfare officer at Villawood, to take care of her son if she died. The boy, however, was shattered by his mother's distancing herself as she pursued her hunger strike and was hospitalized. He believed she had rejected him.

Of the three women, one is known to have left for Austria to marry a Cambodian refugee. It is not known whether the other two were freed or deported.

During the women's hospitalization, protesters gathered to demonstrate for the women's release and called for a government inquiry into the processing of their refugee applications. Staff members of the Australian Service for the Treatment and Rehabilitation of Torture and Trauma Survivors were consulted regarding the women's care. Biro observed that the women's "mental state fluctuated. . . . At times they were withdrawn, depressed, and uncommunicative, and on occasion they were distressed and angry." The women expressed frustration that their pleas for assistance from the hospital staff were frequently met with expressions of their powerlessness to influence asylum outcomes. Physicians and psychiatrists were tripped up by language and cultural barriers, as well as by the women's distrust toward all authorities because of their past exposure to persecution. The women's trust was further crippled by the bewildering array of legal advisors, immigrant officials, and health service staff who attempted to interview them—and by their well-founded fears that whatever information they shared would be passed on to immigration officials.[10]

The mental incompetency diagnoses did tip into the long-standing medical ethics debate regarding whom the force-feeding counter-weapon can be deployed against. In Australia, adults can refuse food or drink without medical intervention if they so stipulate. Prison administrators and doctors need a court order to override a patient's lack of consent. The New South Wales Supreme Court issued an interim order authorizing the Immigration Department to "feed or administer nourishment to the defendants against their will in order to prevent their death or serious bodily damage" and to use "reasonably necessary" force to do so.[11] When some physicians and nurses refused to force-feed the women, the Immigration Department declared the hospital a detention center in order to impose force-feeding, thereby expanding carceral power and scope. Even so, the government acknowledged that medical practitioners could not be compelled to "act in any way contrary to their ethical, moral or religious convictions."[12]

The force-feeding court order specifically related to the Cambodian women was broadened into legislation three years later, in 1995, that allowed medical authorities to force-feed any detainee without his or her consent and without a specific court order. In the government's view, its custodial obligation to prevent suicide and preserve life justified the forcible administration of medical treatment against the consent of a detainee.[13]

In the news, the Australian government portrayed hunger strikes as attempts to manipulate public sympathy. Gerry Hand, Australia's minister for immigration, dismissed hunger strikes as "pointless" in pressuring him to "throw out the rule book" and intervene in the asylum application process. He commented that people who tried to circumvent the process with a hunger strike threat were trying to play him "for a good, old-fashioned Australian sucker."[14] Refugee advocates, on the other hand, critiqued the government's inhumane policies and incarceration regime.

In 2002 at Villawood, a detained Iraqi physician and an Australian psychologist conducted a unique study investigating the collective trauma of detainees. Dr. Aamer Sultan, fleeing persecution in Iraq for providing care to wounded Shiite rebels, arrived by plane in Sydney in May 1999. Australia rejected his asylum application but could not deport him since the two governments had severed diplomatic relations. Instead, Dr. Sultan was detained at Villawood for three years, when he received a three-year temporary protection visa.[15] While at Villawood, Sultan contacted clinical psychologist Kevin O'Sullivan, who was providing mental health services to fifty Villawood detainees on a one-year contract. Using semi-structured interview surveys, O'Sullivan's clinical notes, and Sultan's longitudinal observations, they found that the thirty-three inmates they surveyed, who were detained for an average of two years, were beset by pervasive fear, distrust, and anxiety, resulting in psychotic symptoms. Eighty-five percent had chronic features of depression, and 65 percent had contemplated suicide.[16]

The pervasive mental health crisis arose from the conditions of indefinite detention. Dr. Sultan told a *Los Angeles Times* reporter: "By law you are not a criminal, but you spend the rest of your life in prison.... We are not paying for what we have done. We are paying for what we are. I think we came to a very racist country. I think that we made a fatal mistake."[17]

Detention robbed people of dignity, Biro concluded in a report and subsequent publication, emphasizing that "they lose control of their lives and they feel angry and confused about this."[18] Biro filed a complaint with the immigration department that documented the refugees' experiences, spoke to journalists, and was subsequently fired. In an interview to a reporter, Biro condemned the ongoing helplessness induced by government policy: "You give them nothing to maintain their self-sufficiency, hope and self-esteem. You give them nothing to think about except their problems. In the end, you try to break them in the hope that they'll eventually go back voluntarily. It's a slow and deliberate form of mental torture. In the case of many Cambodians, the Immigration Department has achieved where Pol Pot failed: to break their resolve."[19]

SELF-MUTILATION AT DETENTION CENTERS
AND CAMPS

Fleeing war and repression in their home countries, renewed swells of refugees from Afghanistan, Iran, and Iraq came to Australian shores unauthorized, most arriving on boats. Many of them were placed at the new Woomera detention center, opened in November 1999, and located five hundred kilometers inland from Adelaide. By April 2000, more than fifteen hundred were held in Woomera, far exceeding its capacity of four hundred. The Department of Immigration and Multicultural and Indigenous Affairs contracted with Australasian Correctional Management, a subsidiary of Wackenhut Security Corporation, to manage the facility. The overcrowded, miserable conditions, the hot and dusty climate, and the slow processing of asylum claims fueled the detainees' frustration, and the camp was buffeted by violent protests throughout its three years of operation until it was closed in 2003. As one detainee told a reporter concerning one of the protests: "This protest is about freedom and basic human rights. It is no longer about visas."[20] This evocation of essential freedoms in the news media was intended for the Australian and international public.

In June 2000, over two days of protests, 480 detainees broke out of the center and walked into the township of Woomera. Two months later, three days of riots and fires were suppressed by guards using tear gas and water cannons. The press drew upon reports by nonprofit lawyers and human rights advocates to cover the riots. In November 2000, as many as fifty detainees at Woomera went on hunger strike for two weeks. Ten were hospitalized, several of whom were reportedly force-fed while handcuffed.[21]

The detainees' frustration and despair grew as their detention expanded from months to years. In January 2002, when the Australian government announced a freeze on processing Afghani refugee applications, nearly 370 detainees at Woomera—Afghanis and also Iranians and Iraqis—participated in a mass hunger strike. Between fifty-five and a hundred prisoners sewed their lips during the protest.

This was not the first instance of lip sewing during a hunger strike in an Australian detention center. At the Curtin detention center in Western Australia, during a mass hunger strike in February 2000, a dozen Afghani refugees had sewn their lips together to avoid force-feeding.[22] Lip sewing transformed the form of hunger striking by inscribing the refusal to eat on the striker's own body. The lip sewing usually involved a single hole made in the top lip and another in the bottom lip, with a piece of cloth, string, or bedding threaded through them. The lip sewing was intended to demonstrate both that they were abiding by the hunger strike and that the Australian government had silenced them.[23]

Kon Karapanagiotidis, a lawyer and executive director of the Asylum Seeker Resource Centre in West Melbourne, writing in 2010, recalled a meeting in 2002 with a fifteen-year-old Iraqi at Woomera who had sewn his lips together for a week. The teenager, who had spent three years in detention, said, "They have taken everything else from me and my family. . . . I sew my lips together because my words mean nothing anymore, no one will believe me. I will speak no more with words, my body is all I have left."[24]

Karapanagiotidis also commented on the surge in self-harm incidents—cutting oneself, drinking cleaning products, eating razors, suicide—in detention. He then reversed the source of the horror, saying: "What is horrifying to me these days is not that people sew their lips together but rather that my country proudly creates and runs a detention system that is deliberately built to damage people, to denigrate them and destroy all hope."[25]

Farshid, one of the young detainees interviewed by Lucy Fiske, spoke of how detention turns the detainee into "the lost person, the forgotten person, you don't exist, you cannot change anything and you have no power over anything." From this place of demoralization, Fiske comments, resistance becomes a crucial means for detainees to "experience their own agency, to take a decision not to eat the food on offer, or to create a disturbance and force a response from authorities such as through self-harming or breaking a piece of camp infrastructure. The aim of the protest was less about achieving a change in their environment and more about experiencing self." As Farshid explained, self-mutilation makes "people feel they are real again, they exist, they have power over something—their body. So, blood always has a very powerful message and when people see they can get over their fear and do something, . . . I have power. I can do things."[26] In a system bent on disempowerment, the bleeding self-inflicted cut both announces the power one has seized over one's own body and delivers a visceral cry insisting that the damage of indefinite detention be ended.

The Woomera hunger strike lasted sixteen days, with strikers dragging mattresses outside and lying in the sunlight as daytime temperatures soared to 100°F in January. The government grew apprehensive of media attention on the strike and on January 26 erected a security fence around the refugee camp. A few hours later, security guards shouted at thirty journalists to leave the fence area within half an hour or face arrest. Natalie Larkins, an ABC Adelaide TV reporter, was arrested, charged with trespassing, and freed on bail on condition that she leave Woomera immediately.[27]

On January 29, in a rare instance of hearing directly from one of the detainees, Hassan Varsi spoke to reporters in response to the arrest of Larkins, who was attempting to publicize their predicament: "We, the Afghani people at the Woomera Detention Centre, will unstitch our lips out of respect of the IDAG [Independent Detention Advisory Group] and Australian community and out of sympathy we have for the recently arrested ABC Reporter."[28]

At the end of January, a handful of young Afghani, Iraqi, and Iranian men were released on three-year temporary protection visas. The hunger strike concluded when the government agreed to resume processing Afghani applications. There were no fatalities, and no one was force-fed, though many people needed to be medically rehydrated.[29]

The self-inflicted violence of lip sewing attracted media publicity, news photographers, and camera crews eager to show such a viscerally potent representation of the hunger strike protest. Detention center administrators denied asylum seekers opportunities to speak to the media directly, and the guards screened phone calls. The news media relied on detainee advocates, IDAG members, opposition politicians, and refugee advocates for information.[30]

The government sought to contain the ramifications of this extreme form of protest by coding it as "un-Australian" and thus as proof of the detainees' inability to live in Australian society. Minister for Immigration Philip Ruddock argued that lip sewing is "unknown in our culture" and "offends the sensitivities of Australians." Malcom Farr, a *Daily Telegraph* columnist, argued that lip sewing as an effort to achieve asylum had backfired: "The test is simple: who wants as neighbors people who have stitched shut the mouths of their children?"[31] The so-called test underscored the expression of xenophobia.

The words of a teenage girl, shared through the family attorney, provide rare insight into the thinking of children who hunger strike and consider sewing their lips. In August 2001, after the family's request for asylum was rejected for the second time, Shana, age thirteen, and her brother Parviz, seventeen, went on a hunger strike to protest their conditions. Her brother sewed his lips together and refused to cut the stitches. Their hunger strike lasted for twenty-five days.

In a statement to the attorney, Shana asked: "Is there anybody outside to answer me? . . . Why we shouldn't be loved? Why we shouldn't be part of you? Why we shouldn't see your smile, your care, your open arms instead of those dark officers with black boots and buckles? What is life for us? Where is happiness and childhood?" She said, "We are punished same as criminals and called by numbers, not names. . . . We are same as animal—they feed us in cage. I don't want this food—I want my freedom." Shana also spoke of witnessing trauma among her fellow detainees. "I have seen ill people who hang and cut themselves," she said. "I have seen fire and violence, children and women on the floor when they were crying and screaming and a lot more."[32]

Her father, Hossein, told a *Los Angeles Times* reporter that Shana lost more than twenty pounds during her protest. Shana had been learning English in detention and enjoyed going to school, but after her hunger strike she was prohibited from attending classes. She became "completely withdrawn and spends her time alone, seldom talking or playing with girls her age." In a document prepared for the courts, Hossein said, "In Australia, my children have forgotten how to laugh and have forgotten how to smile.... They have lost every last moment of their childhood and will never be the same again."[33] After three years in the Curtin detention center, the family was released and offered temporary protection status and later asylum.

The hunger strikes and lip-sewing pacts at Woomera, Port Hedland, and Curtin sharpened public scrutiny, led to inquiries from human rights organizations, and hastened long-delayed foster care placements for twelve- to fifteen-year-old boys. In an inquiry, one unaccompanied child revealed that after two days of refusing food and drink, the case officer urgently intervened and notified the child's lawyer, who shortly afterward secured a temporary protection visa. The sequence of actions underscored the Australian government's negligence in regard to unaccompanied children, which came to light only when the youth's protests vexed politicians who preferred to divert accusations of harm to adult asylum seekers.[34]

Minister Ruddock's claim that lip sewing is antithetical to Australian society and locatable as evidence of an "alien" culture is confounded by the surfacing of lip sewing in the 1970s and 1980s as a performative practice by European and American performance artists. In 1976, West German performance artist Uwe Laysiepen, known as Ulay, sewed his lips shut and had his thoughts spoken out by Marina Abramović, a Serbian feminist performance artist. In the unfinished film *A Fire in My Belly* (1986–87), American artist David Wojnarowicz combined video images from Mexico City with a self-portrait of his face with his lips sewn together as a visceral meditation on society's violence to those on its margins and the repressive silencing of gay men and the poor in the AIDS pandemic. More than a decade later, in June 2002, Australian artist Mike Parr took the gesture directly into the political and cultural debate on immigrant detention in his performance piece "Close the Concentration Camps." He sat motionless in the middle of a gallery with his lips cross-stitched, dried blood streaked on his cheek, and his thigh

FIGURE 21. An Iranian refugee has his mouth sewn shut as part of hunger strikes at the border between Greece and Macedonia, November 26, 2015. Credit: Reuters/Yannis Behrakis.

branded with the word "ALIEN" in a direct effort to evoke Nazi extermination camps and the lip-sewing protests at Woomera.[35]

Lip sewing as an elaboration of the hunger strike form recurred in the mid-2010s in Europe in the midst of the refugee crisis of Middle Eastern families crossing the Mediterranean by boat. After reaching the Greek Islands on smugglers' boats from Turkey, thousands of Syrians, Iranians, Iraqis, Bangladeshis, and Pakistanis crossed the Greek mountains, but in November 2015 they were stranded at the Greek-Macedonian border, after a European Union policy blocked further refugee travel in the wake of the Paris terrorist bombing attacks. After a few days of protests, seven Iranian men stitched their mouths shut with string and twine and wrote "Iran" and "freedom" on their faces and chests.[36]

The transmission through the media of viscerally disturbing images of young men's mouths sewn shut was intended to provoke the public. The images commanded the viewer to react: to turn away, express disgust, shudder in revulsion, feel shame, or feel responsibility to remove the threads. The images also raised questions: Who were these young men? Why were they doing this to their bodies? Could they still drink water? Could they still make vocal sounds and attempts at speech? How did they communicate?

Scholar Ron Hoenig commented on how "the image brings home the corporeality of the act of lip sewing. Lips are powerful tokens of the sensory and sensual materiality of the body. They open to allow us to speak, to eat, to drink, to kiss. Through them we express the complexity of our thoughts and the simplicity of our strongest needs—for communication, for nourishment, for tenderness and passion. Stitched lips close off nourishment, language, love. Sealing them in protest externalizes and embodies the silence, amplifies the silencing. Screams the silence."[37]

HUNGER STRIKES IN OFFSHORE DETENTION CENTERS

Beginning in the 1990s, Australia developed procedures to offshore refugees who arrive by boat into detention centers on Christmas Island, an Australian territory; at Manus Island, a military site under the jurisdiction of Papua New Guinea; and in the island nation of Nauru, northeast of Australia. This so-called Pacific Solution was launched in September 2001 when the Australian Parliament passed legislation that excised Australian territories, and thus Christmas Island, from Australia's migration zone, meaning that asylum seekers arriving on Christmas Island could not automatically apply for refugee status. Supporting this scheme, global corporations became involved in the construction and management of immigrant detention centers both offshore and in Australia. The new policy effectively removed refugees out of view while reducing their access to means of appeal or protest. Even though the government shrouded its operations in secrecy and controlled media access, refugee advocates were able to provide the media with reports of hunger strikes, suicides, and protests, as well as widespread abuse and medical and psychological neglect from these offshore camps. The media's attention made these remote sites "hypervisible during crises."[38]

At the Christmas Island detention center, hunger strikes erupted in 2012 and 2013 when detainees were faced with the prospect of being transferred to Manus Island or Nauru, making the possibility of asylum in Australia even more remote. The detention center, built on a former phosphate mining lease, by 2013 had been expanded to house 2,960 people. In mid-January 2014, among the seventy-eight hunger strikers in the men's compound, nine Iranian men stitched their lips together and threatened to stitch their eyelids.

Within a week they were joined by 350 on hunger strike in a family compound. Up to ten people were hospitalized after attempting suicide or self-harming with glass or razor blades. Australian senator Sarah Hanson-Young berated the administration for separating families and for the "toxic culture breeding in these detention centres" where "vulnerable" refugees are "pushed to [the] breaking point." The incarceration of "hundreds of children" was alarming, and Senator Hanson-Young declared that "no child should bear witness to the horrors of long-term detention and the desperation it causes." Immigration minister Scott Morrison vowed that the crisis would be quickly resolved because of upgraded "security infastructure" and new "procedures to assist, manage and de-escalate events," including transferring detainees to Manus and Nauru, which drove the detainee protests in the first place.[39] The crisis erupted anew six months later, when 375 asylum seekers were on hunger strike and seven men stitched their lips together.[40]

The Manus Island Regional Processing Centre was situated on Los Negros Island, in Manus Province, a remote island north of the main island of Papua New Guinea. The location had been used for naval patrolling operations by the Japanese, then the United States, and then Australia, until it was handed over to Papua New Guinea following its independence from Australia in 1974. The Australian government continued to use the island to support maritime patrol of international shipping lanes. From 2001 the Australian government developed Manus Island as a detention facility. Successive Australian governments negotiated with Papua New Guinea to open and close the facility temporarily, to finance its expansion, and, after 2012, to resettle Manus refugees in Papua New Guinea.

The bleak conditions of the Manus Island detention center and equally bleak future for the detainees prompted multiple uprisings throughout its existence. Reports of riots and murder as well as physical and sexual abuse, inadequate medical care, neglect, and suicides drew the attention of the UN, Australian NGOs, Papua New Guinea legislators, and the Australian press.

In December 2014, four men—two Iranian, one Iraqi, and one Lebanese—who had been held in detention for more than a year sewed their lips together as part of a mass hunger strike in the compound. The strikers were protesting the "catastrophic conditions," the overbearing tropical heat, overcrowding, "filthy" toilets, and "horrible" food.[41] By January 2015, more than seven hundred asylum seekers, two-thirds of the total at Manus Island, were on hunger strike, outraged by the publicized vow of the newly appointed immigration minister, Peter Dutton, that the Manus Island detainees would "never arrive

FIGURE 22. The sister of a hunger-striking Egyptian asylum seeker speaks at a protest outside the Department of Immigration and Citizenship, Sydney, Australia, January 21, 2015. Credit: Richard Milnes/Alamy Live News.

in Australia" and instead would be permanently settled in Papua New Guinea. As many as fourteen men sewed their lips together.

In January 2015, Australians went on twenty-four-hour sympathy fasts, publicly declaring on placards their solidarity with the hunger strikers at Manus Island. Throughout 2015, the Refugee Action Coalition organized large-scale rallies and demonstrations in cities across Australia to close Manus Island, to end all mandatory and offshore detention, and to restore normal refugee assessment processes in Australia so that credible fear interviews, reviews, and the assigning of temporary visas and services could be offered to asylum seekers domestically and proximately to major cities. Former detainees and refugee family members already in Australia addressed crowds and shared their relatives' experiences of detention at Manus and Nauru. Investigations and reports of detainees attempting suicide or cutting themselves, medical crises requiring emergency hospitalization, and brutality in detention inflamed public concern and led to more demonstrations.

A Manus Island detainee who gained international renown was twenty-five-year-old Iranian cartoonist Ali Dorani, better known by his artistic name, Eaten Fish. His ordeal began when the smuggler's boat transporting him from Indonesia to Australia was intercepted at sea on August 6, 2013.

His pen name was inspired by his experience of being plucked from the sea upon entering Australian waters: "I'm like a fish bone. . . . Gotten from the sea. Eaten and thrown away for so long." In February 2017, Eaten Fish went on an independent nineteen-day hunger strike. He informed the detention center administrators that he was protesting his treatment in the camps. He alleged that he had been the victim of sexual assaults by guards and other detainees and then was forced to remain housed with those who had attacked him.[42] Eaten Fish was supported by an international community of cartoonists who publicized his hunger strike and the abuses that had provoked it.[43]

Ten months before his strike, international press notoriety and domestic legal challenges had shaken Papua New Guinea's willingness to permit the detention center to continue. On April 26, 2016, the Supreme Court of Papua New Guinea ruled that the Manus Island detention center breached the constitutional rights to personal liberty and was thus illegal. The following day, Prime Minister Peter O'Neill announced that the processing center would be closed and the Australian government would need to make "alternative arrangements for the asylum seekers." Yet for another three years the camp remained in operation while its inhabitants were beset with violence and uncertainty. At one point the Papua New Guinea Defence Force were accused of firing shots into the camp, resulting in a class-action settlement in Australian courts against the Australian government and private contractors that brought additional pressure to close the camp. However, the outcome for the detainees, who included Iranian, Iraqi, Rohingya, and Sri Lankan men, remained unclear.

The Manus Island facility closed officially on October 31, 2017. However, for the nearly sixty men stranded there, being released in Papua New Guinea was fraught with fear of reprisals by hostile locals. Some were taken voluntarily or forcibly removed to transitional facilities on Manus Island, which lacked "running water, electricity or security fences."[44]

Eaten Fish was likely held at one of these temporary facilities. After four years in detention, he left Manus Island when he was given refuge in Norway in December 2017. He had succeeded against great odds because of his unique voice as a cartoonist. He could narrate his trauma and vulnerability with morbid humor, and his cartoons circulated via digital media to an international community of cartoonists and activists. The intercession of lawyers, human rights activists, physicians, and artists adept at using the levers of digital social media and the digital press made it possible for select individuals to be ushered to refugee resettlement, but rarely if ever in Australia.

In 2016 policy shifts and refugee swaps were made between Australia and the United States. But the process became caught in political turbulence when President Trump sought to renege on the deal that President Obama made with Australian Prime Minister Trumbull to swap out 1,250 asylum seekers in Manus and Nauru detention for Central Americans in U.S. detention. In 2019 the pace of swaps quickened, and by April 2021, 940 former detainees were resettled in the United States and more than 1,223 were temporarily in Australia for medical treatment or in transit.[45]

DIAGNOSING TRAUMA TO AID REFUGEES

Where words alone failed, the detainees used bodily defiance through hunger strikes and self-mutilation as political acts of protest against the Australian government's policy. Faced with the reality of their rightlessness, detainees in Australia's offshore detention centers escalated their actions to insist upon their voices and actions being heard. As Fiske observed, "whether the immediate goals of the protest were achieved or not, detainees' [*sic*] sought to exercise control over their own bodies; to re-establish sovereignty of self against the omnipotence of the sovereign state which detained them."[46] Without nonprofit medical and human rights investigations and reporting, it would have been impossible to inform sympathetic members of the Australian and international public and arouse their demonstration against the brutality of detention.

The government took mass amnesty off the table, but policy pivots created a means for detainees to be discharged from offshore detention and into medical treatment in Australia, Papua New Guinea, or Taiwan. This set the stage for transit to camps before being relocated to welcoming countries around the globe. In 2019 several hundred detainees were approved for medical treatment in Australia through short-term legislation that stipulated two physicians' recommendations for medical evacuation in a bid to ensure that medical necessity overrode security interests. A diagnosis of illness, either physical or mental, could deliver transport out of remote detention and into medical care in Australia. Exposing the Australian government's and the private corporations' imposition of harm and trauma fed public sympathy for the detainees, but the political campaign to stop detention altogether fell short.

Across a century, diagnoses of mental illness had contradictory impacts on prisoners. In the early twentieth century, British and American suffragists believed they were threatened with rightlessness if given a mental illness diagnosis and sent to the asylum, where they feared that their own decision-making about their treatment would be ignored and they might never be heard from again. By contrast, the Australian human rights advocates and medical professionals insisted that the already rightless refugees were plunged into mental distress, dysfunction, and illness by indefinite incarceration, aggravating the trauma of their journey. Since they were already rightless and forgotten, the refugee protesters turned violence on their own bodies in a cry for aid. Medical and mental health aid in Australia appeared as a pathway to public care and concern, and potentially an avenue out of limbo.

Some migrant detainees seized the moment by reshaping their hunger striking, introducing lip sewing as a visible and visceral signal of protest. This uncloaked the Australian government's remote detention that had made them unseen. These fierce protests inscribed on their bodies a solemn defiance to not be silenced. The media attention and the solidarity protests in Australian cities were aimed at shaming the government and breaking the logjam in slow-churning administrative bureaucracy, but also at overturning policy. The Australian government eventually did allow medical treatment and multilateral diplomatic negotiations to restart refugee processing. Despite these adjustments, the punitive deterrence strategy weathered the political backlash. When the United States and Australia accepted the refugees each other had caged, it lent credence to the suspicion that enforcing deterrence outstripped ensuring humanitarian refuge. Both governments punished captives and kept their lives suspended in a bureaucratic maze of their own devising and subject to their own political requirements.

Advocates could perceive only one way out of the carceral tomb that off-shore detention had become: to clutch at the right to receive care. The detained sought treatment, care, and a life in the everyday world outside detention—be it in a hospital or in transition housing—as long as it served their integration into a country of refuge. If they could be less rightless, they could possibly dwell in and join a new and beneficial social fabric.

TEN

Captives in U.S. Detention and Their Networks of Resistance and Solidarity

IN 2017 AND 2018, the news was dominated by disturbing stories of Central American and Mexican migrant children, separated from their parents, being kept in cages in Texas detention centers. These children and adults were the latest captives in a systemic shift in U.S. immigration policy that began in the 1980s when the United States, European nations, and Australia expanded detention to manage the unauthorized arrival of asylum seekers. The number of immigrants and asylum seekers held in detention grew from approximately two thousand in 1981 to almost half a million in 2012,[1] mirroring the rise in the U.S. prison population from approximately 330,000 in 1980 to nearly 2.2 million in 2018.[2] In turn, criminalizing immigration entry as a felony, tightening punitive outcomes in the immigration bureaucracy, and supporting detention through legislative mandates and multibillion-dollar pools of funding generated windfall gains for private corporations and revenue streams for beleaguered municipalities. Caging immigrants became a ticket to steady revenue growth.

Although the meanings of the terms have often been collapsed for political or policy reasons, *immigrant* and *refugee* are distinct categories with separate legal histories governing their respective classification and rights. In the United States, *immigrant* refers to migrants who have obtained legal visa status prior to entry, while *refugee* refers to migrants who have arrived in the United States (either authorized or unauthorized) to escape political persecution or extraordinary hardship in their home country. The Immigration Act of 1965 enumerated categories of migrants who could be prioritized for entry, including those individuals with desirable skills or education, those with U.S. citizen or permanent resident family members, and refugees.

What happened in detention centers was largely shrouded from public scrutiny. The federal government and the private prison corporations controlled access to the detainment facilities and rarely released information to the public willingly. Through legal defense, only charities, pro bono lawyers, and family members could learn about the experiences of detainees. The legal advocacy, human rights, and religious charitable organizations created a network of immigrant defense and, with publicity and organized demonstrations, directed media attention to the crises of life and death, emphatically hunger strikes, occurring in detention centers. The racial and national-origin inequities that kept many refuge seekers caged indefinitely enflamed a political crisis over immigrants and galvanized efforts by the relatively rightful in the United States to gather on behalf of rightless detainees.

THE HAITIAN CRISIS AND THE SHAPING OF U.S. REFUGEE POLICY

Prior to 1981, the U.S. Immigration and Naturalization Service (INS) had enforced a policy of detaining only those migrants deemed likely to abscond or who posed a security risk.[3] However, as the decade progressed, the modern U.S. system for mandatory detention began to take shape as the INS, under the Carter and Reagan administrations, began systematically apprehending the growing numbers of undocumented Cuban and Haitian refugees arriving in Florida. In response to Cuba's economic stagnation and political repression, some 125,000 Cubans arrived, beginning with the April 1980 Mariel boatlift. In 1978 and 1979, as repression and violence in Haiti under the Duvalier dictatorship increased, the numbers of Haitian refugees journeying the six hundred miles by boat to Florida's shores grew significantly.

Many of these refugees were placed at the Krome Service Processing Center, a decommissioned air force missile facility thirty miles west of Miami. Located at the edge of the Everglades, the Krome center was, at first, a jumble of tents and makeshift buildings thrown up on vacant land. After the Dade County Public Health Department issued health and sanitary code violations against Krome and urged its closure, the INS assured local and state officials that it would transfer the detainees to detention centers out of state. However, with the uptick in Haitian arrivals in November and December 1980, the Krome center was reactivated, its hangars and repair buildings converted into barracks and dining facilities.[4]

Since 1954, Haitians applying for political asylum in the United States had routinely been released on parole, after public health screening, to sponsoring relatives or voluntary agencies while their refugee claims were pending. Even so, Haitian applications for asylum were overwhelmingly denied, clearly for political reasons. In 1980 and 1981, 90 percent of the refugees admitted to the United States were fleeing communist regimes in Southeast Asia, the USSR, Cuba, and Eastern Europe. In the same period, asylum applications by refugees from right-wing, anticommunist, authoritarian regimes in Latin America, primarily Haitians and Salvadorans, were overwhelmingly denied, unless individuals could document a direct connection to an opposition political party or the press. These denied refugee applicants were characterized as "economic immigrants," migrating to improve their livelihood, even when evidence detailed their experiences of persecution in their home countries.

To assist the detained refugees, in the late 1970s, legal service projects were set up by lawyers, religious activists, and ethnic organizations in Florida, Texas, Arizona, and California to assist with the high demands for legal representation. In California, Florida, and Texas, civil rights lawyers filed class-action cases to establish basic due process rights for detainees and challenge asylum procedures. During the next decade these cases created national standards for processing the asylum claims of individuals from El Salvador, Guatemala, and Haiti.

In 1979, the Haitian Refugee Center and eight individual Haitians brought a class-action suit on behalf of over four thousand Haitians in southern Florida's U.S. District Court, alleging that the INS and the Justice Department had violated the Haitians' rights to due process by conducting only cursory interviews to assess their claims of persecution in Haiti and by expediting the processing for their deportation. In July 1980, District Court Judge James Lawrence King found that the INS, in its treatment of the plaintiffs, had "violated the Constitution, the immigration statutes, international agreements, INS regulations and INS operating procedures. It must stop."[5] He ordered the INS to submit a new processing procedure and to stay further deportations. The INS appealed to delay changing its procedures; however, deportations were slowed.

Then, on May 20, 1981, the Reagan administration secretively issued a directive to the INS that unilaterally imposed indefinite detention on all excludable aliens. The INS applied this policy almost exclusively to Haitians, essentially turning Krome into a long-term detention center. Meanwhile,

Cubans' applications for parole were expedited, and most Cubans continued to be released on parole from Krome. This blatant difference in treatment became a key issue fueling protests by Haitians through the 1980s, alongside the indefinite detention.[6]

That summer, Krome became severely overcrowded, outstripping its capacity of 524. Florida's governor, Bob Graham, filed suit against the federal government to enforce minimum health, hygiene, and safety standards. In response, the INS increased the cap on Krome's population to one thousand and began to transfer many Haitians to detention facilities elsewhere in the country. Florida demanded that no Haitians be released in Florida unless they were reuniting with family and that no new INS facilities be built there.[7]

Even so, the overcrowded conditions persisted and, coupled with the indefinite detention and differential treatment compared with Cubans, inflamed the situation at Krome. In September 1981, a large number of Haitian detainees went on hunger strike in protest. INS officials began removing the strike leaders to other camps. Haitians resisted by throwing food and rocks. Some escaped through a hole cut in the chain-link, barbed-wire-topped fence. Though preceded by numerous smaller hunger strikes and demonstrations, this large-scale protest caught the guards flat-footed, and they used tear gas to quell the demonstration. Afterward, INS officials identified the "instigators of the disturbance," recaptured the escaped detainees, and transferred 120 Haitians to a federal prison in Otisville, New York. Twelve Border Patrol agents were added to Krome's twenty-six-member security detail.[8]

The week before Christmas, a hunger strike at Krome mushroomed into demonstrations both inside and outside the barbed wire fence.[9] Members of Miami's Haitian community traveled the thirty miles west to the detention center and, for a week, held daily demonstrations in solidarity with the Krome strikers—chanting, waving placards, and peacefully confronting INS officers. They called for the compassionate release of detainees before Christmas, a demand underscored by Miami's Haitian leaders in telegrams and petitions to the White House. What both the demonstrators outside and the asylum seekers inside wanted was a return to the earlier policy of granting Haitians swift parole so they could live with families and friends in Miami while awaiting their asylum case hearings. Edward McCarthy, Roman Catholic Archbishop of Miami, appealed to President Reagan for the detainees' "humane" release, saying that the Haitians had come to "these shores seeking freedom, liberty and justice."[10] Archbishop McCarthy also performed separate masses at the detention center for the 677 Haitian men and seventy Haitian women being held there.

On Christmas Eve Day, when these efforts had brought no change, in an appeal for compassion from Christian Americans, 727 Haitians refused breakfast and lunch. The same day, nearly two-thirds of the 186 Haitian refugees held at the Federal Medical Center in Lexington, Kentucky, refused meals to protest their incarceration. Archbishop McCarthy called the hunger strike "a very human reaction to the very inhuman conditions" of detention and family separation.[11]

Tensions escalated both inside and outside Krome. On Sunday, December 27, seven hundred Haitian exiles and sympathizers gathered outside the detention center, stormed the perimeter fence, and hurled stones and bottles at police, who responded with tear gas. Meanwhile, nearly 110 male Haitian detainees escaped from Krome, even as guards used batons to subdue them. Police arrested nine of the demonstrators outside the camp and charged them with unlawful assembly. The hunger strike ended on December 29 after rumors of intensifying punishments for hunger strikers spread and the escaped detainees were captured. According to spokesperson Beverly McFarland, the INS had posted notices in Haitian Creole encouraging the detainees to feel "free to eat without fear of punishment," but Haitians both inside and outside saw the notices as attempts to threaten hunger strikers with retaliation, including summary deportation.[12]

Hunger strikes at Krome continued to erupt, all protesting the same issues: the slow processing of asylum cases and indefinite detention. They often ended with assurances that application processing would be expedited and living conditions improved—assurances that went unfulfilled. In 1984 a new group of 115 Haitian refugees at Krome, "calling for 'a collective suicide,'" undertook a hunger strike for more than seven days. One of the medical professionals monitoring the strikers called Krome a "Reagan concentration camp."[13]

The U.S. government blamed the delayed disposition of asylum proceedings on the dozen class-action lawsuits filed on behalf of Haitian detainees in federal courts. Advocates for the Haitians countered that without the lawsuits, the United States would wrongly deport the detainees as unauthorized economic immigrants, thereby ineligible for refugee protections.

In 1985, the U.S. Supreme Court case *Jean v. Nelson* invalidated the 1981 policy of mandatory detention for its targeting of Haitian nationals. Supreme Court Justice William Rehnquist, writing for the seven-judge majority, argued

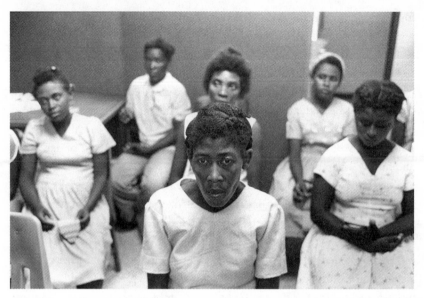

FIGURE 23. Haitian women detainees in Krome Service Processing Center, Miami, Florida, 1981. Credit: Gary Monroe/Duke University Libraries.

that the attorney general's parole authority "must be neutral as to race or national origin" and agreed with the lower court that demanded that the INS create a nondiscriminatory "detention rule or regulation."[14] In response, the Reagan administration chose to apply mandatory detention to all unauthorized migrants, a decision buttressed by congressional legislation and budget authorizations. The U.S. Immigration Control and Reform Act of 1986 made immigrants who entered prior to 1982 eligible for amnesty, and all those who came after were "illegal" and thus subject to detainment and deportation. Since amnesty was now a one-time opportunity in the past, while deportation was ongoing, the distinction between "legal" and "illegal" cemented federal policing, punitive detention, and deportation as a cornerstone of U.S. immigration policy. This inaugurated the modern system of mandatory detention for asylum seekers at the U.S. border, collapsing the category of refugee asylum seekers into the general category of unauthorized immigrants.[15]

To support this new policy, the budget for INS border enforcement and detention systems ballooned from $1 billion in 1985 to $4.9 billion in 2002.[16] In 1983 the Mass Immigration Emergency Plan required that ten thousand immigration detention beds be ready for use at any given time. Hoping to exploit the opportunity, private prison corporations began lobbying Congress to enable the INS to contract with them to build and run immigration deten-tion centers.[17] Meanwhile, increased border patrol and U.S. marshals increased the capture and detention of unauthorized immigrants, which led to overcrowded INS facilities, fueling the INS to further subcontract to pri-vate corporations and local jails to increase detention capacity. Part of a broader tough-on-crime policy and prison expansion in the United States, immigration mandatory detention, overcrowding, and subcontracting fed each other, snowballing into further expansion, detention, and expense.[18]

The expansion of indefinite detention policies led to further institutional abuses. In October 1990, Cheryl Little, an attorney and director of the Haitian Refugee Center, submitted a report to the district INS director that included complaints at Krome of arbitrary isolation, strip searches, limited access to telephones, arbitrary denial of access to bathrooms, and lack of proper medical care. There were reports of rape and assault as well as psycho-logical abuse at the hands of the guards, in addition to hunger strikes and two suicide attempts in a single week.[19]

Six months later, in April 1991, Florida Rural Legal Services issued press releases detailing the culture of intimidation present at Krome. When a group of nineteen detainees held in the camp for four months were trans-ferred instead of paroled, other Krome detainees went on hunger strike, even as they feared reprisals and being singled out for punitive transfers to other camps. To discourage the strike, all detainees were required to appear at the cafeteria at mealtimes, and hunger strikers had to sit and wait until all those eating had finished. Shortly afterward the hunger strike dwindled.[20]

The INS continued to insist that conditions were normal. Krome admin-istrator Constance Weiss denied allegations of violence and human rights abuses, explaining that at Krome "there is no institutional policy of brutal-izing people," and rhetorically adding, "Why would we want to run a place where we beat the hell out of people?" However, refugee advocacy groups and immigration lawyers argued that miserable conditions, indefinite confine-ment, and brutality were intentionally deployed at Krome to discourage other potential refugees from coming to the United States and to hasten the detainees' willingness to be deported. Since oversight of the detention center was limited to sporadic media attention about the protests and slow-moving federal court cases, fresh groups of asylum-seeking detainees were being pushed into desperation.[21]

After the Haitian Refugee Center, in federal court in 1991, won a tempo-rary restraining order against forced repatriation, the George H. W. Bush administration instructed the Coast Guard to intercept Haitian boat arrivals and incarcerate them in camps at Guantánamo military base, creating an offshore diversion in order to facilitate their deportation. More than thirty-four thousand passed through the six makeshift, barbed-wire-fenced sub-camps at Guantánamo. A third were slowly relocated to U.S. camps, but most were repatriated to Haiti, while a smaller number diagnosed with HIV were quarantined.[22]

In 1992 legendary African American dancer and choreographer Katherine Dunham, at the age of eighty-two, went on a sympathy strike, insisting that she would fast until President Bush designated the Haitians as political refugees. "The lives of those people who half drown in those little boats are being equated to animals," she said in an interview. "It means I have to declare out-and-out war." For six weeks, Dunham subsisted on juice, tea, and water at her home in East St. Louis. Her protest fast made national and international headlines and brought Democratic presidential candidates to her home. The recently deposed president of Haiti, Jean-Bertrand Aristide, visited her home and successfully begged her to end her strike.[23]

Despite the visibility of a celebrity sympathy hunger strike, the INS continued to arbitrarily burden Haitians with harsher standards and parole denials, claiming that it was pursuing a humane refugee parole policy nationwide. The differential treatment of Haitians and Cubans was never starker than in January 1993, when fifty-two Cubans who hijacked a Cuban commuter flight and diverted it to Miami were released from Krome within forty-eight hours. Immediately afterward, 119 Haitian men and forty Haitian women, confined at Krome for months, engaged in an eight-day hunger strike in protest. Specifically, the Haitians were upset that the Cubans were perceived as political refugees while they were seen as "economic refugees," even though they had fled their country because of political persecution. They also complained of ill treatment by the Krome staff. In a letter distributed to the press, the strikers claimed that "all Haitian refugees in Krome are ready to eat with our family who wait for us in the USA. We want our freedom like the Cubans. Our family are waiting for us."[24]

The hunger strikers believed they would die in the days ahead and that no one on the outside would know. However, rumors of the hunger strike breached Krome's fences. Mayor Xavier Suarez of Miami called for the Haitian detainees' immediate parole into the custody of relatives or church groups and for them to receive the same speedy parole review as provided to

Cubans. Other advocates communicated to journalists and politicians that "lives could well be lost or health seriously and permanently impaired."[25]

Cheryl Little wrote to the INS to substantiate the hunger strikers' protest of "arbitrary and unfair parole policies at Krome" despite their meeting all the conditions for parole, including the "credible fear" assessments.[26] Journalist Robert Steinback, in an article in the *Miami Herald,* repudiated the way the United States "flouted its own laws" and "defied international law" and warned that only public outrage might change the outcome for the asylum seekers. "Until then," he argued, "one can only hope that the strikers can endure the burn of hunger—and the rest of us can endure the burn of injustice."[27] "The basic problem is that there are no rules," said Joan Friedland, an immigration lawyer. "Everything is discretionary" in both the detention centers and the refugee processing system.[28]

What the repeated crises for Haitian detainees revealed is that the designation of refugee versus economic immigrant is a political decision. Since the 1960s, Cold War anticommunist sentiments in the United States had favored Cubans as special status refugees, offering them an expedited review process and federal benefits to establish residency in the United States, while asylum seekers fleeing violence and persecution in other Caribbean and Central American countries were trapped in systems of prolonged detention. Even as the U.S. government used the case of the Haitian refugees to establish an elaborate system of mandatory indefinite detention for all immigrants and refugees, it continued to selectively enforce these policies for political purposes, bulwarked by racialized justifications.

In 1994, the Clinton administration established a new camp in Guantánamo to hold intercepted Haitians and Cubans and dismantled a thirty-year policy of immediate amnesty for Cubans. Both strategies advanced a strategy of offshoring migrant detention. The United States and Cuba ironed out a deal for a regular immigration channel for twenty thousand Cubans, while the more than fifteen thousand Haitians were either resettled in other countries or repatriated, either voluntarily or by force.[29]

In 1996, laws were passed increasing the list of "crimes of moral turpitude," including nonviolent drug charges, for which both legal immigrants and undocumented noncitizens could be subjected to mandatory detention and deportation. As the grounds for detainment increased, so did the number of detainees. In 2003, when the INS was restructured as Immigration and Customs Enforcement (ICE) and placed under the Department of Homeland

Security (DHS), Congress approved more funds for "detention bed space *and for criminally prosecuting immigration offenses.*"[30] A law passed in 2004 directed the DHS to increase the daily immigrant detainee bed capacity by eight thousand annually. In 2005 the bed count reached eighteen thousand.[31] By 2018 it had grown to 40,500. The budget to subcontract with corporations and local prisons to build and operate detention centers also swelled. The federal budget for the DHS ballooned from $700 million in 2005 to $2 billion in 2015. This mill of criminalization, capture, and indefinite detention more than doubled the annual number in detention from 198,037 in 2002 to 478,000 in 2012. Deportations increased from about 165,000 in 2002 to almost 400,000 annually from 2009 to 2014.[32]

The escalating criminalization and detention of immigrants, some of whom had lived in the United States for years and even decades, seeded the conditions for hunger strikes in protest of detention and conditions at the privately managed detention centers in the 2010s.

SEPARATED FAMILIES AND THOUSANDS OF DETAINEE HUNGER STRIKERS

Since detainees' families were frequently of mixed immigration and citizenship status—some family members were citizens, others were recent immigrants—the escalation in capture and detention often split families across both citizenship status and generations. Hunger strikes then became a means to illustrate how detention caused crises not just for individuals but for families. Month after month, new strikes sparked instances of imperiled families being cleaved apart. Because U.S. immigration and refugee law had historically supported family reunification both across generations and laterally, advocates and immediate family members claimed kinship as an emotionally durable tie to the detainee and also to free them from the bureaucratic snare.

In February 2014, six family members and supporters undertook a two-week hunger strike camped outside an ICE office in Phoenix, in solidarity with relatives on hunger strike in nearby Eloy Detention Center. One of the solidarity strikers, Anselma Lopez, told a reporter that her thirty-year-old son Elder, one of the Eloy hunger strikers and the father of two U.S. citizen children, had spent almost three years in the Eloy center after being arrested while at work at a McDonald's. "I'm fasting for my grandchildren as well because if my son gets deported, they won't be able to see him again," she said.[33]

More than a thousand miles away, the following month, more than a thousand people detained at the Northwest Detention Center (NWDC) in Tacoma, Washington, declared a hunger strike. Activists formed the NWDC Resistance, advocating for the detainees and documenting their activities in "A Hunger Strikers Handbook," published three years later, in April 2017. The handbook was both a primer and a historical account of the 2014 hunger strike, offering detainee testimonials of the detention conditions that precipitated the strike and the strategies for hunger striking and communicating to allies.

One Tacoma detainee explained the reason for the strike: "They are treating us like animals. I'll hunger strike. I won't miss the cold beans or the worms." The detainees built solidarity among themselves for the strike, selecting a date to begin and sharing information with families and supporters outside. On March 7, 2014, twelve hundred people stopped eating, remaining in their beds through breakfast and refusing lunch or dinner. Designing the strike to suit the conditions and intent, most of these strikers took part in a relay of short-term fasts; only a few endured throughout.[34] The strikers' demands were to improve substandard food and conditions, increase their meager pay of one dollar an hour for work at the facility, reduce the exorbitant commissary prices, and allow unbonded releases so that detainees' families would not be placed in financial jeopardy. An eight-page handwritten letter to President Obama urged him to "use his presidential authority and order a total stop to the unjust deportations that are separating families, destroying homes, and bringing uncertainty, insecurity and unhappy futures to our children, our loved ones."[35]

The strikers, though sequestered in the detention center, did not go unheard. At the rallies and protests outside, organizers read aloud letters the strikers had written. The NWDC Resistance also set up live phone calls with the strike organizers inside that were broadcast on portable speakers outside. At a rally on April 5—one of many nationwide that day to mark the two million deportations estimated to have occurred during the Obama administration—an activist read out a letter from the hunger strikers that underscored the gravity of the decision to forgo food: "We have a profound respect for food, we honor it, we know that it is necessary and vital for many here and in the rest of the world, but to make it known that we are here, that we exist, it seems like the only alternative to say, 'we are here' [presentes]." The strikers felt solidarity for "an infinite number of compañeros and compañeras detenidos" across the United States, combining "our voices, together with

FIGURE 24. Cover of "A Hunger Strikers Handbook," April 2017, written by the NWDC Resistance. Courtesy of Megan Ybarra.

yours, so that our echo will have greater resonance, as it includes every time more women and men convinced that it is inhumane to destroy families." The indefinite detention and looming threat of deportation imperiled "honest and hardworking people" and caused an "uncertain future for our children." The speech concluded with a callout cry by the crowd: "Not one more! Ya basta [stop]!"[36]

Inside the detention center, the hunger strikers faced threats by the guards of force-feeding. One hunger striker spoke to a reporter of guards threatening them with "seeing medical and get tubes down our throats and be force-fed. I'm not an animal. It's a cruel way to grab somebody, hold them down and put a tube down their throat. We are here to fight our cases and get back to our families. We aren't here to be tortured." Strike organizers were placed in solitary confinement, their family visiting times were shortened, and some were transferred to other facilities. In protest, Maru Mora Villalpando, an immigrant rights lawyer and founder of Latino Advocacy, reached out to Washington state officials to create an independent monitoring and negotiation process for the detainees and oversight of both ICE and the detention center administration.

On May 1, after fifty-six days, the hunger strike ended. By drawing public attention to the strike, the NWDC Resistance had averted force-feeding from occurring, though not solitary confinement and transfers. Some conditions in the prison did change after the strike, including lower commissary prices. And some strikers were released and reunited with their families. However, family separation continued as a dominant theme in subsequent detainee hunger strikes in Texas, Louisiana, and California.

Within weeks of the NWDC hunger strike, detainees at Joe Corley Detention Center in Conroe, Texas, initiated a hunger strike to protest their treatment.[37] At one point, more than 120 men were on hunger strike at Corley. Hunger strikers were placed in smaller group cells to break up communication and weaken solidarity. Some were reportedly shackled at the ankles and wrists and connected by the waist to steel beds with no blankets or pillows. Sandra Bonilla, the wife of one detainee, said in a translated statement that her husband phoned her one morning with news of ICE's plans to deport him to Honduras two days later. She said, "They're trying to disappear my husband. . . . If [detainees] ask for better, they try to get rid of them. My husband should be home with our family, not in detention. He doesn't want to be treated like a dog, and so they're punishing him even more."[38]

From 2015 to 2019, over fourteen hundred people went on hunger strike at more than eighteen detention facilities across the United States. The detainees at these centers included thousands of women and children who were fleeing the escalating gang murders and violence in El Salvador, Honduras, and Guatemala. In response, the United States expanded the use of family detention rather than releasing minor children to the custody of a parent or relative. In 2014–15, more than twenty-five hundred women and children were detained together at family detention centers across the country.

In March 2015, seventy-eight young mothers went on hunger strike at Karnes County Residential Center, southeast of San Antonio, Texas, where up to three hundred women and children were awaiting decisions on their asylum petitions. In a statement issued in Spanish and translated into English, they collectively protested in the "name of mothers" and beseeched authorities to let them "be set free with [their] children." The women blamed their children's loss of well-being, which included weight loss, deteriorating health, and depression, on the misery of incarceration. They also contested the "unjust" procedures that could refuse them asylum and deport them back to "the place where they could even lose their life."[39]

Three of the hunger-striking mothers were taken to the medical clinic and held overnight with their children, while nurses and guards warned that they would lose custody of their children for participating in the strike. They were warned that self-starvation would diminish their "brain functioning" and could cause them to be judged "unfit guardians for their children."[40]

As the threats to separate the women from their children became known in the media, advocates, lawyers, and judges began to challenge the grounds on which a detention center could serve as a viable place for children to stay. Federal Judge Dolly Gee ruled in July 2015 that the U.S. government must abide by the 1990s Flores Settlement that required licensed facilities for detained children. The DHS asserted that the detention centers where women and children were held were safe for children, but because of the centers' prison configuration, exceptions to the Texas state rules for child-care-appropriate facilities had been requested. Seventeen months later, in December 2016, Travis County District Court Judge Karin Crump intervened, ruling that the detention facilities were unable to "protect the health, safety, and well-being of children" since the requested exceptions would have allowed more than four occupants to a room, allowed children to be in rooms with unrelated adults, and allowed older boys and girls to sleep in the same room.[41]

Immediately after this court ruling, the private contractors and ICE summarily freed more than five hundred women and children from Karnes and Dilley detention centers, busing them to the San Antonio bus station on a wet, frigid December night while migrant advocates scrambled to provide them with shelter, food, and emergency care. The Interfaith Welcome Coalition, a network that supports refugees, and the Refugee and Immigrant Center for Education and Legal Services (RAICES) asked the community for donations of money, winter clothing, new underwear and socks, children's toys, and other items, while the Interfaith Welcome Coalition bought $1,700 worth of inflatable mattresses and bedding. When the RAICES refugee shelter had filled up, families were shuttled to the San Antonio Mennonite Fellowship church, where the children slept on pews or donated mattresses. Several children continued to wear their detention center identification tags, and many mothers still wore ankle monitors.[42] Although ICE had dumped the welfare of the women and children on social service organizations, its carceral surveillance managed to extend beyond the detention center walls.

MIGRANT SOLIDARITIES

The migration routes through Central America and Mexico were also traveled by several thousand undocumented immigrants from South Asia who fled persecution in their home countries, making their way to ports in Ecuador, Brazil, and Panama and then to Central American countries. In 2013 the U.S. Border Patrol received more than a thousand requests for asylum annually from Indian, Pakistani, and Bangladeshi youths and adult men.[43] These South Asians joined the disparate populations of asylum seekers in detention centers across the United States, where they were subjected to the same kind of treatment and similarly resorted to hunger striking in protest.

On October 14, 2015, in a detention center in El Paso, Texas, fifty-four asylum seekers, primarily from Bangladesh, refused food for seven days. They had passed their "credible fear" interviews, which made them eligible for release to U.S. relatives until their asylum cases could be heard, but had not been released. They were protesting their confinement, lack of access to health care or medical staff, the absence of Bengali-speaking interpreters, harsh treatment from guards, and the threat of possible deportation. Guards strip-searched and humiliated the hunger strikers, and placed their leaders in solitary confinement. By the time the hunger strike ended, seven of the strikers were in critical medical condition.[44]

A week later, fourteen Bangladeshi and Indian detainees started a hunger strike at LaSalle ICE Processing Center in Louisiana. On October 29, a statement from the LaSalle 14 was released by DRUM (Desis Rising Up and Moving), a New York–based South Asian immigrant and labor advocacy organization. The statement said: "We came to this country to save our lives, but this country treated us like animals and held us in detention for months and years. . . . Even though for the last 12 days we were in a hunger strike, no ICE officer treated us like humans." The officers threatened the strikers that if one of them died, the others would be charged for the death. This threat brought an end to the strike but did not deter the detainees' quest for "immigration justice and freedom."[45]

On the night of October 28, not long after the LaSalle strike began, twenty-seven women, mostly from Central America and Mexico, began a hunger strike at the Hutto Residential Center in Taylor, Texas. On November 4, twenty-six asylum seekers at the Adelanto detention facility in San Bernardino County, California, stopped eating to protest their prolonged imprisonment. The Adelanto hunger strikers included a man fleeing antigay violence in Ghana and others escaping religious and political persecution in Pakistan, Nepal, and Bangladesh. They were protesting the slow processing of their asylum cases, delayed bond hearings, and exorbitant bond demands. The hunger strike in Adelanto ended when one of the men collapsed.

Fahd Ahmed, executive director of DRUM, emphasized in a press interview that the dire conditions in detention ignited "a wildfire of hunger strikes spreading across the country," erupting out of "a deep-rooted problem in the immigration system" and "a failure of humanity." The hundreds of detainees were emboldened to put their bodies on the line, with the assistance of advocates and lawyers who communicated the detainees' struggles to supporters and the media and who coordinated information across different detention centers.[46]

SUPPORT NETWORKS OF SOLIDARITY

Since detainees could not speak publicly for themselves, they relied on networks of solidarity to make visible the crisis of U.S. detention policies. These networks drew together immigration advocates, human rights lawyers, university legal clinics, ethnic organizations, and Catholic, Muslim, and Sikh service organizations. They would advocate for detainees, and when hunger strikes erupted, they became a vital channel of support for detainees and their U.S.-based family members. The organizations tapped their community networks to raise funds and attract media attention for striking detainees. They also provided legal services for detainees to navigate the asylum system and for social welfare services to support those who were released on parole awaiting asylum decisions.

During hunger strikes, advocates mobilized their networks to share letters, petitions, and information from the detainees with journalists, using press releases and social media to keep communities and the public informed. They also organized pickets and demonstrations in front of detention centers and ICE offices. Using another strategy, the Sikh Freedom Ride leveraged a van caravan and religious identity to create a spectacle of public protest along an eleven-hundred-mile route. Organized by the Jakara youth movement in Fresno, California, the caravan was launched to spotlight the plight of hunger-striking Punjabi asylum seekers languishing for more than eight months in an El Paso detention center, in spite of passing their "credible fear" interviews. Deep Singh, cofounder of Jakara, explained that the Fresno-based Mexican American and Hmong groups fighting ICE deportation inspired their actions and underlined their common experiences with state surveillance, immigration deportation, and incarceration.

Creating protest flash points across time and space along the route, the caravan stopped at Southern California Sikh religious and humanitarian institutions to rally support for the Punjabi detainees. At a rally in the Los Angeles community of Artesia, they shared the stage with Latinx and South Asian activists. After driving through the night, the caravan reached the El Paso detention center, where some youths were able to interview detainees and later share their stories with local and digital media, to publicize the caravan's journey and build a coalition with other solidarity organizations for immigrants from Mexico, Central America, and the Middle East.[47]

These social justice alliances put into practice scholar Cathy Cohen's call to build coalitions that recognize racial, ethnic, spiritual, and sexual differences yet provide bridges for common action in response to oppression at the hands of immigration policing and incarceration. Rather than allowing identity to limit collective purpose, the youth networks emphasized intersectional practices of alliance building to confront the criminalizing and incarceration of immigrants and people of color.[48]

FIGURE 25. Family members and activists begin a five-day hunger strike outside the Federal Building in Los Angeles, California, September 30, 2020, to call for the release of detainees at the Adelanto immigration detention center. Credit: Eugene Garcia/EPA-EFE/Shutterstock.

The benefits and challenges of alliance building reverberated in the decision by three Latinx activists, Deyaneira García, Jorge Gutierrez, and Jennicet Gutiérrez, in May 2016 to launch a hunger strike in a city park outside the Santa Ana Jail after months of protests and negotiations on behalf of transgender immigrants facing deportation. Supporting transgender detainees to include them in the fold of community protection required multifaceted campaigns and alliances across immigrant, queer, and trans communities of color. Protesting alongside members of immigrant, trans, and queer support organizations, the three activists demanded that ICE end the detention of transgender immigrants. They also challenged the Santa Ana City Council to terminate its contract with ICE to hold trans immigrants in sixty-four-bed segregated "pods" facilities, specifically designed to detain trans and queer women. Transgender activist Jennicet Gutiérrez emphasized in her press interview, published in *Latina,* the vulnerability of transgender women to being "targeted" and "murdered" in detention in general.[49] Jorge Gutierrez, a thirty-one-year-old transgender immigrant rights advocate who founded Familia:TQLM, repudiated the City of Santa Ana's questionable financial decision to build a new prison, incurring $27 million in debt and necessitating that the city contract with ICE to harvest $7 million a year for holding trans and queer immigrants. Gutierrez argued that detention is disastrous for "our queer and trans brothers and sisters." He spoke on their behalf: "We are harassed, we are made fun of, we are threatened, we are misgendered. We are denied medical access" and threatened with solitary confinement. Their protest fast in front of the jail, he said, was part of a larger struggle to protect communities and families, and a national fight to stop raids and deportations and to close down detention centers.[50]

In each of these solidarity campaigns, political activism provided a diagnosis of the U.S. prison system's pervasive inhumanity and underlined connections between mass incarceration in the criminal justice system and the mushrooming use of civil detention for immigrants. Both policies resulted in large-scale incarceration of black and brown people. Solidarity protests were a way to create hope for another future through coalitions of diverse groups, family arrangements, and communities.

SEPARATED FAMILIES AND DEMANDS FOR REUNIFICATION

The crisis of family separation was revived in 2017 when, under the Trump administration, ICE began holding greater numbers of migrant children in custody, refusing to release them to live with family members and other sponsors. In 2018 the Trump administration established a "zero tolerance" policy that criminalized migrant entry regardless of asylum claims—leading to forcible separation of migrant parents and children by ICE and holding of children in cages and tent cities at McAllen and other South Texas locations.

In response, in June 2018, the national nonprofit Break Bread Not Families joined with La Unión del Pueblo Entero and the Texas Civil Rights Project to organize a twenty-four-hour public relay fast over twenty-four days to honor the estimated twenty-four hundred children separated from their parents. Participants in the solidarity fast included television and media celebrities as well as McAllen politicians.

Later that summer, political and legal pressure forced the DHS to reunite separated families, though they remained held in detention. The Karnes County Residential Center held reunited fathers and their children, while reunited mothers and their children were sent to the South Texas Family Residential Center in Dilley.

On August 2, 2018, RAICES reported that fifty fathers had taken to sitting on the facility's soccer field to protest recent separations from their children and other injustices.[51] A Honduran father, speaking in Spanish on a phone from inside Karnes, explained that indefinite detention and the likelihood of deportation had propelled the men to stage a hunger strike: "Everyone has agreed that we will stop eating. . . . We need to know if we will be deported or allowed to remain in this country. We are asking the government to free us. We are not criminals."[52]

ICE downplayed what it called the "brief sit-in" and disputed the claim made by RAICES that a hunger strike was part of the protest. However, advocacy organizations reported that three hundred men and three hundred boys were participating in the protest, with the adults not eating or drinking and the children refusing to participate in school activities. On August 15, tensions rose again between the fathers and ICE officials shortly after the fathers were reunited with their children. An ICE officer said the guards had stepped in to stop "disruptive behavior," but advocates described the event as "backlash against migrants who had been speaking out about their conditions." Sixteen men were arrested, transferred to another facility, and, when brought back the next day, threatened with permanent separation if they continued the disruption.[53]

Punishing migrants by separating families and isolating children became a flash point for everyone. Some detained parents said they freely agreed to be deported in order to rejoin their children. Others said they were coerced into signing voluntary removal papers, with their child used as leverage—a move ICE denied. The media coverage depicted the parents and their children as pawns of ICE and highlighted the children's welfare.

In February 2019, against the backdrop of President Trump's rally for building a border wall in El Paso, national and international media became aware of long-term hunger strikes by a dozen Punjabi and Cuban men seeking asylum that began in late December 2018 at the El Paso detention center.[54] They protested that they were being denied bond and parole, while detainees from other countries were being released. In early January 2019, Congresswoman Veronica Escobar had visited the El Paso detention center and publicly declared the conditions "unacceptable. . . . El Paso and our country are better than this."[55] By then, some of the men had been on hunger strike for more than two weeks. ICE sought court orders for medical staff to draw blood and urine samples, and it hydrated and fed six of the hunger strikers nonconsensually.[56] Little had been known about the strike until forcible feeding was implemented and testimony appeared in the media of the visceral and painful experiences of the prisoners.

By February 3, nine men were being force-fed at El Paso. Singh, a twenty-two-year-old identified only by his last name, described the abusive treatment: "They tie us on the force-feeding bed, and then they put a lot of liquid into the tubes, and the pressure is immense so we end up vomiting it out. We can't talk properly, and we can't breathe properly. The pipe is not an easy process, but they try to push it down our noses and throats." They made daily requests for basic items such as pillows and wheelchairs to help them move through the facility. Singh reported losing fifty pounds since beginning the strike.[57] The nasogastric tubes remained in their nasal passages twenty-four hours a day. The tubes, being too large for some individuals, caused nasal bleeding and pain. Many hunger strikers had wounds and lesions in their throats and nasal passages, and were also suffering from rectal bleeding and bleeding while vomiting, as well as persistent stomach pain. Some had difficulty breathing and speaking.[58] Amrit Singh, uncle of two of the protesters, reported that his nephews, after being on hunger strike for a month, suffered from persistent vomiting and nosebleeds due to the force-feedings, as well as the health effects of a hunger strike.[59] These physical traumas, characteristic of force-feeding in so many other contexts, became publicized as similar to the experiences of Guantánamo prisoners.

In February, lawyers were able to get a non-prison physician to examine the force-fed prisoners. Based on this physician's report during closed-door court hearings, the force-feeding was stopped. Forty-nine Democratic lawmakers, led by Escobar and Congresswoman Suzanne Bonamici, demanded an investigation into the force-feeding and inhumane treatment.[60] ICE defended its actions as "monitoring food and water intake" and as necessary "for health and safety." In the course of its defense, ICE detailed other hunger strikes concurrently occurring across its system, until then not known through the media. At the time ICE issued its report, none were being force-fed.[61]

After nearly two months, the hunger strikers at El Paso resumed eating, having been promised they would be released on parole. Jasvir Singh, who had been on hunger strike for seventy-four days and force-fed for thirteen days, did not speak for more than a week because of the painful effects of the nasogastric tube. He and Rajandeep Singh, who had been force-fed for twenty-nine days, were released in April. They were transferred to another center in Washington State, and then were suddenly released on bond. After being held in custody for over eight months, these two men were set free.[62]

Ultimately, the crisis of immigration detention is a crisis created by the state, using the language of "illegality" to justify turning a civil offense of undocumented entry into a crime. The requests for asylum at the U.S. border were made in good faith. Both by international treaty and by legislation, the U.S. government was obliged to offer refuge, to review claims expeditiously, and to swiftly free detainees and allow them to live, work, and study in U.S. society while the more rigorous review transpired. Instead, the United States reversed its own policies and reneged on its obligations by criminalizing refugee seekers and normalizing the use of cages and indefinite detention.

The experience of indefinite detention produces conditions of desperation that push detainees to hunger strike as a last resort. At the center of the strike are demands for access to the UN-approved refugee review process, including the ability to post reasonable bond, rather than being criminalized as "illegal," "unauthorized," and summarily deported back to the country they have fled. These flashes of resistance to incarceration are detainees' attempts to claim their voice and be heard, rather than remaining sequestered and unseen. Far from wanting to defy the state, these women, men, and children seek the state's protection and refuge, enlisting attorneys and advocates and willing to follow the bureaucratic steps required. Public demonstrations and vigils on behalf of hunger-striking detainees communicate a community's embrace of families that have been separated by the state according to citizen status. The process of creating human connection between U.S. citizens and those holding immigrant status humanizes the plight of the individual hunger striker within a national narrative of immigrant family reunification. It underscores that the state's detention-and-deportation strategy is not supported by all the citizens and that there are U.S. communities and parts of civil society that seek to provide these immigrants refuge.

Support networks for the incarcerated refugee applicants are buoyed by a vision of society that is infused with human rights, dignity, and benevolence. Drawn from faith communities, schools, social justice, labor, feminist, LGBTQ, immigrant, and ethnic communities, they join to combat the government's punitive policies that reject refugee arrivals at the border. In many ways, theirs is a strategy to restore and make robust the civic organizations and supports that were created after World War II and that grew, in the 1970s to 1990s, to create temporary support within communities for those in asylum processing.

The question of trust is a central paradox for all sides. Supporters of ICE fundamentally mistrust the motives, histories, or contexts that migrants say have propelled them to seek refuge in the first place. By contrast, the solidarity networks share the detainees' stories of trauma, violence, and exploitation while in U.S. detention. They and the detainees themselves distrust assurances from the U.S. government and its private contractors that conditions will be improved or that asylum proceedings will be just. Refuge seekers are wary of the guards' reprisals, ICE agents' deportation threats, and asylum judges' hostility, and they recognize that their fate is tied to navigating their way through the bureaucratic maze with the aid of advocates.

The solidarity networks mobilize wider public support for refuge seekers for a national political purpose: to reorder government and political priorities that for forty years have built prisons of fear and distrust to contain unanticipated, unplanned, and irregular migration. The flow of human migration—fleeing violence, war, political repression, famine, and environmental devastation—grows month by month, decade by decade. National security states have expended billions in infrastructure to block the migrants and in policing and surveillance to apprehend and cage them.

The carceral infrastructure tests but does not destroy the sense of solidarity that materializes among detained migrants and their advocates and supporters. Instead, the networks of solidarity emboldened in the fight against detention are knitting a different vision of society: a mutual social mesh that embraces detainees with United States citizens, immigrants with residents, enveloping them in a common responsibility. For both the relatively rightful and the precariously caged refuge seekers, the pro-immigrant slogan "No Estan Solos/You Are Not Alone" materializes a groundswell of care and compassion as a vision for the world they aim to create and for a different kind of government that can sustain such a world.

Conclusion

HUNGER-STRIKING CONTINGENCIES

HUNGER STRIKING IS CONTINGENT AND UNPREDICTABLE. Like any oppositional move against state power and carceral power, it is a gamble. Every outcome depends on prior conditions that hinge on other conditions in an endless cascade, drawing interconnections and impact from forces that range from the proximate to the global. Since the outcome is not predetermined, hunger striking does not follow a telos, an ultimate object or aim. There are moves and possibilities at every juncture, and the trajectory of history is up for grabs.

The hunger strike phenomenon marshals the human body to communicate over prison barricades to the public. The bodily and visceral experiences of hunger are, for the strikers, sourced in the human body—in its parts and its fullness; in the mouth, tongue, throat, digestive tract, and stomach; in the physicality and feeling of refusing to eat. Their experiences are enveloped in the sense of smell, and in sensitivity to noise and temperature. The representations of hunger striking are likewise centered on the emaciated body in a medical bed, with tubes inserted into the alimentary tract, or lips sewn together—while also grasping the conditions of captivity and constraint and the striker's adversary, both immediate and far away.

The hunger strike is a tool that can take different forms, adaptable to the needs of the historical moment and communicated in evolving, experimental ways that enable the striking prisoner to be heard and understood beyond the walls of the prison. Strikers engage and shape the form of the hunger strike in ways that can be grasped and responded to with both feeling and reason. The hunger strike form is shaped by all kinds of creators—journalists, lawyers, artists, sympathizers, activists, political allies, critics, physicians and nurses, and state authorities. Following the striker's instigation of the phenomenon, witnesses—in proximity and at a remove—seize the form, carry it, and reshape it using many different media across platforms to rematerialize it outside the prison. Naming the phenomenon a hunger strike brings it into focus for people, who may puzzle over the behavior they observe before deciding how to respond.

The hunger strike itself is not always the spark that leads to change. Rather, it is a declaration that the existing situation is untenable and change is needed. The hunger strike constellates forces that may or may not cause change to occur. *Refusal to Eat* has revealed what is catalytic about this communication, and why it can move and motivate not only a reaction but new possibilities. The hunger strike communicates values of dignity and personal autonomy, ethics of life and death, and qualities of stamina and determination. The assumptions that guide it include the harrowing value of individual agony, that protest has purpose, and that this is a last-ditch effort, possibly leading to death.

The most consistent and persuasive forms of hunger strike are laced into an individual heroic story that conveys the personal experience of agony. Striking bodies are identified and distinguished by voice, spirit, and name. The focus on individual rights, on self-evidence, and on naming the person matters for the story's intelligibility in liberal society, holding greater attention than the experiences of a mass—a class, the rabble, the poor—who are perceived as expendable. Drawing on and deploying personal story and context evokes questions: Whose dignity is valued and whose is under siege? Who possesses moral force to shame the state? Who lacks credibility, moral force, and leverage upon the state and society? What strategies are necessary to amass leverage when one has little or none?

The hunger-striking story is effective when it offers realistic details from the prisoner's cell, conveying the true-to-life immediacy and urgency of prison conditions. It seeks to show publicly what the state purposefully shrouds from view. The hunger strike form contours the bodily protest both in prison and outside as it expresses the prisoner's voice beyond walls. Hungering is about converting a sense of personal agony into a social agony that is communally felt, imagined, and experienced.

Voice is the vehicle by which the materiality of hunger striking can be heard outside the prison walls. Making the prisoner's voice heard is an achievement of the hunger strike form. The picketing, public procession, placards and banners, the shouts and excitable speech, the display of photographs and the calling out of names that follow once the prisoner's voice is heard publicly announce the strike inside. These, as well as vigils, sympathy fasts, and funeral processions, are attempts to shame the state authorities.

The attention to voice raises questions of what and who is heard, who listens, and what they are listening for. Can the hunger striker speak? This epistemological question—as Gayatri Spivak discerned in regard to the subaltern—asks on what terms the prisoner is heard by, and intelligible to, the audience of the rulers and the rights-bearing. This is a challenge that bears on the speech, values, assumptions, and status of the speaker.[1]

The status of rightlessness bears even more heavily on necessitating intermediaries—the advocates and lawyers who transmit the communication in forms and media that can reach an audience. The purpose is to carry the message of hunger striking as guided by deliberation and reason. The hunger striker has a goal or purpose that she or he is reaching for that becomes readily informed by a repertoire of demands on the state to remedy prison conditions and/or address political demands. The challenge is to the state's rule and its accountability to justice. The striker calls out injustice and frames her or his refusal as a political demand for democratic representation and answerability. What is truly unpredictable is the potential that the hunger strike can rouse a widespread and far-reaching hunger for another world, for demonstrable change from the world in which one is sequestered.

Carceral power isolates. It disempowers collective action and social power. State regimes through their carceral powers reinforce that the prisoner is disobeying the rules and that this is an individualized problem or pathology. The prisoner is scolded for rule-breaking. The strategy is to make *disobeying* the problem, not the rules themselves, which are thus shielded from the direct challenge the prisoner has waged.

Hunger striking has both defensive and offensive capabilities. It is reactive to prison punishment and conditions, and yet proactive in amassing and enduring a challenge for a long period. Whether as an individual event or done at scale, the protest upsets prison routines and compels change. The state regimes, again and again across the century, discovered that in spite of their onrush of carceral weapons and penal discipline to subdue the prisoner, their powers could not penetrate some quality of being in hungering that is elusive to state control.

The hunger strike reveals the ultimate contest between the state and the prisoner, that of life and death. What the hunger strike does for the prison is bring death into uneasy proximity to the living. Death on hunger strike is rare. It is greatly feared, it is anticipated, but it is not the common outcome.

Across the span of a century, most all of the hunger strikes to the death have been by men—Irish prisoners both in Britain and Ireland, in India, among the Kurds and leftist dissidents in Turkish prisoners. Is this because of the strikers or the captors? Is this because the state is more indifferent to men or to prisoners jailed for violence and sabotage? Yet there is a great deal of hustle, second-guessing, strategizing, and intervention to prevent death or to forestall it. The vast majority have survived the hunger strike because death was averted through negotiation, intervention, or a ceasing and turning away by the striker. The hunger strike is therefore not the end. It may be the beginning to an end, but that end is not inevitably death.

Whether a hunger strike achieves its purpose, whether it is a success or a failure, seems to rest with vital contingencies such as whether the hunger strike can attach to the larger crises of democracy, accountability, and representation to challenge the legitimacy of rule. This is easier to achieve when the strike in prison is connected with organized political demonstration and insurgency. Success rather than failure also seems to be more likely when an oppositional prisoner solidarity infrastructure has been created.

Perhaps the more expansive and existential question is this: Is it possible to end hunger strikes? From the vantage point of the state, the carceral solution to hunger striking is forcible feeding and more repression. As we have seen, through a century of every twist and turn of their implementation, neither is a solution. Both spill into a quagmire.

In order to end hunger strikes, we need to abolish the structures that fuel hunger striking. Can one abolish the infrastructures of capture and confinement, of detention, camps, and prison, that seed hunger striking as public protest? Reforming prisons and detention is unlikely to solve the problem because it does not address the underlying causes of harm and violence.

The hunger strike as a protest will persist, evolve, mutate as long as the conditions promoting the crisis of democracy and inequity persist, as long as the state strategy of rightlessness targets and deprives many from equitable possibility and confines them indefinitely. What abolition requires, according to activist and scholar Mariame Kaba, is the reduction of the state's powers of oppression. The question, then, is what it would take to build anew a society where prison and detention are not necessary. To dispute, resist, and reject the status quo is necessary if one seeks to imagine a society that eliminates indefinite detention, that decriminalizes human movement, that eases access to courts, and that makes it possible for prisoners to be heard directly.[2]

Hunger striking as a practice creates an inevitable wasting and emptying of the body's vitality as bodily processes slow down over time, leading to the collapse of organs, the diminution of senses. This debility and folding inward, however, in public can paradoxically create externalizing energy and passion, attracting interest and creative actions.

Public visibility is critical oxygen to the hunger strike phenomenon. The medium of photography has become vital to the materialization of the hunger strike outside of prison. Instead of being represented by a statistic, protesters can carry or display an everyday portrait of the hunger striker, providing a visual register of their humanity and dignity, usually prior to imprisonment. Journalists and supporters can also circulate the photographic documentation of the scene of protest. These images, transmitted through media to spectators across space and time, fashion a sense of the collective who stand up for the hunger striker, or mourn the striker's debility and perhaps death, all the while challenging the state's status quo policies of incarceration.

The aesthetics of protest emanate most potently in the actual assembling of the crowd, in the expressiveness of banners, posters, speeches, chants, and songs, in the actions of protestors and police. The prison is materialized outside its own walls through participants who wear prison jumpsuits or dress. In the first decades of the twentieth century, images of mass rallies and funeral processions circulated in photographs and newsreels—documenting protest communities in different regions, sometimes spanning the globe. Yet even the latest high-tech videos from the early twenty-first century cannot fully convey the immediate sensorial experience of the live protest—the smells, taste, noise, bustle, and adrenalin of the crowd. The momentum of the demonstrations generates more political upheaval.[3]

In the public marches, vigils, pickets, and funeral processions, the assemblies of people who support and mourn the hunger strikers breach the boundaries of who counts as "the people," seeking outer limits. Public solidarity with prisoners and detainees builds through news media and communication networks, tapping into a mobilization of already existing movements and organizations and forging new canopies of political opposition to state power. The new avenues of communication rupture the state's secrecy around the conditions of the captives and generate new demands and forums for public accountability.

The hunger strike's battle against inequality drives a wedge into the crisis of states and their uneven enactment of democracy across the century. For instance, the transatlantic American and British suffragist movements' demands for inclusion capitalized on the spectacle of suffering white women before white empires. In Ireland and in India, the hunger strike embraced anticolonial and anti-imperial rebellion and seeded the idea of national sacrifice as expressed through gendered bodies. In the U.S. internment camp at Tule Lake and in South Africa, those caged in detention without charge used hunger strikes to fight against state violence, repression, and racial injustice. Relentlessly, the U.S. and Australian state powers imposed mass incarceration to indefinitely detain migrants. The crisis of democracy, in these cases, lies in how the citizen opponents of immigrant detention want their societies and governments to change.

For those denied rights and those mobilizing on behalf of strikers, attempts must be made to breach the chasm between the rights-bearing and the rightless. Migrants seeking refuge and their advocates must draw on and communicate individual stories of family separation and psychic and physical peril to accomplish the release of the mass of asylum seekers from carceral bureaucracy. Confronting the state and the status quo produces infinite possibilities. In the early twenty-first century, some U.S. citizens have expressed dismay and outrage at the expansion of the carceral state as they witness the indefinite caging of refuge seekers and those incarcerated at Guantánamo. In protest, they call out "not in our name," "not our government," and work to forge a new oppositional solidarity, committed to disavowing and dismantling the structures of criminalization and incarceration that undergird the government's practice.

A hunger strike conveys desperate measures. It is tried when one has exhausted all else. It is the final weapon. And, as we have seen, the conditions and trajectories of hunger striking are incredibly varied. Enacting a hunger strike over a duration is about choice, planning, and determination, as well as self-bargaining to control bodily impulse and self-discipline to endure noneating hour by hour, day by day. The decision to strike is renewed constantly. The strike can evolve and change in terms of duration and whether it is endured alone or in company. It can be started and stopped, turned into a relay among strikers, echoed in sympathy fasts outside the prison. It is also contingent on conditions, including the response of fellow prisoners and prison authorities.

Within a particular campaign, the hunger strike is often the ulimate tool that drives a climactic event. But when we zoom out and look at the overall life span of the person who uses the tool of the hunger strike, it may represent only one instance of the individual's human endurance over an epoch of political battles. This was strikingly true in the cases of Alice Paul, Mary MacSwiney, Gandhi, and Nelson Mandela, as well as Irom Sharmila, Shaker Aamer, and Eaten Fish: all were tireless in expressing purpose and significance in their life's work, beyond their endurance of hunger striking.

The carceral system involves spatial confinement—a geography of institutions and sites of caging, isolation, and punishment. But the protest of the hunger strike can penetrate the prison walls and take up space outside. If the revolt within the prison and the revolt outside are joined, then the challenges for the state escalate.

The carceral system also involves time, as imposed by the prison sentence. A hunger strike, however, claims time in a different dynamic. The strike is a durational performance in which the prisoners, bit by bit, take back both their body and their time. The violence of the state is understood as discipline, coded as routine and necessary to maintain order in the prison. The striker refuses this routine.

The state may control space, but it is vulnerable to temporality, vulnerable to the destabilization that is the striking prisoner's objective—to shake things up. The state is vulnerable because it cannot anticipate and control every contingency. The striking prisoner disrupts the time sentence and time stamps that are in the prison's control. The state tries to stabilize the uprising, to manage the disorder, to calculate how to wall off unwelcome outcomes of the strike. The authorities may calculate that they can wait the protest out, that they can contain its impact.

The stakes of seizing time, seizing the moment from the state, are vast. History can veer onto a different trajectory. Past resolves and political impasses can thaw, recasting the present. And what seemed impossible can become another, possible future.

INTRODUCTION

1. According to the *Oxford English Dictionary* online, the first reference was in a November 1889 *Century Magazine* article, a "narrative of the hunger-strike of the four women in the prison of Irkutsk." Significantly, the Russian word to describe the protest is голодовка (or *golodofka*), which literally means "famine strike" or "famine fast," linking the protests of prisoner self-starvation with the deprivations of recurrent peasant famines. In Gaelic, there are words for ritual fasting (*Troscadh*) and starvation for justice (*Cealachan*), and in Sanskrit a word (*Dhurna*) for exacting justice by fasting at the doorstep, all of which have been interpreted to be culturally specific antecedents for the modern practice of hunger striking. The word combination "hunger strike" has been translated from English into languages as diverse as Gaelic (*stailc ocrais*), Hindi (भूख हड़ताल), French (*grève de la faim*), Spanish (*huelga de hambre*), Arabic (إضرابعنالطعام), and Japanese (ハンスト).

2. Marie Gottschalk, *Caught: The Prison State and the Lockdown of America* (Princeton University Press, 2014); Naomi Murakawa, *The First Civil Right: How Liberals Built Prison America* (Oxford University Press, 2014); Ruth Wilson Gilmore, *Golden Gulag: Prisons, Surplus, Crisis, and Opposition in Globalizing California* (University of California Press, 2007); Frank Dikötter and Ian Brown (eds.), *Cultures of Confinement: A History of the Prison in Africa, Asia, and Latin America* (Cornell University Press, 2007).

3. Dominique Moran, Nick Gill, and Deirdre Conlon (eds.), *Carceral Spaces: Mobility and Agency in Imprisonment and Migrant Detention* (Routledge, 2013); Jenna M. Lloyd and Alison Mountz, *Boats, Borders, and Bases: Race, the Cold War, and the Rise of Migration Detention in the United States* (University of California Press, 2018); Alison Mountz, *The Death of Asylum: Hidden Geographies of the Enforcement Archipelago* (University of Minnesota Press, 2020); Jenna M. Lloyd, Matt Mitchelson, and Andrew Burridge (eds.), *Beyond Walls and Cages: Prisons, Borders, and Global Crisis* (University of Georgia Press, 2012).

4. Michel Foucault, *Discipline and Punish: The Birth of the Prison,* trans. Alan Sheridan (Vintage Books, 1977); David Garland, *Punishment and Modern Society: A Study in Social Theory* (Oxford University Press, 1990); Dominique Moran, *Carceral Geography: Spaces and Practices of Incarceration* (Ashgate, 2015).

5. Padraic Kenney, *Dance in Chains: Political Imprisonment in the Modern World* (Oxford University Press, 2017), 3–6.

6. Giorgio Agamben, *Homo Sacer: Sovereign Power and Bare Life,* trans. Daniel Heller-Roazen (Stanford University Press, 1998).

7. Hannah Arendt, *Origins of Totalitarianism* (1951); A. Naomi Paik, *Rightlessness: Testimony and Redress in U.S. Prison Camps since World War II* (University of North Carolina Press, 2016), 1–3.

8. Banu Bargu, *Starve and Immolate: The Politics of Human Weapons* (Columbia University Press, 2014), 6, 65, 81.

9. Maud Ellmann, *The Hunger Artists: Starving, Writing, and Imprisonment* (Harvard University Press, 1993), 3.

10. Barbara H. Rosenwein, "Worrying about Emotions in History," *American Historical Review* 107, no. 3 (2002): 821–45; Jan Plamper, "The History of Emotions: An Interview with William Reddy, Barbara Rosenwein, and Peter Stearns," *History and Theory* 49, no. 2 (2010): 237–65.

11. Diana Taylor, "Trauma in the Archive," in Elspeth H. Brown and Thy Phu (eds.), *Feeling Photography* (Duke University Press, 2014), 239–51, 249.

12. Michael Gershon, *The Second Brain: The Scientific Basis of Gut Instinct and a Groundbreaking New Understanding of Nervous Disorders of the Stomach and Intestine* (New York: HarperCollins, 1998).

13. Elizabeth A. Wilson, *Gut Feminism* (Duke University Press, 2015), 5, 40–43.

14. Sara Ahmed, "Affective Economies," *Social Text* 22, no. 2 (2004): 117–39.

15. Lauren Berlant, "Thinking about Feeling Historical," *Emotion, Space, and Society* 1, no. 1 (2008): 4–9; Berlant, *Cruel Optimism* (Duke University Press, 2011).

16. Neel Ahuja, *Bioinsecurities: Disease Interventions, Empire, and the Government of Species* (Duke University Press, 2016), 24; Sharon P. Holland, Marcia Ochoa, and Kyla Wazana Tompkins, "On the Visceral," *GLQ: A Journal of Lesbian and Gay Studies* 20, no. 4 (2014): 391–406, 395.

17. For instance: Kevin Grant, *Last Weapons: Hunger Strikes and Fasts in the British Empire, 1890–1948* (University of California Press, 2019); Tim Pratt and James Vernon, "'Appeal from This Fiery Bed . . .': The Colonial Politics of Gandhi's Fasts and Their Metropolitan Reception," *Journal of British Studies* 44, no. 1 (2005): 92–114; Pranab Kumar Chatterjee, "The Hunger-Strike Movement of the Andaman Prisoners in 1937 and National Response," *Proceedings of the Indian History Conference* 40 (1979): 662–69; Francis J. Costello, *Enduring the Most: The Life and Death of Terence MacSwiney* (Brandon Book Publishers, 1995); Neeti Nair, "Bhagat Singh as 'Satyagrahi': The Limits to Non-Violence in Late Colonial India," *Modern Asian Studies* 43, no. 3 (2009): 649–81.

18. Ian Miller, *A History of Force Feeding: Hunger Strikes, Prisons and Medical Ethics, 1909–1974* (Palgrave Macmillan, 2016); Kevin Grant, "Fearing the Danger

Point: The Study and Treatment of Human Starvation in the United Kingdom and India, c. 1880–1974," in Marshall D. McCue (ed.), *Comparative Physiology of Fasting, Starvation, and Food Limitation* (Springer, 2012), 365–77; Corinna Howland, "To Feed or Not to Feed: Violent State Care and the Contested Medicalization of Incarcerated Hunger-Strikers in Britain, Turkey and Guantanamo Bay," *New Zealand Sociology* 28, no. 1 (2013): 101–16; Mary Anne Kenny, "Force-Feeding Asylum Seekers," *Alternative Law Journal* 27, no. 3 (2002): 107–12; Michelle C. Velasquez-Potts, "Carceral Oversight: Force-Feeding and Visuality at Guantánamo Bay Detention Camp," *Public Culture* 31, no. 3 (2019): 581–600.

19. Bargu, *Starve and Immolate;* Patrick Anderson, *So Much Wasted: Hunger, Performance, and the Morbidity of Resistance* (Duke University Press, 2010); Gürcan Koçan and Ahmet Önçü, "From the Morality of Living to the Morality of Dying: Hunger Strikes in Turkish Prisons," *Citizenship Studies* 10, no. 3 (2006): 349–72.

20. Leith Passmore, "Force-Feeding and Mapuche Autonomy: Performing Collective Rights in Individual Prison Cells in Chile," *Journal of Latin American Cultural Studies* 23, no. 1 (2014): 1–16; Macarena Gómez-Barris, "Mapuche Hunger Acts: Epistemology of the Decolonial," *Transmodernity* 1, no. 3 (2012): 120–32.

21. David Beresford, *Ten Men Dead: The Story of the 1981 Irish Hunger Strike* (Atlantic Monthly Press, 1997); Thomas Hennessey, *Hunger Strike: Margaret Thatcher's Battle with the IRA, 1980–1981* (Irish Academic Press, 2014); Allen Feldman, *Formations of Violence: The Narrative of the Body and Political Terror in Northern Ireland* (University of Chicago Press, 1991).

22. Raffaela Puggioni, "Speaking through the Body: Detention and Bodily Resistance in Italy," *Citizenship Studies* 18, no. 5 (2014): 562–77; Johanna Siméant, "Who Clamours for Attention—and Who Cares? Hunger Strikes in France from 1972 to 1992," *La Lettre de La Maison Française d'Oxford* 10 (1998): 98–119; Johanna Siméant and Christophe Traïni, *Bodies in Protest: Hunger Strikes and Angry Music* (Amsterdam University Press, 2016); Patricia Schor and Egbert Alejandro Martina, "The Alien Body in Contemporary Netherlands: Incarceration and Force-Feeding of Asylum Seekers," October 14, 2013, http://criticallegalthinking.com/2013/10/14/alien-body-contemporary-netherlands-incarceration-force-feeding-asylum-seekers/.

23. Audra Simpson, "The State Is a Man: Theresa Spence, Loretta Saunders and the Gender of Settler Sovereignty," *Theory and Event* 19, no. 4 (2016): 1–30.

24. Ralph Armbruster-Sandoval, *Starving for Justice: Hunger Strikes, Spectacular Speech, and the Struggle for Dignity* (University of Arizona Press, 2017); Diane Wilson, *An Unreasonable Woman: A True Story of Shrimpers, Politicos, Polluters, and the Fight for Seadrift, Texas* (Chelsea Green, 2005).

25. Patrick Anderson, "There Will Be No Bobby Sands in Guantánamo Bay," *PMLA* 124, no. 5 (2009): 1733; Anderson, *So Much Wasted,* 10; Feldman, *Formations of Violence,* 237; Bargu, *Starve and Immolate;* Ellmann, *Hunger Artists;* Amanda Machin, "Hunger Power: The Embodied Protest of the Political Hunger Strike," *Interface: A Journal for and about Social Movements* 8, no. 1 (2016): 157–80; Ewa Płonowska Ziarek, "Bare Life on Strike: Notes on the Biopolitics of Race and Gender," *South Atlantic Quarterly* 107, no. 1 (2008): 89–105.

26. Lynn Hunt, *Inventing Human Rights: A History* (W. W. Norton, 2007), 19–34.

27. For a broader framework of race and empire and state power, see Nikhil Pal Singh, *Race and America's Long War* (University of California Press, 2017); Kris Manjapra, *Colonialism in Global Perspective* (Cambridge University Press, 2020).

28. James Hevia, *The Imperial Security State: British Colonial Knowledge and Empire-Building in Asia* (Cambridge University Press, 2012); Fabian Klose, *Human Rights in the Shadow of Colonial Violence: The Wars of Independence in Kenya and Algeria* (University of Pennsylvania Press, 2013); Alfred McCoy, *Policing America's Empire: The United States, the Philippines and the Rise of the Surveillance State* (University of Wisconsin Press, 2009); Stuart Shrader, *Badges without Borders: How Global Counterinsurgency Transformed American Politics* (University of California Press, 2019).

29. Samuel Moyn, *The Last Utopia: Human Rights in History* (Harvard University Press, 2010), 117.

CHAPTER ONE

1. Alex Keyssar, *The Right to Vote: The Contested History of Voting in the United States* (Basic Books, 2000, 2009); Daniel Immerwahr, *How to Hide an Empire: A History of the Greater United States* (Farrar, Straus, Giroux, 2019).

2. Ellen Carol DuBois, *Suffrage: Women's Long Battle for the Vote* (Simon and Schuster, 2020); Sarah Hunter Graham, *Woman Suffrage and the New Democracy* (Yale University Press, 1996).

3. Laura E. Nym Mayhall, *The Militant Suffrage Movement: Citizenship and Resistance in Britain, 1860–1930* (Oxford University Press, 2003), 5; Adam Przeworski, "Conquered or Granted? A History of Suffrage Extensions," *British Journal of Political Science* 39, no. 2 (2009): 291–321.

4. Linda J. Lumsden, *Rampant Women: Suffragists and the Right of Assembly* (University of Tennessee Press, 1997), 25–26.

5. Parliamentary Archives, HC/SA/SJ/10/12/20.

6. Parliamentary Archives, HC/SA/SJ/10/12/21.

7. *London Evening Standard,* July 9, 1909.

8. F. W. Pethick-Lawrence, "The Treatment of Suffragettes in Prison," W.S.P.U. Leaflet No. 59, W.S.P.U. Collection (ca. 1909), Museum of London; Kevin Grant, *Last Weapons: Hunger Strikes and Fasts in the British Empire, 1890–1948* (University of California Press, 2019), 3, 43, 50, 55.

9. Teresa Billington-Greig, "A Criticism of Militancy," in Carol McPhee and Ann Fitzgerald (eds.), *The Non-Violent Militant: Selected Writings of Teresa Billington-Greig* (Routledge, 1987), 190. The essay was first published in 1911.

10. Kevin Grant examines the context of Russian exiles and British suffragists in London cooperating and sharing political ideas and tactics in 1909. Kevin Grant, "British Suffragettes and the Russian Method of Hunger Strike," *Comparative Stud-*

ies in Society and History 53, no. 1 (2011): 113–43; Grant, *Last Weapons*, 51–54; David Wrobel, "Considering Frontiers and Empires: George Kennan's Siberia and the U.S. West," *Western Historical Quarterly* 46, no. 3 (2015): 285–309.

11. *New Age,* "Notes of the Week," July 15, 1909.

12. Letter written to Mrs. Pankhurst from Lucy Carr Shaw, including an extract of a letter from her brother George Bernard Shaw, August 2, 1909, in Cathy Gordon's private collection, https://imageevent.com/bluboi/suffragette?p=21&n=1&m=-1&c=3&l=0&w=1&s=0&z=2.

13. Emmeline Pankhurst, *My Own Story* (Hearst's International Library, 1914), 150.

14. Annie Kenney, *Memories of a Militant* (Edward Arnold, 1924), 145.

15. Mayhall, *Militant Suffrage Movement,* 53–55.

16. Kenney, *Memories of a Militant;* Lisa Tickner, *The Spectacle of Women: Imagery of Suffrage Campaign, 1907–14* (Chatto and Windus, 1987), 104.

17. Evelyn Hilda Burkitt, Birmingham Prison September 20, 1909, Medical Officer Report, British Archives, Kew HO 45/10417/183577.

18. George Kennan, *Siberia and the Exile System, vol. 2* (Cambridge University Press, 2012), 239, n1; Kennan, "In Heaven, God; in Okhotsk, Koch," *Outlook,* September 1, 1906: 28.

19. Assistant Secretary, Home Office Confidential, September 20, 1909, to Governor of the Birmingham Prison, British Archives, Kew HO 45/10417/183577.

20. Evelyn Hilda Burkitt, Birmingham Prison September 20, 1909, Medical Officer Report, British Archives, Kew HO 45/10417/183577.

21. Ellen Barwell, Birmingham Prison September 20, 1909, Medical Officer Report, British Archives, Kew HO 45/10417/183577.

22. *Scotsman,* "Two Suffragettes Released: Hunger Striker's Prison Experiences," October 18, 1909.

23. John O'Callaghan, "Mrs Pankhurst to Begin in Boston," *Boston Globe,* October 21, 1909.

24. Letter to Captain C. M. Gonne from Men's Political Union for Women's Enfranchisement, 28 Berry Street Liverpool, January 5, 1910, Papers of Alice Paul, 1785–1985, Great Britain: correspondence, summons, judgement, 1909–1912, http://pds.lib.harvard.edu/pds/view/53709391 seq. 3.

25. *New York Times,* "Miss Paul Describes Feeding by Force: American Suffragette in Holloway Jail Lay Abed the Whole of 30-Day Sentence. Refused Prison Clothes. Three Wardresses and Two Doctors Held Her While Food Was Injected Through Nostrils. Now Released," December 10, 1909, 1.

26. *Washington Post,* "Harsh to Yankee Girl," November 21, 1909.

27. *New York Times,* "Miss Paul Describes Feeding by Force," December 10, 1909, 1; Letter to Captain C. M. Gonne from Men's Political Union for Women's Enfranchisement.

28. *New York Times,* "Miss Paul Describes Feeding by Force," December 10, 1909, 1.

29. Alice Paul to Tacie Paul, 27 December 1909, Alice Paul Papers 2:29, cited in Mary Walton, *A Woman's Crusade: Alice Paul and the Battle for the Ballot* (St. Martin's Griffin, 2010), 31.

30. *Philadelphia Tribune*, "Alice Paul Talks. Hunger Striker Describes Forcible Feeding," January 22, 1910.

31. *Spokane Daily Chronicle*, "Men Begin Starvation Strike: Refuse to Eat Nice Hot Breakfast," November 6, 1909, 1; *Spokane Press*, "Will Police Use Stomach Pump," November 6, 1909; *Baltimore Sun*, "Pankhurst Friends Over," November 11, 1909, 2; *Baltimore Sun*, "Starvation Strike Fails," November 11, 1909, 2.

32. *San Francisco Chronicle*, "Prefer Bread and Water Diet to Work," November 7, 1909, 29; Joyce Kornbluh, *Rebel Voices: An IWW Anthology* (Charles H. Kerr, 1998), 95–97.

33. Agnes Thecla Fair, "Miss Fair's Letter Dated November 11, 1909," *Workingman's Paper*, November 20, 1; *Workingman's Paper*, "The Disgrace of Spokane," November 13, 1.

34. *Arizona Republican*, "A Woman Orator Jailed at Spokane," November 7, 1909.

35. *Spokane Daily Chronicle*, "Starvation Strike Is Over; Beg for Food and Eat Like Wild Creatures," November 12; Associated Press, "I.W.W. Martyrs Still Refuse to Eat," *San Diego Union and Daily Bee*, November 9, 1909.

36. Constance Lytton, *Prisons and Prisoners* (William Heinemann, 1914), 234–58.

37. *Philadelphia Tribune*, "Alice Paul Talks. Hunger Striker Describes Forcible Feeding," January 22, 1910.

38. Alice Paul to Tacie Paul, 31 August 1909 and 25 September 1909, Alice Paul Papers 2:29, cited in Walton, *Woman's Crusade*, 29; J.D. Zahniser and Amelia R. Fry, *Alice Paul: Claiming Power* (Oxford University Press, 2014).

39. Katherine H. Adams and Michael L. Keene, *Alice Paul and the American Suffrage Campaign* (University of Illinois Press, 2008), 190.

40. Inez Haynes Gillmore [aka Irwin], *The Story of the Woman's Party* (Harcourt, Brace, 1921), 473.

41. *New York Times*, "White House Picketers Sentenced," September 26, 1917.

42. "Police Court," October 21, 1917, National Woman's Party Papers, Library of Congress; and *Suffragist*, "Seven Months," October 27, 1917; cited in Doris Stevens, *Jailed for Freedom* (Boni and Liveright, 1920), 280–81.

43. Alice Paul, *New York Tribune*, October 23, 1917; cited in Stevens, *Jailed for Freedom*, 281.

44. Zahniser and Fry, *Alice Paul*, 282–83.

45. *New York Times*, "Miss Alice Paul on Hunger Strike," November 7, 1917.

46. Alice Paul to Dora Lewis November 1917, National Woman's Party Papers, Library of Congress; *New York Evening World*, "Hunger Strike," November 7, 1917.

47. Stevens, *Jailed for Freedom*, 221–22.

48. Ibid., 220.

49. Ibid., 223.

50. Adams and Keene, *Alice Paul and the American Suffrage Campaign.*

51. Stevens, *Jailed for Freedom,* 223.

52. Ibid., 224.

53. Ibid.

54. Ibid.

55. Ibid., 225.

56. Gillmore, *Story of the Woman's Party,* 245; Adams and Keene, *Alice Paul and the American Suffrage Campaign,* 169.

57. Statement of Miss Lucy Burns, smuggled out of Occoquan by Miss Katherine Morey of Boston, Wednesday, November 14, National Woman's Party Records, Library of Congress.

58. Adams and Keene, *Alice Paul and the American Suffrage Campaign,* 206, 208; Zahniser and Fry, *Alice Paul,* 291.

59. Eleanor Clift, *Founding Sisters and the Nineteenth Amendment* (Wiley, 2003), 152.

60. National Woman's Party, statement, November 17, 1917; *Suffragist,* "The Government Holds the Ringleader," November 24, 1917, National Woman's Party Records, Library of Congress.

61. Zahniser and Fry, *Alice Paul,* 293–94.

62. Correspondence between Mullowney and Zinhkham, November 26–28, 1917, National Woman's Party Papers, Library of Congress; *New York Times,* "Suffrage Pickets Freed," November 28, 1917; *Chicago Tribune,* "Hunger Strike Wins," November 28, 1917; Zahniser and Fry, *Alice Paul,* 294–95.

63. Stevens, *Jailed for Freedom,* 241.

64. Circular Letter, November 9, 1917, National Woman's Party Records, Library of Congress.

65. Telegram, National Woman's Party Records, Library of Congress.

66. Circular Letter from National Woman's Party, Lucy Burns, November 9, 1917, with comments in margins from Edna Dunning, November 1917, National Woman's Party Records, Library of Congress.

67. Letter to Miss Burns from Chicago Illinois from Cora Howland from Chicago, November 12, 1917, National Woman's Party Records, Library of Congress.

68. Fannie A. Bivans, a lawyer from Decatur, Illinois, typed a letter to Miss Lucy Burns, National Woman's Party November 12, 1917, National Woman's Party Records, Library of Congress.

69. Circular Letter from National Woman's Party, Lucy Burns, November 9, 1917, with comments in margins from Mrs. Edward Rider, Letter from Evelyn Barr Brock and Mrs. Marcus J. Brock, National Woman's Party Records, Library of Congress.

70. Christabel Pankhurst, *Unshackled: The Story of How We Won the Vote* (Hutchinson, 1959).

71. Johanna Alberti, *Beyond Suffrage: Feminists in War and Peace, 1914–1928* (Macmillan, 1989); Cheryl Law, *Suffrage and Power: The Women's Movement, 1918–1928* (I.B. Tauris, 1997); Anna Muggeridge, "The Missing Two Million: The

Exclusion of Working-Class Women from the 1918 Representation of the People Act," *French Journal of British Studies* 23, no. 1 (2018).

72. Christine A. Lunardini, *From Equal Suffrage to Equal Rights: Alice Paul and the National Woman's Party, 1912–1928* (NYU Press, 1986), 152.

73. Alice Paul Oral History, Bancroft Library, University of California Berkeley, Regional Oral History Office, Suffragists Oral History Project. Interview Conducted by Amelia R. Fry, November 24–26, 1972, University of California Regents, 1976, 56–57.

74. Scholars in more recent times have explored the role of emotions and affect in political moments; see, for example, Deborah Gould, *Moving Politics: Emotion and ACT UP's Fight Against AIDS* (University of Chicago Press, 2009); Johanna Siméant and Christophe Traïni, *Bodies in Protest: Hunger Strikes and Angry Music* (Amsterdam University Press, 2016).

75. Stevens, *Jailed for Freedom,* vii–viii.

76. Amanda Machin, "Hunger Power: The Embodied Protest of the Political Hunger Strike," *Interface: A Journal for and about Social Movements* 8, no. 1 (2016): 157–80, 159.

77. Barbara Green, *Spectacular Confessions: Autobiography, Performative Activism, and the Sites of Suffrage, 1905–1938* (St. Martin's Press, 1997), 104.

78. James Scott, *Weapons of the Weak: Everyday Forms of Peasant Protest* (Yale University Press, 1987).

79. Janet Raye, "Hellraisers Journal: Agnes Thecla Fair, Hobo Poet and 'The Good Angel of Labor,'" February 17, 2017, www.weneverforget.org/hellraisers-journal-agnes-thecla-fair-hobo-poet-and-the-good-angel-of-labor-memorialized-by-alfred-d-cridge/.

CHAPTER TWO

1. Anne E. Parsons, *From Asylum to Prison: Deinstitutionalization and the Rise of Mass Incarceration after 1945* (University of North Carolina Press, 2018); Kathleen Jones, *Asylums and After: A Revised History of the Mental Health Services from the Early 18th Century to the 1990s* (Athlone Press, 1993).

2. W. W. Gull, "Anorexia Nervosa (Apesia Hysterica, Anorexia Hysterica)," *Transactions of the Clinical Society of London* 7 (1874): 22–28; Joan Jacobs Brumberg, *Fasting Girls: The History of Anorexia Nervosa* (Vintage Books, 2000).

3. Michel Foucault, *Folie et déraison: Histoire de la folie à l'âge classique* (Paris: Plon, 1961); Andrew Scull, *The Most Solitary of Afflictions: Madness and Society in Britain 1700–1900* (Yale University Press, 1993); David Rothman, *The Discovery of the Asylum: Social Order and Disorder in the New Republic,* 2nd ed. (Routledge, 2002).

4. Richard Michael Fox, *Drifting Men* (Leonard and Virginia Woolf, 1930), 119.

5. M. K. Gandhi, *Ethics of Fasting* (Indian Printing Works, 1944), 89–90; *Harijan,* "Hunger Strike," August 19, 1939.

6. Fox, *Drifting Men,* 119.

7. Mary Gordon, *Penal Discipline* (Routledge Kegan Paul, 1922), 234–35.

8. *Leigh v. Gladstone,* 26 T.L.R. 139 (K.B. 1909).

9. "Prison Doctors and the Home Office," *British Medical Journal* 2, no. 2555 (December 18, 1909), 1765–66.

10. J. S. Edkins, "Fasting Prisoners and Compulsory Feeding," *British Medical Journal* 2, no. 2544 (October 2, 1909), 1099.

11. "Fasting Prisoners and Compulsory Feeding," *British Medical Journal* 2, no. 2544 (October 2, 1909), 997–98; *British Medical Journal,* "Fasting Prisoners and Compulsory Feeding," *British Medical Journal* 2, no. 2546 (October 9, 1909), 1175–76; Edward Thompson et al., "Fasting Prisoners and Compulsory Feeding," *British Medical Journal* 2, no. 2546 (October 16, 1909), 1191–93.

12. Agnes F. Savill, C. W. Mansell Moullin, and Sir Victor Horsley, "Preliminary Report on the Forcible Feeding of Suffrage Prisoners," *Lancet* 180, no. 4643 (August 24, 1912): 549–51.

13. Frank Moxon, "What Forcible Feeding Means," London, Women's Press, 1914 Ellen Isabel Jones Papers 7EIJ/2, Women's Library, London School of Economics.

14. Flora Murray, "Torture in the Twentieth Century," London, Women's Press, 1913 Ellen Isabel Jones Papers 7EIJ/2, Women's Library, London School of Economics.

15. "Doctors as Torturers: The Medical Profession Exploited by the Government," London, Women's Press, 1914 Ellen Isabel Jones Papers, 7EIJ/2, Women's Library, London School of Economics.

16. Murray, "Torture in the Twentieth Century," London, Women's Press, 1913 Ellen Isabel Jones Papers 7EIJ/2, Women's Library, London School of Economics.

17. E. D. Kirby, "Forcible Feeding," *British Medical Journal* 2, no. 2556 (December 25, 1909), 1826.

18. House of Commons Hansard, October 1, 1909, vol. 11, cc1636–7W; British Archives, Kew HO 45/10417/183577.

19. House of Commons Hansard, October 1, 1909, vol. 11, cc1636–7W, cc2183–5.

20. G. H. Colt, "The Gag," *Lancet* 170, no. 4389 (October 12, 1907): 1011–17.

21. Leif Svalesen, *The Slave Ship Fredensborg* (Indiana University Press, 2000), 114.

22. Marcus Rediker, *The Slave Ship: A Human History* (Penguin Books, 2008), citing the testimony of Thomas Trotter in Sheila Lambert (ed.), *House of Commons Sessional Papers of the Eighteenth Century, vol. 73* (Scholarly Resources, 1975), 83, 88, 92.

23. Thomas Clouston, "Forcible Feeding," *Lancet* 100, no. 2570 (November 30, 1872): 797–98.

24. Fox, *Drifting Men,* 117–18; cited in Ian Miller, *A History of Force Feeding: Hunger Strikes, Prisons and Medical Ethics, 1909–1974* (Palgrave Macmillan, 2016), 134.

25. Constance Lytton, *Prisons and Prisoners* (William Heinemann, 1914), 268–69.

26. E. Sylvia Pankhurst, "Forcibly Fed: The Story of My Four Weeks in Holloway Gaol," *McClure's Magazine,* August 1913, 87–93.

27. The *Manchester Guardian* published its version of Pankhurst's account on March 26, 1913. E. Sylvia Pankhurst, *The Suffragette Movement: An Intimate Account of Persons and Details* (Longmans, Green, 1931).

28. Roni Chernoff, "History of Tube Feeding: From Ancient Times to the Future," *Nutrition in Clinical Practice* 21 (2006): 408–10; Max Einhorn, *The Duodenal Tube and Its Possibilities* (W. B. Saunders, 1920).

29. Eamon O'Duibhir, Bureau of Military History WS1474, 15, Republic of Ireland, Military Archives Dublin, www.militaryarchives.ie/collections/online-collections/bureau-of-military-history-1913-1921/reels/bmh/BMH.WS1474.pdf.

30. Lytton, *Prisons and Prisoners,* 270.

31. Frank Vassilyadi, Alkistis-Kira Panteliadou, and Christos Panteliadis, "Hallmarks in the History of Enteral and Parenteral Nutrition: From Antiquity to the 20th Century," *Nutrition Clinical Practice* 28, no. 2 (2013): 209–17.

32. Assistant Secretary, Home Office to Governor of the Birmingham Prison, September 20, 1909, British Archives, Kew HO 45/10417/183577; Laura Harkness, "The History of Enteral Nutrition Therapy," *Journal of the American Dietetic Association* 102 (2002): 399–404.

33. Miller, *History of Force Feeding,* 72–73.

34. Ibid., 73–74.

35. Fox, *Drifting Men,* 117–18.

36. Eamon O'Duibhir, Bureau of Military History WS1474, 15.

37. Kevin Grant, "Fearing the Danger Point: The Study and Treatment of Human Starvation in the United Kingdom and India, c. 1880–1974," in Marshall D. McCue (ed.), *Comparative Physiology of Fasting, Starvation, and Food Limitation* (Springer, 2012): 365–77.

38. Eamon O'Duibhir, Bureau of Military History WS1474, 26–27.

39. Fanny Parker, alias Janet Arthur, published in "Another Prison Infamy," *Votes for Women* (1914), National Records of Scotland reference: HH16/43/6.

40. Ibid.

41. Ibid.

42. June Purvis, "June Purvis Challenges Assumptions That the Force-Feeding of Hunger-Striking Suffragettes Was Merely Extremely Unpleasant," *Times Higher Education Supplement* no. 1225 (April 26, 1996): 21.

43. Parker, "Another Prison Infamy."

44. Ibid.

45. Gordon, *Penal Discipline,* 234–35.

46. Bliss, D. W., "Feeding per Rectum: As Illustrated in the Case of the Late President Garfield and Others," *Medical Record,* July 15, 1882.

47. J. W. A. Mackenzie, "The Nutrient Enema," *Archives of Disease in Childhood* 18, no. 93 (March 1943): 22–27; "Rectal Alimentation," *Nature* 118, no. 2980 (1926): 858–59; Julius Friedenwald and Samuel Morrison, "A History of the Enema," *Bulletin of the History of Medicine* 8, no. 2 (February 1940): 239–76; A. Rendle Short and H. W. Bywaters, "Amino-Acids and Sugars in Rectal Feeding," *British Medical Journal* 1, no. 2739 (June 28, 1913): 1361–67.

48. David Dellinger, *From Yale to Jail: The Life Story of a Moral Dissenter* (Pantheon, 1993).

49. Letter from Raymond Dellinger to James Bennett, October 28, 1943, RG 129, Box 23, Folder 1, National Archives at College Park, Maryland.

50. Letter from James Bennett to Raymond Dellinger, October 30, 1943, RG 129, Box 23, Folder 1, National Archives at College Park, Maryland.

51. Judge Webber Wilson, U.S. Board of Parole, David Dellinger case transcript, February 7, 1944, RG 129, Box 23, Folder 1, National Archives at College Park, Maryland.

52. Murray, "Torture in the Twentieth Century."

53. Eamon O'Duibhir, Bureau of Military History WS1474, 16.

54. Inquest Report of the Jury on the Death of Thomas Ashe (Dublin: Fegus O' Conor, ca. 1917), "Account of the Force-Feeding in Mountjoy Prison resulting in the Death of Thomas Ashe 20–25 September 1917," Austin Stack and Nora Ashe MS 44,612, National Library of Ireland.

55. "Register of Criminal Prisoners on Hunger Strike, 1913–1940," British Archives, Kew, PCOM 2/465.

56. Miller, *History of Force Feeding*, 128.

57. Ibid., 71.

58. Joe Sim, *Medical Power in Prisons: The Prison Medical Service in England, 1774–1988* (Open University Press, 1990), 178–79.

CHAPTER THREE

1. How democracy and voting rights were enacted differed widely under dominion status. In Canada and South Africa dominions, voting denials continued for non-propertied men, all women, all indigenous people, and most Asian and African peoples. Australia, however, universalized white male suffrage and advanced white women's suffrage. Julie Evans, Patricia Grimshaw, David Phillips, and Shurlee Swain, *Equal Subjects, Unequal Rights: Indigenous Peoples in British Settler Colonies, 1830–1910* (Manchester University Press, 2003); Marilyn Lake and Henry Reynolds, *Drawing the Global Colour Line: White Men's Countries and the Question of Racial Equality* (Cambridge University Press, 2008).

2. The historical context for British rule over Ireland, the Irish Home Rule movement, and the partition of Ireland in the following paragraphs is drawn from Alvin Jackson, *Home Rule: An Irish History, 1800–2000* (Oxford University Press, 2003); Alan O'Day, *Irish Home Rule, 1867–1921* (Manchester University Press, 1998); Alvin Jackson (ed.), *The Oxford Handbook of Modern Irish History* (Oxford University Press, 2014); R. F. Foster, *Modern Ireland: 1600–1972* (Penguin Books, 1989); A. T. Q. Stewart, *The Narrow Ground: Aspects of Ulster, 1609–1969* (Blackstaff Press, 1997).

3. Louise Ryan, "Traditions and Double Moral Standards: The Irish Suffragists' Critique of Nationalism," *Women's History Review* 4, no. 4 (1995): 487–503; Louise

Ryan and Margaret Ward (eds.), *Irish Women and the Vote: Becoming Citizens* (Irish Academic Press, 2007); Margaret Ward, "Conflicting Interests: the British and Irish Suffrage Movements," *Feminist Review* 50, no. 1 (1995): 127–47.

4. Charlotte H. Fallon, *Soul of Fire: A Biography of Mary MacSwiney* (Mercier Press, 1986), 19–22.

5. Dave Hannigan, *Terence MacSwiney: The Hunger Strike That Rocked the Empire* (O'Brien Press, 2010); D. M. Lesson, *The Black and Tans: British Police and Auxiliaries in the Irish War of Independence, 1920–21* (Oxford University Press, 2011), 188.

6. P. S. O'Hegarty, *A Short Memoir of Terence MacSwiney* (Talbot Press, 1922), 90.

7. Muriel MacSwiney, Bureau of Military History, WS 637, 15, Republic of Ireland Military Archives, Dublin.

8. O'Hegarty, *Short Memoir of Terence MacSwiney*, 90.

9. Hannigan, *Terence MacSwiney*.

10. Muriel MacSwiney, Bureau of Military History, WS 637, 16.

11. Friar Dominic O'Connor's statement quoted in O'Hegarty, *Short Memoir of Terence MacSwiney*, 92.

12. Sean McConville, *Irish Political Prisoners, 1848–1922: Theatres of War* (Routledge, 2003), 745.

13. Francis Costello, *Enduring the Most: The Life and Death of Terence MacSwiney* (Brandon, 1995), 160; Fannon, *Soul of Fire*, 46–47.

14. *Observer,* August 22, 1920; quoted in Hannigan, *Terence MacSwiney*, 127.

15. *New York Times,* "Irrepressible Ireland," October 26, 1920; Paige Reynolds, *Modernism, Drama, and the Audience for Irish Spectacle* (Cambridge University Press, 2007), 137.

16. Annie MacSwiney diary, Terence MacSwiney Papers P48B/421, University College Dublin Special Collections.

17. Ibid.

18. Ibid.

19. Ibid.

20. Ibid.

21. *Guardian and Observer,* "Death of Lord Mayor of Cork," October 26, 1920.

22. *Rochester Democrat and Chronicle,* "Cork Jail Hunger Striker Dies," October 18, 1920.

23. *New York Times,* "Hunger Striker Dies in Cork Jail after 68-Day Fast," October 18, 1920; *New York Times,* "Joseph Murphy Dies of 76 Days' Hunger Strike, the Second Prisoner to Succumb in Cork Jail," October 26, 1920.

24. *New York Times,* "Pope Shows Deep Regret," October 27, 1920; *New York Times,* "MacSwiney a Martyr, Leaders' Views Here," October 26, 1920; *Scotsman,* "A City of Mourning," October 30, 1920; *New York Times,* "Great Throng Here Honors MacSwiney," November 1, 1920; *Boston Daily Globe,* "60,000 at Worchester MacSwiney Service," November 1, 1920; *Washington Post,* "10,000 in Cortege: Washington Pays Great Tribute to Sacrifice of MacSwiney," *Washington Post,*

November 1, 1920; *Toronto Daily Star,* "Mass for Mr. MacSwiney," November 3, 1920; *Boston Daily Globe,* "Parade of 30,000 Mourns Irish Martyrs Tribute Paid by 100,000 on Commons," November 1, 1920.

25. *New York Times,* "MacSwiney a Martyr."

26. *Scotsman,* "The Late Lord Mayor of Cork," October 29, 1920.

27. Ibid.

28. *Scotsman,* "City of Mourning."

29. British Pathé, "Death of Lord Mayor of Cork," newsreel, 1920, www.youtube.com/watch?v = IpJl3L33nv8; "Funeral of Terence MacSwiney, Cork Mayor," Film 90937 (1920), Huntley Film Archives, www.youtube.com/watch?v= 0zRnDNyp218.

30. *New York Times,* "Great Throng Here Honors MacSwiney."

31. *New York Times,* "30,000 Bostonians March for MacSwiney," November 1, 1920.

32. Reynolds, *Modernism, Drama, and the Audience for Irish Spectacle,* 154.

33. Anthony Bradle, "Nation, Pedagogy, and Performance: W. B. Yeats's *The King's Threshold* and the Irish Hunger Strikes," *Literature & History* 18, no. 2 (Autumn 2009): 20.

34. W. B. Yeats, *The King's Threshold: Manuscript Materials,* ed. Declan Kiely (Cornell University Press, 2005), 417, 429, 434.

35. The book included articles he contributed to the *Irish Freedom* newspaper from 1911 to 1913.

36. Everett Jenkins, *Pan-African Chronology III: A Comprehensive Reference to the Black Quest for Freedom in Africa, the Americas, Europe and Asia, 1914–1929* (McFarland, 2011), 305.

37. Hannigan, *Terence MacSwiney.*

38. Sarmila Bose and Eilis Ward, "'India's Cause Is Ireland's Cause': Elite Links and Nationalist Politics," in Michael Holmes and Denis Holmes (eds.), *Ireland and India: Connections, Comparisons, Contrasts* (Folens, 1997), 55.

39. *Boston Daily Globe,* "Mary MacSwiney on Hunger Strike," November 7, 1922.

40. *Irish Independent,* "The Misses MacSwiney," November 23, 1922.

41. State Paper Office, Dublin S 1369/9 National Archive of Ireland (NAI).

42. Ibid.

43. Ibid.

44. Ibid.

45. *Irish Times,* "Miss Mary MacSwiney and Dr Cohalan," November 25, 1922.

46. Logue to Cosgrave, November 15, 1922, S 1369/9 NAI.

47. *Irish Times,* "Miss MacSwiney and Dr Colahan."

48. Logue to Cosgrave, November 15, 1922, S 1369/9 NAI.

49. Ibid.

50. Fallon, *Soul of Fire,* 90; *Irish Times,* "Miss Mary MacSwiney," November 18, 1922, 7.

51. At the time, Seán MacSwiney was fighting the Irish Free State government and evading capture, and their other two sisters were nuns in the United States and Japan.

52. *Irish Times,* November 21, 1922; Fallon, *Soul of Fire,* 91.

53. British Pathé, "Miss Mary MacSwiney," newsreel, 1922, www.youtube.com /watch?v=9xT4Qd2_n7c.

54. *Evening Herald* (Dublin), "Message from Mountjoy Prison to the People of Ireland," November 15, 1922.

55. Journalist and fiction writer Dorothy Macardle published an account of her Irish Civil War experiences, *Earth-Bound: Nine Stories of Ireland* (1924), and a historical account of 1916–1926 political history, *The Irish Republic* (1937).

56. "Vigil: A Journal of Mountjoy," November 23, 1922, entry of Dorothy Macardle jail journals, pp. 15–16, de Valera Papers P/150/1658, University College Dublin Archives.

57. Ibid.

58. Ibid.

59. *Irish Independent,* "Miss MacSwiney, TD, Released—Now in Nursing Home," November 28, 1922; Fallon, *Soul of Fire,* 92–93.

60. Letter from Miss MacSwiney to Madame Humphries, Wednesday, November 29, 1922, de Valera Papers P/150/1658, University College Dublin Archives.

61. P. S. O'Hegarty, *The Victory of Sinn Féin* (Talbot Press, 1924); Rosemary Cullen Owens, *A Social History of Women in Ireland, 1870–1970* (Gill and Macmillan, 2005), 126.

62. Bryan Fanning, *Histories of Irish Future* (Bloomsbury, 2015).

63. Michael Biggs, "The Rationality of Self-Inflicted Sufferings: Hunger Strikes by Irish Republicans, 1916–1923," *University of Oxford Sociology Working Papers 2007,* 403; James Healy, "The Civil War Hunger-Strike—October 1923," *Studies: An Irish Quarterly Review* 71 (1982): 213–26 (see esp. 214).

64. Healy, "Civil War Hunger-Strike—October 1923," 215.

CHAPTER FOUR

1. There is dispute about Nani Gopal Mukherjee's age. In his memoir, *The Story of My Transportation for Life* (Sadbhakti Publications, 1950), Vinayak Damodar Savarkar refers to him as a "16 or 17 year old Bengali Brahmin lad," whereas James Campbell Ker, a colonial civil servant in British criminal intelligence, identified Mukherjee as twenty years of age in his British India government publication *Political Trouble in India, 1907–1917.* Historian Kevin Grant has most recently sided with Ker's information as more authoritative. The difference in age bears on a moral debate about prison treatment for underage youths versus adult convicts. See Grant, *Last Weapons: Hunger Strikes and Fasts in the British Empire, 1890–1948* (University of California Press, 2019), 179, fn. 16.

2. Savarkar, *Story of My Transportation for Life,* 167, 169, 175; Vikram Sampath, *Savarkar: Echoes from a Forgotten Past, 1883–1924* (Viking, 2019), 307–9.

3. Grant, *Last Weapons,* 106–9; Maia Ramnath, *From Haj to Utopia: How the Ghadar Movement Charted Global Radicalism* (University of California Press, 2011); Seema Sohi, *Echoes of Mutiny: Race, Surveillance, and Indian Anticolonialism in North America* (Oxford University Press, 2014); Tim Harper, "Singapore, 1915, and the Birth of the Asian Underground," *Modern Asian Studies* 47, no. 6 (November 2013): 1782–1811.

4. *Times of India,* "Votes for Women: Forcible Feeding Meeting of Protest," October 28, 1909.

5. Grant, *Last Weapons,* 108.

6. Shahid Amin, *Event, Metaphor, Memory: Chauri Chaura, 1922–1992* (University of California Press, 1994).

7. Mohandas K. Gandhi, *An Autobiography: The Story of My Experiments with Truth,* trans. Mahadev Desai (Beacon Press, 1993), 430.

8. "The Fast," in Gandhi, *Autobiography,* 430–34.

9. These were published as weekly installments, first in Gujarati in Gandhi's magazine *Navajivan* (New Life) in 1924 and later translated by Gandhi's secretary, Mahadev Desai, into English and published in Gandhi's English-language newspaper, *Young India.* The installments were combined in Gandhi's *Autobiography,* in two volumes, published first in Gujarati (1926, 1928) and then in English (1927, 1929). It was then retranslated into English in 1939 and published worldwide in 1940. Ramachandra Guha, *Gandhi: The Years That Changed the World, 1914–1948* (Knopf, 2018), 266–69, 280; Gandhi, *Autobiography.*

10. Nirmal Kumar Bose, *Studies in Gandhism* (Indian Associated Publishing, 1947), 175; Joan V. Bondurant, *Conquest of Violence: The Gandhian Philosophy of Conflict* (University of California Press, 1965), 37; M. K. Gandhi, *Ethics of Fasting* (Indian Printing Works, 1944); Parama Roy, *Alimentary Tracts: Appetites, Aversions and the Postcolonial* (Duke University Press, 2010), 103–4; Banu Bargu, "Gandhi's Fasts," blog post, November 29, 2017, http://blogs.law.columbia.edu/uprising1313/banu-bargu-gandhis-fasts/?cn-reloaded=1.

11. M. K. Gandhi, *Collected Works of Mahatma Gandhi, vol. 23* (Government of India, Publications Division, 1999), 419–20.

12. Grant, *Last Weapons,* 104; Sampath, *Savarkar.*

13. Savarkar, *Story of My Transportation for Life,* 177, 374–75; Sampath, *Savarkar,* 437–38.

14. Grant, *Last Weapons,* 104–5.

15. Savarkar, *Story of My Transportation for Life,* 267–68.

16. Ibid.

17. C. S. Venu, *Jatin Das (The Martyr)* (Madras: C. S. Cunniah, 1930), 31.

18. Neeti Nair, "Bhagat Singh as 'Satyagrahi': The Limits to Non-violence in Late Colonial India," *Modern Asian Studies* 43, no. 3 (May 2009), 649–81 (see esp. 660–66).

19. Malwinder Jit Singh Waraich, *Bhagat Singh: The Eternal Rebel* (Government of India, Ministry of Information and Broadcasting, 2007), 116.

20. Ibid., 119–23.

21. Venu, *Jatin Das,* 35–36.

22. Ibid., 41.

23. British Pathé, "Revolutionary Jatin Das Funeral at Lahore," newsreel, 1929, www.youtube.com/watch?v = aK9kuLDSlaA.

24. Venu, *Jatin Das,* 39–47.

25. Ibid., 1.

26. Muhammad Ali Jinnah, speech, September 12 and 14, 1929, in Central Assembly; Neeti Nair, *Changing Homelands: Hindu Politics and the Partition of India* (Harvard University Press, 2011), 122–23.

27. Bose, *Indian Struggle,* 179.

28. Mahatma Gandhi, "Letter to Bhupendra Nath Banerjee," October 8, 1929; in Gandhi, *Collected Works, vol. 47,* 215; Lati Mani, *Contentious Traditions: The Debate on Sati in Colonial India* (University of California Press, 1998).

29. Bose, *Indian Struggle,* 180.

30. Mahatma Gandhi, "My Silence," *Young India,* October 10, 1929; reprinted in Gandhi, *Collected Works, vol. 47,* 264.

31. The "Declaration of Independence of India" was passed by the Indian National Congress on December 19, 1929, and publicly read throughout India on January 26, 1930. See www.satyagrahafoundation.org/purna-swaraj-the-declaration-of-the-independence-of-india/.

32. Grant, *Last Weapons,* 121; D. A. Low, *Eclipse of Empire* (Cambridge University Press, 1993), 154–55.

33. Taylor C. Sherman, *State Violence and Punishment in India* (Routledge, 2010); Pramod Kumar Srivastava, "Resistance and Repression in India: The Hunger Strike at the Andaman Cellular Jail in 1933," *Crime, Histoire et Sociétés/Crime, History and Society* 7, no. 2 (2003): 81–102.

34. Pranab Kumar Chatterjee, "The Hunger-Strike Movement of the Andaman Prisoners in 1937 and National Response," *Proceedings of the Indian History Congress* 40 (1979): 662–69.

35. Sherman, *State Violence,* 103–5.

36. Telegrams from Governor of Bengal to Secretary of State, July 7 and 11, 1939, British Library, India Office Records (IOR), Coll 115/3B; "Hunger strike by political prisoners in Bengal jails," Reference: IOR/L/PJ/8/492 (July to September 1939).

37. Sugata Bose, *His Majesty's Opponent: Subhas Chandra Bose and India's Struggle against Empire* (Belknap Press of Harvard University Press, 2011).

38. *Harijan,* "Bengal Political Prisoners," July 15, 1939.

39. *Harijan,* "To Bengal Prisoners," August 5, 1939; Gandhi, *Ethics of Fasting,* 89–90.

40. *Harijan,* "Hunger Strike," August 19, 1939.

41. "Speech at the All India Congress C. Meeting," Bombay, August 8, 1942, in Gandhi, *Collected Works, vol. 76,* 392.

42. Guha, *Gandhi,* 641–51.

43. *Times* (London), August 10, 1942, 3. A similar statement was made by the Government of India itself on August 7 or 8. Nicholas Mansergh (ed.), *Transfer of Power, vol. 2* (London: HMSO, 1970), 600–603; Gandhi, *Collected Works, vol. 76,* 463–66.

44. Paul Greenough, "Political Mobilization and the Underground Literature of the Quit India Movement, 1942–44," *Social Scientist* 27, no. 7/8 (1999): 11–47; P. N. Chopra (ed.), *Quit India Movement: British Secret Report* (Thomson Press, 1976), 10.

45. Bipan Chandra, Mridula Mukherjee, Aditya Mukherjee, Sucheta Mahajan, and K. N. Panikkar, *India's Struggle for Independence, 1857–1947* (Penguin, 2003).

46. M. K. Gandhi to Lord Linlithgow, December 31, 1942, in Gandhi, *Collected Works, vol. 77,* 50–51.

47. Ibid., 56.

48. *Hindu,* "An Explanation," February 27, 1943.

49. Gandhi, *Autobiography;* Guha, *Gandhi;* Joseph Lelyveld, *Great Soul: Mahatma Gandhi and His Struggle with India* (Vintage Books, 2011).

50. *New York Times,* "Gandhi Starts Fast to Protest Arrest," March 16, 1943.

51. *Chicago Daily Tribune,* "Gandhi Starts Hunger Strike to Last 21 Days: Protests His Confinement behind Barbed Wire," February 11, 1943.

52. Letter to Secretary of State for India from Dr. John B. Primmer, February 23, 1943, and response, IOR L/PJ/7/5285.

53. *Indian Express,* "Gandhiji Breaks Fast," March 4, 1943; "Talk before Breaking 21 Day Fast," in Gandhi, *Collected Works, vol. 77,* 70–71.

54. Mohandas Gandhi, *Bapu Ke Ashirwad,* November 26, 1944.

CHAPTER FIVE

1. Richard Drinnon, *Keeper of Concentration Camps: Dillon S. Myer and American Racism* (University of California Press, 1987), 78–79.

2. Dorothy S. Thomas and Richard Nishimoto, *The Spoilage: Japanese-American Evacuation and Resettlement during World War II* (University of California Press, 1946).

3. Drinnon, *Keeper of Concentration Camps,* 80.

4. Ibid., 90–95. See also Takashi Fujitani, *Race for Empire: Koreans as Japanese and Japanese as Americans during World War II* (University of California Press, 2011).

5. Thomas and Nishimoto, *Spoilage,* 62–63, 105–7.

6. Jeffery F. Burton, Mary M. Farrell, Florence B. Lord, and Richard W. Lord, *Confinement and Ethnicity: An Overview of World War II Japanese American Relocation Sites* (University of Washington Press, 2002), 289.

7. Thomas and Nishimoto, *Spoilage,* 106.

8. Ibid., 128–46; Michi Nishiura Weglyn, *Years of Infamy: The Untold Story of America's Concentration Camps* (University of Washington Press, 1996), 160–65;

Commission on Wartime Relocation and Internment of Civilians, *Personal Justice Denied: Report of the Commission on Wartime Relocation and Internment of Civilians* (University of Washington Press, 1997; originally published in 1982–83), 247; FBI Investigation of the Tule Lake Relocation Center, November 12–December 10, 1943, p. 460, Folder 1.4, Box 14, Japanese American Internment Case Files, RG 118, National Archives Pacific Region; Tule Lake Reports JERS R161/F448; Rosalie Hankey, field notes, November 20, 1943, JERS 93/265, Bancroft Library, University of California (UC) Berkeley.

9. Greg Robinson, *A Tragedy of Democracy: Japanese Confinement in North America* (Columbia University Press, 2009), 193–94; *Washington Post,* "Tule Lake Riot Was Exaggerated, WRA Chief Says," November 14, 1943; Thomas and Nishimoto, *Spoilage,* 158; Commission on Wartime Relocation and Internment of Civilians, *Personal Justice Denied,* 247; Drinnon, *Keeper of Concentration Camps,* 111; FBI report, August 2, 1945, 162a–d, Torture at Tule Lake, concerning the cases of Tokio Yamane, Tom Yoshio Kobayashi, and Koji Todoroki, RG 60, Entry 38B, WWII FBI Files 62–69030–710, Box 81, 650/230/32/38/5, National Archives; Barbara Takei, "Legalizing Detention: Segregated Japanese Americans and the Justice Department's Renunciation Program," in *A Question of Loyalty: Internment at Tule Lake* (Shaw Historical Library, 2005), 75–105.

10. Thomas and Nishimoto, *Spoilage,* 150–51.

11. United Press International, "Martial Law Rules Japs in Tule Lake," *Los Angeles Times,* November 14, 1943; *Los Angeles Times,* "Work or Starve Rule Being Used by the Army," November 14, 1943.

12. Thomas and Nishimoto, *Spoilage,* 156; War Relocation Authority (WRA), "Tule Lake Incident: Report of Talks by Colonel Verne Austin," University of California, Los Angeles (UCLA) Special Collections.

13. Ibid., 158.

14. Commission on Wartime Relocation and Internment of Civilians, *Personal Justice Denied,* 247; Drinnon, *Keeper of Concentration Camps,* 137–41; FBI report, August 2, 1945, 162a–d, Torture at Tule Lake, concerning the cases of Tokio Yamane, Tom Yoshio Kobayashi, and Koji Todoroki, RG 60, Entry 38B, WWII FBI Files 62–69030–710, Box 81, 650/230/32/38/5, National Archives; Takei, "Legalizing Detention."

15. "Kibei" in Gary Okihiro (ed.), *Encyclopedia of Japanese American Internment* (ABC-CLIO, 2013), 88–89.

16. Fujitani, *Race,* 140–46.

17. Eileen H. Tamura, *In Defense of Justice: Joseph Kurihara and the Japanese American Struggle for Equality* (University of Illinois Press, 2013).

18. Thomas and Nishimoto, *Spoilage,* 156; Greg Robinson, *A Tragedy of Democracy: Japanese Confinement in North America* (Columbia University Press, 2009), 193–94.

19. Gary Y. Okihiro, "Tule Lake under Martial Law: A Study in Japanese Resistance," *Journal of Ethnic Studies* 5, no. 3 (1977): 71–85, 77.

20. Ibid.

21. Thomas and Nishimoto, *Spoilage,* 177–79; John Tateishi, *And Justice for All: An Oral History of the Japanese American Detention Camps* (University of Washington Press, 1999), 114–18.

22. Box 43, Folders 7–8, Verne Austin Papers, UCLA Special Collections.

23. "Stockade Prisoners Rebellion investigation by Sgt Yeramian," December 31, 1943, Box 43, Folders 7–8, Verne Austin Papers, UCLA Special Collections.

24. Petition submitted to Henry L. Stimson, Secretary of War, by Tule Lake residents. December 7, 1943, Box 43, Folder 8, Verne Austin Papers, UCLA Special Collections.

25. "Record of Events. January 1944" and "A notice issued by Lieutenant L.G. Schaner, Provost Marshal. January 3, 1944 Physical Description: Re: Food," Box 43, Folder 8, Verne Austin Papers, UCLA Special Collections.

26. "Edwards Memorandum, January 4, 1944," "Statement of Harry Nogawa to Sergeant Sam Yeramian, investigator, January 3, 1944, Re: Troublemakers, " and "Letter, Austin to Ernest Kozuma, member in the negotiating committee. January 4, 1944 re A meeting of camp residents to be held January 5, 1944," Box 43, Folder 8, Verne Austin Papers, UCLA Special Collections.

27. Hiroyoshi Tsuda to Sergeant Sam Yeramian, investigator, January 5, 1944, Box 43, Folder 8, Verne Austin Papers, UCLA Special Collections.

28. Archivally, the transcript exists through the collaboration of WRA and academic social science research and collection by University of California scholars and is archived at UC Berkeley's Bancroft Library. These reports and correspondence became the sources for a series of social science publications, including Thomas and Nishimoto's *The Spoilage,* that documented Japanese American behavior, social and individual loss, carceral removal, and rehabilitation into assimilated American subjects or damaged subjects expelled and repatriated to Japan.

29. A. Naomi Paik, *Rightlessness: Testimony and Redress in U.S. Prison Camps since World War II* (University of North Carolina Press, 2016), 3.

30. "Hiroyoshi Tsuda to Sergeant Sam Yeramian, investigator, January 5, 1944" and "Report of the Informal Interview of the Divisional Responsible Men and the Detained Stockade Internees, January 14, 1944," p. 4, Box 43, Folder 8, Verne Austin Papers, UCLA Special Collections.

31. Tatsuo Ryusei Inouye, "Tule Lake Stockade Diary," ed. Martha Nakagawa, trans. Masumi Izumi, UCLA Asian American Studies Center (2018); see chap. 13, "End of Hunger Strike," www.suyamaproject.org/wp-content/uploads/2018/05 /Inouye_Diary_Chap13_End_Hunger_Strike.pdf. I am grateful that Inouye's daughter, Nancy Oda, made available to me a preliminary translation of this diary in 2015.

32. Ibid.

33. Ibid.

34. W. R. LaFleur, "Hungry Ghosts and Hungry People: Somaticity and Rationality in Medieval Japan," in *Fragments for a History of the Human Body, vol. 1* (Zone Books, 1989), 270–303 (see esp. 274).

35. Inouye, "Tule Lake Stockade Diary."

36. Ibid.

37. Informal Interview of the Divisional Responsible Men, Box 43, Folder 8, Verne Austin Papers, UCLA Special Collections.

38. Drinnon, *Keeper of Concentration Camps.*

39. Thomas and Nishimoto, *Spoilage,* 292; *San Pedro News Pilot,* "Tule Japs Denied Rights, Charge," July 14, 1944; *Christian Science Monitor,* "Counsel Rights Seen Denied to Japanese," July 14, 1944; *American Civil Liberties Union News,* "Tyranny Reigns at Tule Lake," August 1944; American Civil Liberties Union of Northern California records, MS 3580, California Historical Society; Bancroft MSS 78/177 c; Stockade Cases 1944, Box 21, Folders 1–5, Wayne M. Collins Papers, Bancroft Library, UC Berkeley.

40. WRA Manual, "Administrative Separation of Residents within Center," Section 110.15 April 26, 1944; Thomas and Nishimoto, *Spoilage,* 286.

41. Thomas and Nishimoto, *Spoilage,* 372.

42. Ibid., 293–94.

43. Yoshiyama, "Diary since the Hunger Strike," July 18–August 25, 1944, Japanese American Evacuation and Resettlement Records, Bancroft MSS 67/14 c Reel 184 Frame:0643, Folder R 26.30, Bancroft Library, UC Berkeley.

44. Thomas and Nishimoto, *Spoilage,* 294–95.

45. Ibid., 296.

46. Bancroft MSS 78/177 c 16t, Wayne M. Collins Papers, Suffragists Oral History Project, Bancroft Library, UC Berkeley.

47. Yoshiyama, "Diary."

48. Ibid.

49. Ibid.

50. Ibid.

51. Ibid.

52. *Newell Star,* "Stockade: Isolation Area Empty: Occupants Return Home," August 31, 1944.

53. Inouye, "Tule Lake Stockade Diary."

54. Cynthia Eller, *Conscientious Objectors and the Second World War: Moral and Religious Arguments in Support of Pacifism* (Praeger, 1991); John D'Emilio, *Lost Prophet: The Life and Times of Bayard Rustin* (University of Chicago Press, 2003); David Dellinger, *From Yale to Jail: The Life and Times of a Moral Dissenter* (Wipf and Stock, 1993).

55. *Crisis,* "Seabee Hunger Strike Investigated," April 1945, 110–11; *New York Times,* "Ends Navy Hunger Strike," March 5, 1945; Norman Houston of the Los Angeles Branch of the NAACP, 34th Construction Battalion and violence against black Seabees, Papers of the NAACP, Part 09: Discrimination in the U.S. Armed Forces, Series A: General Office Files on Armed Forces' Affairs, 1918–1955.

56. Jewish Telegraphic Agency (JTA), "Refugees Detained at La Spezia Call Hunger Strike; Insist on Sailing for Palestine," April 10, 1946, www.jta.org/1946/04/10 /archive/refugees-detained-at-la-spezia-call-hunger-strike-insist-on-sailing-for -palestine; *Miami News,* "Jewish Refugees End Hunger Strike," April 11, 1946; Jewish

Telegraphic Agency, "Passover Prayers for the Strikers Recited by Thousands under Open Sky," April 18, 1946, www.jta.org/1946/04/18/archive/palestine-leaders-resting-after-winning-hunger-strike-for-admission-of-refugees.

57. "Vienna Students in Sympathy Strike," JTA Vienna, March 12, 1937; "Wilno Jewish Students to Combat Segregation Efforts," JTA Warsaw, February 12, 1937.

58. Bob Matthews, "How Long Can a Human Fast," *Afro-American* (Baltimore), September 26, 1961; Thomas Gaither, *Jailed-In* (New York: League for Industrial Democracy, 1961); Issac B. Rebert, "Three Negroes of Hunger Strike," *Sun* (Baltimore), September 12, 1961; Dan Ridout, "Maryland's Court Case Marked by Hunger Strike," *Chicago Daily Defender,* October 23, 1961; *Chicago Daily Tribune,* "Hunger Strike Woman Moved to Hospital," February 16, 1960; Baker E. Morten, "Ex-Track Star Continues Jail Fast; Pickets Protest," *Chicago Defender,* February 3, 1960; Charles Layne, "Passive Resistance in Elkton, Maryland," *Philadelphia Tribune,* September 26, 1961.

CHAPTER SIX

1. Even though the Union Party received more than 11 percent more votes, the parliamentary election system, which favored rural over urban districts, gave control to the National Party.

2. "Pass laws" were an internal passport system employed in Cape Colony and later Transvaal that regulated and controlled the movement and residency of non-white laborers, and were applied to black Africans, Indians, Chinese, and Coloured people. In 1952, pass laws were aimed at black men and institutionalized nationally, limiting access to residences, labor, and public accommodations.

3. Michael Savage, "The Imposition of Pass Laws on the African Population in South Africa, 1916–1984," *African Affairs* 85, no. 339 (April 1986): 181–205.

4. Hilda Bernstein, "Diary of a Detainee," *Africa South in Exile* 5, no. 2 (1961): 24–47.

5. Ibid., 28–29.

6. Toni Strasburg, *Holding the Fort: A Family Torn Apart* (Kwela Books, 2019).

7. Ibid., 81–82.

8. Bernstein, "Diary of a Detainee," 41; Strasburg, *Holding the Fort,* 109.

9. Bernstein, "Diary of a Detainee," 42.

10. Ibid., 44.

11. Ibid.

12. Ibid.

13. Ibid., 46-47.

14. Strasburg, *Holding the Fort,* 153–54.

15. Indres Naidoo (as told to Albie Sachs), *Robben Island: Ten Years as a Political Prisoner in South Africa's Most Notorious Penitentiary* (Vintage Books, 1983), 164; Fran Lisa Buntman, *Robben Island and Prisoner Resistance to Apartheid* (Cambridge University Press, 2003), 45.

16. Naidoo, *Robben Island,* 165.

17. Moses Dlamini, *Hell-Hole, Robben Island: Reminiscences of a Political Prisoner in South Africa* (Africa World Press, 1984), 181.

18. Ibid., 182.

19. Naidoo, *Robben Island,* 165.

20. Ibid., 166.

21. Dlamini, *Hell-Hole,* 182.

22. Naidoo, *Robben Island,* 167.

23. Nelson Mandela, *Long Walk to Freedom* (Little, Brown, 1994), 368.

24. Naidoo, *Robben Island,* 169.

25. Ibid., 172.

26. Dlamini, *Hell-Hole,* 185.

27. Naidoo, *Robben Island,* 172.

28. Mandela, *Long Walk,* 369.

29. Ibid.

30. Ibid.

31. Naidoo, *Robben Island,* 174

32. Mandela, *Long Walk,* 369.

33. Natoo Babenia, *Memoirs of a Saboteur: Reflections on My Political Activity in India and South Africa* (Mayibuye Books, 1996), 161.

34. Buntman, *Robben Island and Prisoner Resistance,* 6–7.

35. Hilda Bernstein, *No. 46—Steve Biko* (International Defence and Aid Fund, 1978).

36. Barney Pityana, *Bounds of Possibility: Legacy of Steve Biko and Black Consciousness* (Zed Books, 1992), 80.

37. Xolela Mangcu, *Biko: A Life* (I.B. Tauris, 2014), 262; Donald Woods, *Biko* (Henry Holt, 1987), 214.

38. For example, Robin Wright, "Jimmy Kruger: Afrikaner under Fire," *Washington Post,* September 25, 1977; *Afro-American* (Baltimore, MD), "'Cold' to Death of Leader, S. African Cracks," September 24, 1977, 16.

39. Lindy Wilson, *Steve Biko* (Ohio State University Press, 2012), 11; Derick Silove, "Doctors and the State: Lessons from the Steve Biko Case," *Social Science and Medicine* 30, no. 4 (1990): 417–29.

40. Dorian Lynskey, "Nelson Mandela: The Triumph of the Protest Song," *Guardian,* December 6, 2013.

41. Nelson Mandela, "A Tribute to Stephen Bantu Biko," foreword to Mangcu, *Biko: A Life,* 7–9. The speech was likely delivered at the 25th anniversary of his death in 2002.

42. G. R. McLean and Trefor Jenkins, "The Steve Biko Affair: A Case Study in Medical Ethics," *Developing World Bioethics* 3, no. 1 (2003); Derrick Silove, "Doctors and the State: Lessons from the Biko Case," *Social Science and Medicine* 30 (1990): 417–29; Lawrence Baxter, "Doctors on Trial: Steve Biko, Medical Ethics, and the Courts," *South African Journal on Human Rights* 1 (1985): 137–51.

43. Dr. I. Surve, "Keynote Address Delivered at Rhodes University at Service for Detainees on Hunger Strike," National Medical and Dental Association [NAMDA] Collection AL3182 A1.11.10, South African History Archive [SAHA], University of Witwatersrand.

44. Matthew Chaskalson, Karen Jochelson, and Jeremy Seekings, "Rent Boycotts, the State, and the Transformation of the Urban Political Economy in South Africa," *Review of African Political Economy* 14, no. 40 (1987): 47–64.

45. P. Eric Louw, *The Rise, Fall, and Legacy of Apartheid* (Praeger, 2004), 152.

46. Don Foster (with Dennis Davis and Diane Sandler), *Detention and Torture in South Africa: Psychological, Legal and Historical Studies* (D. Philip, 1987), 154.

47. Human Rights Commission, "Detainees Hunger Strike at Diepkloof Prison," Press Release, Unlock Africa's Jails Campaign, January 25, 1989, Michigan State University Special Collections.

48. Press Release on Detainees in Diepkloof Prison, February 4, 1986, Detainees' Parents Support Committee (DPSC) Papers, AG 2523, L2, Historical Papers Research Archive, University of Witwatersrand; Erik Van Ees, "South African Prisoners Go on Hunger Strike," *Chicago Tribune,* February 16, 1986.

49. DPSC, Press Release, February 25, 1986, AG 2523 L1 and L2, Historical Papers Research Archive, University of Witwatersrand.

50. Alan Cowell, "600 in a South African Prison Said to Be on Hunger Strike," *New York Times,* August 16, 1986.

51. Human Rights Commission, "Detainees Hunger Strike at Diepkloof Prison."

52. "Tutu and Mkhatshwa Join Solidarity Fast [November 29, 1985]," *South African History Online,* www.sahistory.org.za/dated-event/tutu-and-mkhatshwa-join-solidarity-fast.

53. Surve, "Keynote Address"; NAMDA AL3182 A1.11.10, SAHA, University of Witwatersrand.

54. DPSC, Press Release, "Statement on Official Emergency Detention Statistics," May 2, 1987, Historical Papers Research Archive, University of Witwatersrand.

55. Johannesburg Prison Press Statement, January 23, 1989, AG2523 Q2.1 file 1, Historical Papers Research Archive, University of Witwatersrand; Sidla Ekhaya, *We Shall Eat at Home: The Detainees' Hunger Strike in Pietermaritzburg, 1989* (Detainees Aid Committee, 1990), 2–3.

56. Janet Heard, "192 Detainees Now Believed to Be Refusing Food," *Star,* February 7, 1989.

57. Johannesburg Prison Press Statement, January 30, 1989, AG 2523 Q2.1 file 1, University of Witwatersrand; *Cape Argus,* "53 More in Jail Strike Says Smuggled Letter," February 2, 1989; Mzimkulu Malunga, "Hunger Strike," *Weekly Mail,* February 3, 1989.

58. Johannesburg Prison Press Statement, February 6, 1989, SAHA AG 2523 Q2.1 file 1, Historical Papers Research Archive, University of Witwatersrand.

59. Prof. Clive Rosendorff, Press Statement, February 8, 1989, Adler Collection, Witwatersrand Medical School.

60. Christopher Merrett, "Emergency of the State Detention without Trial in Pietermaritzburg and the Natal Midlands, 1986–90," *Natalia* 41 (2011): 10–33.

61. "St Albans Prison—Press Statement," February 1989, SAHA File PD—F04.2.1.4, South African History Archive, University of Witwatersrand; Karen Evans, "Over 100 E. Cape Detainees Join Strike," *Weekly Mail,* February 10, 1989; Kin Bentley, "PE Lawyers Sending Vlok Strike Memo," *Herald* (Port Elizabeth), February 10, 1989.

62. Philip Kuzwayo, "We Knew We Had One Way of Getting Out—by Starving Ourselves to the Limit," *New Africa,* March 1989 ("Trial Edition"), 8–9.

63. Ibid.

64. Ibid.

65. *Star,* "7 Hunger Strikers Taken to Hospital from Diepkloof," February 9, 1989; *Cape Argus,* "7 Hunger Strikers Being Drip-Fed in Hospital," February 9, 1989; Max Coleman (ed.), *A Crime against Humanity: Analysing the Repression of the Apartheid State* (D. Philip, 1998), 140.

66. Ineke van Kessel, *Beyond Our Wildest Dreams: The United Democratic Front and the Transformation of South Africa* (University of Virginia Press, 2000).

67. Tony Stirling and Arthur Kemp, "Hunger Strike Is Spreading," *Citizen* (Johannesburg), February 10, 1989; Press Statement to U.S. and British Embassies from Albany Black Sash, February 15, 1989, AG2523 Q2.1 File 2, Pt3, Historical Papers, University of Witwatersrand.

68. *Natal Witness,* February 16 and 18, 1989, cited in Christopher Merrett, "Emergency of the State: Detention without Trial in Pietermaritzburg and the Natal Midlands, 1986–90," *Natalia* 41 (2011): 22.

69. Eleanor Singer and Jacob Ludwig, "South Africa's Press Restrictions[:] Effects on Press Coverage and Public toward South Africa," *Public Opinion Quarterly* 51, no. 3 (1987): 315–34.

70. Richard Sergei [*sic*], "South Africa/Mandela Bodyguards/Hunger Strike," *ABC Evening News,* February 9, 1989, Vanderbilt Television News Archive, Vanderbilt University.

71. Tom Masland, "Hunger Strike Futile, South Africa Says," *Chicago Tribune,* February 10, 1989; John D. Battersby, "Hunger Strikes Grow in South African Prisons," *New York Times,* February 10, 1989; Janet Heard, "Police Ban Lawyers' Protest Meeting," *Star,* February 12, 1989.

72. Martha Teichner, "South Africa/Hunger Strike," *CBS Evening News,* February 13, 1989, Vanderbilt Television News Archive; Peter Jennings, "South Africa/Hunger Strike," *ABC Evening News,* February 13, 1989, Vanderbilt Television News Archive; Janet Heard and Sally Sealey, "Sympathy Mounts for Detainees," *Star,* February 11, 1989.

73. Martha Teichner, "South Africa/Mandela/Hunger Strike," *CBS Evening News,* February 16, 1989, Vanderbilt Television News Archive; Cathy Withiel,

"Judge Orders Confiscated Tape Can Be Transmitted," *Citizen* (Johannesburg), February 14, 1989.

74. South African Catholic Bishops Conference, "Response to Further Restrictions on Peaceful Protests," February 14, 1989, AG 2523 Q2.1, File 2, pt 2, Historical Papers, University of Witwatersrand.

75. NAMDA, Press Statement on Hunger Strike, February 14, 1989 NAMDA, SAHA Archives, University of Witwatersrand.

76. *Cape Times,* "Vlok Pledge on Detainees Minister's Bid to End Hunger Strike," February 14, 1989; Mike Robertson and Dianna Games, "Vlok Agrees to Meet Churchmen and Lawyers as Hunger Strike Worsens," *Business Day,* February 14, 1989; Andre Koopman and Charl de Villiers, "Detainees' Parents Meet Vlok," *Cape Times,* February 15, 1989; *Star* (Johannesburg), "Hope for Many Detainees after Lawyers' Discussions with Vlok," February 15, 1989.

77. Scott Kraft, "Hunger Strike Ends," *Los Angeles Times,* February 17, 1989.

78. Teichner, "South Africa/Mandela/Hunger Strike."

79. *Star* (Johannesburg), "Hope for Many Detainees."

80. Kraft, "Hunger Strike Ends."

81. Associated Press, "Hunger Strike Wins Freedoms for Detainees," *Tennessean,* February 17, 1989.

82. Erik Larsen, Chris Vermaak, and Sapa, "Suspend Hunger Strike Call to Critically Ill Detainees," *Citizen,* February 16, 1989; *Star* (Johannesburg), "Optimism for Ending Hunger Strike Deadlock," February 16, 1989; *Cape Argus,* "Diepkloof Hunger Strike Off," February 16, 1989; *Daily Dispatch* (East London, South Africa), "Churchmen Call Off Strike for 2 Weeks," February 17, 1989.

83. *Cape Argus,* "123 Join Hunger Strike in Durban," February 18, 1989; Quraish Patel, "300 More Join Strike," *Sunday Tribune* (Durban), February 19, 1989; Louise Flanagan, "Now the Fort Detainees Won't Take Food," *Weekly Mail* (Johannesburg), February 17, 1989.

84. "Detention under Three Emergencies: A Report of the Natal Midlands, 1986–1989," Detainees Aid Committee, Pietermaritzburg (August 1989), SAHA F.04.1.0.5, South African History Archive, University of Witwatersrand; Janet Heard, "'High-Spirited' Detainees Talk to Press at Hospital," *Star,* February 21, 1989; *New Nation,* "We'll Resist Jail," February 23, 1989; Themba Molefe, "We Won't Go Back," *Sowetan,* February 24, 1989; Bryan Pearson, "More City Hunger Strikers in Hospital," *Natal Witness,* March 1, 1989.

85. "Release our Detainees" flyer, Thomas Winslow Papers, BC 1210 E7, University of Cape Town Special Collections; "Hunger Strike Crisis: A NUSAS-SRC Perspective," ca. February 1989, NAMDA South African History Archive, University of Witwatersrand; *Cape Argus,* "Detainees: Less Than 10% Freed," February 27, 1989; *Cape Times,* "D-Day Today for Hunger-Strikers," March 2, 1989.

86. Jo-Anne Collinge, "Further Hunger Strikes Reported," *Star,* March 8, 1989; Jo-Anne Collinge, "Reports of 'New' Hunger Strike at Pretoria Central," *Star,* March 14, 1989; *Cape Argus,* "Hunger Strike Resumed on Reef," March 8, 1989;

Cape Times, "17 Modderbee Hunger Strikers Send Vlok Letter," March 9, 1989; *New Nation,* "Transeki Hunger Strike," March 30, 1989.

87. TransAfrica Fund, "National Detainees Day Observed across the United States," March 10, 1989.

88. Hunger Strike, No 1 10, March 1989, Human Rights Commission, AG 2523 Q2.1 File 2 pt 2, South African History Archive, University of Witwatersrand.

89. Scott Kraft, "4 South African Detainees Flee Hospital," *Los Angeles Times,* March 21, 1989.

90. William Claiborne, "4 South African Prisoners Flee, Seek Refuge in Bonn's Embassy," *Washington Post,* March 21, 1989.

91. Ibid.

92. *Herald* (Port Elizabeth), "All on Hunger Strike Being 'Centralised,'" March 29, 1989; *Star* (Johannesburg), "Detainees on Hunger Strike to Be Moved to Free State," March 28, 1989; *Cape Times* (Cape Town), "First Hunger Striker Moved to Bloemfontein," March 31, 1989.

93. John D. Battersby, "South Africa to Tighten Controls on Detainees," *New York Times,* March 30, 1989.

94. *National Catholic Reporter,* "Procession Bears Cross for African Political Prisoners," April 7, 1989, 9.

95. *National Catholic Reporter,* "Church Leaders Renegotiate to End Hunger Strike," April 7, 1989, 9.

96. *Citizen,* "Boesak Threat to Resume Death Fast," April 5, 1989.

97. Mandela, *Long Walk,* 369.

98. *South China Morning Post,* "HK Students Join Hunger Strike," May 16, 1989, 11; Sheryl Wudunn, "Hunger Strikers, Heart of China Protest," *New York Times,* May 19, 1989, 1, 10; *Times of India,* "China Disbands Illegal Groups," June 17, 1989, 24; Daniel Southerland, "China's Spring Rebellion: Will the Turmoil Return?," *Washington Post,* August 20, 1989, 1; Chong-Pin Lin et al., "Tiananmen Square Hunger Strike Declaration," *World Affairs* 152, no. 3 (December 1, 1989): 148–50.

99. Jane Howard, "Jail Protest Grows after Kurds Die," *Guardian,* August 5, 1989, 9; *Jerusalem Post,* "Prison Hunger Strike Is New Blow to Turkey's Human Rights Record," August 9, 1989, 3; Rasit Gurdiek, "Fears for Fasting Turkish Prisoners," *Times,* August 15, 1989, 8; *Boston Globe,* "Turkish Prisoners End Hunger Strike," August 20, 1989, 27; Banu Bargu, *Starve and Immolate: The Politics of Human Weapons* (Columbia University Press, 2014); Patrick Anderson, *So Much Wasted: Hunger, Performance, and the Morbidity of Resistance* (Duke University Press, 2010).

100. Tom Lodge, *Mandela: A Critical Life* (Oxford University Press, 2007).

CHAPTER SEVEN

1. David McKittrick and David McVea, *Making Sense of the Troubles: The Story of the Conflict in Northern Ireland* (New Amsterdam Press, 2002); Ronnie Munck,

"The Making of the Troubles in Northern Ireland," *Journal of Contemporary History* 27, no. 2 (April 1992): 211–29.

2. André Wynen, WMA Secretary General, "The Physician and Torture," *World Medical Association* 28, no. 2 (1981): 18.

3. *Irish Times*, "Detainees Allege Torture," August 18, 1971; Danny Kennally and Eric Preston (eds.), *Belfast, August 1971: A Case to Be Answered* (Independent Labour Party, 1971).

4. Samantha Newbery, *Interrogation, Intelligence and Security: Controversial British Techniques* (Manchester University Press, 2015), 1.

5. Ibid., 87–90.

6. Report of the Enquiry into Allegations against the Security Forces of Physical Brutality in Northern Ireland Arising out of Event on the 9th August, 1971 ("Compton Report") Cmnd. 4823, November 1971; Report of the Committee of Privy Counsellors Appointed to Consider Authorised Procedures for the Interrogation of Person Suspected of Terrorism ("Parker Report") CMnd. 4901, March 1972; Samantha Newbery, "Intelligence and Controversial British Interrogation Techniques: The Northern Ireland Case, 1971–2," *Irish Studies in International Affairs* 20 (2009): 103–19.

7. "Compton Report," 1 (emphasis in original); André Wynen, WMA Secretary General, "The Physician and Torture," *World Medical Association* 28, no. 2 (1981): 18; Peter Vesti and Niels Johan Lavik, "Torture and the Medical Profession: A Review," *Journal of Medical Ethics* 17, Supplement (1991): 4–8.

8. Newbery, *Interrogation;* Newbery, "Intelligence and Controversial British Interrogation Techniques," 106–10.

9. Laurence McKeown, *Out of Time: Irish Political Prisoners, Long Kesh, 1972–2000* (Beyond the Pale, 2001), 28; Danny Morrison, "Introduction," in Danny Morrison (ed.), *Hunger Strike: Reflections* (Elsinor, 2020), 15.

10. *Republican News*, "Support the Hunger Strikers," June 11 and 18, 1972; Richard English, *Armed Struggle: The History of the IRA* (Oxford University Press, 2003), 193; Barry Flynn, *Pawns in the Game: Irish Hunger Strikes, 1912–1981* (Collins Press, 2011), 131–38; John Ó Néill, "The 1972 Hunger Strike," *Treason Felony Blog*, February 21, 2017, https://treasonfelony.wordpress.com/2017/02/21/the-1972-hunger-strike/.

11. Anthony S. Mathews, *Freedom, State Security and the Rule of Law: Dilemmas of the Apartheid Society* (University of California Press, 1986), 237–38.

12. McKeown, *Out of Time*, 14.

13. Allen Feldman, *Formations of Violence: The Narrative of the Body and Political Terror in Northern Ireland* (University of Chicago Press, 1991), 149.

14. Price and Price vs. Home Office, April 2, 1974, pp. 1–2, TS84/22, British National Archives.

15. Tom Williams, Home Office, January 16, 1974, to Duncan Watson, Treasury Solicitor's Office, TS84/22, British National Archives.

16. Suzanne Breen, "Marian Price Interview: Old Bailey Bomber Ashamed of Sinn Fein," *Village*, December 7, 2004.

17. Price and Price vs. Home Office, April 2, 1974, pp. 1–2, TS84/22, British National Archives.

18. Breen, "Marian Price Interview."

19. Price and Price vs. Home Office, April 2, 1974, pp. 1–2, TS84/22, British National Archives.

20. Breen, "Marian Price Interview."

21. Letter from Tom Williams, Home Office, Whitehall, January 16, 1974, to Duncan Watson Treasury Solicitor's Office, TS 84/22, British National Archives.

22. Ibid.

23. Ian Miller, *A History of Force Feeding: Hunger Strikes, Prisons and Medical Ethics, 1909–1974*. (Palgrave Macmillan, 2016), 216.

24. Dr. R. I. K. Blyth, Principal Medical Officer, Brixton Prison to Governor of Brixton Prison, January, 1974, TS 84/22, British National Archives.

25. *Venceremos Sisters: Prison Writings of the Price Sisters* (Cathal Brugha Cumann, undated, ca. 1974), 9–10, Linen Hall Library, Belfast, Ireland, P4474.

26. British Medical Journal, "Medicolegal: Inquest on Hunger Striker," *British Medical Journal* 3, no. 5922 (July 6, 1974): 52–53.

27. House of Commons Hansard, "Artificial Feeding of Prisoners Statement," July 17, 1974, vol. 877, cc451-5.

28. *Irish Times,* "Effect of Force-Feeding Like Multiple Rape," March 11, 1974, 8.

29. British Medical Journal, "Ethical Statement: Artificial Feeding of Prisoners," *British Medical Journal* 3, no. 5922 (July 6, 1974): 52–53.

30. World Medical Association, "Declaration of Tokyo—Guidelines for Physicians Concerning Torture and Cruel, Inhuman or Degrading Treatment or Punishment in Relation to Detention and Imprisonment" (adopted by the 29th World Medical Assembly, 1975), www.wma.net/en/30publications/10policies/c18/ (accessed November 11, 2011).

31. Hernán Reyes, "Medical and Ethical Aspects of Hunger Strikes in Custody and the Issue of Torture," *Research in Legal Medicine* 19, no. 1 (1998).

32. Miller, *History of Force Feeding,* 220.

33. David Beresford, *Ten Men Dead: The Story of the 1981 Irish Hunger Strike* (Atlantic Monthly Press, 1997), 15; McKeown, *Out of Time,* 37.

34. Thomas Hennessey, *Hunger Strike: Margaret Thatcher's Battle with the IRA, 1980–1981* (Irish Academic Press, 2014), 459.

35. McKeown, *Out of Time,* xi.

36. Ibid., 16.

37. Feldman, *Formations of Violence,* 174.

38. Ibid., 220; Begoña Aretxaga, "Striking with Hunger: Cultural Meanings of Political Violence in Northern Ireland," in Joseba Zulaika (ed.), *States of Terror: Begoña Aretxaga's Essays* (Center for Basque Studies, University of Nevada, 2005); McKeown, *Out of Time;* Padraig O'Malley, *Biting at the Grave: The Irish Hunger Strikes and the Politics of Despair* (Beacon Press, 1990).

39. Bobby Sands, "Birth of a Republican," *Republican News,* December 16, 1978, 6.

40. McKeown, *Out of Time,* 18.

41. Atkins to Prime Minister, November 15, 1979, TNA CJ4/3025, British National Archives; Hennessey, *Hunger Strike,* 68.

42. Ibid.

43. McKeown, *Out of Time,* 77–78.

44. Bobby Sands, "Prison Diary" (first seventeen days of hunger strike), www .bobbysandstrust.com/writings/prison-diary.

45. Hennessey, *Hunger Strike,* 180; Note on the Meeting on Thursday, April 16: Medical Aspects of the Current Hunger Strike, TNA CJ4/3627, British National Archives; James LeMoyne, "Sands' Mother: 'He Is Prepared for the End,'" *Washington Post,* May 1, 1981.

46. Begoña Aretxaga, *Shattering Silence: Women, Nationalism, and Political Subjectivity in Northern Ireland* (Princeton University Press, 1997), 109–10; O' Malley, *Biting at the Grave,* 119.

47. Beresford, *Ten Men Dead,* 79; O'Malley, *Biting at the Grave.*

48. *Chicago Tribune,* "Bobby Sands and Mahatma Gandhi," April 28, 1981.

49. Feldman, *Formations of Violence,* 219, 238.

50. Ibid., 242.

51. Morrison, "Introduction," 21.

52. Beresford, *Ten Men Dead,* 156, 158.

53. *An Phoblacht/Republican News,* "Double Death Inside," May 30, 1981; Peggy O'Hara, *An Phoblacht/Republican News,* June 12, 1981, cited in Hennessey, *Hunger Strike,* 239–40.

54. Ibid.

55. Ibid.

56. "Siobhan" was a pseudonym for a prominent Republican who was interviewed by Begoña Aretxaga (*Shattering Silence,* 104).

57. Peggy O'Hara, *An Phoblacht/Republican News,* cited in Hennessey, *Hunger Strike,* 241.

58. McKeown, *Out of Time,* 79.

59. Ibid., 81–83.

60. Hennessey, *Hunger Strike.*

61. Miller, *History of Force Feeding,* 228.

CHAPTER EIGHT

1. Michel Foucault, *The History of Sexuality: An Introduction, vol. 1,* trans. Robert Hurley (Vintage Books, 1978), 137–38; Michel Foucault, "Society Must Be Defended," in *"Society Must Be Defended": Lectures at the College de France, 1975–1976,* ed. Mauro Bertani and Alessandro Fontano, trans. David Macey (Picador, 2003), 239–64.

2. "Voluntary Total Fasting," March 1990, National Medical and Dental Association Collection A1.11.10, New Folder 2, South African History Archive, University of Witwatersrand.

3. W. J. Kalk and Yosuf Veriava, "Hospital Management of Voluntary Total Fasting among Political Prisoners," *Lancet* 337, no. 8742 (1991): 660–62.

4. W. J. Kalk, M. Felix, E. R. Snoey, and Y. Veriava, "Voluntary Total Fasting in Political Prisoners: Clinical and Biochemical Observations," *South African Medical Journal* 83, no. 6 (1993): 391–94; G. R. Keeton, "Hunger Strikers: Ethical and Management Problems," *South African Medical Journal* 83, no. 6 (1993): 380–81; "Metabolic and endocrine effects of voluntary total fasting," University of Witwatersrand Application to the Committee for Research on Human Subjects (1990), June 18, 1991, University of Witwatersrand Hospital, Adler Museum of Medicine Archives.

5. Michael Peel, "Hunger Strikes: Understanding the Underlying Physiology Will Help Doctors Provide Proper Advice," *British Medical Journal* 315, no. 7112 (1997): 830.

6. Kalk and Veriava, "Hospital Management"; Peel, "Hunger Strikes," 829–30.

7. Hisham M. Mehanna, Jamil Moledina, and Jane Travis, "Refeeding Syndrome: What It Is, and How to Prevent and Treat It," *British Medical Journal* 336, no. 7659 (June 26, 2008): 1495–98.

8. World Medical Association (WMA) Declaration of Tokyo, 1975.

9. Dr. A[ntónio] Gentil Martins, Malta > Period 2 > PDFs > 1989 > Miami, Digital Files, World Medical Association Archives, Ferney-Voltaire, France.

10. WMA Declaration of Malta on Hunger Strikers, 1991. In the WMA deliberations, a paper defending medical rescue was reviewed prior to implementing the Malta declaration. S. A. Strauss, "Legal Questions Surrounding Hunger Strikes by Detainees and Prisoners," *Medicine and Law* 10 (1991): 211–18.

11. Dr. A[ntónio] Gentil Martins, Malta > Period 2 > PDFs > 2001 > Divonne, Digital Files, World Medical Association Archives, Ferney-Voltaire, France.

12. WMA Declaration of Malta on Hunger Strikers, revised by the 57th WMA General Assembly, Pilanesberg, South Africa, October 2006.

13. C. J. Jackson, 1984 Report, CJ4/5319 (TNR), National Archives, London. Emphasis added.

14. 28 C.F.R. Subpart E—Hunger Strikes, Inmate, Title 28—Judicial Administration, Part 549 Medical Services E Inmate Hunger Strikes [45 FR 23365, April 4, 1980, as amended at 59 FR 31883, June 20, 1994].

15. Ibid. § 549.65.

16. U.S. Department of Justice, Federal Bureau of Prisons, July 29, 2005, OPI: HSD/HSS P5562.05, Subject: Hunger Strikes, www.bop.gov/policy/progstat /5562_005.pdf.

17. Karen J. Greenberg, *The Least Worst Place: Guantanamo's First 100 Days* (Oxford University Press, 2009), 187–95.

18. Clive Stafford Smith, *The Eight O'Clock Ferry on the Windward Side: Seeking Justice in Guantanamo* (Nation Books, 2017), 204–5. Bisher al-Rawi was an Iraqi child who fled with his parents to Britain from the Saddam Hussein regime in the 1980s. After his arrest in November 2002 on a business trip to Gambia, he was detained by the CIA and transported to Bagram Air Base in Afghanistan in December, where he was imprisoned underground and in total darkness for weeks. In

March 2003, he was put in U.S. military custody in Guantánamo, where he was held until March 30, 2007.

19. Quoted in Susan Okie, "Glimpses of Guantanamo: Medical Ethics and the War on Terror," *New England Journal of Medicine* 353, no. 24 (2005): 2530; Steven Miles, *Oath Betrayed: America's Torture Doctors* (University of California Press, 2009), 111.

20. Declaration of Dr. John S. Edmondson, Affadavit in *Majid Abdulla Al Joudi et al. vs. George W. Bush,* U.S. District Court, 2005 para. 16, http://humanrights .ucdavis.edu/projects/the-guantanamo-testimonials-project/testimonies/testimony-of-military-physicians/edmondson_affidavit.pdf.

21. Ibid., para. 9.

22. Safety Restraint Chair Inc., Denison, Iowa, www.restraintchair.com/; Mahvish Rukhsana Khan, *My Guantánamo Diary: The Detainees and the Stories They Told Me* (Public Affairs, 2008), 215; George Annas, *Worst Case Bioethics: Death, Disaster and Public Health* (Oxford University Press, 2010), 60; Yasmin Ibrahim and Anita Howarth, "Hunger Strike and the Force-Feeding Chair: Guantanamo Bay and Corporeal Surrender," *EPD: Society and Space* 32, no. 2 (2019): 294–312.

23. Eric Schmitt and Tim Golden, "Force-Feeding at Guantánamo Is Now Acknowledged," *New York Times,* February 22, 2006; see also George J. Annas, "Hunger Strikes at Guantanamo: Medical Ethics and Human Rights in a 'Legal Black Hole,'" *New England Journal of Medicine* 355, no. 13 (2006): 1377–82.

24. Schmitt and Golden, "Force-Feeding at Guantánamo."

25. Michelle Shephard, "Force-Feeding an End to Guantanamo Dissent," *Toronto Star,* April 8, 2006.

26. Tim Golden, "Tough U.S. Steps in Hunger Strike at Camp in Cuba," *New York Times,* February 9, 2006.

27. Benedict de Spinoza, *The Ethics,* trans. R. H. M. Elwes, Project Gutenberg, 2003, III, 6, www.gutenberg.org/files/3800/3800-h/3800-h.htm.

28. Tim Golden, "Guantánamo Detainees Stage Hunger Strike," *New York Times,* April 9, 2007.

29. Senate Select Intelligence Committee, "Report on Torture: Committee Study of the Central Intelligence Agency's Detention and Interrogation Program" (2014), 84.

30. Ibid., 391, fn. 584.

31. Ibid., 82, 83, 107, 114–15.

32. Physicians for Human Rights, "CIA Torture Report Highlights Unnecessary Medical Procedure," https://phr.org/news/cia-torture-report-highlights-unnecessary-medical-procedure (accessed June 4, 2019).

33. Ibid.; Erik Wemple, "On CNN, Former CIA Director Michael Hayden Defends a 'Medical Procedure,'" *Washington Post,* December 11, 2014; Dianne Feinstein, "Fact Check: CIA's Use of Rectal Rehydration, Feeding Not Medical Procedures," Press Release, December 12, 2014, www.feinstein.senate.gov/public /index.cfm/press-releases?ID=e8f730c3-43c8-4931-94f6-c478f25d8bbb.

34. Shaker Aamer, "Shaker Aamer: 'I Want to Hug My Children and Watch Them as They Grow,'" *Observer* (London), April 20, 2013.

35. Ibid.

36. Samir Naji al Hasan Moqbel, "Gitmo Is Killing Me," *New York Times,* April 14, 2013.

37. Carol Rosenberg, "AMA Opposes Force Feedings at Guantanamo," *Miami Herald,* April 30, 2013.

38. Joint Task Force Guantanamo Bay, Cuba—Joint Medical Group, "Standard Operating Procedure: Medical Management of Detainees on Hunger Strike" (SOP), March 5, 2013, 2, www.aele.org/law/gitmo-force-feed.pdf.

39. Foucault, *History of Sexuality,* 137–38; Michel Foucault, "Society Must Be Defended," in *"Society Must Be Defended": Lectures at the Collège de France, 1975–76* (Picador, 2003), 38.

40. Thomas Lemke, *Biopolitics: An Advanced Introduction,* trans. Eric F. Trump (NYU Press, 2011), 5.

41. Foucault, *History of Sexuality,* 137–38.

42. Joint Task Force Guantanamo Bay, SOP, 3, 5.

43. Ibid., 6, 15–16.

44. Ibid., 17.

45. Ibid.

46. Janet Bovin, "Viewpoint: Nurse's Refusal to Force Feed Gitmo Prisoners Triggers Debate," *American Nurse,* December 1, 2014; Janet Bovin, "A Look inside Guantanamo Bay," *Nursing Spectrum,* March 14, 2007.

47. Carol Rosenberg, "Navy Nurse Who Refused to Force-Feed at Guantánamo Keeps His Job," *Miami Herald,* May 13, 2015.

48. Anja K. Peters, "Force Feeding Is in the Interests of the State, Not Its Prisoners" (letter to the editor), *Nursing Standard* 28, no. 50 (August 13, 2014); Jeanne Lenzer, "Nurse Refuses 'Criminal' Force Feeding of Guantanamo Detainees," *British Medical Journal* 349 (July 18, 2014): g4712.

49. Carol Rosenberg, "Top Nursing Group Backs Navy Nurse Who Wouldn't Force Feed at Guantanamo," *Miami Herald,* November 18, 2014; Senator Dianne Feinstein, Letter to Senator Chuck Hagel, March 31, 2015, www.feinstein.senate .gov/public/index.cfm/press-releases?ID=1698FAAD-8B9A-474A-BF37-EF2CF-416BFD0; Rosenberg, "Navy Nurse Who Refused to Force-Feed."

50. Daniel Lakemacher quoted in Peter Jan Honigsberg, *A Place outside the Law: Forgotten Voices from Guantanamo* (Beacon Press, 2019), 124–25, 180.

51. Spencer S. Hsu, "Judge Again Orders U.S. to Release Guantanamo Bay Force-Feeding Videos," *Washington Post,* October 27, 2015.

52. Charlie Savage, "Videos of Force-Feeding at Guantánamo Will Stay Secret, Court Rules," *New York Times,* March 31, 2017; U.S. Court of Appeals, District of Columbia Circuit, *Jihad Dhiab, and Shaker Aamer, Appellees v. Donald J. Trump et al.,* appellants No 16=5011, Decided March 31, 2017.

53. Honigsberg, *Place outside the Law,* 180.

54. The video was uploaded on July 8, 2013, to the *Guardian* newspaper's *YouTube* channel, where it has more than eight million views as of this writing:

"Yasiin Bey (aka Mos Def) Force Fed under Standard Guantánamo Bay Procedure," www.youtube.com/watch?v=z6ACE-BBPRs;.

55. Jonathan Hodgson, "Guantanamo Bay: The Hunger Strikes," *Art Journal* 73, no. 2 (2014): 5–13.

56. Mark Townsend, "The Making of Guantánamo Bay: The Hunger Strikes," *Guardian*, October 12, 2013.

57. Mustafa Khalili, Guy Grandjean, and Sherbert and Fonic, "Guantánamo Bay: The Hunger Strikes," video animation, www.theguardian.com/world /video/2013/oct/11/guantanamo-bay-hunger-strikes-video-animation. A version with Arabic subtitles was distributed on the *Al Jazeera* website.

58. Minnie Vaid, *Iron Irom: Two Journeys* (Rajpal, 2013), 18–24; Deepti Priya Mehrotra, *Burning Bright: Irom Sharmila and the Struggle for Peace in Manipur* (Penguin Books India, 2009), 67–77; Shubh Mathur, "Life and Death on the Borderlands: Indian Sovereignty and Military Impunity," *Race and Class* 54, no. 1 (2012): 33–49.

59. Mark Hay, "What Does a 16-Year Hunger Strike Do to Your Body?," *Vice*, August 12, 2016.

60. Vaid, *Iron Irom*, 28.

61. Mehrotra, *Burning Bright*, 100

62. Vaid, *Iron Irom*, 76.

63. "A Life-Affirming Fast," *Economic & Political Weekly* 28, no. 12 (March 23, 2013): 9; Mehrotra, *Burning Bright*, 101.

64. Rahul Karmakar, "Fasting Irom Sharmila 'Ate' a Rich and Balanced Diet, Thrice a Day," *Hindustan Times*, August 10, 2016.

65. Uri McMillan, "Objecthood, Avatars and the Limits of the Human," *GLQ: A Journal of Lesbian and Gay Studies* 21, no. 2–3 (June 2015): 224–27.

66. Organization of Minorities in India, "15 Year Hunger-Striker Irom Sharmila: 'Repeal India's AFSPA or I Die of Starvation,'" November 18, 2015, www .minoritiesofindia.org/15-year-hunger-striker-irom-sharmila-repeal-indias-afspa-or-i-die-of-starvation/.

67. Neha Tara Mehta, "Indian Court Tackles Extrajudicial Killings in Manipur," *Al Jazeera*, July 24, 2016.

68. Organization of Minorities in India, "15 Year Hunger-Striker Irom Sharmila."

69. Harriet Sherwood, "Palestinian Prisoner Khader Adnan Ends 66-Day Hunger Strike," *Guardian*, February 21, 2012.

70. Visualizing Palestine, "Hunger Strikes" (poster), 2012, http://s3.amazonaws .com/VP2/visuals/en/3e9f1a96a48a5514de26f2928baf528a.jpg?2015.

71. Letter from the Jasim Jamal, Qatar to the United Nations Secretary-General, August 7, 1980, http://unispal.un.org/UNISPAL.NSF/0/EB23F5850A2A0845052 566CC004F1345.

72. Israeli Medical Association, *The Physician's Guide to Treating the Detainee/ Prisoner on Hunger Strike*, June 2014, www.ima.org.il/Ima/FormStorage/Type8 /IMAHungerEN.pdf; Azadeh Shahshahani and Priya Arvind Patel, "From Pelican

Bay to Palestine: The Legal Normalization of Force-Feeding Hunger-Strikers," *Michigan Journal of Race & Law* 24, no. 1 (2018): 1–14.

73. Jesse Lempel, "Force-Feeding Prisoners on Hunger Strike: Israel as a Case Study in International Law," *Harvard International Law Journal*, https://harvardilj.org/2016/12/force-feeding-prisoners-on-a-hunger-strike-israel-as-a-case-study-in-international-law/.

74. Jack Khoury, "Israel's High Court Finds Force Feeding Constitutional: 'A Hunger Striker Is Not an Ordinary Patient,'" *Haaretz,* November 9, 2016; *Israel Medical Association et al. v. Knesset et al.,* HCJ 5304/15, September 11, 2016.

75. Zvi Bar'el, "Force-Feeding Debate Misses Point on Israel's True Transgression," *Haaretz,* June 25, 2014.

76. Paige St. John, "Team Solitary: Four Inmates at Pelican Bay Prison Organized the Statewide Prison Hunger Strike despite Being Housed in Isolation Units," *Los Angeles Times,* July 29, 2013; *Los Angeles Times,* "Doctors Clash on Feeding by Force," August 21, 2013; Tom Hayden, "How Will California's Prison Hunger Strike End?," *Nation,* August 27, 2013; Keramet Reiter, "The Pelican Bay Hunger Strike: Resistance within the Structural Constraints of a US Supermax Prison," *South Atlantic Quarterly* 113, no. 3 (2014): 579–611.

77. *In Re application of the Department of Homeland Security, Immigration and Customs Enforcement, v. Anwar Hossain et al.,* U.S. District Court, Southern District of Florida, Case Number15-24560, December 21, 2015.

78. Alexandra Martinez, "Judge's Order to Force-Feed Ten Hunger-Strikers at Krome Sparks Immigration Protest," *Miami New Times,* December 28, 2015.

79. Foucault, *History of Sexuality,* 144.

80. Corinna Howland, "To Feed or Not to Feed: Violent State Care and the Contested Medicalization of Incarcerated Hunger-Strikers in Britain, Turkey and Guantanamo Bay," *New Zealand Sociology* 28, no. 1 (2013): 101–16, 109.

81. Batsheva Sobelman, "Israel Passes Contentious Law Allowing Force-Feeding of Inmates," *Los Angeles Times,* July 30, 2015.

82. Diaa Hadid, "Worried That Fasting Palestinian Prisoner Could Die, Israel Releases Him," *New York Times,* June 29, 2015.

83. Carol Rosenberg, "Military Bans Big Macs, Other Treats at Guantanamo Legal Meetings," *Miami Herald,* May 26, 2015.

84. Department of Defense, Joint Task Force, Guantanamo, "Memorandum: Modification of Rules Regarding Detainee Legal and Periodic Review Board Meetings," May 14, 2015, www.documentcloud.org/documents/2086844-memorandum-re-modification-to-rules-for-detainee.html.

85. Rosenberg, "Military Bans Big Macs."

CHAPTER NINE

1. Lucy Fiske, *Human Rights, Refugee Protest and Immigration Detention* (Palgrave Macmillan, 2016), 11.

2. Hannah Arendt, *The Origins of Totalitarianism* (Harcourt, 1968), 293, 295, 296.

3. Janet Phillips and Harriet Spinks, "Immigration Detention in Australia," Department of Parliamentary Services Research Paper, 2013.

4. Patricia Hyndman, "The Australian Migration Legislation Amendment Act 1989," *International Journal of Refugee Law* 1, no. 4 (1989): 546–49.

5. Ronald Kessels and Maritsa Efitimiou, "Effects of Incarceration," in Mary Crock (ed.), *Protection or Punishment? The Detention of Asylum Seekers in Australia* (Federation Press, 1993), 93; Alison Mountz, *Seeking Asylum: Human Smuggling and Bureaucracy at the Border* (University of Minnesota Press, 2010), xv.

6. *South China Morning Post,* "Canberra Unmoved by Fast," March 11, 1992; Ron Skinner, "Somali Refugees End Hunger Strike," Green Left, June 26, 1991, www.greenleft.org.au/content/somali-refugees-end-hunger-strike.

7. Robert Milliken, "Voyage of Hope Ends in Despair for Boat People," *Independent,* February 2, 1993; Evan Gottsman, *Cambodia after the Khmer Rouge: Inside the Politics of Nation Building* (Yale University Press, 2002).

8. Andrew Biro communicated with the women before and during the hunger strikes and documented their experiences while keeping their names anonymous. We know their names only because of their legal cases. See Biro, "A Welfare Worker's Experience," in Crock, *Protection or Punishment?;* and Derrick Silove et al., "Ethical Considerations in the Management of Asylum Seekers on Hunger Strike," *JAMA* 267, no. 5 (1996): 412.

9. Biro, "Welfare Worker's Experience."

10. Ibid.; Silove et al., "Ethical Considerations."

11. *Department of Immigration, Local Government and Ethnic Affairs v. Gek Bouy Mok,* Supreme Court of New South Wales Equity Division, Powell J, 4982 of 1992, 30 September 1992, unreported, cited in Mary Anne Kenny, "Force-Feeding Asylum Seekers," *Alternative Law Journal* 27, no. 3 (2002): 107–12; *Mok Gek Bouy v. the Minister of Immigration, Local Government and Ethnic Affairs and Malcolm Paterson* [1993] Federal Court of Australia [FCA] 545; (1993) 47 FCR 1 (15 November 1993).

12. M. Millett, "Hunger Strikers Can Be Fed by Force," *Sydney Morning Herald,* October 13, 1992; *Sydney Morning Herald,* "Demonstration Backs Hunger-Strike Women," November 12, 1992.

13. Silove et al., "Ethical Considerations," 411, 412; Kenny, "Force-Feeding Asylum Seekers," 109–10; Millett, "Hunger Strikers Can Be Fed by Force."

14. *Sunday Age* (Melbourne), "Hand to Stay Firm on Migration Rules," March 24, 1992.

15. *Sydney Morning Herald,* "Freed Asylum Seeker Looks for Australia's Soul," October 9, 2002; Margot O'Neill, *Blind Conscience* (University of New South Wales Press, 2008).

16. A. Sultan and K. O'Sullivan, "Psychological Disturbances in Asylum Seekers Held in Longterm Detention: A Participant-Observer Account," *Medical Journal of Australia* 175 (2001), 593–96.

17. Richard Paddock, "The 'Crime' of Being a Young Refugee," *Los Angeles Times,* January 5, 2002.

18. Biro, "Welfare Worker's Experience," 96.

19. Robert Milliken, "Voyage of Hope Ends in Despair for Boat People," *Independent,* February 2, 1993.

20. Sean Scalmer, "Hunger-Strikes, Lip-Sewing, and 'Un-Australian' Protest: Supporting Information," January 29, 2002, radio transcript, www.abc.net.au /radionational/programs/perspective/sean-scalmer/3496904.

21. ABC News, "Woomera Detainees Force-Fed," November 29, 2000, radio transcript, www.abc.net.au/am/stories/s218002.htm.

22. Ron Hoenig, "Reading Alien Lips: Australian Print Media Depictions of Asylum Seekers and the Construction of National Identity," in Barbara Baird and Damien W. Riggs (eds.), *The Racial Politics of Bodies, Nations and Knowledges* (Cambridge Scholars, 2009), 140–43.

23. Julie Wolfram Cox and Stella Minahan, "Unravelling Woomera: Lip Sewing, Morphology and Dystopia," *Journal of Organizational Change Management* 17, no. 3 (2004): 292–301.

24. Kon Karapanagiotidis, "Sewing Lips Together a Final Plea for Help," Asylum Seeker Resource Centre, www.asrc.org.au/2010/11/21/sewing-lips-together-a-final-plea-for-help/.

25. Ibid.

26. Fiske, *Human Rights, Refugee Protest and Immigration Detention,* 55.

27. Reporters Without Borders, "Reporters Without Borders Annual Report 2003—Australia," www.refworld.org/docid/46e6914720.html (accessed August 18, 2019).

28. Rebecca Di Girolamo, "Detainees Agree to Unsew Lips," *Australian,* January 29, 2002.

29. Christopher Kremmer, "Asylum Seekers Encounter New World outside Fences," *The Age,* January 22, 2002.

30. Hoenig, "Reading Alien Lips," 147.

31. Scalmer, "Hunger-Strikes."

32. Paddock, "'Crime' of Being a Young Refugee."

33. Ibid.

34. Human Rights and Equal Opportunity Commission (Sydney), *A Last Resort? National Inquiry into Children in Immigration Detention* (April 2004), 156, 157, 215, 259

35. Amelia Jones, "Performing the Wounded Body: Pain, Affect and the Radical Relationality of Meaning," *Parallax* 15, no. 4 (2009): 45–67; Jennifer Tyburczy, "Queer Acts of Recovery and Uncovering: Deciphering Mexico through Archival Ephemera in David Wojnarowicz's *A Fire in My Belly,*" *Text and Performance Quarterly* 35, no. 1 (2015): 4–23; Sarah Austin, "Mike Parr and the Discursive Rupture: The Condemned and Punished Body as a Political Strategy in *Close the Concentration Camps,*" *Double Dialogues* no. 6 (Winter 2005), www.doubledialogues.com/article

/mike-parr-and-the-discursive-rupture-the-condemned-and-punished-body-as-a-political-strategy-in-close-the-concentration-camps/.

36. Patrick Kingsley, "Stranded Migrants Sew Mouths Shut in Protest against Balkan Border Controls," *Guardian,* November 23, 2015; Lizzie Dearden, "Refugee Crisis: Stranded Iranian Asylum Seekers Sew Their Mouths Shut in Protest at Greek-Macedonian Border," *Independent,* November 23, 2015.

37. Hoenig, "Reading Alien Lips," 133.

38. Mountz, *Seeking Asylum,* xvii.

39. Paige Taylor, "Lips Stitched, Dozens on Hunger Strike on Christmas Island," *Australian,* January 16, 2014; Ian Rintoul, "Refugee Hunger Strike in Australia's Brutal Christmas Island Detention Centre," *Socialist Worker,* January 21, 2014; Sophie Tedmanson, "Asylum Seekers Stitch Their Mouths Shut as Tensions Rise on Christmas Island," *Daily Mail* (UK), January 16, 2014.

40. *Sydney Morning Herald,* "Asylum Seekers on Christmas Island Stitch Lips Together in Hunger Strike," June 2, 2014.

41. Ben Doherty, "Four Asylum Seekers on Manus Sew Lips Together as Part of Mass Hunger Strike," *Guardian,* December 3, 2014.

42. "How Eaten Fish Survived Four Years in Refugee Detention with His Cartoons, Social Media and a Network of Activist Friends," *PRI: The World,* December 22, 2017, www.pri.org/stories/2017-12-22/how-eaten-fish-survived-four-years-refugee-detention-his-cartoons-social-media; Joshua Robertson, "Eaten Fish: Iranian Asylum Seeker and Cartoonist Ends Manus Island Hunger Strike," *Guardian,* February 18, 2017.

43. Binoy Kampmark, "Eaten Fish and the Refugee Crisis: Cartoons, Brutality and Manus Island," *Counterpunch,* September 13, 2016, www.counterpunch.org/2016/09/13/eaten-fish-and-the-refugee-crisis-cartoons-brutality-and-manus-island. See also "Australia's Cartoonists Rally to 'Save Eaten Fish,'" Cartoonists Rights International Network, https://cartoonistsrights.org/2E1g5.

44. Ben Doherty, "Manus Detention Centre Cleared of All Refugees and Asylum Seekers," *Guardian,* November 24, 2017.

45. Refugee Council of Australia, "Offshore Processing Statistics," www.refugeecouncil.org.au/operation-sovereign-borders-offshore-detention-statistics/4/.

46. Fiske, *Human Rights, Refugee Protest and Immigration Detention,* 124.

CHAPTER TEN

1. Center for Migration Studies, "Immigration Detention: Behind the Numbers," February 13, 2014, http://cmsny.org/immigration-detention-behind-the-record-numbers/.

2. U.S. Department of Justice, Bureau of Justice Statistics, "Prisoners in 1980," www.bjs.gov/content/pub/pdf/p80.pdf; U.S. Department of Justice, Bureau of

Justice Statistics, "Correctional Populations in the United States 2017-18," August 2020, www.bjs.gov/content/pub/pdf/cpus1718.pdf.

3. Niels Frenzen, "US Migrant Interdiction Practices in International and Territorial Waters," in Bernard Ryan and Valsamis Mitsilegas (eds.), *Extraterritorial Immigration Control: Legal Challenges* (Martinus Nijhoff Publishers, 2010), 377; Michael Welch, *Detained: Immigration Laws and the Expanding I.N.S Jail Complex* (Temple University Press, 2002), 107.

4. Alfonso Chardy, "A Look inside Krome: From Cold War Base to Immigrant Detention Facility," *Miami Herald,* October 6, 2015; Mario Rivera, *Decision and Structure: U.S. Refugee Policy in the Mariel Crisis* (University Press of America, 1991), 144–45.

5. *Haitian Refugee Center v. Civiletti,* 503 F.Supp. 442 (S.D.Fla. 1980); *Refugee Center v. Smith,* 676 F.2d 1023 (5th Cir. 1982).

6. Robert L. Steinback, "Hunger Strike Exposes Biased Asylum Policy," *Miami Herald,* January 5, 1993; Carl Lindskoog, *Detain and Punish: Haitian Refugees and the Rise of the World's Largest Immigration Detention System* (University of Florida Press, 2018); Jana K. Lipman, "'The Fish Trusts the Water, and It Is in the Water That It Is Cooked': The Caribbean Origins of the Krome Detention Center," *Radical History Review* 2013, no. 115 (2013): 115–41.

7. Jenna M. Loyd and Alison Mountz, *Boats, Borders, and Bases: Race, the Cold War, and the Rise of Migration Detention in the United States* (University of California Press, 2018), 72–75.

8. Raymond Bonner, "U.S. Transfers 120 Haitians to Prison in New York State," *New York Times,* September 5, 1981.

9. Also in December, two hundred Haitians at Fort Allen, Puerto Rico rioted, and one hundred Border Patrol agents were flown in to suppress the uprising. *New York Times,* "U.S. Aides and Haitians' Lawyers Discuss Riot in Puerto Rico Camp," December 22, 1981.

10. *New York Times,* "Haitians at 2 Detention Sites Refusing to Eat and to Talk," December 25, 1981.

11. Ibid.

12. Gregory Jaynes, "Haitians in Detention Drop Hunger Strike; 100 Escape Facility," *New York Times,* December 30, 1981; *Globe and Mail,* "100 Refugees Flee Detention Centre: Miami Police Seeking Escaped Haitians," December 29, 1981; Jaynes, "Haitians in Detention."

13. *New York Times,* "Aliens Held in Miami Go on a Hunger Strike," February 1, 1984.

14. *Jean v. Nelson,* 472 U.S. 846 (1985); *Louis v. Nelson,* 544 F. Supp. 973 (S.D. Fla. 1982).

15. Michael Flynn, "How and Why Immigration Detention Crossed the Globe," *Working Paper 8* (Geneva: Global Detention Project, 2014), www.refworld.org /pdfid/545b41254.pdf.

16. David Dixon and Julia Gelatt, "Immigration Enforcement Spending since IRCA," Migration Policy Institute, November 2005, 1.

17. Kristina Karin Shull, "'Nobody Wants These People': Reagan's Immigration Crisis and America's First Private Prisons" (UC Irvine, 2014), https://escholarship.org/uc/item/4v54x9hp; ACLU, "Banking on Bondage: Private Prisons and Mass Incarceration," www.aclu.org/banking-bondage-private-prisons-and-mass-incarceration; Michael Flynn and Cecilia Cannon, "The Privatization of Immigration Detention: Towards a Global View," Global Detention Project, 2009, www.refworld.org/pdfid/545b37394.pdf.

18. Patrisia Macías-Rojas, *From Deportation to Prison: The Politics of Immigration Enforcement in Post–Civil Rights America* (NYU Press, 2016), 54–61; Roxanne Lynn Doty and Elizabeth Shannon Wheatley, "Private Detention and the Immigration Industrial Complex," *International Political Sociology* 7, no. 4 (2013): 426–43.

19. Letter from Cheryl Little, Haitian Refugee Center, October 18, 1990, to Richard Smith, District Director INS, 1992, AIJC Krome, Box 9, American Immigrant Justice Collection, Duke University Special Collections; Mark Dow, *American Gulag: Inside U.S. Immigration Prisons* (University of California Press, 2004), 55–60.

20. "Unsigned statement of Haitian Detainee," 1991, and letter from Cheryl Little, Florida Rural Legal Services, to Carol Chase, Acting District Director, INS, Miami, January 3, 1993, Duke, AIJC Krome, 1992, Boxes 7 and 9, American Immigrant Justice Collection, Duke University Special Collections.

21. Larry Rohter, "'Processing' for Haitians Is a Time in a Rural Prison," *New York Times*, June 21, 1992.

22. A. Naomi Paik, "Representing the Disappeared Body: Hunger Strikes at Guantánamo," *Humanity: An International Journal of Human Rights, Humanitarianism, and Development* 9, no. 3 (2018); A. Naomi Paik, "Carceral Quarantine at Guantánamo: Legacies of U.S. Imprisonment of Haitian Refugees, 1991–1994," *Radical History Review* 115, no. 1 (2013): 142–68.

23. *New York Times*, "On Her Toes," March 15, 1992; *New York Times*, "Haitian Leader Meets Hunger Striker in U.S.," March 17, 1992. Two years later, Randall Robinson, the director of TransAfrica, went on a similar solidarity hunger strike in opposition to the Clinton administration's policies toward Haiti. See *Jet*, "Randall Robinson to Stay on Hunger Strike until Clinton Changes Policy toward Haiti," May 2, 1994, 5–6.

24. Mike Clary, "Haitians Fasting to Protest Hero's Welcome for Cubans," *Los Angeles Times*, January 4, 1993.

25. Florida Rural Legal Services, January 6, 1993, Box 7, American Immigrant Justice Collection, Duke University Special Collections.

26. Letter from Cheryl Little, Florida Rural Legal Services, to Carol Chase, Acting District Director, INS, Miami, January 3, 1993, Box 7, American Immigrant Justice Collection, Duke University Special Collections.

27. Robert L. Steinback, "Hunger Strike Exposes Biased Asylum Policy," *Miami Herald*, January 5, 1993.

28. Larry Rohter, "'Processing' for Haitians Is a Time in a Rural Prison," *New York Times*, June 21, 1992.

29. Paik, "Carceral Quarantine at Guantánamo."

30. Macías-Rojas, *From Deportation to Prison*, 69.

31. National Immigrant Justice Center, www.immigrantjustice.org/staff/blog/immigration-detention-bed-quota-timeline; Gretchen Gavett, "Map: The U.S. Immigration Detention Boom," *PBS Frontline*, October 18, 2011, www.pbs.org/wgbh/frontline/article/map-the-u-s-immigration-detention-boom/.

32. Center for Migration Studies, "Immigration Detention: Behind the Numbers," http://cmsny.org/immigration-detention-behind-the-record-numbers/.

33. David Iaconangelo, "Arizona Anti-Deportation Activists Enter Second Week of Hunger Strike," *Latin Times*, February 24, 2014; Matthew Hendley, "People with Family in Immigration Lockup Go on Hunger Strike Outside Phoenix ICE Office," *Phoenix New Times*, February 18, 2014.

34. NWDC Resistance, "A Hunger Strikers Handbook," April 2017, https://antipodeonline.org/sapa-1516-ybarra/ (see pp. 15–16).

35. Ibid., 18; Jolinda Stephens, "Prison Hunger Strike to End Deportations," *Tribuno del Pueblo* (Chicago) 41, no. 3 (2014), www.tribunodelpueblo.org/2014/05/prison-hunger-strike-end-deportations/.

36. NWDC Resistance, "A Hunger Strikers Handbook," 22.

37. Angélica Cházaro and Dan Berger, "What's behind the Hunger Strike at Northwest Detention Center," *Seattle Times*, March 19, 2014.

38. Candice Bernd, "Retaliation Measures Taken at Texas Migrant Jail over Hunger Strike," *Truthout*, March 28, 2014, https://truthout.org/articles/retaliation-measures-taken-at-texas-detention-facility-as-detainees-resume-hunger-strike-in-tacoma/.

39. Wil S. Hylton, "A Federal Judge and a Hunger Strike Take on the Government's Immigrant Detention Facilities," *New York Times Magazine*, April 10, 2015; Cristina Parker, "Women in Karnes Family Detention Camp Start Work Strike and Fast for Holy Week! Demanding Freedom!," Grassroots Leadership, http://grassrootsleadership.org/blog/2015/03/breaking-women-karnes-family-detention-camp-start-work-strike-and-fast-holy-week.

40. Hylton, "Federal Judge and a Hunger Strike"; Amanda Sakuma, "Hunger-Striking Immigrant Moms and Kids Allege Retaliation," *MSNBC*, April 3, 2015, www.msnbc.com/msnbc/supporters-allege-retaliation-against-hunger-striking-moms-and-kids.

41. Cindy Carcamo, "Judge Blasts ICE, Says Immigrant Children, Parents in Detention Centers Should Be Released," *Los Angeles Times*, July 25, 2015; *Flores v. Johnson*, 212 F. Supp. 3d 864 (C.D. Cal. 2015); Peter Gorman, "No Family Left Behind," *Fort Worth Weekly*, December 8, 2016; Philip G. Schrag, *Baby Jails: The Fight to End the Incarceration of Refugee Children in America* (University of California Press); Claudio J. Perez, "How U.S. Policy Has Failed Immigrant Children: Family Separation in the Obama and Trump Eras," *Family Law Quarterly* 54, no. 1 (Spring 2020): 37–66.

42. Michael Barajas and Alex Zielinski, "Why Is ICE Releasing Hundreds of Women and Children from Family Detention Centers?," *San Antonio Current*,

December 5, 2016; Nigel Duara, "Hundreds of Women and Children Are Released from Texas Immigration Detention Facilities," *Los Angeles Times,* December 6, 2016.

43. Caitlin Dickson, "How the U.S. Sold Out Indian Asylum Seekers on the Border," *Daily Beast,* August 11, 2014.

44. Esther Yu Hsi Lee, "The Hunger Strike You Haven't Heard About," *Think Progress,* October 21, 2015, https://thinkprogress.org/the-hunger-strike-you-havent-heard-about-1c3f72570545/; Sunita Sohrabji, "Asylum Seekers End Hunger Strike at Texas ICE Facility," *India West,* October 30, 2015.

45. Sunita Sohrabji, "South Asian Asylum Seekers End Hunger at ICE Facility," *India West,* November 13, 2015.

46. Sunita Sohrabji, "'Wildfire' of Hunger Strikes by Asylum Seekers Detained at ICE Facilities," *India West,* December 4, 2015.

47. Ezra David Romero, "Caravanning to El Paso, Fresno Sikhs Protest Year-Long Detention," *Valley Public Radio,* April 25, 2014, http://kvpr.org/post /caravanning-el-paso-fresno-sikhs-protest-year-long-detention.

48. Cathy Cohen, "Punks, Bulldaggers, and Welfare Queens: The Radical Potential of Queer Politics?," *GLQ: A Journal of Lesbian and Gay Studies* 3, no. 4 (1997): 437–65.

49. Raquel Reichard, "Immigrant & LGBT Rights Leaders Start Hunger Strike to #EndTransDetention," *Latina.com,* May 18, 2016.

50. Tina Vasquez, "Hunger Strikers to ICE: End Transgender Immigrant Detention," May 17, 2016, *Rewire News Group,* https://rewire.news/article /2016/05/17/hunger-strikers-ice-transgender-immigrant/.

51. Dara Lind, "What We Know about a Reported Hunger Strike by Fathers in Immigration Detention," *Vox,* August 2, 2018, www.vox.com/2018/8/2/17641208 /immigrant-strike-detention-families-separation.

52. John Burnett, "Detained Fathers Turn to Hunger Strike," *NPR,* August 2, 2018, www.npr.org/2018/08/02/634909493/detained-fathers-turn-to-hunger-strike.

53. Emma Platoff, "After 'Disturbance' at Immigrant Detention Center, 16 Migrant Fathers Taken Away Overnight," *Texas Tribune,* August 17, 2018.

54. Daniel Borunda, "Immigrants on Hunger Strike Being Force-Fed at El Paso ICE Detention Center," *El Paso Times,* January 30, 2019; Geneva Sands and Priscilla Alvarez, "ICE Force-Feeding Detainees amid Ongoing Hunger Strike in Texas," *CNN Wire Service,* January 31, 2019.

55. Veronica Escobar, Twitter post, January 2, 2019, 5:14 P.M., https://twitter .com/RepEscobar/status/1091142795912536070; Sunita Sohrabji, "Following 80-Day Hunger Strike, 2 Sikh Asylum Seekers Released," *India West,* May 10, 2019.

56. Sarah Harvard, "US Border Crisis: ICE Officials Force-Feeding Immigrants on Hunger Strike in Texas Detention Centre," *Independent Digital News & Media,* 2019; Borunda, "Immigrants on Hunger Strike"; Garance Burke, "UN: US Force-Feeding Immigrants May Breach Torture Agreement," *AP News,* February 7, 2019.

57. Garance Burke and Martha Mendoza, "Detainee on Hunger Strike Details Force-Feeding," *AP News,* February 3, 2019.

58. Michelle Chen, "Immigrants Are Fighting for Their Rights Even behind Bars," *Nation,* February 15, 2019; *India West,* "Sikh Coalition Files Complaint Alleging Ill-Treatment of Indian Asylum Seekers in ICE Detention Centers," April 9, 2019.

59. Garance Burke and Martha Medoza, "ICE Force-Feeding Detainees on Hunger Strike," *AP News,* January 31, 2019.

60. *Florida Daily Post,* "ICE Force-Feeding Immigrants Detainees [*sic*] on Hunger Strike," February 20, 2019, https://floridadailypost.com/ice-force-feeding-immigrants-detainees-hunger-strike.

61. Garance Burke and Martha Mendoza, "Lawmakers Seek Probe of ICE Force-Feeding of Immigrants," *AP News,* February 19, 2019.

62. Sunita Shorabji, "Following 80-Day Hunger Strike, Two Sikh Asylum Seekers Release from ICE Custody in New Mexico," *India West,* April 22, 2019; Robert Moore, "Two of the Asylum-Seekers Who Were Force-Fed at an El Paso Detention Center Are Now Free," *Texas Monthly,* April 11, 2019; *Florida Daily Post,* "ICE Force-Feeding."

CONCLUSION

1. Gayatri C. Spivak, "Can the Subaltern Speak?," in Cary Nelson and Lawrence Grossberg (eds.), *Marxism and the Interpretation of Culture* (University of Illinois Press, 1988), 271–313.

2. John Duda, "Toward the Horizon of Abolition: A Conversation with Mariame Kaba," https://thenextsystem.org/learn/stories/towards-horizon-abolition-conversation-mariame-kaba. See also Angela Y. Davis, *Are Prisons Obsolete?* (Seven Stories Press, 2003).

3. Jim Aulich, "Conclusion: Reflections on Protest and Political Transformation since 1789," in Aidan McGarry et al. (eds.), *The Aesthetics of Global Protest: Visual Culture and Communication* (Amsterdam University Press, 2020), 269–92.

SELECTED BIBLIOGRAPHY

ARCHIVES

Berkeley, California

Bancroft Library, University of California
    Japanese American Evacuation and Resettlement Records
    Suffragists Oral History Project
    Wayne M. Collins Papers

Cape Town, South Africa

University of Cape Town Special Collections
    Thomas Winslow Papers

College Park, Maryland

National Archives and Records Administration
    Records of the Bureau of Prisons

Dublin, Ireland

National Archives of Ireland
    State Paper Office
University College Dublin Archives
    Mary MacSwiney Papers
    Terence MacSwiney Papers
    Éamon de Valera Papers

Durham, North Carolina

Duke University Special Collections
   American Immigrant Justice Collection

East Lansing, Michigan

Michigan State University Special Collections

Ferney-Voltaire, France

World Medical Association Archives

Johannesburg, South Africa

University of Witswatersrand
   South African History Archive
      The National Medical and Dental Association Collection
      The Lawyers for Human Rights Collection
   Historical Papers Research Archive
      Detainees' Parents Support Committee Records
Alder Museum of Medicine, University of Witswatersrand Medical School

London, United Kingdom

The British Library
   India Office Records
The National Archives
London School of Economics
   Women's Library Collection
Parliamentary Archives

Los Angeles, California

UCLA Library Special Collections
   Japanese American Research Project Collection
   Verne Austin Papers

Nashville, Tennessee

Vanderbilt Television News Archive

Sacramento, California

California State University Library
  Japanese American Archival Collection

Washington, D.C.

Library of Congress
  National Woman's Party Records

PRIMARY SOURCES

Babenia, Natoo. *Memoirs of a Saboteur: Reflections on My Political Activity in India and South Africa.* Bellville, South Africa: Mayibuye Books, 1996.

Barnes, Djuna. "How It Feels to Be Forcibly Fed." *New York World Magazine,* September 6, 1914.

Bernstein, Hilda. "Diary of a Detainee." *Africa South in Exile* 5, no. 2 (1961): 25–47.

———. "Diary of a Detainee." In M. J. Daymond, Dorothy Driver, Sheila Meintjes, Leloba Molema, Chiedza Musengezi, Margie Orford, and Noboantu Rasebotsa. *Women Writing Africa, vol. 1: The Southern Region,* 263–68. New York: Feminist Press at the City University of New York, 2003.

Billington-Greig, Teresa. "A Criticism of Militancy." In *The Non-Violent Militant: Selected Writings of Teresa Billington-Greig,* ed. Carol McPhee and Ann Fitzgerald. New York: Routledge, 1987.

Bose, Nirmal Kumar. *Studies in Gandhism.* Calcutta: Indian Associated, 1947.

Bose, Subhas Chandra. *The Indian Struggle, 1920–1942.* Edited by Sisir Kumar Bose and Sugata Bose. New York: Oxford University Press, 1997.

Breen, Suzanne. "Marian Price Interview: Old Bailey Bomber Ashamed of Sinn Fein." *Village,* December 7, 2004.

Clouston, T. S. "Forcible Feeding." *Lancet* 100, no. 2570 (1872): 797–98.

Colt, G. H. "The Gag." *Lancet* 170, no. 4389 (1907): 1011–17.

Commission on Wartime Relocation and Internment of Civilians. *Personal Justice Denied: Report of the Commission on Wartime Relocation and Internment of Civilians.* Seattle: University of Washington, 1997.

The Death of Thomas Ashe: A Full Report of the Inquest. Dublin: J.M. Butler, 1917.

Dellinger, David. *From Yale to Jail: The Life Story of a Moral Dissenter.* Eugene, OR: Wipf and Stock, 1993.

Dlamini, Moses. *Hell-Hole, Robben Island: Reminiscences of a Political Prisoner in South Africa.* Trenton, NJ: Africa World Press, 1984.

Einhorn, Max. *The Duodenal Tube and Its Possibilities.* Philadelphia: W.B. Saunders, 1920.

Fox, Richard Michael. *Drifting Men*. London: Hogarth Press, 1930.

Friedenwald, Julius, and Samuel Morrison. "The History of the Enema with Some Notes on Related Procedures." *Bulletin of the History of Medicine* 8, no. 2 (1940): 239–76.

Gandhi, Mohandas K. *An Autobiography: The Story of My Experiments with Truth*. Translated by Mahadev Desai. Boston: Beacon Press, 1993.

———. *Collected Works of Mahatma Gandhi*. New Delhi: Government of India, Publications Division, 1999.

———. *Ethics of Fasting*. Lahore: Indian Printing Works, 1944.

Hayes Irwin, Inez. *The Story of the Woman's Party*. New York: Harcourt, Brace, 1921.

Inouye, Tatsuo Ryusei. "Tule Lake Stockade Diary, November 13, 1943—February 14, 1944." Translated by Masumi Izumi. The Suyama Project, University of California, Los Angeles Asian American Studies Center, 2018. http://www.suyamaproject.org.

Kellogg, John Harvey. *The New Dietetics, What to Eat and How: A Guide the Scientific Feeding in Health and Disease*. Battle Creek, MI: Modern Medicine, 1921.

Kennally, Danny, and Eric Preston, eds. *Belfast, August 1971: A Case to Be Answered*. London: Independent Labour Party, 1971.

Kenney, Annie. *Memories of a Militant*. London: Edward Arnold, 1924.

Lytton, Constance. *Prisons and Prisoners*. London: William Heinemann, 1914.

Mackenzie, J. W. A. "The Nutrient Enema." *Archives of Disease in Childhood* 18, no. 93 (1943): 22–27.

Mandela, Nelson. *Long Walk to Freedom: The Autobiography of Nelson Mandela*. New York: Little, Brown, 1994.

McCabe, James D. *Our Martyred President: The Life and Public Services of Gen. James A. Garfield, Twentieth President of the United States*. Philadelphia: National Publishing Company, 1881.

"Medicolegal: Inquest on Hunger Striker." *British Medical Journal* 3, no. 5922 (July 6, 1974): 52–53.

Naidoo, Indres. *Robben Island: Ten Years as a Political Prisoner in South Africa's Most Notorious Penitentiary*. Edited by Albie Sachs. New York: Vintage Books, 1983.

O'Hegarty, P. S. *A Short Memoir of Terence MacSwiney*. Dublin: Talbot Press, 1922.

———. *The Victory of Sinn Féin*. Dublin: Talbot Press, 1924.

Pankhurst, Christabel. *Unshackled: The Story of How We Won the Vote*. London: Hutchinson, 1959.

Pankhurst, E. Sylvia. "Forcibly Fed: The Story of My Four Weeks in Holloway Gaol." *McClure's*, August 1913, 87–93.

———. *The Suffragette Movement: An Intimate Account of Persons and Ideals*. London: Longmans, Green, 1931.

Pankhurst, Emmeline. *My Own Story*. New York: Hearst's International Library, 1914.

Paul, Alice. Alice Paul Oral History. Interview by Amelia R. Fry, November 24, 1972. Bancroft Library, University of California—Berkeley, Regional Oral History Office, Suffragists Oral History Project.

"Rectal Alimentation." *Nature* 118, no. 2980 (1926): 858–59.

"Report of the Committee of Privy Counsellors Appointed to Consider Authorised Procedures for the Interrogation of Person Suspected of Terrorism (Parker Report)." London: Her Majesty's Stationery Office, March 1972.

"Report of the Enquiry into Allegations against the Security Forces of Physical Brutality in Northern Ireland Arising out of Event on the 9th August, 1971 (Compton Report)." London: Her Majesty's Stationery Office, November 1971.

Sands, Bobby. "Birth of a Republican." *Republican News,* December 16, 1978.

Savarkar, Vinayak Damodar. *The Story of My Transportation for Life.* Bombay: Sadbhakti, 1950.

Schnitker, Maurice A., Paul E. Mattman, and Theodore L. Bliss. "A Clinical Study of Malnutrition in Japanese Prisoners of War." *Annals of Internal Medicine* 35, no. 1 (1951): 69–96.

Senate Select Committee on Intelligence. "Committee Study of the Central Intelligence Agency's Detention and Interrogation Program." Brooklyn, NY: Melville House, 2014.

Short, A. Rendle, and H. W. Bywater. "Amino-Acids and Sugars in Rectal Feeding." *British Medical Journal* 28, no. 1 (1913): 1361–67.

Stevens, Doris. *Jailed for Freedom.* New York: Boni and Liveright, 1920.

Strasburg, Toni. *Holding the Fort: A Family Torn Apart.* Cape Town: Kwela Books, 2019.

Tateishi, John, ed. *And Justice for All: An Oral History of the Japanese American Detention Camps.* Seattle: University of Washington Press, 1984.

U.S. Department of War. "Hospital Diets." Washington, DC: Government of the United States, 1941.

Venceremos Sisters: Prison Writings of the Price Sisters. Andersonstown, UK: Cathal Brugha Cumann, 1974.

Venu, C. S. *Jatin Das (The Martyr).* Madras: C.S. Cunniah, 1931.

Waraich, Malawinder Jit Singh. *Bhagat Singh: The Eternal Rebel.* New Delhi: Government of India, Ministry of Information and Broadcasting, 2007.

Yeats, W. B. *The King's Threshold: Manuscript Materials.* Edited by Declan Kiely. Ithaca, NY: Cornell University Press, 2005.

SECONDARY SOURCES

Ackerman, Alisa R., and Rich Furman. "The Criminalization of Immigration and the Privatization of the Immigration Detention: Implications for Justice." *Contemporary Justice Review* 16, no. 2 (2013): 251–63.

Adams, Katherine H., and Michael L. Keene. *Alice Paul and the American Suffrage Campaign.* Urbana: University of Illinois Press, 2008.

Agamben, Giorgio. *Homo Sacer: Sovereign Power and Bare Life.* Translated by Daniel Heller-Roazen. Stanford, CA: Stanford University Press, 1998.

Ahmed, Sara. "Affective Economies." *Social Text* 22, no. 2 (2004): 117–39.

———. *The Cultural Politics of Emotion.* New York: Routledge, 2004.

Ahuja, Neel. *Bioinsecurities: Disease Interventions, Empire, and the Government of Species.* Durham, NC: Duke University Press, 2016.

Alberti, Johanna. *Beyond Suffrage: Feminists in War and Peace, 1914–28.* London: Palgrave Macmillan, 1989.

Amin, Shahid. *Event, Metaphor, Memory: Chauri Chaura, 1922–1992.* Berkeley: University of California Press, 1994.

Anderson, Patrick. *So Much Wasted: Hunger, Performance, and the Morbidity of Resistance.* Durham, NC: Duke University Press, 2010.

———. "There Will Be No Bobby Sands in Guantánamo Bay." *PMLA* 124, no. 5 (2009): 1729–36.

Annas, George J. "Hunger Strikes at Guantanamo: Medical Ethics and Human Rights in a 'Legal Black Hole.'" *New England Journal of Medicine* 355, no. 13 (2006): 1377–82.

Arendt, Hannah. *The Origins of Totalitarianism.* New York: Harcourt, Brace, 1951.

Aretxaga, Begoña. *States of Terror: Begoña Aretxaga's Essays.* Edited by Joseba Zulaika. Reno: Center for Basque Studies, University of Nevada, 2005.

Armbruster-Sandoval, Ralph. *Starving for Justice: Hunger Strikes, Spectacular Speech, and the Struggle for Dignity.* Tucson: University of Arizona Press, 2017.

Aulich, Jim. "Conclusion: Reflections on Protest and Political Transformation since 1789." In *The Aesthetics of Global Protest: Visual Culture and Communication,* ed. McGarry Aidan, Erhart Itir, Eslen-Ziya Hande, Jenzen Olu, and Korkut Umut, 269–92. Amsterdam: Amsterdam University Press, 2020.

Bargu, Banu. "Gandhi's Fasts." Blog post, November 29, 2017. http://blogs.law.columbia.edu/uprising1313/banu-bargu-gandhis-fasts/?cn-reloaded=1.

———. *Starve and Immolate: The Politics of Human Weapons.* New York: Columbia University Press, 2014.

Baxter, Lawrence. "Doctors on Trial: Steve Biko, Medical Ethics, and the Courts." *South African Journal on Human Rights* 1 (1985): 137–51.

Beresford, David. *Ten Men Dead: The Story of the 1981 Irish Hunger Strike.* New York: Atlantic Monthly Press, 1997.

Beveridge, Allan. "Voices of the Mad: Patients' Letters from the Royal Edinburgh Asylum, 1873–1908." *Psychological Medicine* 27, no. 4 (1997): 899–908.

Biggs, Michael. "The Rationality of Self-Inflicted Sufferings: Hunger Strikes by Irish Republicans, 1916–1923." *Sociology Working Papers,* 2007.

Biro, Andrew. "A Welfare Worker's Experience." In *Protection or Punishment? The Detention of Asylum Seekers in Australia,* ed. Mary Crock. Sydney: Federation Press, 1993.

Bondurant, Joan V. *Conquest of Violence: The Gandhian Philosophy of Conflict.* Berkeley: University of California Press, 1965.

Bose, Sarmila, and Eilis Ward. "'India's Cause Is Ireland's Cause': Elite Links and Nationalist Politics." In *Ireland and India: Connections, Comparisons, Contrasts,* ed. Michael Holmes and Dennis Holmes, 52–73. Dublin: Folens, 1997.

Bose, Sugata. *His Majesty's Opponent: Subhas Chandra Bose and India's Struggle against Empire.* Cambridge, MA: Harvard University Press, 2011.

Bradley, Anthony. "Nation, Pedagogy, and Performance: W. B. Yeats's The King's Threshold and the Irish Hunger Strikes." *Literature and History* 18, no. 2 (2009): 20–33.

Brown, Ian, and Frank Dikötter. *Cultures of Confinement: A History of the Prison in Africa, Asia, and Latin America.* Ithaca: Cornell University Press, 2007.

Brown, Judith M. *Gandhi: Prisoner of Hope.* New Haven, CT: Yale University Press, 1989.

Brumberg, Joan Jacobs. *Fasting Girls: The History of Anorexia Nervosa.* New York: Vintage Books, 2000.

Buntman, Fran Lisa. *Robben Island and Prisoner Resistance to Apartheid.* New York: Cambridge University Press, 2003.

Burton, Jeffrey F., Mary M. Farrell, Florence B. Lord, and Richard W. Lord. *Confinement and Ethnicity: An Overview of World War II Japanese American Relocation Sites.* Seattle: University of Washington Press, 2002.

Cacho, Lisa Marie. *Social Death: Racialized Rightlessness and the Criminalization of the Unprotected.* New York: NYU Press, 2012.

Campbell, Brian, Laurence McKeown, and Felim O'Hagan, eds. *Nor Meekly Serve My Time: The H-Block Struggle, 1976–1981.* Belfast: Beyond the Pale, 1994.

Chaskalson, Matthew, Karen Jochelson, and Jeremy Seekings. "Rent Boycotts, the State, and the Transformation of the Urban Political Economy in South Africa." *Review of African Political Economy* 14, no. 40 (1987): 47–64.

Chatterjee, Pranab Kumar. "The Hunger-Strike Movement of the Andaman Prisoners in 1937 and National Response." *Proceedings of the Indian History Conference* 40 (1979): 662–69.

Chernoff, Ronni. "An Overview of Tube Feeding: From Ancient Times to the Future." *Nutrition in Clinical Practice* 21, no. 4 (2006): 408–10.

Clift, Eleanor. *Founding Sisters and the Nineteenth Amendment.* Hoboken, NJ: Wiley, 2003.

Cohen, Cathy. "Punks, Bulldaggers, and Welfare Queens: The Radical Potential of Queer Politics?" *GLQ: A Journal of Lesbian and Gay Studies* 3, no. 4 (1997): 437–65.

Coleman, Max, ed. *A Crime against Humanity: Analysing the Repression of the Apartheid State.* Johannesburg: D. Philip, 1998.

Costello, Francis J. *Enduring the Most: The Life and Death of Terence MacSwiney.* Co. Kerry, Ireland: Brandon, 1995.

Cullen Owens, Rosemary. *A Social History of Women in Ireland, 1870–1970.* Dublin: Gill and Macmillan, 2005.

Das, Veena. "Language and Body: Transactions in the Construction of Pain." *Daedalus* 125, no. 1 (1996): 67–91.

Doty, Roxanne Lynn, and Elizabeth Shannon Wheatley. "Private Detention and the Immigration Industrial Complex." *International Political Sociology* 7, no. 4 (2013): 426–43.

Drinnon, Richard. *Keeper of Concentration Camps: Dillon S. Myer and American Racism.* Berkeley: University of California Press, 1987.

Duda, John, and Mariame Kaba. "Towards the Horizon of Abolition: A Conversation with Mariame Kaba." 2017. https://thenextsystem.org/learn/stories/towards-horizon-abolition-conversation-mariame-kaba.

Ellmann, Maud. *The Hunger Artists: Starving, Writing, and Imprisonment.* Cambridge, MA: Harvard University Press, 1993.

English, Richard. *Armed Struggle: The History of the IRA.* New York: Oxford University Press, 2003.

Espiritu, Yen Le. *Body Counts: The Vietnam War and Militarized Refuge(es).* Oakland: University of California Press, 2014.

Fallon, Charlotte H. *Soul of Fire: A Biography of Mary MacSwiney.* Cork, Ireland: Mercier Press, 1986.

Fanning, Bryan. *Histories of the Irish Future.* New York: Bloomsbury, 2015.

Feldman, Allen. *Formations of Violence: The Narrative of the Body and Political Terror in Northern Ireland.* Chicago: University of Chicago Press, 1991.

Fiske, Lucy. *Human Rights, Refugee Protest and Immigration Detention.* London: Palgrave Macmillan, 2016.

Flynn, Barry. *Pawns in the Game: Irish Hunger Strikes, 1912–1981.* Cork, Ireland: Collins Press, 2011.

Foster, Don (with Dennis Davis and Diane Sandler). *Detention and Torture in South Africa: Psychological, Legal and Historical Studies.* Cape Town: D. Philip, 1987.

Foucault, Michel. *Discipline and Punish: The Birth of the Prison.* Translated by Alan Sheridan. New York: Vintage Books, 1977.

———. *The History of Sexuality: An Introduction, vol. 1.* Translated by Robert Hurley. New York: Vintage Books, 1978.

———. *"Society Must Be Defended": Lectures at the Collége de France, 1975–1976.* Translated by David Macey. Edited by Mauro Bertani and Alessandro Fontana. New York: Picador, 2003.

Frenzen, Niels. "US Migrant Interdiction Practices in International and Territorial Waters." In *Extraterritorial Immigration Control: Legal Challenges,* ed. Bernard Ryan and Valsamis Mitsilegas, 369–90. Leiden, Netherlands: Martinus Nijhoff Publishers, 2010.

Fujitani, Takashi. *Race for Empire: Koreans as Japanese and Japanese as Americans during World War II.* Berkeley: University of California Press, 2011.

Garland, David. *Punishment and Modern Society: A Study in Social Theory.* Oxford: Oxford University Press, 1990.

Gershon, Michael D. *The Second Brain: The Scientific Basis of Gut Instinct and a Groundbreaking New Understanding of Nervous Disorders of the Stomach and Intestines.* New York: HarperCollins, 1998.

Ghosh, Durba. *Gentlemanly Terrorists: Political Violence and the Colonial State in India, 1919–1947.* New York: Cambridge University Press, 2017.

Gilmore, Ruth Wilson. *Golden Gulag: Prisons Surplus, Crisis and Opposition in Globalizing California.* Berkeley: University of California Press, 2007.

Gómez-Barris, Macarena. "Mapuche Hunger Acts: Epistemology of the Decolonial." *Transmodernity* 1, no. 3 (2012): 120–32.

Gottschalk, Marie. *Caught: The Prison State and the Lockdown of America.* Princeton, NJ: Princeton University Press, 2014.

Gould, Deborah B. *Moving Politics: Emotion and ACT UP's Fight against AIDS.* Chicago: University of Chicago Press, 2009.

Grant, Kevin. "British Suffragettes and the Russian Method of Hunger Strike." *Comparative Studies in Society and History* 53, no. 1 (2011): 113–43.

———. "Fearing the Danger Point: The Study and Treatment of Human Starvation in the United Kingdom and India, c. 1880–1974." In *Comparative Physiology of Fasting, Starvation, and Food Limitation,* ed. Marshall D. McCue, 365–77. Berlin: Springer, 2012.

———. *Last Weapons: Hunger Strikes and Fasts in the British Empire, 1890–1948.* Oakland: University of California Press, 2019.

———. "The Transcolonial World of Hunger Strikes and Political Fasts, c. 1909–1935." In *Decentring Empire: Britain, India and the Transcolonial World,* ed. Durba Ghosh and Dane Kennedy, 243–69. New Delhi: Orient Longman, 2006.

Green, Barbara. *Spectacular Confessions: Autobiography, Performative Activism, and the Sites of Suffrage, 1905–1938.* New York: St. Martin's Press, 1997.

Greenberg, Karen J. *The Least Worst Place: Guantanamo's First 100 Days.* New York: Oxford University Press, 2010.

Greenough, Paul R. "Political Mobilization and the Underground Literature of the Quit India Movement, 1942–44." *Social Scientist* 27, no. 8 (1999): 11–47.

Gregg, Melissa, and Gregory J. Siegworth, eds. *The Affect Theory Reader.* Durham, NC: Duke University Press, 2010.

Guha, Ramachandra. *Gandhi: The Years That Changed the World, 1914–1948.* New York: Alfred A. Knopf, 2018.

Hannigan, Dave. *Terence MacSwiney: The Hunger Strike That Rocked an Empire.* Dublin: O'Brien Press, 2010.

Harper, Tim. "Singapore, 1915, and the Birth of the Asian Underground." *Modern Asian Studies* 47, no. 6 (2013): 1782–1811.

Healy, James. "The Civil War Hunger-Strike: October 1923." *Studies: An Irish Quarterly Review* 71, no. 283 (1982): 213–26.

Hennessey, Thomas. *Hunger Strike: Margaret Thatcher's Battle with the IRA, 1980–1981.* Dublin: Irish Academic Press, 2014.

Hodgson, Jonathan. "Guantanamo Bay: The Hunger Strikes." *Art Journal* 73, no. 2 (2014): 5–13.

Hoenig, Ron. "Reading Alien Lips: Australian Print Media Depictions of Asylum Seekers and the Construction of National Identity." In *The Racial Politics of Bodies, Nations and Knowledges,* ed. Barbara Baird and Damien W. Riggs, 133–54. Newcastle, UK: Cambridge Scholars, 2009.

Hoffenberg, Raymond. "Doctors and Society—The Biko Lecture." *South African Medical Journal* 84, no. 5 (1994): 245–49.

Holland, Sharon P., Marcia Ochoa, and Kyla Wazana Tompkins. "On the Visceral." *GLQ: A Journal of Lesbian and Gay Studies* 20, no. 4 (2014): 391–406.

Howland, Corinna. "To Feed or Not to Feed: Violent State Care and the Contested Medicalization of Incarcerated Hunger-Strikers in Britain, Turkey and Guantanamo Bay." *New Zealand Sociology* 28, no. 1 (2013): 101–16.

Hyndman, Patricia. "The Australian Migration Legislation Amendment Act 1989." *International Journal of Refugee Law* 1, no. 4 (1989): 546–49.

Jain, Meenakshi. *Sati: Evangelicals, Baptist Missionaries, and the Changing Colonial Discourse.* New Delhi: Aryan Books, 2016.

Jenkins, Everett, Jr. *Pan-African Chronology III: A Comprehensive Reference to the Black Quest for Freedom in Africa, the Americas, Europe and Asia, 1914–1929.* Jefferson, NC: McFarland, 2001.

Kalk, W. J., M. Felix, E. R. Snoey, and Y. Veriava. "Voluntary Total Fasting in Political Prisoners: Clinical and Biochemical Observations." *South African Medical Journal* 83, no. 6 (1993): 391–94.

Kalk, W. J., and Yosuf Veriava. "Hospital Management of Voluntary Total Fasting among Political Prisoners." *Lancet* 337, no. 8742 (1991): 660–62.

Keeton, G. R. "Hunger Strikers: Ethical and Management Problems." *South African Medical Journal* 83, no. 6 (1993): 380–81.

Kenney, Padriac. *Dance in Chains: Political Imprisonment in the Modern World.* New York: Oxford University Press, 2017.

Kessels, Ronald, and Maritsa Efitmiou. "Effects of Incarceration." In *Protection or Punishment? The Detention of Asylum Seekers in Australia,* ed. Mary Crock. Sydney: Federation Press, 1993.

Koçan, Gürcan, and Ahmet Önçü. "From the Morality of Living to the Morality of Dying: Hunger Strikes in Turkish Prisons." *Citizenship Studies* 10, no. 3 (2006): 349–72.

LaFleur, William R. "Hungry Ghosts and Hungry People: Somaticity and Rationality in Medieval Japan." In *Fragments for a History of the Human Body, vol. 1,* ed. Michel Feher, Ramona Naddaff, and Nadia Tazi. New York: Zone Books, 1981.

Law, Cheryl. *Suffrage and Power: The Women's Movement, 1918–1928.* London: I.B. Tauris, 1997.

Lee, Rachel C. *The Exquisite Corpse of Asian America: Biopolitics, Biosociality, and Posthuman Ecologies.* New York: NYU Press, 2014.

Leeson, D. M. *The Black and Tans: British Police and Auxiliaries in the Irish War of Independence.* New York: Oxford University Press, 2011.

Lelyveld, Joseph. *Great Soul: Mahatma Gandhi and His Struggle with India*. New York: Vintage Books, 2011.

Lemke, Thomas. *Biopolitics: An Advanced Introduction*. Translated by Eric F. Trump. New York: NYU Press, 2011.

Lindskoog, Carl. *Detain and Punish: Haitian Refugees and the Rise of the World's Largest Detention System*. Gainesville: University of Florida Press, 2018.

Lodge, Tom. *Mandela: A Critical Life*. New York: Oxford University Press, 2007.

Louw, P. Eric. *The Rise, Fall, and Legacy of Apartheid*. Westport, CT: Praeger, 2004.

Loyd, Jenna M., Matt Mitchelson, and Andrew Burridge, eds. *Beyond Walls and Cages: Prisons, Borders, and Global Crisis*. Athens: University of Georgia Press, 2012.

Loyd, Jenna M., and Alison Mountz. *Boats, Borders, and Bases: Race, the Cold War, and the Rise of Migration Detention in the United States*. Oakland: University of California Press, 2018.

Lumsden, Linda J. *Rampant Women: Suffragists and the Right of Assembly*. Knoxville: University of Tennessee Press, 1997.

Lunardini, Christine A. *From Equal Suffrage to Equal Rights: Alice Paul and the National Woman's Party, 1910–1928*. New York: NYU Press, 1986.

Machin, Amanda. "Hunger Power: The Embodied Protest of the Political Hunger Strike." *Interface: A Journal for and about Social Movements* 8, no. 1 (2016): 157–80.

Macías-Rojas, Patrisia. *From Deportation to Prison: The Politics of Immigration Enforcement in Post–Civil Rights America*. New York: NYU Press, 2016.

Mangcu, Xolela. *Biko: A Life*. New York: I.B. Tauris, 2014.

Mani, Lata. *Contentious Traditions: The Debate on Sati in Colonial India*. Berkeley: University of California Press, 1998.

Mathews, Anthony S. *Freedom, State Security and the Rule of Law: Dilemmas of the Apartheid Society*. Berkeley: University of California Press, 1986.

Mayhall, Laura E. Nym. *The Militant Suffrage Movement: Citizenship and Resistance in Britain, 1860–1930*. New York: Oxford University Press, 2003.

Mbembe, Achille. "Necropolitics." Translated by Libby Meintjes. *Public Culture* 15, no. 1 (2003): 11–40.

McConville, Seán. *Irish Political Prisoners, 1848–1922: Theatres of War*. New York: Routledge, 2003.

McKeown, Laurence. *Out of Time: Irish Republican Prisoners, Long Kesh, 1970–2000*. Belfast: Beyond the Pale, 2001.

McKittrick, David, and David McVea. *Making Sense of the Troubles: The Story of the Conflict in Northern Ireland*. New York: New Amsterdam Press, 2002.

McLean, G. R., and Trefor Jenkins. "The Steve Biko Affair: A Case Study in Medical Ethics." *Developing World Bioethics* 3, no. 1 (2003): 77–95.

McMillan, Uri. "Objecthood, Avatars, and the Limits of the Human." *GLQ: A Journal of Lesbian and Gay Studies* 21, no. 2–3 (June 2015): 224–27.

Mehanna, Hisham M., Jamil Moledina, and Jane Travis. "Refeeding Syndrome: What It Is, and How to Prevent and Treat It." *British Medical Journal* 336, no. 7659 (June 26, 2008): 1495–98.

Mehrotra, Deepti Priya. *Burning Bright: Irom Sharmila and the Struggle for Peace in Manipur.* New Delhi: Penguin Books India, 2009.

Miller, Ian. *A History of Force Feeding: Hunger Strikes, Prisons and Medical Ethics, 1909–1974.* London: Palgrave Macmillan, 2016.

———. "'A Prostitution of the Profession'? Forcible Feeding, Prison Doctors, Suffrage and the British State, 1909–1914." *Social History of Medicine* 26, no. 2 (2013): 225–45.

Mitchell, James K. "Social Violence in Northern Ireland." *Geographical Review* 69, no. 2 (1979): 179–201.

Montiel-Castro, Augusto J., Rina M. González-Cervantes, Gabriela Bravo-Ruiseco, and Gustavo Pacheco-López. "The Microbiota–Gut–Brain Axis: Neurobehavioral Correlates, Health and Sociality." *Frontiers in Integrative Neuroscience* 7 (2013): 1–16.

Moran, Dominique. *Carceral Geography: Spaces and Practices of Incarceration.* Burlington: Ashgate, 2015.

Moran, Dominique, Nick Gill, and Deirdre Conlon, eds. *Carceral Spaces: Mobility and Agency in Imprisonment and Migrant Detention.* New York: Routledge, 2016.

Mountz, Alison. *The Death of Asylum: Hidden Geographies of the Enforcement Archipelago.* Minneapolis: University of Minnesota Press, 2020.

———. *Seeking Asylum: Human Smuggling and Bureaucracy at the Border.* Minneapolis: University of Minnesota Press, 2010.

Muggeridge, Anna. "The Missing Two Million: The Exclusion of Working-Class Women from the 1918 Representation of the People Act." *French Journal of British Studies* 23, no. 1 (2018): 1–15.

Munck, Ronnie. "The Making of the Troubles in Northern Ireland." *Journal of Contemporary History* 27, no. 2 (1992): 211–29.

Murakawa, Naomi. *The First Civil Right: How Liberals Built Prison America.* New York: Oxford University Press, 2014.

Nair, Neeti. "Bhagat Singh as 'Satyagrahi': The Limits to Non-Violence in Late Colonial India." *Modern Asian Studies* 43, no. 3 (2009): 649–81.

———. *Changing Homelands: Hindu Politics and the Partition of India.* Cambridge, MA: Harvard University Press, 2011.

Newbery, Samantha. "Intelligence and Controversial British Interrogation Techniques: The Northern Ireland Case, 1971–2." *Irish Studies in International Affairs* 20 (2009): 103–19.

———. *Interrogation, Intelligence and Security: Controversial British Techniques.* Manchester, UK: Manchester University Press, 2015.

Okie, Susan. "Glimpses of Guantanamo: Medical Ethics and the War on Terror." *New England Journal of Medicine* 353, no. 24 (2005): 2529–34.

Okihiro, Gary Y. "Tule Lake under Martial Law: A Study in Japanese Resistance." *Journal of Ethnic Studies* 5, no. 3 (1977): 71–85.

O'Malley, Padraig. *Biting at the Grave: The Irish Hunger Strikes and the Politics of Despair.* Boston: Beacon Press, 1990.

Paik, A. Naomi. *Rightlessness: Testimony and Redress in U.S. Prison Camps since World War II*. Chapel Hill: University of North Carolina Press, 2016.

Palczewski, Catherine H. "The 1919 Prison Special: Constituting White Women's Citizenship." *Quarterly Journal of Speech* 102, no. 2 (2016): 107–32.

Passmore, Leith. "Force-Feeding and Mapuche Autonomy: Performing Collective Rights in Individual Prison Cells in Chile." *Journal of Latin American Cultural Studies* 23, no. 1 (2014): 1–16.

Peel, Michael. "Hunger Strikes: Understanding the Underlying Physiology Will Help Doctors Provide Proper Advice." *British Medical Journal* 315, no. 7112 (1997): 829–30.

Plamper, Jan. "The History of Emotions: An Interview with William Reddy, Barbara Rosenwein, and Peter Stearns." *History and Theory* 49, no. 2 (2010): 237–65.

Posteraro, Tano S. "Organismic Spatiality: Toward a Metaphysic of Composition." *Environment and Planning D: Society and Space* 32, no. 4 (2014): 739–52.

Pratt, Tim, and James Vernon. "'Appeal from This Fiery Bed . . .': The Colonial Politics of Gandhi's Fasts and Their Metropolitan Reception." *Journal of British Studies* 44, no. 1 (2005): 92–114.

Protevi, John. *Political Affect: Connecting the Social and the Somatic*. Minneapolis: University of Minnesota Press, 2009.

Puggioni, Raffaela. "Speaking through the Body: Detention and Bodily Resistance in Italy." *Citizenship Studies* 18, no. 5 (2014): 562–77.

Ramnath, Maia. *Haj to Utopia: How the Ghadar Movement Charted Global Radicalism and Attempted to Overthrow the British Empire*. Berkeley: University of California Press, 2011.

Rediker, Marcus. *The Slave Ship: A Human History*. New York: Penguin Books, 2008.

Reyes, Hernán. "Medical and Ethical Aspects of Hunger Strikes in Custody and the Issue of Torture." *Research in Legal Medicine* 19, no. 1 (1998).

Reynolds, Paige. *Modernism, Drama, and the Audience for Irish Spectacle*. New York: Cambridge University Press, 2007.

Robinson, Greg. *A Tragedy of Democracy: Japanese Confinement in North America*. New York: Columbia University Press, 2009.

Rose, Nikolas. *The Politics of Life Itself: Biomedicine, Power, and Subjectivity in the Twenty-First Century*. Princeton, NJ: Princeton University Press, 2007.

Rosenwein, Barbara H. "Worrying about Emotions in History." *The American Historical Review* 107, no. 3 (2002): 821–45.

Ryan, Louise. "Traditions and Double Moral Standards: The Irish Suffragists' Critique of Nationalism." *Women's History Review* 4, no. 4 (1995): 487–503.

Ryan, Louise, and Margaret Ward, eds. *Irish Women and the Vote: Becoming Citizens*. Dublin: Irish Academic Press, 2007.

Sampath, Vikram. *Savarkar: Echoes from a Forgotten Past, 1883–1924*. New York: Viking Books, 2019.

Savage, Michael. "The Imposition of Pass Laws on the African Population in South Africa, 1916–1984." *African Affairs* 85, no. 339 (1986): 181–205.

Shah, Nayan. "Feeding Hunger Striking Prisoners: Biopolitics and Impossible Citizenship." In *Biocitizenship: The Politics of Bodies, Governance, and Power,* ed. Kelly E. Happe, Jenell Johnson, and Marina Levina, 155–77. New York: NYU Press, 2018.

———. "Feeling for the Protest Faster: How the Self-Starving Body Influences Social Movements and Global Medical Ethics." In *Science and Emotions after 1945: A Transatlantic Perspective,* ed. Frank Biess and Daniel Gross, 239–62. Chicago: University of Chicago Press, 2014.

———. "Putting One's Body on the Line." *GLQ: A Journal of Lesbian and Gay Studies* 25, no. 1 (Winter 2019): 183–87.

Sherman, Taylor C. "State Practice, Nationalist Politics and the Hunger Strikes of the Lahore Conspiracy Case Prisoners, 1929–39." *Cultural and Social History* 5, no. 4 (2008): 497–508.

———. *State Violence and Punishment in India.* New York: Routledge, 2010.

Silove, Derrick. "Doctors and the State: Lessons from the Biko Case." *Social Science and Medicine* 30, no. 4 (1990): 417–29.

Silove, Derrick, Jackie Curtis, Catherine Mason, and Rise Becker. "Ethical Considerations in the Management of Asylum Seekers on Hunger Strike." *JAMA* 276, no. 5 (1996): 410–15.

Sim, Joe. *Medical Power in Prisons: The Prison Medical Service in England.* Milton Keynes, UK: Open University Press, 1990.

Siméant, Johanna. "Who Clamours for Attention—and Who Cares? Hunger Strikes in France from 1972 to 1992." *La Lettre de La Maison Française d'Oxford* 10 (1998): 98–119.

Siméant, Johanna, and Christophe Traïni. *Bodies in Protest: Hunger Strikes and Angry Music.* Amsterdam: Amsterdam University Press, 2016.

Simpson, Audra. "The State Is a Man: Theresa Spence, Loretta Saunders and the Gender of Settler Sovereignty." *Theory and Event* 19, no. 4 (2016): 1–30.

Singer, Eleanor, and Jacob Ludwig. "South Africa's Press Restrictions Effects on Press Coverage and Public Opinion toward South Africa." *Public Opinion Quarterly* 51, no. 3 (1987): 315–34.

Smith, Clive Stafford. *The Eight O'Clock Ferry on the Windward Side: Seeking Justice in Guantanamo.* New York: Nation Books, 2017.

Sohi, Seema. *Echoes of Mutiny: Race, Surveillance and Indian Anticolonialism in North America.* New York: Oxford University Press, 2014.

Spivak, Gayatri C. "Can the Subaltern Speak?" In *Marxism and the Interpretation of Culture,* ed. C. Nelson and L. Grossberg, 271–313. Urbana: University of Illinois Press, 1988.

Srivastava, Pramod Kumar. "Resistance and Repression in India: The Hunger Strike at the Andaman Cellular Jail in 1933." *Crime, Histoire et Sociétés/Crime, History and Societies* 7, no. 2 (2003): 81–102.

Stanley, Eric A., and Nat Smith, eds. *Captive Genders: Trans Embodiment and the Prison Industrial Complex.* Oakland, CA: AK Press, 2015.

Sultan, A., and K. O'Sullivan. "Psychological Disturbances in Asylum Seekers Held in Longterm Detention: A Participant-Observer Account." *Medical Journal of Australia* 175 (2001): 593–96.

Svalesen, Leif. *The Slave Ship Fredensborg.* Bloomington: Indiana University Press, 2000.

Takei, Barbara. "Legalizing Detention: Segregated Japanese Americans and the Justice Department's Renunciation Program." In *A Question of Loyalty: Internment at Tule Lake,* 75–105. Klamath Falls, OR: Shaw Historical Library, 2005.

Tamura, Eileen H. *In Defense of Justice: Joseph Kurihara and the Japanese American Struggle for Equality.* Urbana: University of Illinois Press, 2013.

Taylor, Diana. "Trauma in the Archive." In *Feeling Photography,* ed. Elspeth H. Brown and Thy Phu, 239–51. Durham, NC: Duke University Press, 2014.

Thomas, Dorothy S., and Richard Nishimoto. *The Spoilage: Japanese-American Evacuation and Resettlement during World War II.* Berkeley: University of California Press, 1969.

Tickner, Lisa. *The Spectacle of Women: Imagery of the Suffrage Campaign, 1907–14.* London: Chatto and Windus, 1987.

van Kessel, Ineke. *Beyond Our Wildest Dreams: The United Democratic Front and the Transformation of South Africa.* Charlottesville: University of Virginia Press, 2000.

Vassilyadi, Frank, Alkistis-Kira Panteliadou, and Christos Panteliadis. "Hallmarks in the History of Enteral and Parenteral Nutrition: From Antiquity to the 20th Century." *Nutrition in Clinical Practice* 28, no. 2 (2013): 209–17.

Velasquez-Potts, Michelle C. "Carceral Oversight: Force-Feeding and Visuality at Guantánamo Bay Detention Camp." *Public Culture* 31, no. 3 (2019): 581–600.

———. "Staging Incapacitation: The Corporeal Politics of Hunger Striking." *Women and Performance* 29, no. 1 (2019): 25–40.

Vesti, Peter, and Niels Johan Lavik. "Torture and the Medical Profession: A Review." *Journal of Medical Ethics* 17 (1991): 4.

Walton, Mary. *A Woman's Crusade: Alice Paul and the Battle for the Ballot.* New York: St. Martin's Griffin, 2010.

Ward, Margaret. "Conflicting Interests: The British and Irish Suffrage Movements." *Feminist Review* 50, no. 1 (1995): 127–47.

Weglyn, Michi Nishiura. *Years of Infamy: The Untold Story of America's Concentration Camps.* Seattle: University of Washington Press, 1996.

Welch, Michael. *Detained: Immigration Laws and the Expanding I.N.S Jail Complex.* Philadelphia: Temple University Press, 2002.

Wilcox, Lauren B. *Bodies of Violence: Theorizing Embodied Subjects in International Relations.* New York: Oxford University Press, 2015.

Wilson, Elizabeth A. *Gut Feminism.* Durham, NC: Duke University Press, 2015.

Wilson, Lindy. *Steve Biko.* Athens: Ohio University Press, 2011.

Wolpert, Stanley. *Gandhi's Passion: The Life and Legacy of Mahatma Gandhi.* New York: Oxford University Press, 2001.

Woods, Donald. *Biko*. New York: Henry Holt, 1987.

Wrobel, David. "Considering Frontiers and Empires: George Kennan's *Siberia and the U.S. West*." *Western Historical Quarterly* 46, no. 3 (2015): 285–309.

Zahniser, J. D., and Amelia R. Fry. *Alice Paul: Claiming Power*. New York: Oxford University Press, 2014.

Ziarek, Ewa Płonowska. "Bare Life on Strike: Notes on the Biopolitics of Race and Gender." *South Atlantic Quarterly* 107, no. 1 (2008): 89–105.

INDEX

Note: Page numbers in *italics* refer to illustrations.

Australian Service for the Treatment and
Rehabilitation of Torture and Trauma
Survivors, 251

Babenia, Natoo, 168
Bangladeshi refugees, 243, 258, 279, 280. *See
also* refugee detainees
Bar'el, Zvi, 242
bare life, as term, 8, 9
Bargu, Banu, 9
Barwell, Ellen, 34, 77
Basic Law: Human Dignity and Liberty
(Israel), 241
Belfast Prison (Northern Ireland), 195
Bengal, India, 111, 125, 126–27. *See also*
India
Bengal Volunteers, 121, 123
Bennett, James, 81
Berlant, Lauren, 12
Bernstein, Hilda, 161–63
Bernstein, Lionel, 161, 164
Besig, Ernest, 149–50, 154
Best, Raymond, 139, 142, 150, 154
Bey, Yasiin, 234–36
Biggs, Michael, 108
Biko, Steve, 168–69
biomedical management. *See* forcible
feeding; medical care and intervention;
psychiatric assessment
biopolitics, 215, 230–32, 242–43. *See also*
forcible feeding
biopower, 215, 230. *See also* bodily
sovereignty
Birmingham Prison (UK), 76–77, 82–83,
112
Biro, Andrew, 251, 253, 329n8
Bivans, Fannie A., 55
Black Consciousness Movement, 168–69
Black Sash (organization), 180
black sites, 225–27
blanket protests, 203, 209
Bloody Sunday (Northern Ireland, 1972),
193
BMA (British Medical Association), 194–
95, 201, 220
bodily sovereignty: forms of resistance and,
203, 237, 245; gut feeling and knowing,
11–13; lip sewing and self-mutilation,

253–59, 260, 261, 264; loss of, 230;
prison power and, 5–7, 109, 244;
through hunger striking, overview, 9,
16, 288–89. *See also* biopower; emotions,
overview; Gandhi, Mohandas
(Mahatma); hunger strike, as form;
medical care and intervention; visceral
communication
Boesak, Allan, 178, 179, *183,* 184
Boesak, Dorothy, *181*
Bonamici, Suzanne, 285
Bonilla, Sandra, 277
Borstal jail, Lahore (India), 121
Bose, Subhas Chandra, 123, 124, 127
Botha, P. W., 171, 177, 189
Branham, Lucy, *58*
Break Bread Not Families (organization),
283
British Army, 112, 192–95
British Empire: control of Ireland by,
86–87, 107–9; democratic participation,
23–24; hunger strikes in, 26–36, 61;
voting rights in, 25–26, 56–57; in WWI,
56. *See also* Home Rule; India; North-
ern Ireland
British India. *See* India
British Indian Army, 112. *See also* India
British suffragists. *See* suffragists
Brixton Prison (UK), 85, 90, 197–99
Brock, Evelyn Barr, 55
Brock, Mrs. Marcus J., 55
Buntman, Fran, 168
Burkitt, Hilda, 31, 33, 34
Burns, Lucy, 37, 42–43, 49–52, *50,* 54–55, 59
Bush administration (U.S.), G. H. W.,
271–72
bushido, 147, 155

California Department of Corrections and
Rehabilitation, 242
Cambodian refugees, 250–52, 253. *See also*
refugee detainees
Canada, 87, 113, 305n1
carceral power: Agamben on, 8; forcible
feeding and, 83–84, 252; hunger strikes
against, 15, 109, 132, 170; mental illness
and, 48; parameters of, 3–5, 288, 290,
294. *See also* prison power, defined

72–73; of South African prisoners, 179, 217–18; techniques used in, 66, 71–72, 198; visual documentation of, 232–36, 239; as weapon of prison power, 5, 7, 32–34; WMA on, 219–20. *See also* hunger strikes; intravenous feeding; medical care and intervention; medical ethics; rectal feeding

Foucault, Michel, 83, 215, 230, 243

Fox, Richard Michael, 68, 69, 73, 77

freedom of speech protests, 23, 37, 39–41, 45, 63, 179

Friedland, Joan, 273

Friends of Irish Freedom, 94

frigidity, 67

Fujitani, Takashi, 140

funeral processions, 94–98, 122–23

gag, 66, 72–75, 198. *See also* forcible feeding

gaki, 147

Gandhi, Mohandas (Mahatma), *118*; arrests and detentions of, 113–14, 128, 129–30; on Das's death, 123, 124; detention of, 115; ethos on fasting, 110, 116–18, 128; fasting by, 110, 113–16, 129–31; on forcible feeding, 68–69; opinion of hunger strikes, 110, 126, 127–28; on Terence MacSwiney's death, 98; work in South Africa, 113, 116, 159. *See also* India

Gannon, James A., 47–48, 51

García, Deyaneira, 282

Gardiner, Gerald, 194

Gardiner, Gwynne, 47–48

Gardiner Parliamentary Committee, 202

Garfield, James, 80

Garvey, Marcus, 98

Gaughan, Michael, 200, 201, 205

Gee, Dolly, 278

gender and hunger striking, 13–14, 85, 119–20, 146, 155, 291

Geneva Convention (1929), 141

Gershon, Michael, 12

Ghadar Party, 112

Ghanian refugees, 280. *See also* refugee detainees

"Gitmo Is Killing Me" (Moqbel), 228, *229*

Gladstone, Herbert, 30, 32, 69, 72

golodofka, 28, 295n1. *See also* hunger strikes

Gordon, Mary, 69, 80

Government of India Act (1935), 125

Graham, Bob, 268

Granada War Relocation Center (U.S.), 138

Grandjean, Guy, 236

Grant, Kevin, 15

Great Britain. *See* British Empire

Greenough, Paul, 129

Grootvlei Prison (South Africa), 182

Group Areas Act (1950), 159

Guantánamo: prisoners at, 215, 220, 222–30, 245, 325n18; refugee detainees at, 272, 273. *See also* United States

Guantánamo Bay: The Hunger Strikes (video), 236

Gupta, J. M. Sen, 123

gut feeling and knowing, 11–13. *See also* bodily sovereignty

Gut Feminism (Wilson), 12

Gutiérrez, Jennicet, 282

Gutierrez, Jorge, 282–83

Haitian Refugee Center (U.S.), 267, 271

Haitian refugees, 266–74. *See also* refugee detainees

Hand, Gerry, 252

Hanson-Young, Sarah, 260

Hardie, James Keir, 72

Harris, Francis, 205

Hasan, Mahmudul, 243

Hassan, Emad, 224

Hayden, Michael, 226

Heart Mountain Relocation Center (U.S.), 149

Heath, Edward, 193

Heffelfinger, Kate, 51, *53*

Henderson, Thelton, 243

Heng, Ly Muy, 250

Her Majesty's Prison Maze. *See* Long Kesh prison (Northern Ireland)

heroism and gender, 119–20, 146, 155

Higgins, Frank, 83

Hind Swaraj (Gandhi), 113

Hindustan Socialist Republican Association (HSRA), 120

Hindu traditions, 116, 123–24, 187. *See also* religious ritual fasting

Hmong refugees, 281. *See also* refugee
detainees
Ho Chi Minh, 98
Hoenig, Ron, 259
Holloway Prison (UK), 23, 27, 37–38, 41, 59,
73
Home Rule, 86–88, 89, 113, 193. *See also*
British Empire; *swaraj*
Honduran refugees, 284. *See also* refugee
detainees
Hong Kong, 112
Horsley, Victor, 70
Hossein (refugee), 257
Howland, Cora, 54
Howland, Corinna, 244
Hughes, Frank, 209
human rights, overview, 18. *See also*
rightlessness
Human Rights Alert, 236
hunger strike, as form, 10–11, 288–89. *See
also* bodily sovereignty; hunger strikes
"A Hunger Strikers Handbook" (NWDC
Resistance), 275, *276*
hunger strikes, 1–3, 288–94; by American
prisoners, 39–41, 63, 156, 220, 222–30,
242–43; by American refugee detainees,
268–69, 274–80, 284–85; by American
suffragists, 23, 37–38, 41–42, 47–52, 64;
by Australian refugee detainees, 250,
254–55, 256, 259–63; by Bangladeshi
asylum seekers, 243; by British suffragists, 26–36, 61; in China, 187–88; class
and, 38–39; by Fair and IWW protesters, 40–41; vs. fasting, 1, 116–17; first
published reference to, 295n1; Gandhi's
opinion of, 110, 126, 127–28; gender and,
13–14, 119–20, 146, 155; gut feeling and
knowing in, 11–13; by Haitian refugee
detainees, 268–69, 271, 272; historical
and global overview of, 14–19; by Holocaust refugees, 156; by Indian prisoners,
110–12, 119, 121–22, 125–28, 132, 236–39,
291; by Irish prisoners, 75–76, 78, 82,
90–94, 100, 107–9; by Japanese internment prisoners, 135–36, 144–48, 151–56;
Mandela's opinion of, 167, 184; by
Northern Ireland prisoners, 195–96,
204–14; by Palestinian prisoners,

239–42, 244–45; physician's responsibility in, 6–7; by Polish students, 156; as
political weapon, 61–65, 131–32, 189–90,
208, 244–45; in Port Hueneme naval
base, 156; prisoner voice in, 5, 9–11,
19–20, 289–90; by Russian revolutionaries, 1, 28–29; by South African prisoners, ix–x, 158, 160–68, 172–84, 186,
189–90; as suicide, accusations of, 70,
90, 101–2, 208; as term, 1, 28, 295n1; by
Turkish prisoners, 188; by Vietnamese
political protester, 156; by wartime
conscientious objectors, 68, 73, 80–81,
82. *See also* fasting; forcible feeding;
media coverage; medical care and intervention; solidarity fasts
"Hunger Strikes" (poster), 239–41
hungry ghost, 147
Hunter, John, 75
Hurley, Denis, 182
Hutto Residential Center (U.S.), 280
hysteria and hysterical, as identifier, 54, 55,
67, 77, 106. *See also* mental asylums;
mental illness; psychiatric assessment

Iacopino, Vincent, 226
ICE (U.S. Immigration and Customs
Enforcement), 273–77, 282, 284, 285,
287
IDAG (Independent Detention Advisory
Group), 256
Illingworth, J. W., 82–83
IMA (Israel Medical Association), 241–42
immigrant, defined, 265, 270. *See also*
asylum seeker, defined; refugee
detainees
Immigration Act (1965), 265
immolation, 1, 91, 123–24
India: hunger strikes in, 110–12, 119, 121,
125–28, 132, 236–39, 291; Malom massacre in, 236; martyrdom in, 122–24;
political movements and protests in,
110, 111, 113–16, 119–21, 124–25, 128–30;
public fasting in, 113, 114, 115–18, 129–31.
See also British Empire; Gandhi,
Mohandas (Mahatma)
Indian National Congress Party, 111, 113,
114–15, 120, 124–25. *See also* India

McKee, Billy, 195, 196

McKeown, Laurence, 211–12

media coverage: of American refugee detainees, 271, 285; of American suffragists, 52, 53–55, 62–63; of Australian refugee detainees, 255–56, 259, 262; of biomedicalization of hunger strikes and forcible feeding, 216; of British suffragists, 34–36, 112; class and, 40–41; of Guantánamo prisoners, 227–30; of Indian prisoners, 122–23, 132; of Irish revolutionary prisoners, 90–91, 95, 103, 112; of Japanese internment prisoners, 148, *149*, 157; of Northern Ireland hunger strikes, 195, 196, 201, 205; of Russian hunger strikes, 1, 28–29; of South African hunger strikes, 172–79, 184–88. *See also* hunger strikes; visual documentation

Medical Association of South Africa (MASA), 170

medical care and intervention: for American prisoners, 221; biopolitical algorithms on, 230–31; British non-intervention policy, 191, 199, 213–14; for Gandhi during fasting, 117, 131; mothers on, 206, 207, 209–11; for Northern Ireland prisoners, 197–202, 206, 207–8; for Paul, 47–48; for South African prisoners, 173, 176; during torture, 194–95, 197; for Tule Lake prison hunger strikers, 144, 152, 153–54; WMA's Declaration of Tokyo on, 176, 179, 201, 217, 219, 220, 221, 231; for WSPU hunger strikers, 31–32. *See also* forcible feeding; psychiatric assessment

medical ethics: of forcible feeding, 70–71, 79–80, 83–84, 93, 199, 201, 228–29; physician's responsibility and, 6–7, 69, 246; psychiatric logics and, 47–48, 66–68. *See also* forcible feeding; rightlessness

Mellet, Leon, 182

mental asylums: forcible feeding in, 66, 73, 80; threat to Paul of, 47, 48, 60; threat to refugee detainees of, 264. *See also* hysteria and hysterical, as identifier; psychiatric assessment

mental illness, 7, 47–48, 66–67, 250–53, 263–64. *See also* depression; hysteria and hysterical, as identifier; suicide

Mexican Americans, protests by, 15, 25, 265, 281. *See also* refugee detainees

Migration Amendment Act (1992), 249

military interrogation and torture, 194–95

Miller, Ian, 77, 83, 202, 214

Mkhatshwa, Smangaliso, 173

Modderbee Prison (South Africa), 172

Mohammed, Khalid Sheikh, 225

Mok, Gek Bouy, 250–51

Moqbel, Samir Naji al Hasan, 227, 228, *229*

Morrison, Scott, 260

Mos Def, 234–36

mothers: fasting and hunger strikes by, 251, 274, 278; first meals after hunger strikes by, 238, 244; on medical intervention of hunger strikers, 206, 207, 209–11

Moullin, Charles Mansell, 70

Mountjoy Prison (Ireland), 75–76, 77, 78, 82, 85, 100–103, *104*

Moxon, Frank, 70

Muhammad Ali Jinnah, 123

Mukherjee, Nani Gopal, 111–12, 119, 308n1

Mullowney, Alexander, 46, 49, 52

Munster Women's Franchise League, 88

Murphy, Patrick Joseph, 94, *96*

Murray, Flora, 71, 81

Muslim religious practices, 116, 187, 222. *See also* religious ritual fasting

mutilation. *See* self-mutilation

Mydans, Carl, 148

Myer, Dillon S., 138, 139, 154

Naidoo, Indres, 164, 165–67, 168

NAMDA (National Medical and Dental Association), 170, 173, 179

Napier, Wilfrid, 182–83

Nat, Ung Bun, 250–51

National Detainees Day (South Africa), 180

National Union of Women's Suffrage Societies (NUWSS), 25–26

Native Americans, 25, 42

Nauru detention center, 259, 263

NAWSA (National American Woman Suffrage Association), 42–43, 57–59

forcible feeding of, 179, 217–18; hunger
strikes during emergency rule, 171–84,
186; at Robben Island, 164–68, 185;
white women, 160–63. *See also* South
Africa
South African Students' Organisation, 169
South Texas Family Residential Center
(U.S.), 283
Soviet Union, 249
Special Powers Act (1922), 193
speculum oris, 72. *See also* gag
Spinoza, 225
Spivak, Gayatri, 290
Sri Lankan refugees, 250, 262. *See also*
refugee detainees
Stagg, Frank, 201–2, 205
St. Albans Prison (South Africa), 175–76
"Standard Operating Procedure: Medical
Management of Detainees on Hunger
Strike" (SOP), 230–31
starvation strike, as term, 41. *See also* hun-
ger strikes
statelessness, 247
state power, defined, 3–4. *See also* carceral
power; prison power, defined
Steinback, Robert, 273
St. Elizabeth's Asylum, 47, 48
Stevens, Doris, 52, 61
Steyn, Colin, 160
St. George's Cathedral, London, 95
Strasburg, Toni, 161
Suarez, Xavier, 272
suffrage. *See* voting rights
The Suffragette (publication), 74
suffragists: criticisms of, 13, 54–55; forcible
feeding of, 32–35, 48, 70, 77; hunger
strikes of American, 23, 37–38, 41–42,
47–52; hunger strikes of British, 27–36,
61; mental health diagnosis of, 66–68,
263; Paul's messaging as, 59–61; picketing campaigns by, 43–46, 49; power of
hunger strikes by, 61–65. *See also* voting
rights
suicide: accusations of hunger strikes as, 70,
90, 101–2; as criminal offense in India,
237; refugee detainees and, 251, 253, 259,
260, 271. *See also* depression; mental
illness

Sultan, Aamer, 252–53
swadeshi movement, 111
swaraj, 113, 114, 124. *See also* Home Rule
sympathy fasts. *See* solidarity fasts
Syrian refugees, 258. *See also* refugee
detainees

Tambo, Oliver, 161, 180
Taylor, Diana, 11
Teichner, Martha, 178
temperance, 25, 36
Texas Civil Rights Project, 283
Thatcher, Margaret, 204, 212
Thusi, Sandile, 183
Tiananmen Square (China), 187–88, 249
Todorki, Koji, 143
Topaz War Relocation Center (U.S.), 138
torture: of Biko, 168–70; by British Army,
193–95, 197, 202; debate on forcible
feeding as, 70–71, 79–80, 83–84, 199,
213; of Guantánamo prisoners, 225–26;
of Terence MacSwiney, 93; UN on, 241;
WMA on, 201. *See also* forcible feeding;
sexual assault; trauma
transgender detainees, 282–83
trauma: of Australian refugee detainees,
250–53; diagnosing, 263–64; personal
messaging on, 59–61, 62–63. *See also*
forcible feeding; mental illness; refugee
detainees; torture
Trump administration (U.S.), 263, 283, 284
Tsuda, Hiroyoshi, 144–45, 146
Tucker, Benjamin, 169
Tule Lake Segregation Center (U.S.):
description of, 138, 141–43; hunger
strikes at, 135–36, 144–45, 150–54;
protest strikes at, 138–39, 142, 148;
stockade, 139, 140, 148–50, *149*. *See also*
Japanese internment prisoners
Turkish prisoners, 188, 220, 291
Tutu, Desmond, *183*; detainee negotiations
by, 177, 179, 180, 184; solidarity fasting
by, 173, 178

UDF (United Democratic Front), 170–71,
173, 177
Ulster Volunteers, 87, 193
Union Party (South Africa), 159, 315n1

United Nations: Convention against Torture, 241; Declaration on Human Rights, 201; Protocol Relating to the Status of Refugees, 248; Refugee Convention, 249, 250

United States: CIA black sites, 225–27; civil rights in, 15, 59, 154, 157, 267; democratic participation in, 23–24; family detention in, 278–79, 283; forced family separation in, 274–77, 283–85, 293; hunger strikes by prisoners in, 39–41, 63, 156, 242–43; hunger strikes by refugee detainees in, 268–69, 274–80, 284–85; hunger strikes by suffragists in, 23, 37–38, 41–42, 47–52, 64; refugee and immigration policies of, 250, 265–74, 283, 286–87; refugee and prison population statistics in, 265, 274; refugee solidarity networks in, 280–83, 286, 287; suspension of prisoner rights in, 220–22; voting rights in, 24–25, 36, 41–45, 57–59. *See also* DHS (U.S. Department of Homeland Security); Guantánamo; ICE (U.S. Immigration and Customs Enforcement); Japanese internment prisoners; refugee detainees; Tule Lake Segregation Center (U.S.)

Unlawful Organizations Act (1960), 160

U.S. Immigration Control and Reform Act (1986), 270

U.S. Naval Station Guantánamo Bay. *See* Guantánamo

U.S. Senate Intelligence Committee, 225, 226

U.S. State Department, 149

vaginal enema, 79

Vaid, Minnie, 237

Varsi, Hassan, 255–56

Venu, C. S., 123

Veriava, Yosuf, 218

Verma, Shiv, 121

Vietnam, 98, 156

Vietnamese refugees, 250. *See also* refugee detainees

Villalpando, Maru Mora, 277

Villawood detention center (Australia), 250, 252–53

visceral communication, 9–13, 15, 288; by Gandhi, 117, 131; by suffragists, 29, 59–61; through diary entries, 155; through images and videos, 256, 258; through lip sewing, 255. *See also* bodily sovereignty; hunger strikes; prisoner voice; visual documentation

visual documentation: of forcible feeding, 232–36, 239; of hunger strikers, 10, 36, 292; of lip sewing, 257–59. *See also* media coverage; visceral communication

Visualizing Palestine (organization), 239, 240

Vlok, Adriaan, 176, 178, 179–80, 184

voting rights: in Australia, 305n1; in British Empire, 25–26, 36, 56–57; in Canada, 305n1; in India, 125; in Ireland, 86, 88, 192; in South Africa, 305n1; in United States, 23, 24–25, 36, 41–45, 57–59. *See also* suffragists

Wackenhut Security Corporation, 254

Waddill, Edmund, 52

Wallace Dunlop, Marion, 23, 26–30, *28*, 32, 64, 81

War on Terror, 222, 225

warriors' code of honor, 147

wartime mobilization, 55–56

Weiss, Constance, 271

Wells, Ida B., 42

White, William, 47

Wilson, Elizabeth, 12

Wilson, Woodrow, 42, 45, 46, 54, 58

Winchester Prison (UK), 197

Winkenwerder, William, Jr., 224–25

Winslow, Rose, 46–47, 51, 52

Winson Green Prison (UK), 32–34, 69, 71

Witness Against Torture event, *234*

WMA (World Medical Association): Declaration of Malta, 219–20, 221; Declaration of Tokyo, 176, 179, 201, 217, 219, 220, 221, 231; on torture by British Army, 193–95

Wojnarowicz, David, 257

Women's Army Auxiliary Corps, 80

Women's Coronation Procession (London, 1911), 26

Founded in 1893,
UNIVERSITY OF CALIFORNIA PRESS
publishes bold, progressive books and journals
on topics in the arts, humanities, social sciences,
and natural sciences—with a focus on social
justice issues—that inspire thought and action
among readers worldwide.

The UC PRESS FOUNDATION
raises funds to uphold the press's vital role
as an independent, nonprofit publisher, and
receives philanthropic support from a wide
range of individuals and institutions—and from
committed readers like you. To learn more, visit
ucpress.edu/supportus.